COMMUNITY POLICING

THEORY AND PRACTICE

COMMUNITY POLICING THEORY AND PRACTICE

LINDA S. MILLER
Bloomington Police Department
Bloomington, Minnesota

KÄREN M. HESS
Normandale Community College
Bloomington, Minnesota

WEST PUBLISHING COMPANY

Minneapolis/St. Paul   New York   Los Angeles   San Francisco

WEST COMMITMENT TO THE ENVIRONMENT

In 1906, West Publishing Company began recycling materials left over from the production of books. This began a tradition of efficient and responsible use of resources. Today, up to 95 percent of our legal books and 70 percent of our college and school texts are printed on recycled, acid-free stock. West also recycles nearly 22 million pounds of scrap paper annually— the equivalent of 181,717 trees. Since the 1960s, West has devised ways to capture and recycle waste inks, solvents, oils, and vapors created in the printing process. We also recycle plastics of all kinds, wood, glass, corrugated cardboard, and batteries, and have eliminated the use of styrofoam book packaging. We at West are proud of the longevity and the scope of our commitment to the environment.

Production, Prepress, Printing nd Binding by West Publishing Company.

 PRINTED ON 10% POST CONSUMER RECYCLED PAPER ∞

Text design: John Edeen
Copyediting: Nancy Porter
Artwork: Carto Graphics
Drawing for Chapter 8: Travis Vaudrin
Composition: Carlisle Communications
Indexing: Christine M. Hess
Cover image: Magoffin Associates
Photo credits follow index

Library of Congress Cataloging-in-Publication Data

Miller, Linda S.
    Community policing : theory and practice / Linda S. Miller, Kären
M. Hess.
       p.   cm.
    Includes index.
    ISBN 0-314-02391-7 (hc.)
    1. Community policing.   2. Public relations—Police.   3. Community
policing —United States—Case studies. 4. Public relations—Police-
-United States—Case studies.   I. Hess, Kären M., 1939-
II. Title.
HV7936.C83M55 1994
363.2'3—dc20
                                                    93-25941
                                                    CIP

CONTENTS IN BRIEF

SECTION **III** _____

PROJECTS AND PROGRAMS: COORDINATED EFFORTS,   341

CONTENTS

SECTION I

AN OVERVIEW,   1

1 THE EVOLUTION OF POLICE-COMMUNITY RELATIONS,   3

2 THE ROLE OF COMMUNITY IN COMMUNITY-ORIENTED POLICING,   31

11 INTERACTING WITH THE MEDIA,   315

SECTION **III** _____

PROJECTS AND PROGRAMS: COORDINATED EFFORTS,   341

14 PROGRAMS FOR YOUTH,   399

15 CRIME PREVENTION PROGRAMS: COLLABORATIVE EFFORTS,   427

LIST OF FIGURES

LIST OF TABLES

LIST OF ACRONYMS

AARP—American Association of
   Retired Persons
ACW—Around the Corner to the
   World
AD—Alzehiemer's disease
ADA—Americans with
   Disabilities Act
AIM—American Indian
   Movement
BIA—Bureau of Indian Affairs
CAT—Combat Auto Theft
CCPP—Citywide Crime
   Prevention Program
CCRP—citizen crime reporting
   program
CHANGE—Citizens Helping
   Austin Neighborhood
   Gang Environment
CIT—crisis intervention team
COPE—Community/Citizen-
   Oriented Police
   Enforcement
CPTED—crime prevention
   through environmental
   design
CRB—civilian review board
CRT—crisis response team
CSO—community service officer
DARE—Drug Abuse Resistance
   Education
DFZ—drug free zone
DSO—deinstitutionalization of
   status offenders
EBD—emotionally/behaviorally
   disabled
ESL—English as a second
   language
FCC—Federal Communications
   Commission
HIV—human immunodeficiency
   virus

HOPE—Homes on Portland
   Enterprise
HUD—Housing and Urban
   Development
IACP—International Association
   of Chiefs of Police
ICD—International Center for
   the Disabled
IHS—Indian Health Service
LD—learning disabled; learning
   disabilities
LEAA—Law Enforcement
   Administration
   Assistance
LULAC—League of United Latin
   American Citizens
MADD—Mothers Against Drunk
   Driving
MALDEF—Mexican American
   Legal Defense and
   Education Fund
NAACP—National Association
   for the Advancement of
   Colored People
NABCJ—National Association of
   Blacks in Criminal
   Justice
NAD—National Association of
   the Deaf
NCH—National Council on the
   Handicapped
NCTI—National Corrective
   Training Institute
NFPP—National Foot Patrol
   Program
NHIF—National Head Injury
   Foundation
NOBLE—National Organization
   of Black Law
   Enforcement Execu-
   tives

NOP—neighborhood-oriented policing

NOVA—National Organization for Victim Assistance

NSA—National Sheriffs Association

OJDP—Office of Juvenile Delinquency Prevention

PAL—police athletic league

PCR—police-community relations

PEP Kids—Parents, Educators, Police, and Kids

PIN—Pager Information Network

PIO—press information officer

PIP—Positive Interaction Program

POMC—Parents of Murdered Children

POP—problem-oriented policing

POST—Peace Officer Standards and Training

PTSD—post traumatic stress disorder

RID—report incidents directly

SAT—Stanford Achievement Test

SODAA—Stop Our Drug and Alcohol Abuse

SWRL—South West Regional Laboratory

TAB—temporarily able-bodied

TDD—telecommunication device for the deaf

TOP—Teens on Patrol

VCAN—Victims Constitutional Amendment Network

VIP—Volunteers in Parole

VIP—Volunteers in Policing

VIS—victim impact statement

VOCA—Victims of Crime Act

VSO—victim statement of opinion

VWPA—Victim/Witness Protection Act

WIN—Women in Need

YGSP—Youth Gang Services Project

ACKNOWLEDGEMENTS

We would like to thank the following individuals for their careful review of the manuscript for this text and for their numerous suggestions for improvement: Michael B. Blankenship, Department of Criminology & Criminal Justice, Memphis State University; W.D. Braddock, Department of Criminal Justice, Boise State University; Vincent Del Castillo, Department of Law and Police Science, John Jay College of Criminal Justice; Burt C. Hagerman, Oakland Community College; Robert Ives, Rock Valley College; James E. Newman, Department of Public Services, Rio Hondo Community College; Carroll S. Price, Social Science Division, Penn Valley Community College; Chester L. Quarles, Criminal Justice Program, Department of Political Science, University of Mississippi; and B. Grant Stitt, Department of Criminal Justice, University of Nevada-Reno; Gary W. Tucker, Department of Criminal Justice, Sinclair Community College.

Thanks also to Penny Parrish for her review of and substantial contribution to the chapter on police-media relations and to Paul Bailey for his review of and contributions to the chapter on communication. Thanks also to Christine Hess for her comprehensive index and for her review of and data entry for the Instructor's Manual that accompanies this text. Finally, a sincere thank you to our editors at West, Robert Jucha, Diane Colwyn, and Peggy Brewington. Any errors in content or expression are the sole responsibility of the authors.

PREFACE

Community policing offers one avenue for making neighborhoods safer. Community policing is not a program or a series of programs. It is a philosophy, a belief that working together, the police and the community can accomplish what neither can accomplish alone. The *synergy* that results from community policing can be powerful. It is like the power of a finely tuned athletic team, with each member contributing to the total effort. Occasionally heros may emerge, but victory depends on a team effort.

Community policing differs from earlier efforts such as team policing, community relations, crime prevention programs, or neighborhood watch programs. Community policing involves a rethinking of the role of the police and a restructuring of the police organization. This text discusses in Section One the evolution of community policing and the changes in our communities and our law enforcement agencies which have occurred.

The text emphasizes developing the interpersonal skills needed to build good relationships with all those the police have sworn "to serve and protect." This includes those who are culturally, racially, or socioeconomically different from the mainstream, those who are physically or mentally disabled, and those who are elderly. It also includes youth, both as victims and as offenders, gangs and gang members, and victims of crime. In addition, interacting effectively with members of the media is vital to the success of community policing. Developing these relationships is the focus of Section Two.

Section Three looks at individual projects and programs, including those which involve coordinated efforts of the police, the entire criminal justice system, and the community. It discusses past successes and failures and emphasizes using a problem-oriented approach to fighting crime and delivering services.

How to Use this Text

The text is structured to enhance understanding and remembering the main concepts. To get the most from this text, first look through the listing of Contents to give yourself a framework. Think about the specific subjects included in the topic of community policing as a whole. Then read the section openers for a closer look at the three broad divisions of the text. Finally, complete the following steps for each chapter:

1. Read the "Do You Know" questions at the beginning of the chapter. These present the chapter objectives in a way that should make you think about your current level of knowledge. For example:
    Do You Know . . . When modern policing began?
2. Read the chapter, highlighting, underlining, or taking notes. Watch for answers to the "Do You Know Questions." Pay special attention to information between rules. For example:

Modern policing began with the formation of the London Metropolitan Police.

Also pay attention to words in bold type. These are key terms which you should be able to define. The definitions should be clear from the text.

3. Read the chapter summary. You will find that you have now read key points three times. This triple-strength approach should take the information from your short-term memory into your long-term memory.
4. To solidify the information, return to the "Do You Know" questions at the beginning of the chapter and answer each question. Write down any questions you have about the information in the chapter.
5. Read the discussion questions at the end of the chapter and think about what you can contribute to a class discussion.
6. Look at the list of key terms and make certain you understand and can define each term. If you do not remember what a specific term means, look it up in the glossary to refresh you memory.

If you follow these steps, and if you periodically review the "Do You Know" questions, you should master the content of this text.

ABOUT THE AUTHORS

Linda S. Miller is a sergeant with the Bloomington Minnesota Police Department. She has been with the department twenty years and is currently heading up the planning, research, and crime prevention division. She has also been a patrol supervisor, a crime prevention officer, a patrol officer, and a police dispatcher. Sgt. Miller is a member of the Minnesota Peace and Police Officers Association, the International Police Association, the Midwest Gang Investigator's Association, the International Association of Women Police, and the Minnesota Association of Women in Police. She was a member of the People-to-People's Women in Law Enforcement delegation to the Soviet Union in 1990. Sgt. Miller is a frequent presenter to community groups and is also an instructor.

Kären M. Hess, PhD, has written extensively in the field of law enforcement and criminal justice. Dr. Hess is a frequent instructor for report writing workshops and seminars for law enforcement agencies. She is a member of the English department at Normandale Community College and president of the Institute for Professional Development. Dr. Hess belongs to the National Criminal Justice Association and the National Council of Teachers of English. She is also a member of the Bloomington Citizens Crime Prevention Association board of directors.

AN OVERVIEW

The community and the police depend upon each other. The common police motto—"To serve and protect"—suggests a target population, individuals requiring service and protection. Most police departments stress the importance of community relations, and many have taken community relations beyond image enhancement and crime prevention programs and have started involving the community in policing itself.

The section looks first at the evolution of police-community relations. Since people first came together in groups, they have had some responsibility for seeing to it that those within the group did as was expected. The United States' method of "preserving the peace," modeled after that used in England, has gone through several stages. The relationship between the community and its police has been severely strained at times, and attempts to improve it have taken several forms. Recently, emphasis on improved public relations and crime prevention has expanded to a more encompassing philosophy of community policing, problem-oriented policing, or a community wellness model in many jurisdictions (Chapter 1).

The focus in Chapter 2 is on the people involved in community-police relations. Who are the members of a community? How do communities differ? How have they changed over the years? What future changes might be anticipated? What aspects of a community must be understood by those working within it? What is expected of community members? What do community members expect?

This section concludes with an in-depth look at the police, who are an important part of any community (Chapter 2). Who are the individuals behind the badges? How have they changed over years? How might they change in the future? How does the public generally view the police? What aspects of the police role contribute to this view?

THE EVOLUTION OF POLICE-COMMUNITY RELATIONS

The police are the public and the public are the police.

—Sir Robert Peel

DO YOU KNOW

- When "modern" policing began?
- What Sir Robert Peel's principles emphasized?
- What the three strategic eras of policing are?
- What the police relationship with the community was in each era?
- What the professional model of policing emphasized?
- What public relations programs established by police departments seek to do?
- What some common types of crime prevention programs are?
- What community policing is?
- What neighborhood-oriented policing is?
- What the focus of problem-oriented policing is?
- What the community wellness concept emphasizes?

INTRODUCTION

Throughout history, societies have established rules to govern the conduct of individuals and have devised punishments for those who broke the rules. The earliest record of an ancient society's need for rules to control human behavior dates back to approximately 2300 B.C. when the Sumerian rulers set forth standards for what was an offense against society. For thousands of years such rules were modified and adapted.

The system of policing and maintaining order in the United States is modeled on the police system developed in England. For hundreds of years before the Norman invasion of England, the Anglo-Saxon kings required their subjects to "keep the peace." These kings found that maintaining the peace required constant vigilance by every member of the realm.

Following the Norman invasion, the responsibility of all free Englishmen to maintain the "public peace" continued. The Frankpledge system required loyalty to the law of the king and mutual responsibility to maintain the peace. By the seventeenth century, law enforcement duties were divided into two separate units, a day watch and a night watch. The day watch consisted of constables who served as jailers and fulfilled other government duties. Citizens worked on the night watch. Each citizen was expected to take a turn watching for fires, approaching bad weather, and disorderly individuals. Some towns also expected the night watchman to call out the time.

If a watchman or any other citizen saw a crime in progress, they were expected to give the **hue and cry,** summoning all citizens within earshot to join in pursing and capturing the wrongdoer. Preserving the peace was the duty of all citizens.

By the end of the eighteenth century, most people with sufficient means paid others to stand their assigned watch for them, marking the beginning of a paid police force and, in effect, the original neighborhood watch.

The system of day and night watchmen was very ineffective. Because wealthy citizens could avoid the watch duty by hiring someone to take their place, those they hired were hesitant to invoke their authority against the well-to-do. According to Richardson (1970, p. 10), by the mid-1700s New York City's night watch was: "A parcel of idle, drinking, vigilant snorers, who never quelled any nocturnal tumult in their lives . . . but would, perhaps, be as ready to join in a burglary as any thief in Christendom."

London Metropolitan Police uniforms have a distinctive look that sets them apart from police departments in other parts of the world.

THE BEGINNING OF "MODERN" POLICE FORCES

The first "modern" police force, the London Metropolitan Police, was founded by Sir Robert Peel in 1829.

"Modern" policing began with the formation of the London Metropolitan Police.

Peel set forth the following principles on which the police force was to be based:

- The duty of the police is to prevent crime and disorder.
- The power of the police to fulfill their duties is dependent on public approval and on their ability to secure and maintain public respect.
- Public respect and approval also mean the willing cooperation of the public in the task of securing observance of the law.
- The police must seek and preserve public favor not by pandering to public opinion, but by constantly demonstrating absolutely impartial service to law.
- The police should strive to maintain a relationship with the public that gives reality to the tradition that the police are the public and the public are the police.

- The test of police efficiency is the absence of crime and disorder, not the visible evidence of police action in dealing with these problems (Inkster, 1992, p. 30).

Peel's principles emphasized the interdependency of the police and the public as well as the prevention of crime and disorder.

Peel envisioned a close relationship between the police and the citizens they served which helped the police maintain order in London.

As originally envisioned by the architects of London's Metropolitan Police—acknowledged to be the first modern police department, a police officer's job was primarily crime prevention and social maintenance, not crime detection. Police were to serve as local marshals who actively maintained order by interacting with the neighborhoods they served (Taft, 1986, p. 21).

At the time the Metropolitan Police Force was established in London, the United States was still operating under a day and night watch system similar to that which had been used in England. In the 1830s several large cities established separate paid day watches. In 1833 Philadelphia became the first city to pay both the day and night watches. Boston followed in 1838 with a six officer police force. In 1844 New York City took the first step toward organizing a big city police department similar to what exists today across the country when it consolidated its day and night watches under the control of a police chief. The police department was modeled on the London Metropolitan Police and Peel's principles. Other cities followed the example set by New York. By 1857 Boston, Chicago, New Orleans, Newark, Cincinnati, Philadelphia, and Baltimore had consolidated police departments, modeled on the Metropolitan Police of London. The new police chiefs of these departments faced the beginning of tremendous personnel problems among their officers. Early professionals found security services in disarray.

What those first chiefs of police found in their newly consolidated forces was a motley, undisciplined crew composed, as one commentator on the era described it, principally of "the shiftless, the incompetent, and the ignorant." Tales abounded of police officers in the 1850s who assaulted their superior officers, who released prisoners from the custody of other officers, who were found sleeping or drunk on duty, or who could be bribed for almost anything (Garmire, 1989, p. 17).

Despite these problems, the citizens considered the police a source of assistance. According to Hageman (1985, pp. 16–17), early police officers' duties included more community assistance and service than might be imagined. Even at the beginning of this century, law enforcement was one of the only services sanctioned by government to help citizens. Welfare, parole, probation, and unemployment offices did not exist. Police in New York, for example, distributed coal to the poor, monitored the well-being of vulnerable children, and made efforts to improve their impoverished homes by connecting them with a private charity, served as probation and parole officers, played a role in establishing playgrounds in the city, and supported charitable organizations.

It was more than a decade after the formation of the first police forces in the United States that attempts were made to require police officers to wear uniforms. The well-known resistance to change by police officers was apparent even then. The rank-and-file reaction against uniforms was immediate. Police officers claimed that uniforms were "un-American" and "a badge of degradation and servitude." In Philadelphia, police officers even objected to wearing badges on their coats. It was a bitter four-year struggle before they were finally persuaded to wear a complete uniform.

In 1856 New York City required its officers to be uniformed, but each local ward could determine the style of dress. The results were that in some sections of the city police officers wore straw hats while in others they wore felt. In some wards summer uniforms were white duck suits. In other wards they were multicolored outfits. A writer of the period complained: "If the police were mustered together, they would look like Falstaff's regiment" (Garmire, 1989, p. 19).

Thus began the challenge of modern policing to provide for the needs of an ever-changing and more complex society while shaping and maintaining a well-trained, competent work force to accomplish that mission.

The task has not been easy. The United States grew and changed rapidly. Cities developed and a very diverse population grew at breakneck speed as cultures met and clashed. Law enforcement officials had to decide how to maintain order in such a society, how much authority to give the police, and how to hold them accountable.

THE STRATEGIC ERAS OF POLICING

According to Kelling and Moore (1991, p. 6) policing in the United States can be divided into three eras.

The three eras of policing are political, reform, and community.

The Political Era

The political era extended into the first quarter of the twentieth century and was the time when police departments were formed. During this era police were closely tied to politics. This was very dissimilar to the situation in England. In England the police were centralized under the King, and the police chief had the authority to fire officers. In the United States, the police were decentralized, under the authority of the municipality in which they worked. The chief had no authority to fire officers; therefore, the police were often undisciplined. "The image of 'Keystone Cops'—police as clumsy bunglers—was widespread and often descriptive of realities in U.S. Policing" (Kelling and Moore, 1991, p. 9).

Police officers usually lived in their community and were members of the majority group. Since foot patrol was the most common policing strategy used, officers became close to the public.

> During the political era the police relationship with the community was intimate.

During the political era, chiefs of police were politically appointed and had a vested interest in keeping those who appointed them in power. Politicians rewarded those who voted for them with jobs or special privileges. This was referred to as the **patronage system,** or the **spoils system,** from the adage "To the victor go the spoils." Under the patronage system, corruption flourished. The effects of this system, according to Pace (1991, p. 132), are still present: "The spoils system extends from street level appointments to the Supreme Court. This includes privileges for the party in power in jobs, prime assignments, and special favors in a police agency, court, or correctional installation."

The inefficiency and corruption of the police led to the second era of policing, the reform era.

The Reform Era

August Vollmer and O. W. Wilson are usually attributed with spearheading the reform movement that called for a drastic change in the way police departments were organized and functioned. This era was often referred to as the **progressive era.**

One basic change during this era was to disassociate policing from politics. Disassociation was accomplished in a variety of ways. In Los Angeles, for example, the chief of police position became a civil service job requiring applicants to pass a civil service test. In Milwaukee the chief of police was appointed for life by a citizen commission.

With the disassociation of policing from politics came a change in emphasis on the role of the police. Citizens began to equate policing with fighting crime. The police considered social service type functions less desirable and avoided them whenever possible.

The relationship between the police and the public also changed during the reform era. As noted by Kelling and Moore (1991, p. 12): "Police leaders in the reform era redefined the nature of a proper relationship between police officers and both politicians and citizens. Police would be impartial law enforcers who related to citizens in professionally neutral and distant terms." Such a relationship is well typified by *Dragnet's* Sgt. Joe Friday and the attitude typified in his line "Just the facts, ma'am." The public viewed the police as professionals who were to remain detached from the citizens they served.

During the reform era the police relationship with the community they served was professionally remote.

During the reform era the concept of the **"thin blue line"** developed. This phrase refers to the line that separates law-abiding, peaceful citizens from the murderous, plundering villains who prey upon them. The phrase also suggests a distance between the police and the public they serve. The "thin blue line," as noted by Kelling and Moore (pp. 12–13), "connotates the existence of dangerous external threats to communities, portrays police as standing between that danger and good citizens, and implies both police heroism and loneliness."

Adding to the distancing of police from the public during the reform era was the replacement of foot patrol with motorized patrol. O. W. Wilson's preventive patrol by squad car coupled with an emphasis on rapid response to calls for service became the dual focus of policing during this era. The police image became one of officers roaring through city streets in high-powered squad cars, lights flashing and sirens wailing. The police were viewed as professional crime fighters. Consequently, policing during the reform era is often referred to as the *professional model*.

The **professional model** emphasized crime control by preventive automobile patrol coupled with rapid response to calls.

The problems faced by the first police administrators did not change much, but under the professional model their answers did. Many police methods were challenged during the 1960s when social change exploded in the United States as the result of several significant events which occurred almost simultaneously. The civil rights movement began in the late fifties as a grassroots movement to change the blatantly unequal social, political, and economic systems in the United States. Confrontations between blacks and the police, who were almost completely male

Antiwar riots and flag burnings in the 1960s pitted police against protesters.

and white, increased during this time. Representing the *status quo* and defending it, the manner in which the police handled protest marches and civil disobedience often aggravated each situation.

Punctuated by the assassinations of President Kennedy, Malcom X, Martin Luther King, Medgar Evers, and Robert Kennedy, the events of the decade were, for the first time in history, documented in detail and viewed by millions of Americans on television. The antiwar movement, based on college campuses, was also televised. When demonstrators at the 1968 Democratic Convention in Chicago were beaten by the Chicago police, the demonstrators chanted, "The whole world is watching." Americans watched what was later termed a police riot, and they were shocked.

Plagued by lack of training and confronted by a confusing array of social movements as well as an emerging drug culture, the police became the "enemy." Officers heard themselves referred to as "pigs" by everyone from students to well-known entertainers. They represented the *status quo,* the establishment, and everything standing in the way of peace, equality, and justice. Police in the sixties were at war with the society they served. Never had the relationship between the law enforcement community and the people it served been so strained.

In addition to the questionable way police handled race riots and antiwar demonstrations in the sixties, several big city police departments were charged with being corrupt at that time. The sixties changed the face of America, and law enforcement was no exception. Studies in the seventies on corruption and criminal behavior among police agencies brought great pressure on the entire criminal justice system to change its methods, attitudes, and image. Media coverage of law enforcement practices educated the public who ultimately demanded change.

The Law Enforcement Assistance Administration (LEAA) was established in 1968 as one response to the negative image of the criminal justice system. Over the next several years LEAA provided billions of dollars to the "war on crime," funding studies and programs for law enforcement.

> *LEAA awarded more than $9 billion to state and local governments to improve police, courts, and correctional systems; to combat juvenile delinquency; and to finance innovative crime-fighting projects.*
>
> *Every state and locality felt the impact of LEAA's nationwide anticrime program. Tens of thousands of programs and projects were supported with LEAA funds, and millions of hours were applied to identify effective, efficient, economical ways to reduce crime and improve criminal justice. Projects were developed to reduce crime, to improve the management and administration of courts, to deploy police officers more effectively, to find jobs for ex-offenders, to sharpen the skills of criminal justice personnel, to give prosecutors better tools to fight crime, and to break the jail-street-crime-jail cycle of the drug addict (Wrobleski and Hess, 1993, pp. 48–49).*

The courts also had a major impact on criminal justice during the 1960s. Several legal decisions limited police powers and clarified the rights of the accused. The 1965 *Miranda* v. *Arizona* decision had a significant impact on police methods. This landmark decision requires police officers to inform suspects of their right to remain silent, to have counsel present, and to have court-appointed counsel if they cannot afford to pay for counsel. Also, suspects must be warned that anything they say may be used against them in a court of law.

Despite these efforts, reported crime increased and the public's fear of crime intensified. An influx of immigrants added to the problems of major cities. The deinstitutionalizing of mental patients caused thousands of mentally disabled individuals to enter the mainstream of America, often without means to support themselves. This, coupled with the return of many Vietnam veterans who found it difficult to reenter society, resulted in a large homeless population.

Another challenge to the effectiveness of the professional model was the Kansas City Preventive Patrol Study. This classic study found that increasing or decreasing preventive patrol efforts had no significant effect on crime, citizen fear of crime, community attitudes toward the police, police response time, or traffic accidents. As noted by Klockars

(1983, p. 130): "It makes about as much sense to have police patrol routinely in cars to fight crime as it does to have firemen patrol routinely in fire trucks to fight fire."

Other research conducted in the 1970s also questioned police effectiveness.

> *Research about preventive patrol, rapid response to calls for service, and investigative work—the three mainstays of police tactics—was uniformly discouraging.*
>
> *Research demonstrated that preventive patrol in automobiles had little effect on crime, citizen levels of fear, or citizen satisfaction with police. Rapid response to calls for service likewise had little impact on arrests, citizen satisfaction with police, or levels of citizen fear. Also, research into criminal investigation effectiveness suggested that detective units were so poorly administered that they had little chance of being effective (Kelling, 1988, p. 4).*

Other reasons for reevaluating police methods were the changing nature of the individuals who became police and their frustration with the traditional role of the patrol officer. As noted by Kelling (1988, p. 4): "Despite pieties that patrol has been the backbone of policing, every police executive has known that, at best, patrol has been what officers do until they become detectives or are promoted. At worst, patrol has been the dumping ground for officers who are incompetent, suffering from alcoholism or other problems, or simply burned out." A change was needed at the patrol level to attract more highly educated and less militaristic recruits. The patrol officer had to become important to the department in accomplishing its mission.

Finally, many businesses and individuals began to hire private security officers to assure their safety. The public assumed that the police alone were unable to "preserve the peace." While some called for greater cooperation between public and private policing, others argued that the public should collaborate with all policing efforts.

A combination of the dissatisfaction with criminal justice and the role of patrol officers, research results, and the trend toward private policing led to the third era of policing—the community era.

The Community Era

In the 1980s many police departments began experimenting with more community involvement in the "war on crime." Also during this decade several cities tested Herman Goldstein's problem-oriented approach to policing. The emphasis in many departments began to shift from crime fighting to crime prevention.

During the community era the police reestablished a close relationship with the community.

Since community-oriented, problem-solving policing appears to be the trend for the 1990s and beyond, these approaches are discussed in detail, following a review of the highlights of the three eras of policing, which are summarized in Table 1.1.

Two important focuses of the community policing era were evident in the later years of the professional model: more public relations programs and crime prevention efforts involving citizens.

TABLE 1.1
The Three Eras of Policing

	Political Era 1840s to 1930s	Reform Era 1930s to 1980s	Community Era 1980s to present
Authorization	politics and law	law and professionalism	community support (political), law and professionalism
Function	broad social services	crime control	broad provision of services
Organizational Design	decentralized	centralized, classical	decentralized, task forces, matrices
Relationship to Community	intimate	professional, remote	intimate
Tactics and Technology	foot patrol	preventive patrol and rapid response to calls	foot patrol, problem solving, public relations
Outcome	citizen, political satisfaction	crime control	quality of life and citizen satisfaction

SOURCE: Summarized from George L. Kelling and Mark H. Moore, "From Political to Reform to Community: The Evolving Strategy of Police." In *Community Policing: Rhetoric or Reality.* Edited by Jack R. Greene and Stephen D. Mastrofski 6, 14–15, 22–23. New York: Praeger Publishers, 1991.

PUBLIC RELATIONS PROGRAMS

During the past several decades, especially in the late 1970s as a result of the widening gap between the police and the public, most police departments began public relations programs. According to Senna and Siegel (1990, p. 206): "For the past 20 years, police agencies have been making an effort to gain the cooperation and respect of the community they serve, or, in other words, to improve **police-community relations (PCR)** (emphasis added)."

The goal of **public relations** programs established by police departments is to improve the image of the police.

Public relations efforts by police departments included hosting department open houses, sponsoring youth athletic leagues, and providing speakers for school and community events. Many police departments have established a public relations office or division and assign specific officers to the public relations effort. Such efforts reflect the growing recognition by police administrators that they need public support. Frequently public relations efforts engage citizens to help the police in their crime prevention efforts.

CRIME PREVENTION PROGRAMS

Crime prevention programs have flourished during the past few decades.

Crime prevention programs that enlist the aid of citizens include operation identification programs, neighborhood or block watch programs, and home and automobile security programs.

Such programs continue to be an integral part of most community efforts and will be discussed in detail in Section Three.

Gradually law enforcement has become more responsive to the public's desire for a different kind of policing. Today there is considerable citizen-police interaction and problem solving. While still resistant to change, police agencies are now more likely to respond to the needs and wishes of the communities they serve. The significant changes in the way police address sexual assault, domestic violence, sexual abuse of children, drunk driving, and missing children attest to this new responsiveness. The public wants the police to be proactive; citizens want police to try to prevent crime in addition to apprehending criminals after a crime has been committed.

Although community relations and crime prevention are integral to most community-oriented programs, more issues are involved in and addressed by community-oriented policing.

COMMUNITY-ORIENTED POLICING: A CLOSER LOOK

While community-oriented policing is considered innovative, its central tenets of involvement with and responsiveness to the community are similar to the principles set forth by Sir Robert Peel in 1829 when he established the London Metropolitan Police. Policing has strayed so far from these principles in the past century, that the concepts central to community-oriented policing seem fresh and sensible today.

> *Viewed from one perspective, it is not a new concept; the principles can be traced back to some of policing's oldest traditions. . . .*
>
> *What is new is the idea that community policing is not a particular program within a department, but instead should become the dominant philosophy throughout the department (Brown, 1989, p. 1).*

Oliver (1992, p. 46) contends: "The current 'buzz' word in law enforcement is community policing." He notes, however, that the term "community policing" is an intangible term, based on intangible ideas.

> *The phrase "community policing" is an all-encompassing idea that focuses on a single goal: reducing crime and public fear. . . .*
>
> *Community policing is an imperceptible term that has no concrete definition or limits (Oliver, 1992, p. 46).*

Indeed, community-oriented policing is many different things to many different people. Weatheritt (1991, pp. 153–54) stresses:

> *Community policing is talked about at a number of levels and it is important to distinguish between them. At one level community policing is about developing a set of programs or activities for police: foot patrol, community-based crime prevention, ways of consulting communities about the kinds of problems they have and the kind of policing they want. The emphasis tends to be on the pragmatic and small-scale. . . . [On a second level] community policing is about promoting better police-public relations and a better police image. . . . It is undertaken because community policing activities are seen as good in themselves. . . .*

Community policing is also about changing the ethos of policing to emphasize notions of service, flexibility, consumer responsiveness, conciliation, consultation, and negotiation.

Weatheritt (1991, p. 172) suggests: "Community policing is an elastic term that is often used to give a superficial coherence to a wide and disparate set of policing activities and various forms of police community dialogue."

According to the Police Executive Research Forum: "Community policing should be seen as part of an on-going reform movement that includes various foundations, educational institutions, urban politicians in non-machine cities, and criminal justice educators" (Manning, 1991, p. 45).

Defining community policing is not without its problems. Trojanowicz and Bucqueroux (1990, p. 5) have a page-long definition that begins like this:

Community policing is a new philosophy of policing, based on the concept that police officers and private citizens working together in creative ways can help solve contemporary community problems related to crime, fear of crime, social and physical disorder and neighborhood decay. The philosophy is predicated on the belief that achieving these goals requires that police departments develop a new relationship with the law-abiding people in the community, allowing them a greater voice in setting local police priorities and involving them in efforts to improve the overall quality of life in their neighborhoods. It shifts the focus of police work from handling random calls to solving community problems.

In other words, where traditionally policing has been **reactive,** responding to calls for service, the trend is for policing to be **proactive,** anticipating problems and seeking solutions to these problems.

This perspective of community policing is shared by Vaughn (1991, p. 35): "Community oriented policing is a philosophy, a style, and a method of providing police service and managing the police organization. It is value based and involves long term institutional change."

Community policing is a philosophy that emphasizes working proactively with citizens to solve crime-related problems and prevent crime.

Community-oriented policing is defined in many ways and includes many approaches such as community policing, neighborhood policing, problem-oriented policing, and policing for community wellness. At the heart of most "new" approaches to policing is a return to the ancient idea of community responsibility for the welfare of society. As noted by former

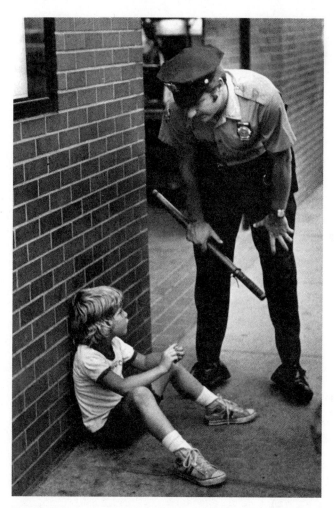

Community policing stresses the importance of interacting with citizens.

New York City Police Commissioner Brown (1990, p. 8): "At the heart of policing is a requirement for understanding between the police and the citizens they are sworn to protect. Put simply, police officers must be *a part* of the community, not *apart* from it." Brown (1991, p. 6) further contends:

> *Permanent interaction between officers and neighborhood residents and merchants is the first step toward identifying the community's problems. When the people of the community get involved and realize they have a voice in improving their quality of life, it creates good will and makes it easier for the police to fulfill their mission. . . .*

We need to solve chronic community problems rather than just react to them. It is time to adopt new strategies to address the dramatic increases in crime and the fear of crime. I view community policing as a better, smarter and more cost-effective way of using police resources.

A need for community involvement is also stressed by VanBlaricom (1989, p. 7):

The traditional police department is an insular organization that responds to citizens' wishes from behind the blue curtain when a crisis of sufficient magnitude erupts to demand political damage control. Community policing changes that approach by bringing the police officers back into the neighborhoods to talk with residents about what they want and how they can lawfully accomplish their goals together.

A comparison of traditional policing and community policing is made in Table 1.2.

Critics of community-oriented policing, however, contend that it is really "nothing new under the sun." As noted by Bayley (1991, pp. 225–26):

It is probably fair to say that community policing in 1988 is more rhetoric than reality. It is a trendy phrase spread thinly over customary reality. Unless this state of affairs changes, the most likely future for community policing is that it will be remembered as another attempt to put old wine into new bottles.

Further, community policing might bring with it several problems.

Potential Problems Associated with Community Policing

Bayley (1991, pp. 226–36) cites several potential problems associated with community policing. First, public safety might decline because the public is not that interested in participating in crime prevention efforts. Second, he suggests that the police may become too soft on crime and lose the ability to control violence in the community. "Can the police put on a velvet glove and keep their iron hand in shape?" asks Bayley (p. 228).

Another potential problem with community policing is that the rationale for having police is diminished. As crime fighters, they were extremely important to communities. If, however, the police prove to be ineffective crime fighters, there is no reason to believe they will be effective crime preventers. Further, the public may become a special interest group for the police. According to Bayley (p. 229): "Community

TABLE 1.2

Comparison of Traditional Policing and Community Policing

Question	Traditional	Community Policing
Who are the police?	A government agency principally responsible for law enforcement.	Police are the public and the public are the police: the police officers are those who are paid to give full-time attention to the duties of every citizen.
What is the relationship of the police force to other public service departments?	Priorities often conflict.	The police are one department among many responsible for improving the quality of life.
What is the role of the police?	Focusing on solving crimes.	A broader problem-solving approach.
How is police efficiency measured?	By detection and arrest rates.	By the absence of crime and disorder.
What are the highest priorities?	Crimes that are high value (e.g., bank robberies) and those involving violence.	Whatever problems disturb the community most.
What, specifically, do police deal with?	Incidents.	Citizens' problems and concerns.
What determines the effectiveness of police?	Response times.	Public cooperation.
What view do police take of service calls?	Deal with them only if there is no real police work to do.	Vital function and great opportunity.
What is police professionalism?	Swift effective response to serious crime.	Keeping close to the community.
What kind of intelligence is most important?	Crime intelligence (study of particular crimes or series of crimes).	Criminal intelligence (information about the activities of individuals or groups).
What is the essential nature of police accountability?	Highly centralized; governed by rules, regulations, and policy directives; accountable to the law.	Emphasis on local accountability to community needs.
What is the role of headquarters?	To provide the necessary rules and policy directives.	To preach organizational values.
What is the role of the press liaison department?	To keep the "heat" off operational officers so they can get on with the job.	To coordinate an essential channel of communication with the community.
How do the police regard prosecutions?	As an important goal.	As one tool among many.

SOURCE: *Implementing Community Policing,* by Malcolm K. Sparrow. U.S. Department of Justice, National Institute of Justice. (November 1988): 8–9.

policing seeks to transform the police from what has been described as 'an army of occupation' into an accepted, unremarkable, and individually responsive part of the community."

Community policing may also adversely increase the power of the police in comparison to that of other governmental agencies. Community policing seeks to build strong ties between the police and the community. Such ties may cause problems, however, when other government officials realize and resent the power police departments and individual officers may have to lobby citizens for financial resources and officer assignments or transfers. Police chiefs nationwide have found themselves in conflict with mayors and city councils as individual police officers lobby for needed resources. A closer relationship between the police and the public may also result in the citizens' increased ability to influence internal department matters.

Another potential problem with community policing is that its emphasis on crime prevention gives police the authority to keep careful watch on individuals in the community. Closely related to this problem is a fear that community policing will increase government surveillance of private citizens. As Bayley (p. 230) states: "Community policing legitimates the penetration of communities by forceful enforcement agents of government."

In addition, community policing, because it promotes adapting policing to local circumstances, may lead to the unequal application of justice. "Local commanders may begin to think it is more important not to alienate loud voices than to protect quiet ones" (Bayley, p. 232). Closely related to this, is the potential that community policing may lessen the protection given to unpopular individuals such as the homeless. It may even lead to vigilantism.

Finally, community policing may worsen a growing dualism in policing; affluent neighborhoods embrace the community-oriented mode while poorer urban areas and ghettos return to an emphasis on law enforcement and crime fighting.

Despite these potential problems, Bayley does not advocate abandoning community policing. Rather, he suggests that if a department adopts community policing as a philosophy, it should be aware of the potential hazards and avoid them. He cautions (p. 236): "Community policing does not represent a small, technical shift in policing; it is a paradigmatic change in the way police operate. It is the most fundamental change in policing since the rise of police professionalism early in this century. Because community policing is serious and fateful, we must be open minded about its potential infirmities as well as its promise." In other words, community policing cannot be considered a cure-all for the problems of crime and fear of crime in our communities.

Similar possible problems associated with community policing are discussed by Wycoff (1991, p. 116):

1. *Illegal Policing.* Community-based officers may become more responsive to local norms than to legal constraints.
2. *Inequitable Policing.* Some groups may benefit more than others from police service.
3. *Politicization of the Police.* Officers might use their community organizing skills and good relationships with the neighborhood to mount a campaign to accomplish political objectives, e.g., salary increases or ouster of an unappreciated judge or chief.
4. *Corruption.* Close contact between police and business people or residents creates possibilities of unacceptable behavior.
5. *Police Intrusion into Private Arenas.* In a democratic society, how effective do we really want our police to be?

Despite these potential problems, Wycoff is also an advocate of community policing. She recalls Peel's 1829 statement that the police are the "only members of the public that are paid to give full-time attention to duties incumbent on every citizen in the interest of community welfare and existence. What we may be seeing is not a new concept under the sun but rather a new sunrise on a fine old concept" (Wycoff, p. 120).

Community policing is usually synonymous with neighborhood-oriented policing.

NEIGHBORHOOD-ORIENTED POLICING

The Houston Police Department has reorganized their organization under a philosophy referred to as neighborhood-oriented policing (NOP).

Neighborhood-oriented policing is a philosophy of policing that stresses police responsiveness and depends on quality day-to-day interactions between the police and the public.

According to Oettmeier and Brown (1991, pp. 126–27):

It is not how good you are, it's how good those people out there think you are that is important. Officers may think they are the best at what they do; however, if the people, the citizens, the community, and the civic groups do not think they are the best or do not think they are doing the job they should be doing, the officers have not accomplished anything positive. . . .

Neighborhood-oriented policing is an interactive process between police officers assigned to specific beats and the citizens that either work or reside in these beats to mutually develop ways to identify problems and concerns and then to assess viable solutions by providing available resources from both the police department and the community to address the problems and/or concern.

Herman Goldstein has developed a very structured, proactive approach to the problems of crime and fear of crime. Goldstein's problem-oriented policing developed, in part, as a response to criticism of the professional model of policing. Like community-oriented and neighborhood-oriented policing, his philosophy is rooted in police and citizen interaction.

PROBLEM-ORIENTED POLICING _____

Goldstein (1990, p. 20) criticizes the professional model of policing as being incident driven: "In the vast majority of police departments, the telephone, more than any policy decision by the community or by management, continues to dictate how police resources will be used." The primary work unit in the professional model is the **incident**, that is, an isolated event which requires a police response. The institution of 911 has greatly increased the demand for police services and the public's expectation that the police will respond quickly.

Goldstein (p. 33) suggests: "Most policing is limited to ameliorating the overt, offensive symptoms of a problem." He suggests that police are more productive if they respond to incidents as symptoms of underlying community problems. Goldstein (p. 66) defines a problem as "a cluster of similar, related, or recurring incidents rather than a single incident, a substantive community concern, and a unit of police business." Once the problems in a community are identified, police efforts can focus on addressing the possible causes of such problems.

Problem-oriented policing requires police to group incidents and, thereby, identify underlying causes of problems in the community.

While problem-oriented policing may be ideal, law enforcement cannot ignore specific incidents. When calls come in, most police departments respond. Problem-oriented policing has a dual focus. First, it requires that incidents be linked to problems. Second, time devoted to "preventive" patrol must be spent proactively, determining community problems and their underlying causes. As noted by Wilson and Kelling (1989, p. 46):

The police know from experience what research by Glenn Pierce, in Boston, and Lawrence Sherman, in Minneapolis, has established:

fewer than 10 percent of the addresses from which the police receive calls account for more than 60 percent of those calls. If each call is treated as a separate incident with neither a history nor a future, then each dispute will be handled by police officers anxious to pacify the complaints and get back on patrol as quickly as possible. . . .

A study of domestic homicides in Kansas City showed that in eight out of ten cases the police had been called to the incident address at least once before; in half the cases they had been called five times *or more.*

A problem-oriented approach relies heavily upon citizen involvement. According to Goldstein (1991, p. 21): "The police must do more than they have done in the past to engage the citizenry in the overall task of policing. . . . A community must police itself. The police can, at best, only assist in that task."

An illustrative analogy can be drawn between a physician and a patient. The physician can examine the patient, take his history, and based on the patient's symptoms, prescribe a treatment. For the patient to recover he must, however, be honest and thorough in describing the symptoms and must follow the prescribed treatment. Further, in medicine as in policing, the best approach is to prevent the illness in the first place. As noted by Wadman and Olson (1990, p. 37): "In order to understand current trends in policing, we should compare the problem of crime with the problem of disease. For centuries, scientists have searched for cures to the various ailments that afflict mankind. It wasn't until the twentieth century that medical science discovered that the best cure was not to have the disease at all." The concept of community wellness is closely associated with problem-oriented policing and with community policing.

COMMUNITY WELLNESS

Just as physicians cannot be blamed for the existence of disease, police cannot be blamed for the existence of crime.

The police can no longer accept total responsibility for our crime problems. Success will be achieved only when the police and the community join forces to develop solutions.

Community wellness is the result of a sharing of responsibility and authority for the causes of crime and for crime itself. . . . Unless the community actively involves itself with its police department

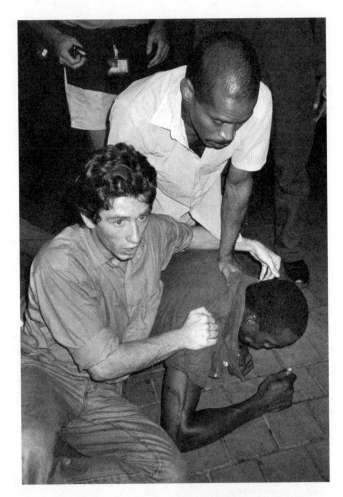

Citizens hold a suspect for police after seeing him snatch a purse.

and the department's attempt to solve community problems, we will forever be mired in reactive, rather than proactive, policing (Nila, 1990, p. 47).

Community wellness emphasizes a proactive partnership between the police and the community to prevent crime.

Wadman and Olson (1990, p. 92) make this analogy: "Much like fighting a forest fire, the wellness concept demands that personnel and equipment be diverted to create the 'firebreaks' that reduce the opportunities for crimes to be committed. This is where the real risks come in." The community wellness approach to policing also recognizes that police must fulfill their "crime fighter" role. In that role, too, however, the relationship between the police and community can be critical.

Regardless of whether police officers respond to incidents, seek symptoms of problems, or both, the public can help or hinder their efforts. Police and community members must discuss and agree to any community involvement program before it is adopted. At times well-meaning individuals and community groups, acting unilaterally, can actually interfere with a police effort and cause unnecessary destruction, injury, and even death.

The dual themes of this book are the manner in which police can build a positive relationship with the community and the subsequent development of crime prevention strategies and programs which the police and community can participate in jointly. Building a positive relationship as the basis for community policing begins with an understanding of the partners involved: the community and the police. These entities are the focus of the next two chapters.

Summary

"Modern" policing began with the formation of the London Metropolitan Police, based on principles set forth by Sir Robert Peel. Peel's principles emphasized the interdependence of the police and the public as well as the prevention of crime and disorder.

Policing in the United States has had three eras: political, reform, and community. During the political era the police relationship with the community was intimate. During the reform era the relationship was professionally remote. During the community era the relationship was again intimate.

During the 1960s and 1970s relations between the police and the public were extremely strained. In an effort to improve relations, many police departments instituted public relations programs. The goal of these programs was to improve the image of the police. Many departments also began crime prevention programs that enlisted the aid of citizens, including such programs as operation identification, neighborhood or block watches, and home and automobile security programs.

In the past decade many police departments have relied on increased community involvement by instituting community policing, neighborhood-oriented policing, problem-oriented policing, and community wellness policing. Community policing is a philosophy that emphasizes working with citizens to solve crime-related problems and prevent crime. Neighborhood-oriented policing is also a responsive style of policing dependent on a good relationship between the police and the public.

Problem-oriented policing requires the police to group incidents so as to identify and solve community problems. Community wellness emphasizes a proactive partnership between the police and the community to prevent crime. Each of these approaches to policing emphasizes the collaborative efforts of the police and the community.

DISCUSSION QUESTIONS

1. From the perspective of law enforcement, what are the strengths and weaknesses of each of the three eras of policing?
2. From the perspective of a citizen, what are the strengths and weaknesses of each era?
3. Is any form of community policing taking place in your community? If so, which?
4. What advantages does community policing offer? Disadvantages?
5. How is the relationship between the police and the public typically portrayed in popular television programs and movies?
6. How is the relationship between the police and the public typically portrayed in the news media?
7. Can you see any evidence of the patronage or spoils system of policing in the 1990s?
8. What are the similarities of community policing, neighborhood policing, and problem-oriented policing?
9. Which form of policing do you believe has the most potential for your community? Why?
10. Have you witnessed any examples of the "thin blue line"?

DEFINITIONS
Can you define the following terms: community policing, community relations, community wellness, hue and cry, incident, neighborhood-oriented policing (NOP), patronage system, police-community relations (PCR), proactive, problem-oriented policing (POP), professional model, progressive era, public relations, reactive, spoils system, "thin blue line."

REFERENCES

Bayley, David H. "Community Policing: A Report from the Devil's Advocate." In *Community Policing: Rhetoric or Reality*, edited by Jack R. Greene and Stephen D. Mastrofski, 126–237. New York: Praeger Publishers, 1991.

Brown, Lee P. "Community Policing: A Practical Guide for Police Officers." *Perspectives on Policing*. (September 1989).

Brown, Lee P. "Community Policing: Its Time Has Come." *The Police Chief*. (September 1991): 6.

Brown, Lee P. "The Police-Community Partnership." *The Police Chief.* (December 1990): 8.

Garmire, Bernard L., ed. *Local Government Police Management.* Mimeographed. Published by the International City Management Association, *Law and Order.* (August 1989).

Goldstein, Herman. *Problem-Oriented Policing.* New York: McGraw-Hill Publishing Company, 1990.

Hageman, Mary Jeanette. *Police-Community Relations.* Beverly Hills: Sage Publications, 1985.

Inkster, Norman D. "The Essence of Community Policing." *The Police Chief.* (March 1992): 28–31.

Kelling, George L. "Police and Communities: The Quiet Revolution." *Perspectives on Policing.* (June 1988).

Kelling, George L. and Moore, Mark H. "From Political to Reform to Community: The Evolving Strategy of Police." In *Community Policing: Rhetoric or Reality,* edited by Jack R. Greene and Stephen D. Mastrofski, 3–25. New York: Praeger Publishers, 1991.

Klockars, Carl B. *Thinking about Police: Contemporary Readings.* New York: McGraw Hill, 1983.

Manning, Peter K. "Community Policing as a Drama of Control." In *Community Policing: Rhetoric or Reality,* edited by Jack R. Greene and Stephen D. Mastrofski, 27–45. New York: Praeger Publishers, 1991.

Nila, Michael J. "Defining the Police Mission: A Community/Police Perspective." *The Police Chief.* (October 1990): 43–47.

Oettmeier, Timothy N. and Brown, Lee P. "Developing a Neighborhood-Oriented Policing Style." In *Community Policing: Rhetoric or Reality,* edited by Jack R. Greene and Stephen D. Mastrofski, 121–34. New York: Praeger Publishers, 1991.

Oliver, Willard M. "Community Policing Defined." *Law and Order.* (August 1992): 46, 56–58.

Pace, Denny F. *Community Relations Concepts.* Placerville, Calif.: Custom Publishing Company, 1991.

Richardson, J. F. *The New York Police.* New York: Oxford University Press, 1970.

Senna, Joseph J. and Siegel, Larry J. *Introduction to Criminal Justice.* 5th rev. ed. St. Paul: West Publishing Company, 1990.

Taft, Philip B., Jr. *Fighting Fear: The Baltimore County COPE Project.* Washington: Police Executive Research Forum, 1986.

Trojanowicz, Robert and Bucqueroux, Bonnie. *Community Policing: A Contemporary Perspective.* Cincinnati: Anderson, 1990.

VanBlaricom, D. P. "Shaking the Pillars of Police Tradition." *Law Enforcement News.* (October 31, 1989): 7.

Vaughn, Jerald R. "Community Oriented Policing . . . You Can Make It Happen." *Law and Order.* (June 1991): 35–39.

Wadman, Robert C. and Olson, Robert K. *Community Wellness: A New Theory of Policing.* Washington: Police Executive Research Forum, 1990.

Weatheritt, Mollie. "Community Policing: Rhetoric or Reality." In *Community Policing: Rhetoric or Reality,* edited by Jack R. Greene and Stephen D. Mastrofski, 153–75. New York: Praeger Publishers, 1991.

Wilson, James Q. and Kelling, George L. "Making Neighborhoods Safe." *The Atlantic Monthly.* (February 1989): 46–49.

Wrobleski, Henry M. and Hess, Kären M. *Introduction to Law Enforcement and Criminal Justice.* 4 rev. ed. St. Paul: West Publishing Company, 1993.

Wycoff, Mary Ann. "The Benefits of Community Policing: Evidence and Conjecture." In *Community Policing: Rhetoric or Reality,* edited by Jack R. Greene and Stephen D. Mastrofski, 103–20. New York: Praeger Publishers, 1991.

CHAPTER **2**

THE ROLE OF
COMMUNITY IN COMMUNITY-
ORIENTED POLICING

*I believe in the United States of America as a
Government of the people, by the people,
for the people . . .*

—American Creed

DO YOU KNOW

- How U.S. citizens established the "public peace"?
- What a social contract is?
- How to define community?
- What the broken window phenomenon refers to?
- What demographics includes?
- How our communities have changed and continue to change?
- What role organizations and institutions play within a community?
- How private policing compares to public policing in terms of
  personnel and budget?
- What power structures exist within a community?
- What the three components of the criminal justice system are?
- What issues in the criminal justice system affect police-community
  relations?
- How the medical model and the justice model view criminals?
- How prevalent civilian review boards are and where they are most
  commonly used?

INTRODUCTION

The opening sentence of the American Creed, adopted by the House of Representatives on April 3, 1918, uses language attributed to Abraham Lincoln in his *Address at Gettysburg,* November 19, 1863: "We here highly resolve that these dead shall not have died in vain; that this nation, under God, shall have a new birth of freedom; and that government of the people, by the people, and for the people, shall not perish from the earth." The philosophy implicit in the American Creed is central to the concept of "community" in the United States. Each community is part of a larger social order.

The U.S. Constitution and Bill of Rights, as well as federal and state statutes and local ordinances establish the "public peace" in the United States.

In the United States individual freedom and rights are balanced with the need to establish and maintain order. The United States was born out of desire for freedom. In fact, Former President Jimmy Carter noted: "America did not invent human rights. In a very real sense, it is the other way around. Human rights invented America."

The importance of individual rights to all citizens is a theme that is central to the following discussion of community. Citizens have established a criminal justice system in an effort to live in "peace," free from crime and violence. The influence of the criminal justice system on police-community relations is discussed later in the chapter. To ensure the peace, citizens of the United States have also entered into an unwritten *social contract.*

The **social contract,** a legal theory, provides that for everyone to receive justice, each person must relinquish some of his freedom.

In civilized society, people cannot simply do as they please. They are expected to conform to federal and state laws, as well as local rules and regulations established by and for the community in which they live. Increased mobility and economic factors have weakened the informal social contract which once helped to keep the peace in our society. As a result the police, as agents of social control, have had to fill the breach, increasing the need for law-abiding citizens to join with the police in making their communities free from drugs and crime. As noted by

Lawrence Massachusetts Police Chief Allen Cole (1989, p. 71): "It is widely accepted that a law enforcement agency is only as successful as the support it receives from the public it serves."

COMMUNITY DEFINED

What does the word *community* bring to mind? To many people it conjures up images of their hometown. To others it may bring images of a specific block, neighborhood or an idyllic small town where everyone knows everyone and they all get along.

Oran (1985, p. 63) defines community as: "A vague term that can include very large or very small areas, groups with common interests." Community has also been defined as a group of people living in an area under the same government. In addition, community can refer to a social group or class having common interests. Community may even refer to society as a whole; the public. This text uses a specific meaning for *community*.

Community refers to the specific geographic area served by a police department or law enforcement agency and the individuals, organizations, and agencies within that area.

Police officers must understand and be a part of this defined community if they are to fulfill their mission. The community may cover a very small area and have a very limited number of individuals, organizations, and agencies; it may, perhaps, be policed by a single officer. Or the community may cover a vast area and have thousands of individuals and hundreds of organizations and agencies and be policed by several hundred officers. According to Goldstein (1990, p. 25), the police tend to use the word community to "describe those affected in any way by the specific problems they are attempting to address, or the program being launched in response to the problem."

In a more philosophical sense, according to Manning (1991, p. 33):" 'Community' represents a sense of integration that people wish, hope, and envision as being a central part of their collective lives." Where such integrated communities exist, people share a sense of ownership and pride in their environment. They also have a sense of what is acceptable behavior, which makes policing in such a community much easier. As noted by Mastrofski (1991, p. 49):

A basis for police action requires that a group of people—say a neighborhood—shares a definition of what constitutes right order, threats to it, and appropriate methods for maintaining it. To the extent that community implies a basis for citizens to work collectively with police to restore and preserve order, it also requires a sense of group identity or attachment—a "we–ness" derived from shared experience and integration.

Community also refers to a sense of integration, of shared values, and a sense of "we-ness."

Klockars (1991, pp. 247–48) suggests: "Sociologically, the concept of community implies a group of people with a common history, common beliefs and understandings, a sense of themselves as 'us' and outsiders as 'them,' and often, but not always, a shared territory."

Unfortunately, many communities lack this "we-ness." In such areas, the police and public served have a "them v. us" relationship. As noted by Goldstein (1990, p. 25): "Areas of cities requiring the most police attention are usually those with few shared values and little sense of community."

In such communities disorder and crime may flourish. In a classic article, "Broken Windows," Wilson and Kelling (1982, p. 31) contend:

Social psychologists and police officers tend to agree that if a window in a building is broken and is left unrepaired, *all the rest of the windows will soon be broken. This is as true in nice neighborhoods as in run-down ones. Window-breaking does not necessarily occur on a large scale because some areas are inhabited by determined window-breakers whereas others are populated by window-lovers; rather, one unrepaired broken window is a signal that no one cares, and so breaking more windows costs nothing. (It has always been fun.)*

The **broken window phenomenon** suggests that if it appears "no one cares," disorder and crime will thrive.

Wilson and Kelling based their *broken window* theory, in part, on research done in 1969 by a Stanford psychologist, Philip Zimbardo. Zimbardo arranged to have a car without license plates parked with its hood up on a street in the Bronx and a comparable car on a street in Palo Alto, California. The car in the Bronx was attacked by vandals within ten minutes, and within twenty-four hours it had been totally destroyed and stripped of anything of value. The car in Palo Alto sat untouched. After a week Zimbardo took a sledgehammer to it. People passing by soon joined in, and within a few hours that car was also totally destroyed. According to Wilson and Kelling (p. 31): "Untended property becomes fair game for

The broken window that remains unfixed gives the impression that no one cares. Crime is likely to flourish in such an environment.

people out for fun or plunder, and even for people who ordinarily would not dream of doing such things and who probably consider themselves as law-abiding."

Broken windows and smashed cars are very visible signs of people not caring about their community. Other less subtle signs include lawns that are not mowed, piles of accumulated trash, and graffiti.

When considering the police-community relationship, it is imperative to determine if a sense of "we-ness" and ownership exists in the community. Developing effective police-community relations is a challenge because, as Mastrofski (p. 65) stresses, the police face a continuous struggle with "the dilemmas of governing communities that are, in fact, complex, ambiguous, diverse, and highly stratified."

This challenge is also emphasized by Weisburd and McElroy (1991, pp. 100–01): "The community is often identified as a resource waiting to be mobilized. Yet, as our findings suggest, community policing police officers are often confronted with settings of severe social disorganization. Such disorganization is not easily transformed into the kind of community organizations envisioned by the community policing philosophy."

It is extremely difficult to maintain a community policing system when the values of groups within a given area clash. For example, controversy may exist between gay communities and orthodox Christian or Jewish communities in the same area. Do each of these communities deserve a different style of policing based on the "community value system?" Do "community" police officers ignore behavior in a community where the majority of residents approve of that behavior, but enforce sanctions against the same behavior in enclaves where that behavior causes tension? These are difficult ethical questions.

Another factor that negates a sense of community is the prevalence of violence. We live in a violent society. The United States was born through a violent revolution. The media emphasizes violence, constantly carrying news of murder, rape, and assault. It seems that if a movie or television program is to succeed, at least three or four people must meet a violent death or suffer some physical injury. The average cartoon that children watch contains more violence than most adults realize. Children learn that violence is acceptable and justified under some circumstances. It is not surprising that violent crimes are increasing more quickly than the size of the population. Citizens expect the police to prevent such violence, but the police cannot do it alone. Individuals must come together to help stop violence and in so doing can build a sense of community.

In addition to understanding the concept of community, it is also important to assess the demographics of the area.

COMMUNITY DEMOGRAPHICS

Demographics refers to the characteristics of the individuals who live in a community.

Demographics includes a population's size, distribution, growth, density, and vital statistics such as average age, education, income, employment rate, and racial makeup.

Although people generally assume that the smaller the population of a community, the easier policing becomes, this is not necessarily true. Small communities generally have less resources. It is also difficult to be the sole law enforcement person being, in effect, on call twenty-four hours a day. A major advantage of a smaller community is that people know each other. A sense of community is likely to be greater in such communities than in large cities such as Chicago or New York.

When assessing law enforcement's ability to police an area, density of population is an important variable to consider. Studies have shown that as population becomes more dense, people become more aggressive. In densely populated areas, people become more territorial and argue more frequently about "turf."

Rapid population growth can invigorate a community, or it can drain its limited resources. Without effective planning and foresight, rapid population growth can result in serious problems for a community, especially if the population growth results from an influx of immigrants or members of an ethnic group different from the majority in that area.

The community's *vital statistics* are extremely important from a police-community partnership perspective. What is the average age of individuals within the community? Are there more young or elderly individuals? How many single parent families are there? What is the divorce rate? What is the common level of education? What is the drop out rate? What is the ratio of blue collar to professional workers in the community? How does the education of those in law enforcement compare?

Income and income distribution is also important. Do great disparities exist? Would the community be described as affluent, moderately well-off, or poor? How does the income of those in law enforcement compare? Closely related to income is the level of employment. How much unemployment exists? How do those who are unemployed exist? Are they on welfare? Do they commit crimes to survive? Are they homeless?

The ethnic makeup of the community is another consideration. Is the community basically homogeneous? A **homogeneous** community is one in which people are all quite similar. A **heterogeneous** community, in contrast, is one in which individuals are quite different from each other. Most communities are heterogeneous. Establishing and maintaining good relations among the various subgroups making up the community is a challenge. Usually one ethnic subgroup will have the most power and control. Consider the consequences if a majority of police officers are also members of this ethnic subgroup.

The existence of *ghettos* in many of our major cities poses extreme challenges for law enforcement. A **ghetto** is an area of a city usually inhabited by individuals of the same race or ethnic background who live in poverty and, to outsiders, apparent social disorganization. According to Pace (1991, p. 43): "Since ghettos house more than 70% of racial or ethnic minorities, the ghetto, minorities, and crime become interrelated and are the focus for most of the anti-crime efforts of the criminal justice system." This is often perceived as a clear bias by law enforcement against members of racial or ethnic minorities.

The Figgie Report (1983, pp. 133–34) identified several elements closely linked to community structure and composition and the causes of crime, including the following:

Hungry ghetto-dwellers search through trash bags for food on West Houston Street in New York City.

- Stability of the community population, especially entailing a lack of lower socioeconomic class transience.
- A history of low unemployment.
- A low population density.

Poverty, unemployment, substandard housing, and inadequate education have all figured into theories on the causes of crime. They are often part of the underlying problems that are manifested in crime.

A RAPIDLY CHANGING POPULATION

Communities have been undergoing tremendous changes in the past quarter century.

> *People of different races, cultures, and languages are coming into closer contact with each other and enormous demands are being made on their understanding and tolerance. Forecasters expect that by the end of the decade, less than 50 percent of the population of the United States will be white. . . .*

> *North America is faced with uncertain economies, overburdened social services and declining educational standards at a time*

when increasingly complex technology demands greater knowledge and sophistication. There are widening class divisions, more broken families and homelessness, growing anger on the part of the disadvantaged, a rise in violent crime and the unpredictable destruction of the international terrorist to contend with (Inkster, 1992, p. 28).

In addition, as noted by McCord and Wicker (1990, p. 30): "The United States is becoming a bifurcated society with more wealth, more poverty, and a shrinking middle class. The gap between the 'haves' and the 'have nots' is widening."

Trojanowicz and Carter (1990, pp. 6–11) note the following changes in the United States and predict they will continue:

- White dominance will end; minorities will increase.
- The elderly population will increase.
- The number of legal and illegal immigrants will increase.

United States Census Bureau projections suggest that African Americans, Hispanics, and Asians together will become the new majority. In addition, the past decade has had an estimated 23 percent increase in the number of Americans aged 65 and older (Exter, 1989). Further, the growing number of both legal and illegal immigrants "flooding into this country," say Trojanowicz and Carter (p. 6), "are of different races, ethnic groups, religions, and cultures. Many do not have even a rudimentary knowledge of the English language." They conclude (p. 11): "Today's challenge is to find new ways for law enforcement to contribute to make the United States a place where all people have an equal chance to secure a piece of the American dream for themselves and their children."

Challenges raised by dealing with members of minority groups, the elderly, and immigrants are discussed in detail later in this text.

ORGANIZATIONS AND INSTITUTIONS

In addition to understanding the demographics of the community and to being able to relate to a great variety of individuals, police officers must also be knowledgeable of the various organizations and institutions within the community and establish effective relationships with them. Brown (1990, p. 8) stresses that effective policing "requires the involvement of agencies other than the police—social services, education, clinics, businesses, employment offices, trash collection—anyone involved in community service."

As noted by Hubert Williams, President of the Police Foundation (1990, p. iv): "A strong network of community organizations and institutions contributes to a system of shared values that does not tolerate criminal behavior. This type of cohesiveness encourages the cooperation of citizens in ways that engender crime control and increase the likelihood that the commission of illegal acts will be detected."

Organizations and institutions can play a key role in enhancing community safety and quality of life.

Sulton (p. 3) stresses that: "Community institutions are the basic fabric from which our complex society is woven." Thus, it is society itself that encourages or discourages conditions related to crime. According to Sulton (p. 1):

All theories of causes of crime share common threads. They assume that crime is a socially defined phenomenon caused by the failure of community institutions to constrain behavior so that it conforms to the law and does not threaten the rights, safety, and lives of others. According to this perspective, crime reduction depends on eradication of the social conditions that produce crime.

A good relationship between the schools in the community and the police is vital to maintaining order. Other organizations and institutions police officers should interact effectively with include the Department of Human Services, health care providers, emergency services providers, and any agencies working with youth. Communities may also have libraries, museums, and zoos that would welcome a good relationship with the police.

The Figgie Report (1983, p. 134) identified a link between community safety and active community organizations, especially churches and volunteer groups that sponsor programs geared toward young people. Such cooperation often poses problems, however, as noted by Wilson and Kelling (1989, p. 52):

The problem of interagency cooperation may, in the long run, be the most difficult of all. The police can bring problems to the attention of other city agencies, but the system is not always organized to respond. In his book Neighborhood Services, *John Mudd calls it the "rat problem": "If a rat is found in an apartment, it is a housing inspection responsibility; if it runs into a restaurant, the health department has jurisdiction; if it goes outside and dies in an alley, public works takes over." A police officer who takes public complaints about rats seriously will go crazy trying to figure out what agency in the city has responsibility for rat control and then inducing it to kill the rats.*

In other words, if responsibility is fragmented, very little gets accomplished.

THE PUBLIC-PRIVATE POLICING INTERACTION

A good relationship between the private security industry and the police is also becoming more important. As noted by Trojanowicz and Bucqueroux (1990, p. 131): "Almost invisibly, private for-profit and nonprofit corporations have been assuming roles that were once almost exclusively the province of the public criminal justice system." They caution that many businesses are turning to private security for their protection and ask: "Does this portend a future where those who have the option choose to ignore the public police in favor of hiring private firms to provide them as much help as they want and can afford?"

Cameron (1991, p. 1) describes the phenomenal growth of the private security industry:

> *According to a new study by the National Institute of Justice, private security already outspends public law enforcement by 73%—and employs two and a half times the workforce, and is expected to increase even more over the next decade. The facts are, spending for private security is $52 billion vs. our $30 billion. And private security agencies employ 1.5 million people vs. our estimated 600,000. The average annual rate of growth in private security is predicted to be 8%, double that of public law enforcement.*

Private policing has two and one-half times the workforce of public policing and outspends law enforcement by 73 percent.

Many communities and even police departments are using **privatization,** contracting with private security agencies or officers to provide services typically considered to be law enforcement functions. Examples of privatization include using non-sworn personnel for parking enforcement, patrolling parks, animal control, prisoner transport, and even, in some instances, prisoner housing. Many police departments are also relinquishing responsibility for responding to home security alarms to private security firms.

The number of false alarms generated by private alarm systems is staggering and severely depletes the resources of many police departments. Jones (1991, p. 24) predicts that by 1995 the United States will

Using multi-image closed-circuit TV sets, a security guard monitors a large high-tech manufacturing facility in Irving, California. Security officers can serve as additional eyes and ears for the police department.

have over 40 million emergency responses to household and business alarm systems and asks: "Will the 800,000 true emergencies out of 40 million runs be worth the staggering cost? There can be no question that there are better ways to utilize such vast resources." He suggests that the Philadelphia experience proved the usefulness of having private alarm companies respond to most such alarms.

> *The Central Police Division has enlisted the support of all those in the private security industry in central Philadelphia—uniformed and non-uniformed security, guards and officers, the hotel industry, alarm companies and the Building Owners and Managers Association. The Philadelphia Parking Association has also joined the Security Watch program. . . .*
>
> *As a result, tangible gains have been made in reducing violent crime, decreasing calls for service involving order-maintenance problems and identifying and eliminating repeat unfounded alarms.*
>
> *The private security sector and the Philadelphia Police Department have formed a true partnership to establish and maintain order in the Center City area (p. 24).*

The need for public and private police forces to establish good working relationships was recognized by the National Institute of Justice in the early 1980s when it began urging cooperation between the agencies and established the Joint Council of Law Enforcement and Private Security Association.

Unfortunately, as noted by Mangan and Shanahan (1990, p. 19): "Police have traditionally viewed private security employees as inadequately trained and ill-paid individuals who could not find other work but were nevertheless allowed to carry a gun." Derogatory names such as "rent-a-cop" and "cop-in-a-box" contribute to this negative perception of private security. Despite this image, Mangan and Shanahan contend that: "Private security has emerged as a major player in the safeguarding of Americans and their property." They call for a "growing partnership between police professionals and private security specialists in a highly technical and changing environment."

ΤΗΕ POWER STRUCTURE

Most communities have both a formal and an informal power structure.

The **formal power structure** includes divisions of society with wealth and political influence such as federal, state, and local agencies and governments, commissions, and regulatory agencies.

The public can usually readily identify the formal power structure. Often policy decisions made at the federal and state level directly affect local decisions. In addition, federal and state funding can directly influence local programs.

The **informal power structure** includes religious groups, wealthy subgroups, ethnic groups, political groups, and public interest groups.

The public cannot as readily identify the informal power structure. The informal power structure includes banks, real estate companies, and other large and influential businesses in a community.

The informal power structure is not merely a few people controlling the masses; rather, the control groups are entire subcultures that influence other subcultures. It has been alleged that four hundred families control the wealth of the United States. Every other subculture is directly affected by this small subgroup (Pace, 1991, p. 121).

Awareness of the way informal groups, especially wealthy and political groups, exercise their ideologies is important for the

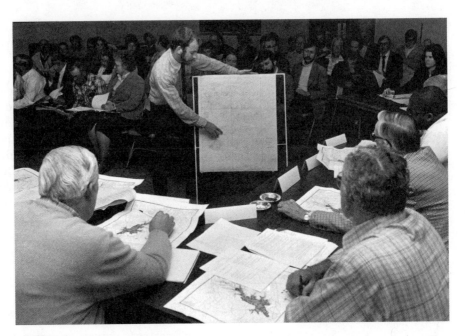

A developer presents a proposal for a new shopping mall to the city council. The formal and informal power structure will influence the council's decision.

> *community relations functionary. The way in which informal group pressure is forced into the formal structure of an organization is a key to understanding why the community at large is often in conflict with the criminal justice system (Pace, pp. 123–24).*

The formal and informal power structure is illustrated in Figure 2.1.

Law enforcement personnel must understand the different subgroups within their jurisdiction and the power struggles that occur among them. Pace (p. 34) suggests: "While democracy may promise equality, the reality is that the majority demands conformity." He further notes: "The reality is that most cultures do not readily adapt to the white, middle-class style of living," but in most communities that is where the power lies.

ıe CRIMINAL JUSTICE SYSTEM

Most people will equate policing or law enforcement with the criminal justice system when, in fact, it is only one part of this system. The other two components, courts and corrections, are much less visible in most communities.

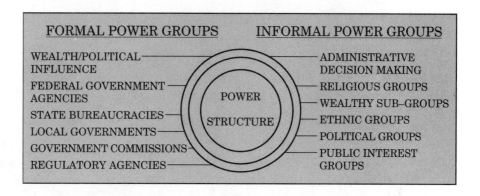

FIGURE 2.1   The Formal and Informal Power Structure

SOURCE: Denny F. Pace, *Community Relations Concepts,* Placerville, Calif.: Custom Publishing Company, 1991: 116. Reprinted by permission.

The three components of the criminal justice system are law enforcement, the courts, and corrections.

Law enforcement is only one segment of the vast criminal justice system which includes the courts and corrections. Because the police are the most visible component of the system, they often become *the* criminal justice system in the eyes of the community.

Many people have a limited understanding of the role the courts and corrections play in crime control. When the perception or the reality is that criminals are not being convicted or are being released early from prison, some people demand more police and ask why they are not doing "their job."

Members of the law enforcement community typically become frustrated and confused by such incidents. Officers become cynical and wonder why they work so hard to make arrests when they see cases dismissed or plea bargained. Officers may also become frustrated when those who are convicted are given a light sentence or perhaps even probation.

Most officers know many career criminals whose behavior has not improved even after they have been through prison, probation, parole, halfway houses, and rehabilitation programs. At times various components of the criminal justice system seem to work against each other. It is important, however, to remember that law enforcement is only one part of the criminal justice process.

In the criminal justice process it is the task of the police to receive reports of, or on their own initiative to detect, law violations, to

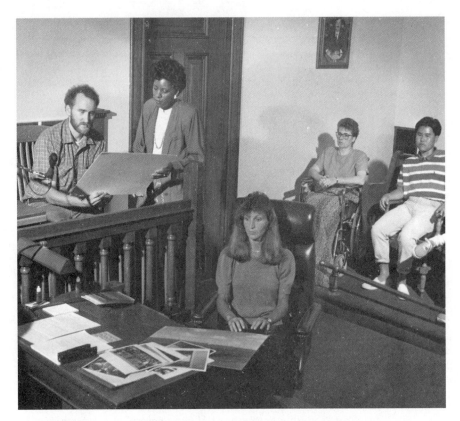

A witness gives testimony in a criminal trial as the court reporter makes a verbatim record.

apprehend those reasonably believed to be responsible for such violations, and to present those apprehended before a court of law for a determination of guilt or innocence. The court, through a time-honored procedure, weighs the charge and the evidence as presented both by an officer of the court who represents the people of the community and by an officer of the court who represents the person accused. If found to be guilty of the charge, the accused either is sentenced by the court to a term of confinement in a county or state (or, in the case of violations of federal statutes, a federal) facility or is permitted to return to the community under close, formal supervision (Garmire, 1989, pp. 22–23).

This system is a "carefully contrived procedure of checks and balances, designed to ensure that no person is accused of a crime and subsequently deprived of freedom of movement without every reasonable step being taken to guarantee fairness and equity in the process" (Garmire, p. 23).

Those who become critical of judges usually do so based on whether they agree with a judge's procedures and sentencing practices. Critics should remember that the system is designed to work the way it does. After all, if we assumed that everyone arrested by the police is guilty of a crime, there would be no need for prosecutors, judges, juries, or courtrooms. The accused could be taken directly to prison.

According to Pace, the public has a negative opinion of the courts because of their failure to process cases promptly, their inconsistency in plea bargaining, and the long tenure accorded to judges. Many believe that the courts provide "assembly-line" justice, and the legal process is filled with delays. Pace (p. 133) also notes: "Justice is an abstraction that may be given a person if he or she is affluent enough to hire the right attorney and outlast the system."

Aspects of the correctional system which have impeded good public relations include failures to reform offenders, the early release of prisoners who are recidivists, and the growing prison population.

The Figgie Report (1983, p. 134) found a relationship between community safety and good criminal justice administration, including strict, fair judges and district attorneys and a good court system. What constitutes good criminal justice administration and a good court system is open to debate. Many issues related to the effectiveness of the criminal justice system are controversial and will affect police-community partnerships. Although many issues are outside police officers' appropriate sphere of action, they affect the system as a whole. Therefore, police officers need to be aware of these issues and their potential impact on the profession.

Controversial issues in the criminal justice system which affect police-community partnerships include plea bargaining, diversion, sentencing, rehabilitation, community alternatives to prisons, victim's rights, and capital punishment.

Plea Bargaining. **Plea bargaining** is a practice by which prosecutors charge a defendant with a less serious crime in exchange for a guilty plea, thus eliminating the time and expense of a trial.

Diversion. **Diversion** is a system operating in most states that "diverts" juvenile status offenders and delinquents from the jurisdiction of the courts, whenever possible. This practice evolved because once juvenile delinquents are labeled they tend to act out and perpetuate that negative role.

Sentencing. Judges have considerable discretion in sentencing. When the community perceives sentences as too lenient, it sparks controversy. Police officers often believe that sentences are too light for serious crimes.

Rehabilitation. One objective of the correction process is rehabilitation, an objective which many have come to believe is an unattainable goal. The **recidivism,** or repeat offense rate of criminal behavior is very high. Greenfeld (1992, p. xvi) reports on a study on prisoners released in 1988. The prisoners were followed for three years. After three years 63 percent had been rearrested for felonies or serious misdemeanors.

Community Alternatives to Prison. Among the alternatives to prison are community supervision programs, including probation or parole, halfway houses, and house arrest. Community supervision is a method of helping offenders become productive, law-abiding members of the community while not adding to the overcrowding of our correctional facilities and the expense of incarceration. These alternatives become especially controversial when a community must determine the location of the facilities. Citizens often have the **NIMBY syndrome,** that is, "not in my backyard."

Victim's Rights. As violent crime increases, a growing number of people are protesting the treatment of victims by the criminal justice system. The law enforcement community has responded to this protest in a number of ways. Interacting with victims is the focus of Chapter 9.

Capital Punishment. The debate continues on the merits and effectiveness of capital punishment as a deterrent to crime and a form of retribution.

Another controversial issue in the criminal justice system is that it has concentrated its efforts on fighting crime to keep the "public peace." Many perceive police officers as armed social workers.

> *It is hard to understand why the American criminal justice system has concentrated its efforts almost solely upon the recognition of individual crimes and the discovery of specific procedures and policies to eliminate each crime. The system has been remiss in developing methods that attack the syndromes of crime (Pace, 1991, p. 5).*

A **syndrome of crime** is a group of signs, causes, and symptoms that occur together to foster specific crimes. The syndromes of crime are central to problem-oriented policing, discussed in detail in Chapter 16.

Another shift within the criminal justice system has been a shift in basic philosophy from a *medical model* to a *justice model.*

The **medical model** sees those who break the law as victims of society; the **justice model** views lawbreakers as responsible for their own actions.

No longer will society take the blame for individual criminals. Justice is served by having individuals be responsible for their own actions and suffer the consequences when they break the law. This change in philosophy is likely to enhance relations between those in the criminal justice system and law-abiding citizens.

CIVILIAN REVIEW BOARDS

"Civilian Review Boards (CRBs), intended to boost public confidence in the process of investigating complaints made by citizens against police, are an increasingly visible feature on the American law enforcement landscape," according to *Law Enforcement News* (April 15, 1991, p. 7). The article quotes Samuel Walker, criminal justice professor at the University of Nebraska, Omaha, who predicts that "increased public attention on police brutality and misconduct because of the videotaped beating of motorist Rodney King by Los Angeles police will result in the establishment of still more civilian review boards."

In a survey of the fifty largest cities in the United States, 60 percent had some form of civilian review (Brown, 1991, p. 6). In contrast, a survey of chiefs of police in towns with populations of 25,000 or less showed that 79 percent did not have such boards and do not want them (Sharp, 1990, p. 98).

Civilian review boards are most common in our largest cities; 60 percent have some form of civilian review.

Supporters of civilian review boards believe that it is impossible for the police to objectively review actions of their colleagues. They emphasize that the police culture demands that police officers support each other, even if they know something illegal has occurred.

Opponents of civilian review boards stress that civilians cannot possibly understand the complexities of the policing profession and that it is demeaning to be reviewed by an external source. As noted by Sharp (1990, p. 6): "People unfamiliar with police procedures can be stumbling blocks to harmonious civilian-police relations. . . . As most police administrators would agree, their jobs are tough enough without having the additional burdens of civilian review boards looking constantly over their shoulders."

Civilian review boards may be good in theory, but are often poor in reality. Pace (1991, p. 250) suggests two problems with citizen review boards:

> *The first problem was that the persons who were pushing for representation on the board were not representative of the community. They were generally the vocal rabble rousers who wished to impose their values upon the community. The second difficulty was, they were operating in a legal vacuum. They could make recommendations, but no one had authority to carry out their decisions. . . .*
>
> *Theoretically, the Citizen Review Board is an ideal vehicle to seek out misdeeds and to reconcile them to the satisfaction of the*

community at large. In practice, they do not function with objectivity, they do not have impartial or specialized investigators to conduct necessary investigations, and they have no power to carry out their decisions.

Civilian review boards are one of the most controversial issues in police work today. Most departments handle officer discipline internally. Complaints against officers are investigated by department personnel who determine whether misconduct occurred.

Police maintain it would be unfair to allow those outside police work to judge their actions, because only police officers understand the complexities of their job and, in particular, how and when force must be used. They stress that few citizens understand such concepts as "command presence" and "verbal force" so often necessary in high risk encounters. As one police sergeant put it: "The public should walk a mile in our combat boots before they judge us."

Citizens demand to be involved in the review process maintain that internal police discipline is tantamount to allowing the "fox to investigate thefts in the chicken coop." According to these citizens, police protect each other and cover up improper or illegal conduct. Citizens believe that this perpetuates abuses and sends a message to brutal officers that their behavior will be shielded from public scrutiny.

In some larger cities, police have lost the power to investigate complaints against fellow officers. The trend is toward more openness and citizen involvement in these matters. Officers should assume that they will be required to be more accountable for their actions. Officers may be held to a higher standard and will need to be prepared to justify their use of force in certain situations.

Successful resolution of this issue requires that the concerns of both the community and the police are addressed. The desired outcome would be that the police maintain the ability to perform their duties without the fear that they will be second-guessed, disciplined or sued by those who do not understand the difficulties of their job, *and* that citizens are not brutally or disrespectfully treated by officers.

Summary

A police-community partnership begins with an understanding of what communities are and how they function. Citizens of the United States have established the "public peace" through the U.S. Constitution and Bill of Rights, as well as through federal and state statutes and local ordinances. They also adhere to a social contract. The social contract, a legal theory, states that for everyone to receive justice, each person must give up some of his or her freedom.

Community refers to the specific geographic area served by a police department or law enforcement agency and the individuals, organizations, and agencies within that area. Community also refers to a sense of integration, of shared values, and a sense of "we-ness." The broken window phenomenon suggests that if it appears "no one cares," disorder and crime will thrive.

Understanding a community requires police to know about its demographics. Demographics includes population or size, distribution, growth, density, and vital statistics such as average age, average education, average income, employment rate, and racial makeup. Three important changes that will alter the demographics of our communities are: (1) white dominance will end; minorities will increase, (2) the elderly population will increase, and (3) the number of legal and illegal immigrants will increase.

Organizations and institutions can play a key role in enhancing community safety and quality of life. The private security industry can play an important role in improving a community's well-being. Private policing has two and a half times the workforce of public policing and outspends law enforcement by 73 percent.

Operating within each community is a power structure that can enhance or endanger police-community relations. The formal power structure includes those with wealth and political influence: federal, state, and local agencies and governments, commissions, regulatory agencies and power groups. The informal power structure includes religious groups, wealthy subgroups, ethnic groups, political groups, and public interest groups.

Also operating within communities and affecting the police-community relationship tremendously is the criminal justice system. The three components of the criminal justice system are law enforcement, the courts, and corrections. Controversial issues in the criminal justice system that affect police-community relations include plea bargaining, diversion, sentencing, rehabilitation, community alternatives to prisons, victim's rights, and capital punishment. The criminal justice system is moving away from a medical model of criminality to a justice model. The medical model sees those who break the law as victims of society; the justice model views lawbreakers as responsible for their own actions.

Civilian review boards are most common in our largest cities; 60 percent have some form of civilian review.

DISCUSSION QUESTIONS _____

1. How would you describe your community?
2. What instances of *broken windows* have you seen in your neighborhood? Other neighborhoods?
3. Can you give examples of the NIMBY syndrome?
4. What major changes have occurred in your community in the past ten years? In your state?

5. Who is included in the power structure in your community?
6. Do you favor the medical model or the justice model for dealing with criminals? Why?
7. How extensively are the services of private security used in your community? Do they cooperate with or compete against the local police?
8. Do you favor use of civilian review boards? Why or why not?
9. What are your views on capital punishment? Do you believe that if a state has capital punishment this reflects negatively on the police?
10. What factors are most important in establishing a "sense of community"?

DEFINITIONS
Can you define these terms: broken window phenomenon, community, demographics, diversion, formal power structure, ghetto, heterogeneous, homogeneous, informal power structure, justice model, medical model, NIMBY syndrome, plea bargaining, privatization, recidivism, social contract, syndrome of crime.

REFERENCES

Brown, Lee P. "The Civilian Review Board: Setting a Goal for Future Obsolescence." *The Police Chief.* (July 1991): 6.
Brown, Lee P. "The Police-Community Partnership." *The Police Chief.* (December 1990): 8.
Cameron, Bruce W. "Goodbye Cops—Hello Security Officers?" *Law and Order.* (December 1991): 1.
Cole, Allen W. "Citizens' Advisory Committees and the Use of Nominal Group Techniques." *The Police Chief.* (November 1989): 71–72.
Exter, Thomas. "Demographic Forecasts—On to Retirement." *American Demographics.* (April 1989).
Figgie Report, The. Part IV: Reducing Crime in America—Successful Community Efforts, 1983.
Garmire, Bernard L. (ed.) *Local Government Police Management.* 2nd rev. ed. Washington, D.C.: Published for the Institute for Training in Municipal Administration by the International City Management Association, 1989.
Goldstein, Herman. *Problem-Oriented Policing.* New York: McGraw-Hill Publishing Company, 1990.
Greenfeld, Lawrence A. *Prisons and Prisoners in the United States.* Washington: Bureau of Justice Statistics, April 1992.
Inkster, Norman D. "The Essence of Community Policing." *The Police Chief.* (March 1992): 28–31.
Jones, Lee A. "The Alarm Industry: Friend or Foe to Police Officers?" *The Police Chief.* (August 1991): 24–27.

Klockars, Carl B. "The Rhetoric of Community Policing." In *Community Policing: Rhetoric or Reality,* edited by Jack R. Greene and Stephen D. Mastrofski, 239–58. New York: Praeger Publishing, 1991.

Mangan, Terence J. and Shanahan, Michael G. "Public Law Enforcement/ Private Security: A New Partnership?" *FBI Law Enforcement Bulletin.* (January 1990): 18–22.

Manning, Peter K. "Community Policing as a Drama of Control." In *Community Policing: Rhetoric or Reality,* edited by Jack R. Greene and Stephen D. Mastrofski, 27–45. New York: Praeger Publishing, 1991.

Mastrofski, Stephen D. "Community Policing as Reform: A Cautionary Tale." In *Community Policing: Rhetoric or Reality,* edited by Jack R. Greene and Stephen D. Mastrofski, 48–67. New York: Praeger Publishing, 1991.

McCord, Rob and Wicker, Elaine. "Tomorrow's America: Law Enforcement's Coming Challenge." *FBI Law Enforcement Bulletin.* (January 1990): 28–32.

Oran, Daniel. *Law Dictionary for Nonlawyers.* 2nd rev. ed. St. Paul: West Publishing Company, 1985.

Pace, Denny F. *Community Relations Concept.* Placerville: Custom Publishing Company, 1991.

"Police Increasingly Face Public Scrutiny Through Civilian Review Boards." *Law Enforcement News.* (April 1991): 7, 11.

Sharp, Arthur G. "Civilian Review Boards May Be a Thing of the Past." *Law and Order.* (September 1990): 97–100.

Sulton, Anne Thomas. *Inner-City Crime Control. Can Community Institutions Contribute?* Washington: The Police Foundation, 1990.

Trojanowicz, Robert and Bucqueroux, Bonnie. "The Privatization of Public Justice: What Will It Mean to Police?" *The Police Chief.* (October 1990): 131–35.

Trojanowicz, Robert C. and Carter, David L. "The Changing Face of America." *FBI Law Enforcement Bulletin.* (January 1990): 6–11.

Weisburd, David and McElroy, Jerome E. "Enacting the CPO Role: Findings from the New York City Pilot Program in Community Policing. In *Community Policing: Rhetoric or Reality,* edited by Jack R. Greene and Stephen D. Mastrofski, 89–101. New York: Praeger Publishing, 1991.

Williams, Hubert. Preface. in *Inner-City Crime Control. Can Community Institutions Contribute?* Washington: The Police Foundation, 1990, iv.

Wilson James Q. and Kelling, George L. "Making Neighborhoods Safe." *The Atlantic Monthly.* (February 1989): 46–52.

Wilson James Q. and Kelling, George L. "The Police and Neighborhood Safety: Broken Windows," *The Atlantic Monthly.* (March 1982): 29–38.

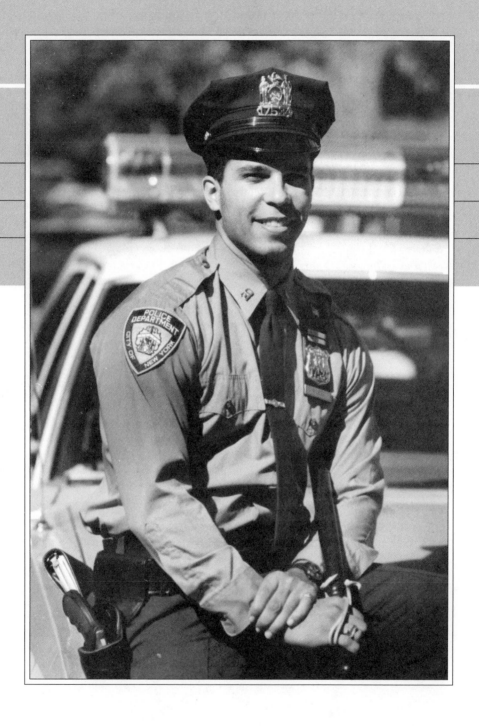

THE ROLE OF POLICE IN COMMUNITY-ORIENTED POLICING

The strength of a democracy and the quality of life enjoyed by its citizens are determined in large measure by the ability of the police to discharge their duties.

—Herman Goldstein

DO YOU KNOW

- How the makeup of the police force has changed in recent years?
- What characteristics are attributed to the police subculture? Which is the dominant characteristic?
- Where the police image comes from?
- What a negative contact is?
- What the public expects of the police?
- What dilemma faces law enforcement?
- What police spend the majority of their time doing?
- What a mission statement is?
- What two aspects of policing profoundly influence the police-community relationship?
- How discretion fits into the community-oriented policing philosophy?
- How the public views use of force by the police?
- What the four paradoxes of coercive power are?
- What three ethics checks are?

INTRODUCTION

Although "police officers" are the professionals discussed in this chapter, the concepts reviewed apply equally to police with different titles such as deputies or sheriffs. While this chapter focuses on police officers as professionals, always remember that police officers are first and foremost individuals. They are sons, daughters, mothers, fathers, brothers, sisters, aunts, uncles, neighbors, and friends. They may belong to community organizations. They may attend local churches. They may be active in politics. Their individual attributes have a great influence on who they are as police officers.

WHO ARE THE POLICE?

Traditionally, police officers were a fairly homogeneous group: white, male, with a high school education and a military background. This has changed; police officers have become a more heterogeneous group.

Today police departments have more minority and female officers. The educational level of the officers is much higher, and fewer have military experience. Police also are as interested in helping people as they are in fighting crime.

As noted by VanBlaricom (1989, p. 7): "The bright, well-educated, and (at least initially) service-oriented young men and women who are recruited into police departments today want to do something about crime besides taking reports of it."

Such changes in the makeup of the police force are fundamental to the community-oriented policing philosophy. As police departments become more representative of the communities they serve, they will be better able to understand the problems they must address. As officers become better educated, they will be better equipped to devise solutions to community problems.

Although the makeup of the police force has changed considerably, police officers still have several things in common that affect how they perceive themselves and their role in society.

THE POLICE SUBCULTURE

The police are a distinct subgroup in their community. They have tremendous power over the citizens they serve and protect. They may face a life-threatening situation at any time. Their lives may depend on each other. They experience situations others would not be likely to understand. As a result, they have developed their own subculture or value system. According to Goldstein (1990, pp. 29–30):

> The strength of the subculture grows out of the peculiar characteristics and conflicting pressures of the job: the ever-present physical danger; the hostility directed at the police because of their controlling role; the vulnerability of police officers to allegations of wrongdoing; unreasonable demands and conflicting expectations; uncertainty as to the function and authority of officers; a prevalent feeling that the public does not really understand what the police have to "put up with" in dealing with citizens; a stifling working environment; the dependence that officers place on each other to get the job done and to provide for their personal safety; and the shared sense of awareness, within a police department, that it is not always possible to act in ways in which the public would expect one to act.

In addition, police work is often unpleasant. Police often have to deal with ugly situations and antisocial behavior. Police are lied to, spit upon, and sworn at. They see unspeakable atrocities. Because of their shared experiences and unique exposure to their community, many police officers develop negative characteristics as coping mechanisms.

Conroy and Hess (1992) describe the responses police officers in a large metropolitan police force gave to the question: "What price did you pay to become a police officer?" The "prices" of becoming an officer are often described as characteristics of the police subculture.

The police subculture has been characterized as including a loss of innocence, cynicism, loneliness, isolation, and a constricted and inappropriate affect.

Police officers have described each characteristic as follows:

- *Loss of Innocence.* I never in a million years would have guessed there was so much violence, so much sadness, so much bitterness, so much anger, so much ugliness out there. It was beyond my comprehension. I would not have guessed it existed to the extent it does. (p. 81)

- *Cynicism.* I can take this uniform off and put it in my locker when I go home, but I've only got one brain. It's the brain I brought with me the first day I came to work, and it's the same brain I got everyday. I don't trust you because you might hurt me. I don't trust you because you're standing out in front of that store because you're a lookout. You're a bad guy until I know otherwise. That's what I learned, and for the last twenty-eight years that's what I've practiced. (p. 95)

- *Loneliness.* I am the loneliest man in the world, the loneliest man in the world. I still had friends, still had people that cared for me, but I was lonely. Nobody was in there with me where it was really terrible. (p. 107)

- *Isolation.* I wasn't close to anybody because I saw myself being in a situation where nobody knew what it was like for me and nobody would understand even if I told them. I thought I was pretty different in my pain and agony. I wasn't close to anybody now that I think about it. (p. 117)

- *Constricted and Inappropriate Affect.* You're required to be very cool and calculating when you dispense your emotions. You can't do it impulsively. I would have a calculated response to any occurrence. (p. 131)

A recurrent theme among the officers interviewed was the inability of the public to understand the police role and a tremendous reliance on the "police family."

A dominant characteristic of the police subculture is isolation and a "them v. us" world view.

The isolation experienced by police is enhanced by the emphasis on patrolling in squad cars. As Conroy and Hess note (1992, p. 121): "As you drive around in your squad car with the windows up, in the winter to stay warm, in the summer to stay cool, you are isolated in your 'cocoon.' Cocoons, however, serve not only to isolate caterpillars as they change to butterflies, but to protect them from predators as well."

Such isolation and "them v. us" world view conflicts with a community-oriented philosophy of policing. As communities move toward a return to foot patrol and to an emphasis on improving police-community relations, police isolation and their world view is likely to change.

Having looked at how the police often see themselves, now focus on how the public often views the police.

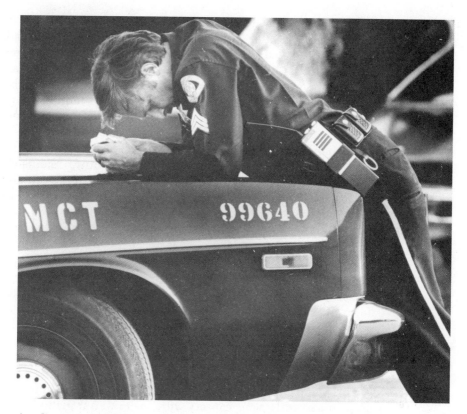

A police sergeant takes time to gather his thoughts after the successful conclusion of a hostage shootout.

THE POLICE IMAGE

How does the public view the police?

- The handsome, fashionable, invincible undercover cops of Miami Vice?
- The laid back, bumbling police department of Mayberry and its two officers, Andy Griffith and Don Knotts?
- Unselfish, fearless heros who protect the weak and innocent? Dirty Harrys?
- Hard-hearted, brutal oppressors of the underclass?
- Corrupt abusers of power, who become part of the criminal world?

Our society has varied images of law enforcement professionals. As noted in Chapter 1, that image is greatly affected by how the public perceives the criminal justice system within which the police function.

Many Americans believe in an ideal justice system in which fairness and equality are guiding principals; truth and justice prevail, and the accused is innocent until proven guilty. Law enforcement professionals are part of this idealized vision; many view police officers and sheriff's deputies as unselfish, fearless, compassionate protectors of the weak and defenseless, who can uncover the truth, bring the guilty to justice, and make things "right."

In contrast, others in our society see a criminal justice system that is neither fair nor just. Some individuals point out that the system employs officers who are overwhelmingly white, middle-class males. They also believe that some officers abuse their power and, in some cases, also abuse those with whom they come in contact in the line of duty.

Sources of the Police Image

An individual's opinion of the police is based on many factors, even a person's driving record. Someone who has received a traffic ticket, drives down the street and sees a squad car directly behind them will probably react differently than an individual who has never received a ticket.

Among the factors that contribute to the police image are television programs, movies, newspapers, magazines, books, the opinions of friends and family, your education, where you live, your economic status, whether you are handicapped, male or female, a member of a minority group, and, most importantly, your contact with the criminal justice system.

The police image is affected by individual backgrounds, the media, and personal experiences with the criminal justice system.

The media has an enormous impact on public opinion. The police image is affected by the manner in which television and newspaper stories present crime and law enforcement activities. Improving police-media relations is the focus of Chapter 11.

Police Work Contributes to the Police Image

Police officers are charged with some of society's most distasteful and dangerous tasks and are allowed to use reasonable force to affect arrests. The nature of police work and the power they are legally permitted to use make the police extremely powerful and contributes to their image.

According to Greene and Mastrofski (1991, p. 192): "In a society aspiring to achieve peace by peaceful means where that is not always possible, the police have been given the responsibility to use force and violence." The inherently negative associations coupled with the use of force are stressed by Klockars (1991, p. 240): "The police are not only

The police uniform with its badge, patches, and gunbelt conveys authority.

fundamentally and irreconcilably offensive in their means to the core cultural aspiration of a modern society [using force to achieve peace], but an ever present reminder that all of these noble institutions, which should make it possible for citizens to live in nonviolent relations with one another and with the state, often come up very short."

The police image is also shaped by police actions and appearance.

The police image is also affected by the police uniform and equipment. The uniform most police officers wear is a very visible reminder of the authority and power bestowed upon police. In fact, officers know that the uniform plays a major part in their ability to gain cooperation and compliance from the public. Much of their authority comes simply from what they are wearing. People recognize and react to visible symbols of authority.

The uniform and its trappings—patches, badges, medals, mace, nightsticks, handcuffs, and guns—can be overwhelmingly intimidating and can evoke negative public responses. Reflective sunglasses and handcuff or gun tie tacks can add to this negative image.

The manner in which police exercise their authority also has an impact on the police image. The attitude of law enforcement officers, their education, their personal image of policing, discipline, professionalism, and interaction with the community have enormous impact on the public's perception of the police.

Seemingly innocent and humorous police novelty items have caused major confrontations between police and the communities they serve. Some police product companies produce calendars, posters, T-shirts, and mugs that support, encourage, and make light of police brutality. Almost always meant to be humorous, the public may not share the same sense of humor. Such items can be immensely destructive to police-community relations. Particularly offensive examples include slogans such as "Brutality, the fun part of police work" and takeoffs on the Dirty Harry line, "Go ahead, make my day."

A few years ago, a black suspect died in police custody as the result of a carotid hold applied by police officers during a struggle. In response to the black community's anger and concern, the chief of police issued an order prohibiting the carotid hold. Already in severe conflict with their chief over several other issues, two officers produced and sold T-shirts within the department that said, "Don't choke'em, smoke'em." The T-shirts went on sale the day of the suspect's funeral. It is not difficult to understand how destructive this was to the police image and community relations in that city as well as in other cities where the media reported these events.

In contrast with this unfortunate incident is the Hug-O-Bear Program which many departments now use. Plush teddy bears are used to calm traumatized children officers encounter in the course of fulfilling their duties. The bears, sometimes donated to the department by community organizations, are often carried in patrol cars and have been invaluable at accident scenes, in child abuse situations, and fires. Programs such as this can reduce the effect of *negative contacts* people may have with the police.

Negative Contacts

Another factor that contributes to the police image and the difficulty in maintaining good community relations is what police commonly refer to as negative contacts.

Negative contacts are unpleasant interactions between the police and the public. They may or may not relate to criminal activity.

While officers have many opportunities to assist citizens, much of what they must do causes people unhappiness. Many people have police contact only when something goes wrong in their lives. Citizens commonly interact with the police when they:

- Receive a traffic citation.
- Have an illegally parked vehicle towed.
- Have a loud party terminated.
- Have been victimized.
- Discuss a child who is in trouble with the law.
- Have a domestic "disagreement" broken up.
- Are arrested for driving while intoxicated (DWI) or some other offense.
- Receive a death notification.

Many more possible scenarios in which citizens become angry or disillusioned occur daily because of the actions police officers must take to perform their duties.

For the most part, the police have no way to eliminate negative contacts and still perform their duties. A major challenge of law enforcement is to build good community relations despite the often adversarial nature of the job. The fact that many negative contacts take place between police and noncriminal individuals, the so-called "average citizen," makes the task especially difficult.

PUBLIC EXPECTATIONS

Otherwise law-abiding citizens who receive traffic tickets or who are arrested for DWI often believe they should be excused and that the police should concentrate on "real" criminals. Most police officers feel that citizens want the law enforced to the letter *except* when it comes to themselves.

The public often demands that the police crackdown on crime, on drunk drivers, and even on traffic violations. For many police departments, the majority of their complaints involve traffic problems. Citizens often demand that police enforce speed laws near their homes. Inevitably, when the police respond by issuing citations to violators, some of those who want the laws to be strictly enforced are ticketed; they often feel betrayed and angry. Somehow, they see their own violation of the speed law as different from that of "teenagers" or "outsiders," and they feel they deserve "a break." Most police officers have been asked, "Why don't you spend your time catching real criminals instead of picking on citizens?"

> People expect the law to be enforced, except when enforcement limits their behavior.

Citizens become incensed when crime flourishes. They hold the police responsible for combatting crime. As noted by Wadman and Olson (1990, p. 27) there is a "dichotomy of the police being held responsible for crime but having little or no authority over its causes." According to Kelling (Morrow, 1991, p. 17): "The terms 'war on crime' and 'war on drugs' encourage and even demand an all-out attack by police upon criminals—no holding back, no quarter given. But like American soldiers in Vietnam, the police are fighting an unwinnable war, assuming large social responsibilities that belong more to politicians than to policemen."

> The police are placed in the dilemma of being expected to win the wars on crime and drugs but are given no control over the causes of these problems. The police cannot win these wars.

This view is also held by Klockars (1991, p. 244):

The fact is that the "war on crime" is a war police not only cannot win, but cannot in any real sense fight. They cannot win it because it is simply not within their power to change those things—such as unemployment, the age distribution of the population, moral education, freedom, civil liberties, ambitions, and the social and economic opportunities to realize them—that influence the amount of crime in any society. Moreover, any kind of real war on crime is something no democratic society would be prepared to let its police fight. We would simply be unwilling to tolerate the kind of abuses to the civil liberties of innocent citizens—to us—that fighting any kind of a real war on crime would inevitably involve.

In addition, when citizens have a problem, they expect the police to help resolve it. In fact, police sociologist Egon Bittner (1974) states that we have police for just that reason—because *"something-ought-not-to-be-happening-about-which-something-ought-to-be-done-NOW!"* Klockars (1985, p. 16) notes that Bittner purposely did not refer to the situation as *illegal* because the police are called upon in many situations that do not involve an illegality. Bittner left the purpose of police involvement wide open: *something ought to be done.*

> People also expect the police to help them when they have a problem or when someone else is causing a problem.

The *NOW* portion of Bittner's explanation refers to the police's unique ability to use force to correct a situation. How and when police actually use force is discussed later in this chapter.

Public expectations and the expectations of those in law enforcement are often at odds. Even within agencies police disagree about what their primary focus should be.

LAW ENFORCEMENT V. SERVICE TO THE PUBLIC

Police departments are often divided on whether their emphasis should be proactive or reactive. Wilson and Kelling (1989, p. 52) reported on a study conducted by the Police Foundation which found that in every department they visited those who were incident-oriented (reactive) spoke "disparagingly of the problem-oriented officers as 'social workers;' some of the latter responded by calling the former 'ghetto blasters.' "

Is the best police officer the one who catches the most "bad guys"? Certainly police departments will continue to apprehend the "bad guys." The crimes they target may, however, contribute to negative police-community relations. The police usually focus on certain kinds of crime, particularly common crimes such as burglary, robbery, assault, and auto theft. The police expect that offenders who commit these crimes might flee or try to avoid arrest in some other way. Police may need to use force to bring the offender to justice.

Police officers generally do *not* enforce white collar crimes. They would not, for example, investigate or arrest a business person for insider trading, price fixing, or cheating on income taxes. According to Garmine (1989, p. 8):

> *Police noninvolvement in most crimes committed in connection with the conduct of business, in the practice of a profession, or in politics seems to be based on a policy choice that, even though not always articulated, is commonly understood among police agencies. According to this understanding, the police have refrained from developing enforcement capacities in these areas of criminal conduct because special enforcement agencies were created when the various crimes were defined in legislation.*

White collar crime involves those who are in business, the professions, or public life—those who tend to be relatively well-to-do, powerful people.

Common crimes could conceivably be committed by anyone, rich or poor. The vast majority of these crimes, however, are committed by those from society's lowest socioeconomic level. Those at or near the poverty level include the majority of our minority populations.

As noted by Klockars (1985, p. 57), since the police officers' domain is the streets: "Those people who spend their time on the street will receive a disproportionate amount of police attention. . . . particularly people who are too poor to have backyards, country clubs, summer homes, automobiles, air conditioning, or other advantages that are likely to take them out of the patrolman's sight."

These facts contribute to the *impression* that the police are focused solely on the kind of crime poor people and minorities commit, hence, the *impression* that they are hostile to those who are poor or members of minority groups. This negative impression does little to foster good community relations.

Police work involves much more than catching criminals. It is a complex, demanding job requiring a wide range of abilities. Studies suggest that 80 percent of police officers' time is spent on nonpunitive activities (Pace, 1991, pp. 20–21). According to Klockars (1985, p. 103): "Over 90 percent of all the problems police attend to are in response to citizen requests for service."

The majority of police actions have nothing to do with criminal law enforcement, but involve *service* to the community.

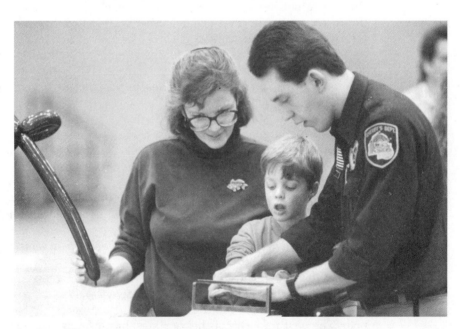

A police officer fingerprints a young boy at a school carnival.

Service to the community includes:

- Peace keeping.
- Preventing suicides.
- Looking for lost or runaway children or vulnerable adults.
- Protecting children and other vulnerable people.
- Maintaining public safety.
- Assisting motorists with disabled vehicles.
- Dealing with emergencies and crisis situations—accidents, and natural disasters.
- Delivering death notifications.
- Resolving conflicts.
- Preventing crime.
- Educating the public.

In fact, defining exactly what police work entails is almost impossible. Most would agree, however, that people have always called the police for help. They call not only about criminal matters, but also about a myriad of situations where they perceive a need for government intervention. The police respond to such calls and usually take whatever action is needed.

It has been said that the police are the only social service agency available twenty-four hours a day, seven days a week and make house calls. What is reasonable to expect of them? One way to clarify the focus of a police department is for the department to adopt a clearly articulated mission statement.

MISSION STATEMENTS

Why do most law enforcement agencies exist? What is their *mission?* The answer is obvious to those who say the purpose is to catch "bad guys." Others believe that the purpose is to prevent crime, or maintain order, or protect the public. Articulating the purpose for an agency's existence helps its members to focus on the same goals and determine how to accomplish their purpose.

A **mission statement** is a written declaration of purpose.

A mission statement is a road map which delineates how an agency will arrive at a desired destination. Without it, a law enforcement agency can wander, appearing inconsistent, inefficient, and purposeless. According to VanMeter (1991, p. 65):

Simply put, a mission is a reason to work. More than just an empty platitude, a mission statement is the standard against which administrators evaluate all decisions and actions. It is the legal foundation for legitimate decision making that affects employment. To be effective, it must be broad enough in scope and sufficient in depth to capture the philosophy, values and goals of the organization.

The mission statement will tell you what the agency's commitment is to the community it serves, how it views its relationship with the community. A mission statement can reveal, rather accurately, the state of police-community relations.

As noted in *Law and Order* (1991, p. 65): "The mission answers the question of why things are done. If it is defined adequately, the agency's decisions and actions will be appropriate as long as they remain based on the mission."

A mission statement can focus a police department's energies and resources. Will the department continue to be reactive and focused on fighting crimes that have already occurred or proactive, focused on identifying problems and attacking those problems? As noted by Wilson and Kelling (1989, p. 49), a community-oriented policing philosophy requires redefining the police mission: "To help the police become accustomed to fixing broken windows as well as arresting window-breakers requires doing things that are very hard for many administrators to do."

Consider the following mission statement of the Madison Wisconsin Police Department:

We believe in the dignity and worth of all people.

We are committed to:

- *Providing high-quality, community-oriented police services with sensitivity*
- *Protecting constitutional rights*
- *Problem-solving*
- *Teamwork*
- *Openness*
- *Continuous improvement*
- *Providing leadership to the police profession*

We are proud of the diversity of our workforce which permits us to grow and which respects each of us as individuals and we strive for a healthful workplace.

How are mission statements developed? A committee, comprised of members of the community and police officers, assesses various police functions. Why would a law enforcement agency include input from the community when it develops its mission statement? Community input improves police-community relations and increases the possibility of an agency accomplishing its missions.

As noted by VanMeter (1991, p. 65): "In public service organizations, the public determines the nature of the mission by identifying the services it expects from the organization. If the expectations go unmet, the public becomes dissatisfied. The organization generally suffers loss of financing, loss of political support and increased interference in day-to-day operations." Or, as Captain Michael J. Nila (1990, p. 43) of the Aurora Illinois Police Department states, the citizen-police committee that developed Aurora's mission statement had "to write a statement that would create a philosophy demanding that the community and the police become one—united by a common goal to enhance the quality of life for all of Aurora." The committee's efforts resulted in the following mission statement:

> *We, the Aurora Police Department, exist to serve all people within our jurisdiction with respect, fairness and compassion. We are committed to the prevention of crime and the protection of life and property; the preservation of peace, order and safety; the enforcement of laws and ordinances; and the safeguarding of constitutional guarantees.*

> *With community service as our foundation, we are driven by goals to enhance the quality of life, investigating problems as well as incidents, seeking solutions and fostering a sense of security in communities and individuals. We nurture public trust by holding ourselves to the highest standards of performance and ethics.*

> *To fulfill its mission, the Aurora Police Department is dedicated to providing a quality of work environment and the development of its members through effective training and leadership (Nila, 1990, p. 43).*

Developing a mission statement that reflects an agency's commitment to the community it serves can be the vehicle to positive, meaningful police-community relations as well as to a more effective police department. It is this mission statement that will, in large part, determine where the agency places its priorities.

No matter where an agency places its priorities, two aspects of how the police accomplish their mission will be critical to police-community relations.

Police use of *discretion* and of *force* profoundly affect police-community relations.

Officers lead an arrested suspect to jail. Being arrested can change a person's life dramatically.

POLICE DISCRETION

Police *do* have broad discretionary powers to enforce the law. Each agency exercises discretion when it establishes its mission, policies, and procedures. Each officer exercises discretion when deciding whether to issue citations or make arrests when laws are violated. Klockars (1985, p. 93) provides a comprehensive definition of police discretion.

A police officer or police agency may be said to exercise **discretion** whenever effective limits on his, her, or its power leave the officer or agency free to make choices among possible courses of action or inaction.

Officers make those choices based on a variety of reasons such as:

- Is there evidence to prove a violation in court?
- Will a good purpose be served by arrest or citation, or is police contact sufficient to end the violation?
- What type of crime and suspect is involved?
- What circumstances exist at the time?

Officers would probably not arrest a stranded motorist in a blizzard who, in danger of freezing to death, breaks into an alarmed commercial building. Nor would they be likely to arrest a driver who develops chest pain and breathing difficulty and drives through a stop sign in an attempt to maneuver off the road. In these cases the value of police discretion, or **selective enforcement,** is clear. It makes sense to most people not to enforce the letter of the law.

Police discretion also poses a problem for police, however, because citizens know that the officer can act subjectively. The person an officer tickets or arrests may feel discriminated against. The public is also concerned that discretion gives the police too much freedom to pick and choose when and against whom they will enforce the law. Citizens worry that discretion allows the police too much room to discriminate against some and overlook the violations of the wealthy and powerful.

Police agencies and officers have broad discretion in deciding which laws to enforce, under which circumstances, and against whom. Some people believe the law should be enforced consistently and in every instance. Most officers, however, believe that such police action would soon be unacceptable, far too harsh, and virtually impossible.

Reasons for Police Discretion

Police departments are bureaucracies subject to rules, regulations, and bylaws that may contribute to irrational and inappropriate behavior. Such regulations limit an officer's ability to use common sense or act in a humane way in certain situations. Such limitations subject the officer to critical media coverage and adverse public opinion. For example, the police strictly upheld the law and towed a car containing a crying and screaming paraplegic girl because the vehicle was parked 15 minutes too long in a restricted zone. Millions of Americans and Canadians viewed this episode on national television.

Discretion is necessary for a number of reasons:

- The statute books are filled with archaic or ambiguous laws.
- Some laws are almost never enforced and no one expects them to be.
- There are not enough police to act on every violation. They must select which laws they will enforce.
- Police prioritize the offenses they act upon: crime is of more concern than a violation of a regulation and serious crime is a greater threat than minor crime. The police act accordingly.
- Discretion is important to maintaining good community relations. If the police were to enforce the letter of the law, community resentment would soon follow. The police need community support if they are to succeed.
- Community standards influence how the police enforce laws. In most urban areas, significant changes have occurred in the past

several years in the enforcement of drunk driving laws. Now violators are routinely arrested and charged; the police rarely overlook this kind of violation.

Morrison (1992, p. 100) notes that: "Vague or ambiguous laws which regulate moral conduct standards too strictly for a majority of the community are another reason for officer discretion." He also notes that: "Discretion can be an effective tool of behavior modification. An untold number of juveniles have been turned around by a sympathetic cop who gave them a break. When used this way, it's good for the police image, too."

Changes in Police Discretion

Law enforcement has responded to an increased public awareness of the dangers of tolerating drunk driving. Agencies, as well as individual officers, have a mandate from the public to strictly enforce DWI laws. Police discretion in this area is limited.

Similar changes have occurred in other areas as well. The public has ceased tolerating crimes that occur among family members. Once among the laws that the public knew the police would not enforce, many police strictly uphold laws against spouse beating and the physical and sexual abuse of children. Again, a significant change in police discretion has occurred in this area.

Community-oriented policing has also had a great impact on police discretion. According to Pratt (1992, p. 99): "Increasingly, police officers are being trusted to use good judgment on the streets in everyday enforcement activities while being subjected to ever-fewer limits and restricting rules. In effect, officers are increasingly being allowed to approach true 'professionalism.'"

Community-oriented policing emphasizes wider use of officer discretion.

In *Terry v. Ohio* (1968), the Supreme Court recognized the role that discretion plays in policing. As noted by Pratt (1992, p. 99), recent court decisions have continued this perspective, recognizing that police officers possess special training and experience that allow them to exercise "wide discretion" in several areas. Among the views expressed in recent decisions are the following:

- Officers are more knowledgeable than most people about human (particularly criminal) behaviors.
- Since officers wear a badge, the public must considers them honest. Police statements are more likely to be true than those made by a suspect.

- Specialized training and experience enable officers to recognize suspicious behavior not apparent to others.
- Based on training and experience, officers can and should take any action reasonably necessary to investigate suspicious activity.
- Officers are exposed to unusual dangers and must, at all times and under all circumstances, act to protect themselves from harm (Pratt, p. 99).

The Downside of Police Discretion

Corrupt officers can wield their discretion in an illegal manner to obtain bribes or payoffs. Officers usually work independently without direct supervision and have tremendous power to decide what action they will take, who they will arrest, and which laws they will enforce.

A corrupt officer can use his power of discretion to obtain payoffs for favorable treatment. As noted by Pollock-Byrne (1989, p. 83):

> *Discretion is a good thing and it is a necessary element of the law, but it also leads to a greater dependence on individual ethical standards in place of rules and laws. . . .*
>
> *Unethical police behavior often arises directly from the power of discretion. Because police officers have the power to select and entrap suspects, they can also make that decision unethically, such as by taking a bribe in return for letting a suspect go. Since they have the power to decide how best to conduct an investigation, they may decide to use this power to entrap and select suspects in a biased or otherwise unfair manner rather than by probable cause.*

Discretion and the Police Image

Unless the police exercise their discretion with care, the community may complain about an actual or perceived abuse of power or discrimination in the way police enforce the law. If the community believes that the police overlook violations committed by a certain segment of society or strictly enforce laws against another, severe community relations problems will develop. As noted by Morrison (1992, p. 100): "The use of discretion by officers in the recent Jeffrey Dahmer case in Milwaukee resulted in an outpouring of criticism for both police and probation officers."

A police agency's policies and procedures, priorities, and the manner in which it equips and assigns its officers indicates how that agency will exercise discretion. Individual officers have the greatest amount of discretion. Police officers often work alone, exercising wide discretion in matters of life and death, honor and dishonor in an environment that is tension filled and often hostile. In addition, within the police bureaucracy, discretion increases as one moves down the organizational hierarchy.

Thus, patrol officers, the most numerous, lowest-ranking, newest to police work, have the greatest amount of discretion. All officers should be acutely aware of the power they wield and the immense impact the exercise of discretion has on the community and the police-community relationship.

While officers often operate independently, without direct supervision, it is important to remember that the community watches how officers perform their duties. The public notes how and when officers enforce the law. Citizens may form opinions about their police department and about all officers in that department based on an individual officer's actions. Perhaps the most critical discretionary decision an officer can make is when and how much force to use.

USE OF FORCE

Police officers are trained for, and equipped to, overcome the resistance they can expect to encounter as they perform their duties. As noted by Garmire (1989, p. 8): "The mandate of the police is to deal with all problems in which force may have to be used, regardless of whether the problems arise out of the criminal law or some other context."

Certain types of criminals, usually those who commit common crimes, are likely to evade arrest, and require the police to find and forcibly take them into custody. Police deal with noncriminal situations which can also require overcoming resistance. Suicidal individuals may require forceful intervention. So might out-of-control mental patients.

The use of force by the police encompasses a wide range of possible actions, from the officer's mere presence to the use of deadly force. The police presence affects a majority of citizens. The police uniform and squad cars are symbols of the officer's power to enforce the law and bring violators to justice—by the use of force if necessary. The visual image of power and authority created by the uniform and equipment facilitates the officer's ability to gain public compliance. The police image is also affected, either positively or negatively, by whether a department develops an authority-heavy image. Care must be taken not to develop such an intimidating image that it alienates the community.

Think about extreme examples you have seen of the *intimidating* police image, perhaps in television programs or movies. Items such as mirrored sunglasses, helmets, billy clubs, handcuffs or gun tie tacks, and black leather sap-type gloves are likely to generate negative emotions and contribute to a sense of fear of or anger toward police.

Uniforms convey a message and often elicit a particular response from the public. For example, many officers feel strongly that wearing an American flag patch on the uniform reduces the number of assaults on police officers.

Controversy on the use of force by police is almost always discussed in terms of police brutality. "There is little doubt," says Pace (1991, p. 70), "that brutality is the criminal justice system's number one community relations problem." The nationally televised Rodney King beating certainly added to this perception.

Police brutality is considered a problem by a large segment of the public. The extent of the problem is perceived differently among urban and suburban, rich and poor, and minority and majority populations. There are valid reasons why different people have different perceptions of the problem. One reason is that the job the police are required to do differs from community to community.

First consider that because the police must intervene in crimes where apprehension is likely to be resisted, most of their enforcement efforts are directed toward "common" criminals. In contrast, white-collar criminals are unlikely to flee or resist. They tend to see their situation as a legal dilemma to be won or lost in court. White-collar criminals are relatively wealthy, have a career, and a place in the community; they have too much to lose to simply flee. Since police enforcement efforts focus on common criminals, who are frequently poor, the most use of force by the police will be directed against this part of the population.

On the other hand, citizens in white suburban areas tend to see the police in different circumstances:

When they report a crime and have been victimized.

When they need assistance after an automobile accident, a medical emergency, when their child is lost, or their car has run out of gas.

When they have locked themselves out of a car or home—or want their home watched.

In each scenario, the police are there to lend assistance. Citizens in suburban areas may never see a police officer use force. The most negative experience they are likely to have with a police officer is receiving a traffic ticket.

When people from these widely separated communities talk about the police, it seems as though they are speaking of entirely different entities. On the one hand, police may be referred to as brutal, racist aggressors while others describe them as professional, helpful, efficient protectors. Which is the true picture of the police?

While the public has many stereotypes of the police, those stereotypes will be shattered or reinforced each time a citizen has personal contact with a police officer. Each individual police contact can have a positive or negative impact on police-community relations.

Most citizens understand and support law enforcement officers' obligation to enforce the law and to use appropriate force when necessary.

All officers have a duty to the profession to encourage public support by professional behavior respectful of each citizen's rights. Sometimes, however, public support of the police does not exist in a community. Lack of support may be the result of the unique characteristics of coercion.

The Paradoxes of Coercive Power

A **paradox** is a seemingly contradictory statement that may, nonetheless, be true. According to Klockars (1985, pp. 124–31) four paradoxes of coercive power affect policing:

- *The paradox of dispossession:* the less one has, the less one has to lose.
- *The paradox of detachment:* the less the victim cares about preserving something, the less the victimizer cares about taking it hostage.
- *The paradox of irrationality:* the more delirious the threatener, the more serious the threat; the more delirious the victim, the less serious the threat.
- *The paradox of face:* the nastier one's reputation, the less nasty one has to be.

The Paradox of Dispossession. This paradox suggests that the police have the most power over those who have the most to lose, usually people in the middle and upper classes who are afraid to lose their material possessions, careers, and reputations. As noted by Klockars (p. 125): "So despite the fact that our possessions, resources, friendships, occupation, reputation, and position in the community appear to give us power to resist being coerced, they actually have the opposite effect." In contrast, "life's losers," those who have little or nothing to lose cannot be easily coerced. Says Klockars: "To coerce the truly dispossessed, police are inclined to threaten to injure the only hostages that such unfortunate people offer: their freedom, such as it is, and their bodies."

The Paradox of Detachment. This paradox is frequently evident in domestic disputes. Things which were once important to those involved in domestic disputes are no longer important. A person's many possessions, career, or reputation are of no importance, if an officer cannot use them to coerce a violent spouse. In such instances police officers try to "re-attach" the person to those possessions. As noted by Klockars (p. 127): "The crucial element is the officer's ability to find something that had once been important to the couple and to talk to them about it in a way that will re-attach them to the value it once had and the hope it represents for the future."

The Paradox of Irrationality. In the line of duty, police encounter many people who are so drunk, mentally ill, terrorized, or traumatized, that they are, according to Klockars (p. 128) "virtually immune to coercive threats." He notes: "If they are so irrational they cannot comprehend a threat, short of actually using coercive force, they cannot be coerced." In such instances officers seek to make the person more rational. Sometimes, however, this is simply not possible. This paradox has further implications for police officers, notes Klockars (p. 120):

> *If police wish to increase their power to coerce rational persons, the paradox of irrationality advises them to appear irrational in their willingness to carry through whatever threats they make. In the paradoxical world of coercive encounters, the police officer who is crazy enough to go any length to carry out a threat (e.g., who is willing to shoot to kill a motorist who refuses to move his car from a no-parking zone) is a police officer any rational person will obey!*

This certainly would do little to foster police-community relations, however.

The Paradox of Face. Some police officers want to have a reputation for being extremely "tough." As one police officer put it: "I was very aggressive and very by-the-book and got the reputation for being an asshole. And knew it, and it didn't bother me. That was part of the job. It's easier to be known as an asshole than to have to be one" (Conroy and Hess, 1992, pp. 126–27).

With power and the authority to use force comes the responsibility to use that power and force not only legally, but also ethically.

ETHICAL POLICING

The tremendous power that policing has over people's lives requires that police officers represent good over evil. To maintain the public trust, police must be men and women of good character who hold foremost the ideals of fairness and justice. The manner in which police use their discretion to enforce the law and solve problems will determine whether the public will view the police as ethical.

It is not always clear in many situations what is the ethical way to act. Officers frequently have their decisions reviewed and questioned after a crisis has passed. Unfortunately, the police have often not been given appropriate guidance in ethical decision-making. Given the complexities of enforcing the law in a diverse population, it is inadequate to teach rookie officers the technical skills of policing and then send them into the community under the assumption they will do the "right thing."

Perhaps a move toward higher ethical standards is reflected by the decision of many police departments to require their police officers to have a college education. There is an increasing need to begin a dialog within the police community on ethics—what ethical behavior is, and how to achieve it in the profession. Incredibly, a discussion of ethics is not a standard part of the training and education of officers. If a prospective officer has a good record, the department assumes he or she meets ethical standards.

One simple adage, set forth by Blanchard and Peale (1988, p. 9), might serve as a starting point for a discussion on ethics: *"There is no right way to do a wrong thing."* They suggest (p. 20) three questions that can be used as personal "ethics checks."

Three ethics-check questions are:

- Is it legal?
- Is it balanced?
- How will it make me feel about myself?

The first question should pose little problem for most officers. Much time is spent on criminal and constitutional law in most law enforcement programs. The focus of the second question is whether the decision is fair to everyone involved, in the short-term and long-term. Does the decision create a win-win situation? The third question is perhaps the most crucial. Would you mind seeing your decision published in the paper? Would you feel good if your friends and family knew about your decision?

Blanchard and Peale (p. 79) suggest the following five principles of ethical power for individuals:

- *Purpose.* I see myself as being an ethically sound person. I let my conscience be my guide. No matter what happens, I am always able to face the mirror, look myself straight in the eye, and feel good about myself.
- *Pride.* I feel good about myself. I don't need the acceptance of other people to feel important. A balanced self-esteem keeps my ego and my desire to be accepted from influencing my decisions.
- *Patience.* I believe that things will eventually work out well. I don't need everything to happen right now. I am at peace with what comes my way.
- *Persistence.* I stick to my purpose, especially when it seems inconvenient to do so. My behavior is consistent with my intentions. As Churchill said, "Never! Never! Never! Never give up!"
- *Perspective.* I take time to enter each day quietly in a mood of reflection. This helps me to get myself focused and allows me to listen to my inner self and to see things more clearly.

Ethical behavior by individual officers and by the department as a whole is indispensable to effective police-community partnerships.

Summary

Today's police departments have changed. They have more minority and female officers. The educational level of the officers is much higher, and fewer have military experience than in years past. Most officers also are as interested in helping people as they are in fighting crime. The police subculture has been characterized as including a loss of innocence, cynicism, loneliness, isolation, and a constricted and inappropriate affect. A dominant characteristic of the police subculture is isolation and a "them v. us" world view.

The police image is affected by individual backgrounds, the media, and personal experiences with the criminal justice system. It is also shaped by what police do and how they look—their uniform and equipment.

Negative contacts are unpleasant interactions between the police and the public. They may or may not involve criminal activity.

People expect the police to enforce the law, except if it adversely impacts them. People also expect the police to help them when they have a problem.

The majority of police actions do not involve criminal law enforcement, rather they are community service oriented. A police department frequently states its purpose in a mission statement, a written declaration of purpose.

Police use of discretion and force will profoundly affect police-community relations. A police officer or police agency may be said to exercise discretion whenever effective limits on his, her, or its power leave the officer or agency free to make choices among possible courses of action or inaction. Community-oriented policing emphasizes wider use of officer discretion.

When police use force, they should keep in mind four paradoxes of coercion:

- The paradox of dispossession: the less one has, the less one has to lose.
- The paradox of detachment: the less the victim cares about preserving something, the less the victimizer cares about taking it hostage.
- The paradox of irrationality: the more delirious the threatener, the more serious the threat; the more delirious the victim, the less serious the threat.
- The paradox of face: the nastier one's reputation, the less nasty one has to be.

Police discretion and authority to use power are balanced by the responsibility to act ethically. Three questions to check police ethical standards are: (1) Is it legal? (2) Is it balanced? and (3) How will it make me feel about myself?

DISCUSSION QUESTIONS

1. What is the image of the police in your community? What factors are responsible for this image? Could the police image be made more positive?
2. What expectations do you have of law enforcement agencies?
3. Does police discretion frequently lead to abuse of alleged perpetrators?
4. Are police officers now more violent and less ethical than their predecessors?
5. Does the image of law enforcement affect its ability to get the job done?
6. What impact does a mission statement have on a department's performance?
7. What should be a department's ideal balance between fighting crime and service to the community?
8. Have you witnessed police exercise their discretion? How did it impress you?
9. Can you give examples of each of the four paradoxes of coercive power as they operate in police work?
10. What decisions commonly made by police officers involve ethical considerations?

DEFINITIONS
Can you define these terms: discretion, mission statement, negative contacts, paradox, selective enforcement.

REFERENCES

Bittner, Egon. "Florence Nightingale in Pursuit of Willie Sutton: A Theory of Police." In *The Potential for Reform of Criminal Justice,* edited by H. Jacob, 17–44. Beverly Hills: Sage, 1974.

Blanchard, Kenneth and Peale, Norman Vincent. *The Power of Ethical Management.* New York: Fawcett Crest, 1988.

Conroy, Dennis L. and Hess, Kären M. *Officers at Risk: How to Identify and Cope with Stress.* Placerville: Custom Publishing Company, 1992.

Garmire, Bernard L. (ed.) *Local Government Police Management.* Published by the International City Management Association, 1989.

Goldstein, Herman. *Problem-Oriented Policing.* New York: McGraw-Hill Publishing Company, 1990.

Greene, Jack R. and Mastrofski, Stephen D. (eds.) *Community Policing: Rhetoric or Reality.* New York: Praeger Publishing, 1991.

Klockars, Carl B. *The Idea of Police.* Newbury Park: Sage Publishing Company, 1985.

Klockars, Carl B. "The Rhetoric of Community Policing." In *Community Policing: Rhetoric or Reality,* edited by Jack R. Greene and Stephen D. Mastrofski, 239–58. New York: Praeger Publishing, 1991.

"Local Government Police Management by the International City Management Association." *Law and Order.* (August 1989): 57–59.

Morrison, Richard D. "Police Discretion—Can We Afford It?" *Law and Order.* (August 1992): 100.

Morrow, Lance. "Rough Justice." *Time.* (April 1, 1991): 16–17.

Nila, Michael J. "Defining the Police Mission: A Community/Police Perspective." *The Police Chief.* (October 1990): 43–47.

Pace, Denny F. *Community Relations Concepts.* Placerville: Custom Publishing Company, 1991.

Pollock-Byrne, Joycelyn M. *Ethics in Crime and Justice: Dilemmas & Decisions.* Pacific Grove: Brooks/Cole Publishing Company, 1989.

Pratt, C. E. "Police Discretion." *Law and Order.* (March 1992): 99–100.

VanBlaricom, D. P. "Shaking the Pillars of Police Tradition." *Law Enforcement News* (October 31, 1989): 7.

VanMeter, D. J. "Mission and its Value." *Law and Order.* (August 1991): 65–66.

Wadman, Robert C. and Olson, Robert K. *Community Wellness: A New Theory of Policing.* Washington: Police Executive Research Forum, 1990.

Wilson, James Q. and Kelling, George L. "Making Neighborhoods Safe." *The Atlantic Monthly.* (February 1989): 46–52.

"Your Agency's Driving Force: Mission and its Value." *Law and Order.* (August 1991): 65.

Building Relationships

With the basic background supplied by Section One, you are ready to look at the interaction occurring between the police and the publics they serve. At the most basic level, police-community relations begin with one-on-one interaction between a police officer and a citizen.

The section begins with a discussion of the interpersonal skills needed to interact effectively with average, mainstream adults. Ensuing chapters discuss specific challenges in dealing with individuals who differ from this norm in some respect: members of minority groups; people who are disabled, including those who are visually or hearing impaired, mentally and emotionally disabled, and those who have epilepsy; the elderly, including those who have Alzheimer's disease and those whose quality of life is reduced because of fear of being victimized; youth, including youth who are learning-disabled, who are in trouble with the law, and who are members of gangs. Interacting with victims of crimes or natural disasters is also discussed.

Although these special populations are discussed separately, overlap often exists. The more differences an individual has from the "norm," the greater the challenge in establishing good relationships. It must always be kept in the forefront that each member of the specific group discussed is first an individual.

Lastly, the section discusses interaction with members of the media, the constitutional issues involved, and how such interactions can help or hinder police-community relations.

BASIC INTERPERSONAL SKILLS

Public cooperation and voluntary compliance with law comes not through law but through positive human contacts.

—Denny Pace (p. 69)

DO YOU KNOW

- How a person's world-view is largely created?
- Why two people may "see" the same thing differently?
- What the most basic rule of semantics is?
- What police officers must recognize in themselves?
- The difference between prejudice and discrimination?
- What empathy is? What levels exist?
- What networks are?
- What the communication process consists of?
- What individual characteristics are important in the communication process?
- What are common barriers to effective communication?
- Why effective listening is often difficult?
- Why police officers may have more barriers to communication than other professionals?
- What can improve communication?
- What the primacy effect is?
- What the four-minute barrier is?
- What two human relations practices used in business might be adopted for improving police-community relations?
- What networking is and how it functions?

A woman executive at a shopping center discovered a minor theft of company property from her company car. The car had been parked outside a police office where several traffic officers took breaks between shifts. The office was not accessible to the public, but had an identification sign on the locked door.

The woman knocked on the door and asked the sergeant who opened it who was responsible for watching the parking area. She also commented on the officers she could see sitting in the room, and suggested they were not doing their jobs. The officers in the room stopped talking with each other and turned their attention to the conversation at the office door.

The sergeant and the woman never got around to discussing the missing item. Instead he responded to her comments with questions. "What do you mean by that?" "What are you trying to say?" She left to tell her supervisor, refusing to file a police report. She soon returned, however, and encountered another officer just outside the office. Their conversation, later characterized as "heated" by witnesses, centered on the woman's suggestion that the officers should do more to prevent theft in the parking lot, implied they were lazy and shirked their responsibilities.

At this point the woman asked to file a police report, and the officer asked her to enter the police office with him to do so. They entered the office, but when the officer suggested they enter a private office away from the hubbub of the break area, she refused to do so. She later said the officer intimidated her by slamming drawers, moving quickly, and ordering her into the room. She feared being alone with him.

The officer's perception of the incident was entirely different. He commented that the woman had a "chip on her shoulder" and an "attitude." She was demanding and impossible to deal with.

After refusing to enter the office to file the report, the woman sat down on a chair in the break area. She was told to either go into the other room and file the report or leave. When she refused to do either, she was escorted from the office and left outside the locked doors. The woman filed a complaint against the police department.

With better communication, this problem and thousands like it could be avoided. Effective communication with the public is vital to good police-community relations. In fact, at the heart of police-community relations are one-on-one interactions between officers and citizens.

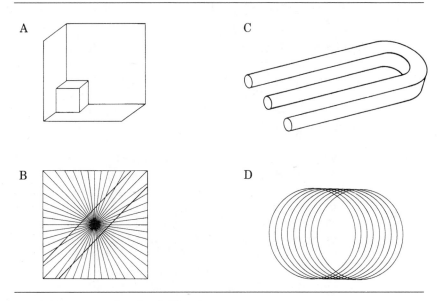

A

C

B

D

FIGURE 4–1   Optical Illusions

A. Is the box inside a room or are there two boxes?
B. Are the lines pulled apart at the center or are they parallel?
C. Where is the center group?
D. Which end is out?

(A. Either is correct; B. Parallel; C. Unknown; D. Either one.)

"Human relations is the thread that holds civilized people together" (Pace, 1991, p. 237).

The following discussion assumes that those involved in the interaction are adults with no serious physical or mental disabilities. Interactions involving individuals with disabilities are discussed in later chapters.

UNDERSTANDING ONESELF

Officers who seek to build effective relationships with the citizens they serve first need to understand themselves and potential barriers to such relationships. They need to recognize their own level of self-esteem as well as the roles they play. Officers need to understand how their view of the world has been shaped and how it affects their interactions with others.

A person's world-view is largely created by what they see and hear as they experience events.

Perception—What Is Seen

One critical aspect of a person's world-view is individual *perception*. According to Hageman (1985, p. 39), **perception** is "the process of giving meaning or organization to experience." Hageman (p. 40) notes that perception is "a complex, dynamic, interrelated composite of processes that involves the human nervous system." Two primary components of this process are the eye and the **sensorium,** that part of the brain that interprets what the eye takes in. Says Hageman (p. 40):

> *The eye takes the energy of certain wavelengths of light and converts it into nerve impulses. It is not the eyes that see. Rather, it is the "perceiver" in the brain, commonly called the sensorium. While the eye can handle stimuli of nearly five million bits per second, the sensorium has limited abilities. The sensorium's resolving power is limited to approximately five hundred bits per second. In short, some stimuli are labeled by the person as important and others as not important. Some stimuli, needless to say, fall by the wayside. The perception is in the "eyes" of the beholder.*

The discrepancy between what the eye takes in (five million bits per second) and what the person actually processes (five hundred bits per second) accounts, in part, for why two witnesses can see the same thing differently.

Two witnesses' sensoriums process different portions of what the eye "sees." According to Hageman (p. 44): "As a general rule, the more objective we are, the more our perceptions mirror the perceptions of others." She gives as an example the fact that if a group of people were given a standard ruler and asked to measure the size of something, they would probably all come up with the same measurement. When no such standard ruler exists, people rely on their limited experiences. Reliance on past experiences may result in prejudices and stereotyping. Later in this chapter you will consider the problems prejudice and stereotyping present to police-community relations. Another aspect of perception is the manner in which people typically categorize and classify their experiences by generalizing in their thoughts and in their language.

Perception—What Is Heard v. What Is Said

In addition to what individuals see, the language they use also shapes their "reality." Individuals in the field of **semantics** research and study meaning of language. According to Hayakawa (1949, pp. 21-22):

> *Words—the way he uses them and the way he takes them when spoken by others—largely shape his beliefs, his prejudices, his*

ideals, his aspirations. They constitute the moral and intellectual atmosphere in which he lives—in short—his **semantic environment.** . . .

It will be the basic assumption of this book [the classic, Language in Thought and Action] that widespread intraspecific co-operation through the use of language is the fundamental mechanism of human survival. A parallel assumption will be that when the use of language results, as it so often does, in the creation or aggravation of disagreements and conflicts, there is something wrong with the speaker, the listener, or both. Human "fitness to survive" means the ability to talk and write and listen and read in ways that increase the chances for you and fellow-members of your species to survive together.

The following are some key assertions of Hayakawa.

- The process by means of which human beings can arbitrarily make certain things *stand* for other things may be called the **symbolic process.** We are, as human beings, uniquely free to manufacture and manipulate and assign values to our symbols as we please. (p. 25)
- Of all forms of symbolism, language is the most highly developed, most subtle, and most complicated. . . . Symbols and things symbolized are independent of each other; nevertheless, we all have a way of believing as if, and sometimes acting as if, there were necessary connections. (p. 27)
- The symbol is NOT the thing symbolized. The four-legged animal that goes "moo" and gives milk is represented in English by three letters arranged to form the word *cow.* Other languages have very different words for the actual animal. The word is NOT the thing; the map is NOT the territory. There is a sense in which we all live in two worlds. First, we live in the world of happenings about us which we know at first hand. But this is an extremely small world. . . . Most of our knowledge, acquired from parents, friends, schools, newspapers, books, conversation, speeches, and radio, is received *verbally.* Call this world that comes to us through words the **verbal world,** as opposed to our own experience, called the **extensional world.** Now this verbal world ought to stand in relation to the extensional world as a *map* does to the *territory* it is supposed to represent. (pp. 21-32)
- Classification. What we call things and where we draw the line between one class of things and another depend upon the interests we have and the purposes of the classification . . . Many of us, for example, cannot distinguish between pickerel, pike, salmon, smelts, perch, crappies, halibut, and mackerel; we say that they are "just fish, and I don't like fish." To a seafood connoisseur, however, these distinctions are real. . . . To a zoologist, even finer distinctions

become of great importance. . . . When we name something, then, we are classifying. The individual object or event we are naming, of course, has no name and belongs to no class until we put it in one. . . . (pp. 209-10)

There are few complexities about classifications at the level of dogs and cats, knives and forks, cigarettes and candy, but when it comes to classifications at high levels of abstraction, for example, those describing conduct, social institutions, philosophical and moral problems, serious difficulties occur. This can be a major source of conflict. When one person kills another, is it an act of murder, an act of temporary insanity, an act of homicide, an accident, or an act of heroism? As soon as the process of classification is completed, our attitudes and our conduct are to a considerable degree determined. We hang the murderer, we lock up the insane man, we free the victim of circumstances, we pin a medal on the hero. Unfortunately, people are not always aware of the way in which they arrive at their classifications. (pp. 211-12)

How do we prevent ourselves from getting into such intellectual blind alleys, or, if we find we are in one, how do we get out again? One way is to remember that practically all statements in ordinary conversation, debate, and public controversy taking the form, "Business is business," "Boys will be boys," and so on, are *not* true. . . .

A simple technique for preventing classification from harming our thinking is the suggestion made by Korzybski to add "index numbers" to our terms, thus: Englishman$_1$, Englishman$_2$ . . .; cow$_1$, cow$_2$, cow$_3$ . . . The terms of the classification tell us what the individuals in that class have in common; **The index numbers remind us of the characteristics left out.** A rule can then be formulated as a general guide in all our thinking and reading: Cow$_1$ is NOT Cow$_2$; Politician$_1$ is NOT Politician$_2$, and so on. This rule, if remembered, prevents us from confusing levels of abstraction and forces us to consider the facts on those occasions when we might otherwise find ourselves leaping to conclusions which we may later have cause to regret. (pp. 212-14)

The simplest and most basic rule of semantics is: Cow$_1$ is NOT Cow$_2$.

Once aware of how perceptions are formed, consider the natural tendency to have preferences and the danger it presents to effective police-community relations.

Preferences, Prejudice, Bias, Stereotyping, and Discrimination

It is important to recognize that no one can be completely objective. Everyone, consciously or unconsciously, has certain preferences and prejudices.

It is critical to self-understanding to recognize preferences, prejudices, and stereotypes.

A **preference** is selecting someone or something over another. You may, for example, prefer to interact with people of your own ethnic background, your own age, or your own economic level.

A **prejudice** is a negative judgment not based on fact; an irrational, preconceived negative opinion. Prejudices are often associated with a dislike of a particular group, race, or religion.

Prejudices are often the result of the classifications discussed earlier. They represent *overgeneralizations,* a failure to consider individual characteristics. According to Hageman (1985, p. 51):

> We as human beings, as part of processing information, have a tendency to prejudge—to classify information into meaningful categories. Prejudgments are natural for human beings, whose eyes are able to receive more bits of stimuli than their brains are able to process. Thus, each one of us is carrying around "preconceived notions" of specific persons or groups of persons. . . .

> These prejudgments do not always involve minority groups, such as blacks and American Indians. Prejudgments can also center on the categories developed and labeled as "old people," "teenagers," "the handicapped," "gay people," and "women."

Prejudices are also referred to as **bias,** a belief that inhibits objectivity. Taken to an extreme, a bias becomes hatred. It is important for law enforcement to understand bias and its extreme form—hate—in order to deal with the increase in bias and hate crimes. The manner in which police should deal with hate crimes is discussed in the next chapter. Prejudices or biases are the result of overgeneral classification or stereotyping.

Stereotyping assumes that all people within a specific group are the same; they lack individuality. Simply because a person is a member of a specific group, that person is thought to have certain characteristics. Common stereotypes associated with nationalities include the French being great lovers, the Italians being great cooks, the Scotch being thrifty, and American Yankees being ingenious.

Often the stereotype of Americans is very negative, as illustrated by an article date-lined *Marne-la-Vallee, France,* when Euro Disneyland opened in France in the spring of 1992:

> Writer Jean Cau dismissed the theme park as "a horror made of cardboard, plastic and appalling colors, a construction of hardened chewing gum and idiotic folklore taken straight out of comic books written for obese Americans. . . ."

Another writer . . . said the park was "a terrifying giant's step toward world homogenization." . . .

A novelist said Euro Disney represented the transformation of culture from craft into industry. "If we do not resist it," he warned, "the kingdom of profit will create a world that will have all the appearance of civilization and all the savage reality of barbarism."

The culture minister, Jack Lang, who as watchdog of French correctness has often bemoaned the invasion of an "American subculture," said he was too busy to attend yesterday's opening. A few days ago, he described Euro Disney as "an enclave of the American leisure industry into France."

Many people have stereotyped police officers. As noted by Conroy and Hess (1992, p. 82), one officer described the television cop syndrome: "They don't see you standing on the street corner in late January directing traffic after an accident. . . . They don't see you down at the medical center with a bite in your arm from some hooker who didn't want you to arrest her . . . . What they see is the TV cop doing all sorts of neat things."

Police officers may also stereotype those with whom they come in contact. As noted by Trojanowicz and Carter (1990, p. 8): "The temptation to generalize from the few to the many is a particularly critical problem for the police." In the traditional mode of policing, officers spend a considerable amount of time dealing with criminals and their victims. Some officers may begin to categorize certain types of individuals as perpetrators. Trojanowicz and Carter (p. 9) note: "Police officers so often see people at their worst, not their best. And because police officers focus so much attention on crime, there is always the danger that they will have a distorted view of who the 'bad guys' are and how many there are of them. This temptation to generalize from a few to the many is a particularly critical problem for the police in the case of immigrants."

An additional danger of stereotyping is that it may become a **self-fulfilling prophecy.** Psychologists tell us that if a person is labeled as being a certain way long enough, the person may come to actually be that way. For example, if you frequently tell a child he is a delinquent, that child may accept the label and actually become a delinquent.

It is a very natural tendency to stereotype people, but a tendency which can be fatal to effective police-community relations. Police officers must first recognize that those they deal with may have formed a stereotype of police officers. It is important for police officers to determine if this is true and, if so, to determine if it is a positive or negative image. Officers must also recognize their own prejudices and be certain they do not lead to discrimination on the job.

Prejudices may lead to **discrimination,** showing a preference or prejudice in treating individuals or groups. Some male traffic officers, for example, are known to issue warnings to females who violate traffic laws and to issue tickets to males for the same violation. Oran (p. 99) defines *discrimination* as: "The failure to treat equals equally; in particular, illegally unequal treatment based on race, religion, sex, age, etc." It is often alleged that members of minority groups receive rougher treatment from police officers than a white person would receive.

Prejudice is an attitude; discrimination is a behavior.

Hageman (1985, p. 55) notes:

The difference between the attitude *reflected in the word "prejudice" and the* overt behavior *of prejudice, as in the word "discrimination," was summed up by an English judge in his comments to nine youths convicted of race rioting in the Notting Hill section of London:*

Think what you like . . . But once you translate your dark thoughts into savage acts, the law will punish you, and protect your victim.

In the United States, the 1964 Civil Rights Act and the 1972 amendment to the Act make it illegal for agencies with fifteen or more employees to discriminate in education, housing, and employment on the basis of race, religion, national origin, or sex. It is critical that police officers understand their own prejudices, biases, and stereotypes and that they avoid any form of discrimination.

UNDERSTANDING OTHERS

As noted by Parker, Meier, and Monahan (1989, p. 78): "To engage in professional work in many areas of life one needs to understand the behavior and motivation of individuals." Understanding others is particularly important in police work. Understanding others does not, however, mean that you sympathize with them or even that you agree with them. Parker, Meier, and Monahan suggest: "Understanding involves sensing the view of others in attempting to grasp a feeling of what their world is like." It is synonymous with *empathy*.

Empathy is understanding another person.

To empathize with someone is to see things from their perspective or, as the saying goes, to put yourself in another's shoes. Parker, Meier, and Monahan (p. 83) describe three levels of empathy: low, moderate, and high:

Low Empathy—*The communicator shows little or no understanding of the most basic part of what the other has communicated, seems out of touch with what the other has said, and responds only from her or his own frame of reference. In* Low Empathy *the first person* subtracts *from the interpersonal encounter.*

Moderate Empathy—*The communicator grasps at least the essential part of the message, and sends a message that fits well with what the other is saying and is essentially interchangeable. The communicator shares with the other an understanding of at least the surface feelings and main content of the message. This communicator has not completely missed the point as in* Low Empathy, *where there may not be even the slightest acknowledgement of what the person has communicated.*

High Empathy—*In deep empathy there is a consistent communication on the part of the communicator that indicates that she or he not only hears the surface message, but is able to sense the underlying feelings and concerns that are barely hinted at in the overt communication of the second person. In* High Empathy, *the communicator's responses are* additive *or* expand on *what the person has stated, and thus allow the second person to explore his or her feelings. In deep empathy, the recipient has a feeling of being able to elaborate on the discussion, and feels truly understood. Communication is opened up; there is an air of excitement about really being heard by the other. This is most important when the police officer or corrections counselor must communicate with distressed persons.*

Parker, Meier, and Monahan (p. 84) give the following example of the levels of empathy when responding to an irate husband involved in a domestic dispute:

Husband: I know damn well she's whoring around, she's never around here when I come home. She's tired, she never prepares supper, doesn't give a crap about me.

(Low Empathy) Officer: When does she come home at night?

(Moderate Empathy) Officer: It really makes you angry that she seems to be fooling around with other men.

(High Empathy) Officer: It makes you madder'n hell to think she's screwing around, but it also hurts a lot because the message is, "I don't care about you."

High empathy does not always require a response. Sometimes knowing when just to listen is important. Parker, Meier, and Monahan

A Detroit police lieutenant talks with a citizen.

(p. 85) stress: "Frequently, just listening attentively allows people to fully express their concerns, which may be extremely helpful in and of itself." Situations perceived as real, are real in their consequences. One secret to effective communications is to attempt to see the world from the other person's perspective.

To empathize with others, you need to adopt the **phenomenological point of view,** which stresses that reality is different for each individual. This point of view is used by Noose (1992, p. 101) in his conceptualization of *networks.*

Networks are the "complex pathways of human interaction that guide and direct an individual's perception, motivation, and behavior."

Such networks are vital to effective communication, including interviewing individuals. According to Noose:

> *Networks represent relationships, links between people, and between people and their beliefs. Without an understanding of these relationships, these networks, it is often quite difficult, and sometimes even impossible, to understand an event or the circumstances that led to it. The answers obtained may have very little in common with the questions asked.*
>
> *All human beings act to create a personal reality, one that allows them to predict and control the world around them. Their associations with others and their own fundamental beliefs all become part of this unique construction of reality. In this way these networks determine how people act and what they will relate when they are questioned. . . .*
>
> *Networks produce the context within which a statement from a complainant, victim, witness or suspect can be most clearly understood.*

Among the most important networks are those which are social: family, neighbors, and friends. Sometimes legal relationships help to form networks such as those between children and their parents or between spouses. In addition to these social networks, there are occupational and professional, political, cultural, and religious networks. Any of these networks can affect how a person views reality as well as what they are willing to communicate about that reality. As noted by Noose (p. 102): "Networks are critically important whenever perception is being questioned." He stresses (p. 103): "Staying informed about the networks that operate within a community is vital for officers who hope to be effective interviewers."

IDENTIFYING THE NATURE OF THE INTERACTION

When making contact with individuals, it is important to know what the purpose of the interaction is. This will, in large part, determine the most effective tone to establish and image to project. Is the contact primarily social—an effort to create good public relations? Is the contact made primarily to seek information—about what? A person? A problem? An incident? Is the contact primarily persuasive—to get an individual to comply with a request? What role must you play? What roles are others playing?

Sometimes, of course, a contact may serve more than one purpose. It may begin as a social contact and turn into one which is persuasive or provides information. Without a clear purpose in mind, however, your communication may not be effective.

Once you consider with whom you are interacting (your audience) and why (your purpose), then focus on how the interaction generally occurs, that is through communication.

THE COMMUNICATION PROCESS

According to George (1985, p. 64): "A **communication** is simply the transfer of information and understanding from one person to another." Depending on the situation, the communication process involves four or five components.

The **communication process** involves a sender, a message, a channel, a receiver, and sometimes feedback.

Communication involves transferring thoughts from one person's mind to another person's mind. The people involved, how well the message parallels the sender's thoughts, and the channel used will all affect the communication.

The sender *encodes* the message in words—spoken or written—and then transmits the message by telephone, fax, letter, in person, or in some other way. The receiver *decodes* the message. The receiver may then provide the sender with some kind of feedback which indicates that the message has been received. Many factors will influence the message.

Individual characteristics that are important in communication include age, education, sex, values, emotional involvement, self-esteem, and language skills.

Imagine, by way of illustration, that people see the world through tinted glasses. The tint represents their particular world view. If the sender of a message sees the world through yellow glasses and the receiver of the message sees the word through red glasses, the message received will be a mixture of the world views of both and will result in a different color—orange.

In addition to the message conveyed through words, a large part of communication occurs as the result of nonverbal communication and body language. UCLA sociologist Albert Mehrabian's research found that the effectiveness with which a face-to-face communication is received depends on the communicator's:

- Look   55 percent
- Sound   38 percent
- Message   7 percent

(Berglund, 1992, p. 2D)

NONVERBAL COMMUNICATIONS AND BODY LANGUAGE

Nonverbal communications include everything other than the actual words in a message such as tone, pitch, and pacing. Sometimes the tone in which something is said makes it obvious the person is being sarcastic. A person who is nervous may speak rapidly in a high pitched voice. Nonverbal communication also includes a person's appearance—how well groomed an individual is and the type of clothing a person wears.

Body language refers to messages conveyed by how a person moves. To test the power of body language, consider what the following say about a person:

Walking—fast, slow, stomping

Posture—rigid, relaxed

Eye contact—direct, indirect, shifting

Gestures—nod, shrug, finger point

Physical spacing—close, distant

Nonverbal Communication and Body Language of Police Officers

The police communicate with the public most obviously through the uniform they wear, the way they wear them, and the equipment they carry.

Police uniforms resemble military uniforms. Frequently navy blue or black, they have accessories such as silver or gold badges, name plates, collar brass, and patches. Police wear leather belts loaded with equipment: hand gun, radio, handcuffs, night stick, mace, and ammunition. Through their uniforms, police officers convey many messages without ever speaking.

The type of uniform is almost universally recognized as that worn by police because, despite variations, police look the same all over the world. Wearing a uniform may be called the ultimate in *power dressing*. Uniforms are authoritative and professional and have an impact on the behavior of the public.

Officers find that they can gain compliance and cooperation from most people very easily on request, even when people would prefer not to cooperate. The public is likely to ignore the same officer who makes the same request while wearing blue jeans and a T-shirt.

Of course, there are ways to change the message the police uniform gives to the public and, consequently, the image the public develops of the department. Consider what the following factors might communicate:

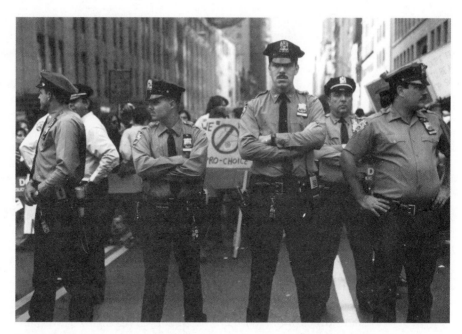

The non-verbal message of the police officers at this pro-choice rally is clear: Don't cross this line.

- Worn, faded, torn, or unkempt looking uniforms.
- Scuffed shoes.
- Mirrored sunglasses.
- Dirty, dented squad cars.
- Handcuff or handgun tie tack.
- Black leather sap gloves.
- Overweight officers.
- Facial hair or long, shaggy, greasy hair.
- Several rings or earrings.
- Long, painted fingernails.
- Chewing gum.
- Playing with nightstick.
- Reading the newspaper while on duty.
- Smoking or eating in the squad car.

Obviously, even if officers wear identical uniforms, individuals will communicate their own messages about their competency, professionalism, and personality.

In addition to understanding such nonverbal messages, many police officers develop their abilities to interpret body language, also called **kinesics,** to such an extent that they can tell when a person is lying or about to become aggressive or flee. They learn to take control of situations by using voice command and authoritative body language.

Other forms of body language are equally important. How officers stand, how they look at those to whom they are talking, whether they smile or frown—all convey a message. A warm smile is said to be the universal language of kindness.

Even a handshake conveys messages. A limp handshake sends one message, a firm handshake another message. Touching, too, can be used to an officer's advantage or disadvantage, as noted by Pace (1991, p. 229):

> *Touching is an important means of communicating willingness to assist, warmth, and sincerity. This gesture has limited use in police communications. Most official situations do not lend themselves to this type of communication. In fact, touching has many negative connotations and is often the catalyst to violent reaction.*

It is worth some time and thought to make sure your appearance and demeanor convey a professional and competent image. Try to eliminate any mannerisms that may give the public the wrong impression about you.

Usually police officers want to convey the impression that they "know their way around." This may actually interfere with effective communication. Noose (1992, p. 105) gives as an example the person who asks directions about how to find a certain store in Boston. If the person is from Boston, the directions given are likely to be brief, with obvious landmarks omitted. If the person is from out of town, however, the directions are likely to be much more detailed. Noose suggests that when interviewing a truthful witness, police officers may want to modify their body language and soften up their "official" language, in a sense pretending to be from out of town. A relaxed manner may result in more in-depth communication and better understanding.

In a confrontational situation, communication skills are also essential. According to Klockars (1985, p. 145): "The police officer's most important tool is his mouth." He notes (p. 146): "The ability to talk in strong, subtle, and sensitive ways, the art of effective rhetoric is essential to the skillful exercise of coercion."

Reading the Nonverbal Messages and Body Language of Others

Police officers, with time and experience, learn to "read" the nonverbal messages and body language of suspects, victims, and witnesses. It is what some call a "sixth sense," and it alerts officers when something is not as it appears or when someone is suspicious, untruthful, afraid, or hesitant. Officers will sometimes call it a "gut feeling" or a nagging suspicion. As many officers have discovered, acting on such inarticulable feelings can pay off.

Criminals are often apprehended because an officer thought they looked suspicious or because something did not "feel right" about a traffic stop or other contact. Many law enforcement officers develop an uncanny ability to spot stolen cars in traffic based on a driver's movements, actions, and driving maneuvers. Officers also learn to read their own "hunches," a very illusive form of communication. Acting on a hunch can save lives, however, as illustrated in the rescue of a driver by an alert, "tuned in" officer.

Officer James Northagen of the Silver Bay Police Department on Lake Superior was on his way to work on a late November night when he noticed tire tracks leading into a snowbank along the edge of the lake. He later said it looked like a vehicle had slipped into a ditch and then driven out. Northagen continued on his way to work, but he kept thinking about the tracks and decided to go back after he started his shift. More than an hour after he first saw the tracks, Officer Northagen looked over the snow bank and saw the wreckage of a pickup truck 60 feet below, in the icy cold water of Lake Superior. The lone occupant was conscious, but pinned in the truck. It took an hour to rescue the man whose head was just barely out of the water for the three hours he was trapped in his truck. (Minneapolis *Star Tribune,* November 22, 1991).

Police officers can tell story after story of nagging and intuitive feelings which they acted on, with similar results.

The REID School of Interviewing and Interrogation trains officers to understand intuitive feelings and the truthfulness of what people communicate. The REID School teaches police officers reliable techniques to determine if a subject is telling the truth based on body language and verbal responses to questions asked by trained interrogators. The REID School's research indicates that certain responses to key questions are very accurate indicators of deception. Police investigators have found such training invaluable; it often results in confessions from guilty people whose lies do not fool the police.

BARRIERS TO EFFECTIVE COMMUNICATION

Because effective communication is so critical to police-community relations, officers should be aware of barriers to effective communication.

Common communication barriers include:

- Prejudices and stereotypes.
- Lack of time.
- Use of jargon.
- Lack of feedback.
- Failure to listen.

Prejudices and stereotypes can greatly interfere with an officer's ability to communicate. Preconceived ideas about a person's truthfulness or "worth" can result in strained relationships with individuals and little or no interchange of ideas. The very language used to refer to others can interfere with communication. For example, would you rather be called a *victim* or a *survivor?* A *cripple* or *physically disabled?*

Lack of time is another barrier to effective communication. Police officers and members of the public are busy. Often neither want to take the time to communicate fully and to establish high empathy. Bad timing can also interfere with communication. Police officers frequently are interrupted by calls for service and need to cut short conversations with others.

The use of **jargon,** the technical language of a profession, is another barrier to communication. Law enforcement has its own special terminology, for example, *alleged perpetrator, modus operandi,* and *complainant.* Officers should avoid using such terms when talking with the public. Officers should also avoid using them in written reports. As noted by Pomerenke (1991, p. 39): "No other profession uses so much jargon and so many acronyms in reports that must be read by people outside the profession than police officers. Many readers, frustrated and confused, ultimately conclude that law enforcement reports are incomprehensible." She gives as an example, the following:

> *R/P informed R/O that VI found apt. entered. A/O and S/O assisted R/O at scene. COMPL/VI (w/f 25yoa 8/15/1945 dob) was taken to Mercy Hosp. TOT was 1135 hrs. VI's veh was transported by TCR.*

Excessive use of jargon and abbreviations can greatly hinder communication.

Lack of feedback can also reduce effective communication. *I know that you believe that you understand what you think I said, BUT I am not sure you realize that what you heard is not what I meant.*

A failure to *listen* is one of the most common and most serious barriers to effective communication. According to Strother (1987, p. 626): "Research has shown that 45% of the total time devoted to communication is spent in listening." Although we spend a great amount of time listening, most people are *not* good listeners. In fact, very few people know how to truly listen. Our educational system develops reading, writing, and speaking skills. The system takes listening skills for granted. Consequently, few people are as good at listening as they could and should be.

One reason for poor listening is the difference between how quickly the human brain can process words and how rapidly most people talk.

Effective listening is difficult because of the gap between how rapidly people talk (125 words per minute) and how rapidly the brain can process those words (500 words per minute). The difference between the speed of speech and the speed of thought creates a false sense of comprehension and promotes mental tangents.

The sense of hearing, like the sense of sight, is physically tremendously slower than the brain's ability to process the information received through the senses.

Other barriers to communication are certain behaviors people can exhibit. Buchholz and Roth (1987, pp. 80-82) note six behaviors that tend to hinder communication.

Behavioral barriers to communication include judging, superiority, certainty, controlling, manipulation, and indifference.

Buchholz and Roth suggest: "These behavior modes are often engaged in innocently and unconsciously, certainly not deliberately by well-meaning people." Often, these behavior modes are trademarks of individuals with low self-esteem.

Judging. "You're wrong." Judging seriously interferes with listening. Rather than focusing on the potential of what someone says, a judgmental person focuses on discrediting what is being said. A person who is quick to judge usually is quite opinionated.

Superiority. An "I'm-more-important-than-you-are" attitude can seriously hinder communication. Flaunting a position of authority hinders communication. Central to this attitude is the feeling that what *I* have to say is ultimately much more important than what is being said by others.

Certainty. "My mind's made up. Don't confuse me with the facts." A person who is convinced of the truthfulness or accuracy of his or her information is generally unable to recognize the possibility of making a mistake.

Controlling. "Let me tell you how this should be done." Few people appreciate being told how to act or what to do. Of course, in certain situations, police officers *must* take control. When officers must have effective personal interaction, however, such control is usually inappropriate and counterproductive.

Manipulation. "Gotcha." It is manipulative to communicate with hidden motives to get people to unknowingly agree or act in a certain way. The manipulator "uses" people.

Indifference. "You're not important. What you think doesn't matter." A person who acts superior often has an indifferent attitude. An officer can convey indifference by the simple act of answering a call for service while talking to someone. To avoid misinterpretation, the officer must take care to explain the necessity of answering the call.

According to Buchholz and Roth (p. 82), other behaviors that inhibit communication include: "facial expressions such as frowning or raising eyebrows, shaking the head, yawning, sighing, leaning back, avoiding eye contact, gazing around the room, taking irrelevant notes, or changing the subject."

Police officers may have more barriers to communication because of the image they convey, their position of authority, and the nature of their work.

COMMUNICATION ENHANCERS

Almost twenty years ago, the National Advisory Commission on Criminal Justice Standards and Goals: Police (1973, p. 407) emphasized the importance of interpersonal communication skills: "Every police agency should immediately develop and improve the interpersonal communications skills of all officers. These skills are essential to the productive exchange of information and opinion between the police, other elements of the criminal justice system, and the public; their use helps officers to perform their tasks more effectively."

The behavioral barriers to effective communication have positive counterparts, that is, behaviors that enhance communication. According to Buchholz and Roth (pp. 82-85), six behaviors can enhance communication.

Behavioral communication enhancers include describing, equality, openness, problem-orientation, positive intent, and empathy.

These behavior modes are typical of individuals with a positive self-image.

Describing. The opposite of judging. "I see it like this." "I hear you saying. . . . " The message sender presents feelings or perceptions that do not judge others as wrong or needing to change.

Equality. The opposite of superiority. "We're on the same team. We're in this together." People's differences are recognized and respected. "Differences in talent, ability, power, and status often exist," say Buchholz and Roth, "but the person who encourages communication seems to attach little importance to these distractors."

Openness. The opposite of certainty. "What do you think? Who has an idea? You've got a good point there. You may be right!" Investigating options rather than steadfastly clinging to the solution greatly enhances communication. People work together toward solutions rather than choosing sides to debate the "best" solution. If people are open, they agree to disagree without being disagreeable.

Problem-orientation. The opposite of controlling. "We're going to have to work this out. We're on the spot and need to come up with an answer." People are encouraged to share their perspectives on a problem. This is an important part of community-oriented, problem-solving policing.

Positive Intent. The opposite of manipulation. "Here's why I'm asking you to do this." Honest, open, candid, sincere behavior promotes communication. People react positively to situations they believe are represented accurately. People usually resent being used or subjected to hidden agendas.

Empathy. The opposite of indifference. "I understand how you feel. I appreciate your concern." Empathy, as discussed previously, is synonymous with understanding others.

Other behaviors that can enhance communication, according to Buchholz and Roth, are: "leaning forward, smiling, nodding, having direct eye contact, sticking to the subject under discussion, and paying full attention." These are also effective *listening* skills, and being an effective listener is an important way to enhance communication.

Active Listening

Officers can use several techniques to improve listening effectiveness. Strother (1987, p. 628) cites the following ten keys to effective listening suggested by the Sperry Corporation:

- Listen for ideas, not facts.
- Judge content, not delivery.
- Listen optimistically.
- Avoid jumping to conclusions.
- Adjust your note-taking to the speaker.
- Concentrate.
- Use excess listening time to summarize the speaker's ideas.
- Work at listening.
- Keep your mind open and your emotions in check.
- Exercise your mind.

Another set of suggestions is made by Fritz (1988):

- Periodically clarify what's being said to you.
- Look for the main points and draw conclusions from them.
- Offer encouragement.
- Separate fact from opinion.
- Avoid interrupting.
- Listen between the lines.
- Notice body language.

Carroll S. Price, in reviewing the manuscript for this book, noted that the primary process of active listening involves a projection: the ability of listeners to project themselves into the shoes of the speaker, so to speak, to not only understand what is being communicated, but *why* the speaker is verbalizing the information and feelings at a specific time.

When speakers realize officers listen to and evaluate what they say carefully, they generally make sure their output is factual and accurate and that their responses are appropriate under the circumstances.

The ability to listen and to assess the situation when communicating can help officers to make the best first impression possible.

THE PRIMACY EFFECT AND THE FOUR-MINUTE BARRIER

According to Reece and Brandt (1987, p. 268): "The way you are treated in this world depends largely on the way you present yourself—the way you look, the way you speak, the way you behave. Although human contact is a challenge, you can learn to control the first impressions you make on others. The key is to become fully aware of the impression you communicate to other people." The first few moments of a personal contact are critical.

The tendency to form impressions of people quickly is called the **primacy effect.**

You can test the primacy effect by asking yourself a few questions. Have you ever walked into a store, been approached by a salesperson, and known almost immediately that you will probably buy something—or will probably *not* buy anything? Have you ever been seated on an airplane next to a stranger and almost immediately wanted to talk to the person—or wanted to get a magazine and bury yourself in it?

First impressions will tend to set the tone for a positive or negative interaction. As Will Rogers so astutely put it, "You never get a second chance to make a first impression."

How long does it take for the primacy effect to occur? Usually in the first four minutes according to Leonard and Natalie Zunin. They have developed the concept of the four-minute barrier.

The **four-minute barrier** is the point in an initial meeting at which most people have formed a positive or negative opinion about the individual with whom they are communicating.

If you can get past the first four minutes of an initial interaction with a person on a positive note, your relationship is likely to be positive. As noted by Reece and Brandt (p. 267): "The general principle is that first impressions establish the mental framework within which a person is viewed, and later evidence is either ignored or reinterpreted."

LESSONS FROM BUSINESS

Changes in technology and in our society have had a profound effect on business. Many businesses have changed their basic approach toward their employees as well as toward their customers. Businesses recognize the importance of service and of good customer relations.

Law enforcement might adopt two practices used successfully in business: networking and seeking customer satisfaction.

Networking

Personal networks were discussed earlier in this chapter as connections individuals have with others in their lives. Consciously establishing such networks has become popular in the business world, with *networking* a popular buzzword. According to Adams (1991, p. 64), networking involves more than simply trading business cards—it requires skill. He cites the definition of networking used by Belinda Plutz, a consultant in New York City.

Networking is the building and keeping of professional relationships for mutual interest and mutual help.

Just as police officers need to communicate with the people in their jurisdiction, they also need to communicate with the institutions and agencies in the area. These include:

- Churches, schools, and business associations such as the Lions, Rotary, and Kiwanias.
- Social service agencies, storefront organizations, and shelters.
- Hospitals, clinics, and emergency care providers.
- City inspectors and licensors.
- Courts and corrections personnel.
- Politicians and members of advisory councils.
- Special interest groups such as MADD.

Finn and Sullivan (1988, p. 1) note:

> *The public repeatedly calls on law enforcement officers for assistance with people who are mentally ill, drunk in public, and homeless. . . . One way of expanding the options for handling these populations is to share responsibility for them with the social service system. Networks between law enforcement agencies and human services agencies can yield substantial benefits not only for the agencies involved, but for individuals who need help.*

As suggested earlier, a community-oriented approach to policing creates a partnership between the police and groups of concerned individuals to address specific community problems. Those involved in the problem may also be part of its solution.

The Citizen as Customer

Law enforcement, like business, might benefit by emphasizing the value of customer service and the time-tested adage "The customer is always right." According to Hart, Heskett, and Sasser (1991, p. 75): "Customers who have bad experiences tell 11 people about it; customers who have good ones tell six."

In a very real sense, citizens are the customers of law enforcement agencies. Couper and Lobitz (1991, p. 17) illustrate this customer-oriented approach: "We will be a police department devoted to maintaining customer satisfaction and getting closer to the people we serve."

The organization must train the people who interact directly with customers, and then it must empower them. That is, it must give them the authority, responsibility, and incentives to recognize, care about, and attend to customer needs. Empowering the bottom of the organizational pyramid can be threatening, especially to middle-level managers, who may view such empowerment as an erosion of their own authority. Empowerment of all members of an organization is absolutely essential to good service recovery. Employees close to the customer are the first to know about problems and are in the best position to determine what can be done to satisfy the customer. (Hart, Heskett, and Sasser, 1991, p. 76)

Law enforcement agencies, like many successful businesses, would benefit from having an empowered work force. It is vital to community-oriented policing to give patrol officers the authority and training necessary to make decisions and to reward them when they do so.

HUMAN RELATIONS GUIDELINES

The ability to listen and understand, to speak and be understood, to communicate the message you intend, both verbally and nonverbally—are at the heart of effective public relations.

Effective human relations goes further than interpersonal communication. The context in which the communication occurs is important. Coffey, Eldefonso, and Hartinger (1982, pp. 180-81) suggest the following guidelines to help police officers make a positive impression and improve interpersonal relationships:

1. Don't be trapped into unprofessional conduct by a threat or a challenge.

2. Make sure everything you do is calculated to enhance your reputation as a good officer—one who is firm, but fair and just.

3. When you are faced with a threat and you can't tell how serious it is, try to "buy time" in which to size up the situation by engaging the person in conversation. Make a comment or ask a question to divert his attention if possible.

4. Don't show hostility even if the other person does. Often a calm and reasonable manner will cause hostility to evaporate, or at least to simmer down.

5. Reduce your "threat" potential. Avoid a grim or expressionless countenance. Be an approachable human being. Too many officers habitually appear gruff and forbidding.

6. Cultivate a pleasant, friendly manner when making nonadversary contacts. Be ready with a smile, a pleasant word, a humorous comment when appropriate.

7. Let your general demeanor, and especially your facial expression and tone of voice, indicate that you respect the other person as a human being.

8. Let other people know by your reception of them that you don't expect trouble from them and that you don't consider them a nuisance. (Maybe you do, but don't let it show.)

9. Show an interest in the other person's problem. Maybe you can't do anything about it, but often it is a great help just to be a good listener.

10. Go out of your way to improve police-community relations. Even though your department may have a unit that specializes in community relations, never forget that you are the real key. The essence of good working relations between the people and the police is to be found in the way you handle yourself.

11. Always leave the people you deal with feeling that they have been treated fairly. When you render a service or react to a request, show some interest and give some explanation. This will promote good feelings, which, if carried on consistently by the entire force, will have the cumulative effect resulting in vastly improved human relations.

12. Try in every way you can to encourage people to work with the police for their own protection. Let the average citizen know that, far from being a threat, you are interested in being of help. Drive home the point that the citizen is threatened by crime and disorder, not by the police.

Summary

A person's world-view is largely created by what they see and hear as they experience events. The discrepancy between what the eye takes in (five million bits per second) and what the person actually processes (five hundred bits per second) accounts, in part, for why two witnesses can see the same thing differently.

Perception is also affected by the words people use to communicate. The most basic rule of semantics is: Cow_1 is NOT Cow_2, that is, each item within a specific class also has individual characteristics.

Effective police-community relations depends on an understanding of oneself and of others. Critical to self-understanding is recognizing preferences, prejudices, and stereotypes. Prejudice is an attitude; discrimination is a behavior. Empathy is understanding another person. Empathy depends, in part, upon determining the other person's networks, the "complex pathways of human interaction that guide and direct an individual's perception, motivation and behavior."

The quality of police-community relations depends largely on the communication process. The process involves a sender, a message, a channel, a receiver, and sometimes feedback. Common communication barriers include prejudices and stereotypes, time, use of jargon, lack of feedback, and failure to listen. Effective listening is difficult because of the gap between how rapidly people talk (125 words per minute) and how rapidly the brain can process those words (500 words per minute). The difference between the speed of speech and the speed of thought breeds a false sense of security and promotes mental tangents. Behavioral barriers to communication include judging, superiority, certainty, controlling, manipulation, and indifference.

Police officers may have more barriers to communication because of the image they convey, their position of authority, and the nature of their work.

Behavioral communication enhancers include describing, equality, openness, problem-orientation, positive intent, and empathy.

When seeking to improve human interactions, officers should keep in mind the tendency to form impressions of people quickly, that is, the primacy effect. The four-minute barrier is the point in an initial meeting at which most people have formed a positive or negative opinion about someone.

Law enforcement might benefit by adopting two practices used successfully in business: networking and seeking customer satisfaction. Networking is the building and keeping of professional relationships for mutual interest and assistance.

Discussion Questions _____

1. What are some of your strong preferences? Might they be called prejudices?
2. Do you prefer to communicate by speaking or writing?

3. Who is included in your network?
4. Do you have a hobby that has a specialized language (jargon)? What words might most people not understand?
5. Three umpires were discussing balls and strikes in baseball. The first said, "I call them like I see them." The second said, "I call them like they are." The third said, "They aren't anything 'til I call them." How does this relate to the study of semantics?
6. What role do euphemisms ("soft" words) play in communication?
7. Give examples illustrating the basic rule learned from semantics: Cow_1 is not Cow_2. Why is the rule important in police work?
8. How does empathy differ from sympathy? When is each appropriate?
9. Can you think of examples of when the four-minute barrier and the primacy effect operated in your life?
10. In what ways might the general public be perceived as "customers" of a police department? What implications does this have?

DEFINITIONS

Can you define these words: bias, body language, communication, communication process, discrimination, empathy, extensional world, four-minute barrier, jargon, kinesics, networking, networks, nonverbal communication, perception, phenomenological point of view, preference, prejudice, primacy effect, self-fulfilling prophecy, semantic environment, semantics, sensorium, stereotyping, symbolic process, verbal world.

REFERENCES

Adams, Michael. "Exchanging Circles." *Successful Meetings*. (April 1991): 64–65.

Berglund, Bob. "Your Message Is Not the Most Important Part of Your Speech." *Star Tribune*. (July 1, 1992): 2D.

Buchholz, Steve and Roth, Thomas. *Creating the High-Performance Team*. New York: John Wiley & Sons, Inc., 1987.

Coffey, Alan; Eldefonso, Edward; and Hartinger, Walter. *Human Relations: Law Enforcement in a Changing Community*. 3rd ed. Englewood Cliffs: Prentice-Hall, Inc., 1982.

Conroy, Dennis L. and Hess, Kären M. *Officers at Risk: How to Identify and Cope with Stress*. Placerville: Custom Publishing Company, 1992.

Couper, David C. and Lobitz, Sabine. "The Customer is Always Right." *The Police Chief*. (May 1991): 17-23.

Finn, Peter E. and Sullivan, Monique. *Police Response to Special Populations: Handling the Mentally Ill, Public Inebriate, and the Homeless*. Washington: National Institute of Justice. January 1988.

Fritz, Roger. *Rate Your Executive Potential.* New York: John Wiley & Sons, Inc., 1988.

George, Claude S. Jr. *Supervision in Action: The Art of Managing Others.* 4th rev. ed. Reston: Reston Publishing Company, 1985.

Hageman, Mary Jeanette. *Police-Community Relations.* Beverly Hills: Sage Publications, 1985.

Hart, Christopher W. L.; Heskett, James L.; and Sasser, W. Earl, Jr. "Surviving a Customer's Rage." *Successful Meetings.* (April 1991): 68-79.

Hayakawa, S. I. *Language in Thought and Action.* New York: Harcourt, Brace & World, Inc., 1949.

Klockars, Carl B. *The Idea of Police.* Newbury Park: Sage Publishing Company, 1985.

Marne-la Vallee, France. "Ooh, la, la! Disney's First Theme Park in Europe Opens Near Paris." *Star Tribune.* (April 13, 1992): 1A, 5A.

National Advisory Commission on Criminal Justice Standards and Goals. *Task Force on Police.* Washington: U.S. Government Printing Office, 1973.

Noose, Gregory A. "Basic Investigative Interviewing Skills: Networking an Interview." *Law and Order.* (March 1992): 101-07.

Oran, Daniel. *Law Dictionary for Nonlawyers,* 2nd rev. ed. St. Paul: West Publishing Company, 1985.

Pace, Denny F. *Community Relations Concepts.* Placerville: Custom Publishing Company, 1991.

Parker, L. Craig, Jr.; Meier, Robert D.; and Monahan, Lynn Hunt. *Interpersonal Psychology for Criminal Justice.* St. Paul: West Publishing Company, 1989.

Pomerenke, Paula J. "Jargon Dangers in Law Enforcement." *Law and Order.* (March 1991): 39.

Price, Carroll S. Letter to author, reviewing the manuscript, 1992.

Reece, Barry L. and Brandt, Rhonda. *Effective Human Relations in Organizations.* 3rd rev. ed. Boston: Houghton Mifflin Company, 1987.

Strother, Deborah Burnett. "On Listening." *Phi Delta Kappan.* (April 1987): 625-28.

Trojanowicz, Robert C. and Carter, David L. "The Changing Face of America." *FBI Law Enforcement Bulletin.* (January 1990): 6-12.

Zunin, Leonard, and Zunin, Natalie. *Contact–The First Four Minutes.*

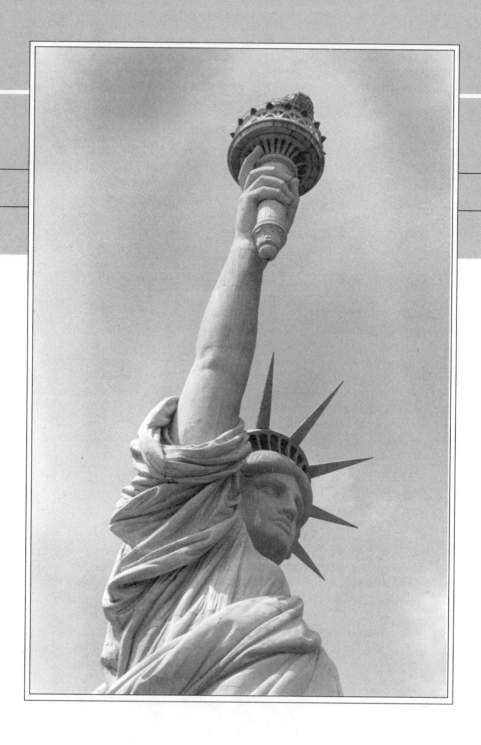

DEALING EFFECTIVELY WITH DIVERSITY

If one were to offer men to choose out of all the customs in the world such as seemed to them the best, they would examine the whole number, and end by preferring their own; so convinced are they that their own usages surpass those of all others.

—Herodotus,
The Persian Wars, Book III, Chapter 38

DO YOU KNOW

- What ethnocentricism is and how it affects police-community relations?
- What are the three schools of thought on what happens when more than one culture inhabits the same territory?
- What has been the dominant culture in the United States?
- What is one of the main barriers frequently associated with ethnic/racial diversity?
- What strategies might be used to communicate more effectively with those who do not speak English?
- What types of diversity are found in the United States?
- What the three basic socioeconomic classes are? What they are based on?
- What the poverty syndrome is?
- What the multi-cultural trap is?
- What a bias or hate crime is?

INTRODUCTION

Police officers need to be aware of the role diversity plays in the community they serve. Law enforcement traditionally has tried to maintain the *status quo*. Diversity is a source of stress for many officers. This need not be the case if officers realize that diversity involves issues that are extremely delicate, sensitive, and important. The questions diversity raises do not have simple answers.

"People of different races, cultures, and languages are coming into closer contact with each other and enormous demands are being made on their understanding and tolerance," says Inkster (1992, p. 28). He notes: "There are widening class divisions, more broken families and homelessness, growing anger on the part of the disadvantaged, and a rise in violent crime." This social unrest presents a significant challenge to police-community relations. It requires "enlightened" police officers, perhaps somewhat like Gulf War commander, General Arnold Schwarzkopf.

During the Gulf War (1991), General Schwarzkopf insisted on American soldiers respecting Islam's religious and cultural values. He was as familiar with the subtleties of Islamic law as he was of the high-tech weaponry and military strategies of the United States. He epitomized the ideal leader—educated, thoughtful, articulate, culturally sensitive, and knowledgeable in several disciplines.

> *These must be the qualities of our police officers if we are to maintain peace, order and a sense of security in society. They must act from a base of knowledge about their profession, about the cultural values of the community in which they work, about people individually and collectively, and about the larger world in which they live. This includes a sensitivity to different cultures and language skills that allow them to communicate with and understand their clients (Inkster, 1992, p. 30).*

CULTURE AND CULTURAL DIVERSITY

Culture is defined as a collection of artifacts, tools, ways of living, values, and language common to a group of people, all passed from one generation to the next. The specific items that make up a culture fall into two broad categories: material and nonmaterial. Material elements of one culture are readily borrowed or adopted by another culture if they are an obvious improvement. This is not the case, however, with the nonmaterial elements involved in "ways of living."

"Ways of living" includes religion, political beliefs, kinship roles, values, and laws, both moral and legal. Diversity is most obvious and sometimes most problematic when different "ways of living" coexist in the same community.

The previous chapter discussed how language (which is an element of culture) shapes the way individuals view the world. The culture itself, also provides a framework or world-view, a **cultural window** through which events are interpreted. Recall the reaction of some of the French nationals to the opening of Euro Disneyland.

Ethnocentrism is the preference of one's own way of life over all others.

People are naturally attracted to others who are similar to themselves. If we surround ourselves with others similar to us, we minimize uncertainty regarding how people will respond to us and we maximize the likelihood we will be in agreement. Minimization of uncertainty motivates people because uncertainty is cognitively uncomfortable. Ethnocentricity and segregation are consequences of our desire to avoid uncertainty.

Several different cultures came to the "New World" and established the United States. As noted by Clement (1992, p. 25): "In a sense, all of us who are not Native Americans are boat people." The United States is a nation of individuals with varying ethnic and racial backgrounds. The sociological literature on ethnic and racial diversity has three schools of thought on the consequences of two or more cultures inhabiting the same geographic area: assimilation, cultural pluralism, and cultural conflict.

Assimilation theorists suggest that our society takes in or assimilates various cultures in what is commonly referred to as a "melting pot."

Assimilation, also referred to as **acculturation,** was, indeed, what happened to the early colonists. Initially the colonists came from various countries with different religions. They settled in specific geographic areas and maintained their original culture, for example, the Pennsylvania Dutch.

The seemingly unlimited resources available and the mutual struggle for survival in the "New World" encouraged colonists to assimilate. Over time, the triple forces of continued immigration, urbanization, and industrialization soon turned the United States into a "melting pot" with diverse cultures from the various colonies merging. The "melting pot" was accomplished relatively painlessly because of the many similarities among the cultures: they looked quite similar physically, they valued religion and "morality," most valued hard work, and, perhaps most important, there was plenty of land for everyone. The "homogenization" of the United States was fairly well accomplished by the mid–1800s. The formerly distinct cultures blended into what became known as an American culture, which was a white, male-dominated, culture of European origin.

Unfortunately, some groups were not as easily assimilated as others. In fact, one group, the Native Americans, were precluded from the developing American culture. Like animals, they were herded onto reservations. Native-Americans have only recently begun to enter into the mainstream of American life. Some Native Americans no longer want to be assimilated—they seek to maintain their culture and heritage. The same is true of many black Americans. It is likely, therefore, that cultural diversity will continue to exist in the United States. Assimilation does not always occur.

An alternative to assimilation is for diverse cultures to peacefully co-exist.

Cultural pluralism suggests there are many melting pots. Some groups are comfortable in one pot, other groups are comfortable in another.

Perhaps the best example of cultural pluralism is the Native American. According to Hageman (1985, p. 99): "American Indians need to be viewed as a nation of tribes. There are 467 recognized Indian tribes and bands in this country with populations ranging from less than 100 to more than 100,000."

Prior to colonization of the United States, the Indian tribes had distinct territories, languages, and cultures. Later, as the settlers took their lands, they joined together in self-defense. In the 1990s, Native Americans are often referred to as a single entity, although the individual tribes still maintain their unique identities.

Cultural pluralism is particularly noticeable when new immigrants arrive in the United States. Usually, instead of attempting to assimilate into the mainstream of America, immigrants seek out others from their homeland, resulting in Chinatowns, Little Italys, Little Greeces, and, most recently, Hmong communities.

According to Hirsch (1988, p. 95): "The dominant model of American pluralism has been that of the **'hyphenated America'**: the Italian-American, the Polish-American, the Afro-American, the Asian-American, and so forth."

Cultural pluralism rests on the assumption that diverse cultures can coexist and prosper. In the 1990s the view that diversity strengthens a society is widely held by members of the public. In Oakland, California,

The All Nation Singers chant in appreciation to the city of Berkeley, California during the first Indigenous Peoples Day in October of 1992. Indigenous Peoples Day is an alternative celebration of Columbus Day. Native Americans from around the country came to participate in the all day event.

for example, members of the community consider the social studies textbooks antihistorical, because they describe the United States as a "common culture," created by waves of immigrants. As noted by Epstein (1992, p. 636): "Once you have decided that the story of America is the story of Europeans escaping events like the potato famine and seeking a better way of life, then you are only telling that part of American history which fits that version. The story of African-Americans and Native Americans is not that story; they were not voluntary immigrants seeking a better life. Our story is the story of a continuous, never-ending struggle for justice and human values within this country."

Indeed, peaceful coexistence, is not always the reality.

The **cultural conflict** theory suggests that diverse cultures that share the same territory will compete with and attempt to exploit one another.

Such cultural conflict was common between the early settlers and the Native American tribes. Conflict was also common between the white immigrants and the black slaves they imported from Africa. From 1619 to 1860 more than six million Africans were involuntarily transported to the American colonies (Hageman, 1985, p. 83).

The hostile treatment of Japanese-Americans during World War II was also rooted in cultural conflict. Following the attack on Pearl Harbor, many Americans believed that the Japanese-Americans were a national threat. Over 110,000 Japanese, the great majority of whom were American-born citizens, were forced by the government to sell their homes and businesses and then placed in internment camps.

Cultural conflict can currently be seen in growing tensions between specific ethnic groups as they compete for the limited remaining resources available. In Minnesota, for example, only Native Americans are allowed to harvest wild rice or to spear fish. The Mille Lacs band of Chippewa has sued Minnesota, claiming treaty rights allow them to fish outside their reservation without state regulation. Native Americans are also currently lobbying to be allowed to take motorboats into the wilderness area to enhance their guide business.

Organizations working for women's rights, grey power, and gay power make it clear that the United States is, indeed, a culturally pluralistic nation. Assimilation, cultural pluralism, and cultural conflicts are all realities in the 1990s in the United States, presenting a formidable challenge for those who must maintain the "public peace." It is a greater challenge to develop "communities" and to enlist their aid to maintain the peace if there is a language barrier.

NON-ENGLISH OR LIMITED ENGLISH SPEAKING INDIVIDUALS

In some parts of the country it is common for officers to deal with non-English speaking people or those who speak English as a second language. Try to imagine performing a car-stop on a vehicle filled with people who do not understand anything you are saying and you cannot understand them. The language barrier can make just getting the job done safely very difficult, to say nothing of maintaining positive police-community relations.

> The language barrier is a major problem in police interactions with some ethnic/racial groups.

As noted by Sharp (1991, p. 95): "Roughly two-thirds of the departments responding recently to a poll focusing on language barrier problems indicated that they encounter difficulties from time to time." Sharp notes: "A cardinal maxim affecting police work is that emergencies can happen anywhere, at any time. All emergencies are bad. They grow worse when the responders and victims do not speak the same language."

In addition, as noted by Hinkle (1990, p. 23), when police interact with those who do not speak English, the officer is in a difficult situation:

> *A citizen (or even a non-citizen) who speaks no English is protected by the same constitutional guarantees as anyone else. This means that delays in the judicial process, delayed response to emergencies, apparent unconcern or lack of proper attention (medical and otherwise) or any of the other problems that may arise from lack of communication place the officer and everyone of his supervisors at risk of a lawsuit.*

Hinkle suggests that ideally officers would be bilingual, speaking English and the language of the main ethnic minority in the area. It is usually not possible, however, for officers to be bilingual. An alternative is to learn the words and phrases used most frequently in policing in the other language. Hinkle notes that soldiers in foreign countries have little trouble issuing simple commands to the locals. If you were to learn ten new words a day, in one year your working vocabulary would be 3,650 words. This vocabulary would be sufficient to understand most communications and to convey your own messages in most situations.

Officers could also benefit from a plasticized guide of the most common words and phrases along with their pronunciations. One such guide, *Speedy Spanish for Police Personnel,* includes words and phrases needed for, among other situations: routine traffic stops, D.U.I., burglary/theft reports, victim/witness interrogation, Miranda Warning & Waiver, domestic disputes, medical care, and booking/body search. Table 5.1 is a page from such a guide.

Until recently, Spanish was the primary language officers needed to learn. In the past few decades, however, refugee influxes from the former Soviet Union, Ethiopia, Poland, Romania, and of course, Asia, have added to the challenge. As one physician noted: "The result is waiting rooms that sound like Towers of Babel, clinics that look like U.N. lobbies, and doctors who don't know where to begin" (Clement, 1992, p. 25). Police officers may also be frustrated by the same situation.

Clement (p. 26) describes a physician's difficulty dealing with a Hmong patient and her interpreter who also spoke limited English. The doctor wanted to draw blood for a test. The interpreter, however, could not make the distinction between "test" and "taste." Said Clement: "For a long time, we had to fight the myth that our doctor wanted to drink the blood. And when we asked for urine and stool specimens, they just laughed." Police officers could encounter a similar difficulty in a D.U.I. incident.

TABLE 5.1
Communication Aid for Officers Interacting with Spanish-Speaking Individuals

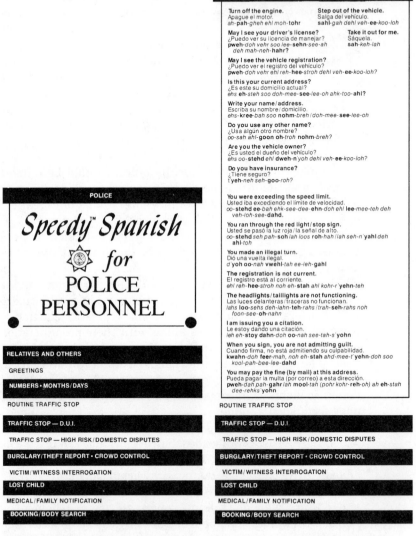

ROUTINE TRAFFIC STOP

Turn off the engine.
Apague el motor.
*ah-***pah***-gheh ehl moh-***tohr***

Step out of the vehicle.
Salga del vehículo.
*sahl-gah dehl veh-***ee***-koo-loh*

May I see your driver's license?
¿Puedo ver su licencia de manejar?
pweh*-doh vehr soo lee-***sehn***-see-ah
deh mah-neh-***hahr***?*

Take it out for me.
Sáquela.
sah-keh-lah

May I see the vehicle registration?
¿Puedo ver el registro del vehículo?
pweh*-doh vehr ehl reh-***hee***-stroh dehl veh-***ee***-koo-loh?*

Is this your current address?
¿Es este su domicilio actual?
*ehs **eh***-steh soo doh-mee-***see***-lee-oh ahk-too-***ahl***?*

Write your name/address.
Escriba su nombre/domicilio.
*ehs-***kree***-bah soo **nohm***-breh/doh-mee-***see***-lee-oh*

Do you use any other name?
¿Usa algún otro nombre?
*oo-sah ahl-***goon** *oh-troh* **nohm***-breh?*

Are you the vehicle owner?
¿Es usted el dueño del vehículo?
*ehs oo-***stehd** *ehl* **dweh***-n yoh dehl veh-***ee***-koo-loh?*

Do you have insurance?
¿Tiene seguro?
*t'***yeh***-neh seh-***goo***-roh?*

You were exceeding the speed limit.
Usted iba excediendo el límite de velocidad.
*oo-***stehd** *ee-bah ehk-see-dee-***ehn***-doh ehl* **lee***-mee-teh deh veh-loh-see-dahd.*

You ran through the red light/stop sign.
Usted se pasó la luz roja/la señal de alto.
*oo-***stehd** *seh pah-soh lah loos roh-hah/lah seh-n'***yahl** *dehl* **ahl***-toh*

You made an illegal turn.
Dió una vuelta ilegal.
*d'***yoh** *oo-***nah** *v***wehl***-tah ee-leh-***gahl***

The registration is not current.
El registro está al corriente.
*ehl reh-***hee***-stroh noh eh-***stah** *ahl kohr-r'***yehn***-teh*

The headlights/taillights are not functioning.
Las luces delanteras/traceras no funcionan.
lahs **loo***-sehs deh-lahn-teh-rahs/trah-***seh***-rahs noh foon-see-***oh***-nahn*

I am issuing you a citation.
Le estoy dando una citación.
*leh eh-***stoy** *dahn-doh oo-nah see-tah-s'***yohn***

When you sign, you are not admitting guilt.
Cuando firma, no está admitiendo su culpabilidad.
kwahn*-doh* **feer***-mah, noh eh-***stah** *ahd-mee-t'***yehn***-doh soo kool-pah-bee-lee-dahd*

You may pay the fine (by mail) at this address.
Pueda pagar la multa (por correo) a esta dirección.
pweh*-dah pah-***gahr** *lah* **mool***-tah (pohr kohr-***reh***-oh) ah eh-stah dee-rehks* **yohn***

POLICE	
Speedy™ Spanish	
for	
POLICE	
PERSONNEL	
RELATIVES AND OTHERS	
GREETINGS	
NUMBERS • MONTHS/DAYS	
ROUTINE TRAFFIC STOP	ROUTINE TRAFFIC STOP
TRAFFIC STOP — D.U.I.	TRAFFIC STOP — D.U.I.
TRAFFIC STOP — HIGH RISK/DOMESTIC DISPUTES	TRAFFIC STOP — HIGH RISK/DOMESTIC DISPUTES
BURGLARY/THEFT REPORT • CROWD CONTROL	BURGLARY/THEFT REPORT • CROWD CONTROL
VICTIM/WITNESS INTERROGATION	VICTIM/WITNESS INTERROGATION
LOST CHILD	LOST CHILD
MEDICAL/FAMILY NOTIFICATION	MEDICAL/FAMILY NOTIFICATION
BOOKING/BODY SEARCH	BOOKING/BODY SEARCH

Reprinted by permission from *Speedy Spanish For Police Personnel,* Santa Barbara: Baja Books.

Strategies to help improve communication with non-English speaking individuals include (1) learning the language or at least common words and phrases; (2) using a language guide; (3) having a list of local language teachers who could serve as interpreters; and (4) subscribing to the Language Line.

In an effort to improve communications with non-English speaking individuals police could maintain a list of teachers of various foreign languages at local high schools, colleges, and universities. Another option is to subscribe to AT&T's *Language Line*. According to Sharp (1991, p. 99):

> *This service, which is the only one of its kind in the world, allows police to get immediate translations of 143 different languages 24 hours a day, seven days a week, 365 days a year. . . . They can place calls from any phone to seek assistance via an 800 number.*

Police departments that subscribe to the Language Line service are issued language identification cards listing all the languages the service can translate. The cards are written in the native script of each language so non-English speakers can indicate their language to officers.

An article in *Law Enforcement News* ("Parlez-vous Miranda Warnings? p. 3) described a typical instance in which the Language Line was invaluable to police:

> *Officers in San Jose who arrived at the home of a Vietnamese woman found her badly beaten on the kitchen floor and found a man cowering behind furniture. Neither spoke English. The officers did not jump to conclusions, but dialed the Language Line Service instead. As a result, they were able to learn from the woman that she had been beaten by her husband. The man hiding was her brother, who had been frightened by the fight and hid himself.*

Police departments must recognize and plan for the language barrier because, as noted by Sharp (p. 99): "There are currently between 12 and 22 million non-English speaking people living in the United States. Another 40 million visit the country every year. Immigration quotas account for approximately 800,000 more entering each year." Rachlin (1992, p. 101) notes:

> *Although a police agency may never have a need for Maihili or Waray-Waray or Azerbaijani, it can never be sure when it will need Toyshanese or Linqala or . . . Punjabi. With its battery of professional interpreters, the Monterey-based AT&T Language Line Services operations center can readily identify virtually any language presented to them and have an interpreter on the line before you can say "Peter Perpetrator picked a pocket of pickled peppers."*

ᴸTURAL DIVERSITY AND OTHER ᴿRIERS TO COMMUNICATION

It is important for police officers to be aware of other cultural differences. For example, in some Asian cultures, only the oldest family member will deal with the police on behalf of the entire family. In the last few years many immigrants have come from Southeast Asia. Often victims of discrimination and crime, there is a tendency for them to not seek police assistance or report crimes. Many, in fact, especially the elderly, fear the police. In one Texas community, for example, an officer was giving a Vietnamese man involved in an accident a ride home. Sensing the man's fear, the officer smiled and tried to put him at ease. The man just stared at him and said in his broken English, "Police very mean. Police in Vietnam. . . ." and then shaped his hand like a gun and held it to his own head (Rachlin, 1992, p. 100).

Cultural norms often dictate that family problems be solved within the community. One good illustration exists among the Hmong people of Southeast Asia. If a Hmong woman is raped, she is unlikely to report it because in her culture the custom is that the rapist, if discovered, is forced to marry his victim. There is, however, great trust among the Hmong people. Such trust can lead to difficulties as noted by deFiebre (1992, p. 1A): "Thriftiness, traditions of trust and a lack of financial sophistication lead many immigrants from Asian and other Third World nations to avoid mainstream American banks and rely on other vehicles to save money." The cultural backgrounds of these people leaves them extremely vulnerable to scams.

Other examples of cultural barriers to communication come from the Native American culture. According to Day (1992, p. 15) making direct eye contact in the Ojibwa culture is a sign of disrespect or outright defiance. He notes: "To show respect they may appear disinterested, present a flat affect, avoid eye contact, say very little, and offer only tangential or indirect responses." A police officer could easily misinterpret such a response.

Eye contact, in fact, varies greatly among different cultures. Most African-Americans prefer indirect eye contact while listening, and direct eye contact while speaking as a sign of attentiveness and respect. The opposite is true of most people of European descent, who prefer direct eye contact during listening and indirect eye contact during speaking as signs of attention and respect. To Hispanics, avoidance of direct eye contact is sometimes a sign of attentiveness and respect, but sustained direct eye contact may be interpreted as a challenge to authority.

Other cultural differences in nonverbal communication can result in misunderstanding. For example, hissing to gain attention is common for Hispanics, but to whites hissing is usually considered impolite and indicates contempt. A slap on the back in the white culture usually indicates friendliness; a slap on the back in Asian or Vietnamese cultures is usually insulting.

The American "okay" sign—thumb and forefinger forming a circle, fingers point up, is considered an obscene gesture in Brazil. This same gesture means *money* in Japanese and *zero* or *worthless* in French. There is great potential for miscommunication between members of different groups.

Police officers should determine what racial/ethnic minorities reside in their jurisdiction and learn what cultural values they might misunderstand. Indeed, what is legal in some cultures may be illegal in the United States.

CULTURAL DIVERSITY AND THE LAW

A few specific examples will show how legal problems might result from cultural diversity. According to Dr. Thomas W. Day (1992, p. 15): "More than one Southeast Asian family has been investigated for child abuse after health professionals noted the skin lesions caused by traditional coin rubbing treatment." The practice of "coining" involves rubbing warm oil and coins across the skin and often results in long, red bruises.

According to deFiebre (1991, p. 1B): "Many Asians are frustrated by child-abuse laws that prohibit severe corporal punishment and a juvenile-justice system that shies away from jailing first offenders."

Another cultural difference that causes problems is that the Hmongs have no age restriction on marriage. Gustafson and Prince (1991, p. 1A) described the situation of a Hmong man who married a twelve-year-old girl after paying her parents $2,000. He was charged with third-degree criminal sexual conduct for having sexual relations with a minor because state law prohibited anyone under sixteen to be married, even with parental consent. According to his lawyer, "I think he's having some difficulty understanding why something accepted in Hmong culture is wrong to do here."

Before considering more problems that result from cultural differences, consider two other forms of diversity in the United States, religious diversity and socioeconomic diversity.

> In addition to cultural diversity (including racial/ethnic diversity), the United States also has religious and socioeconomic diversity.

RELIGIOUS DIVERSITY

Many of those who came to America did so to escape religious persecution. The colonists' desire for religious freedom is inherent in our Bill of Rights. The First Amendment protects, among other freedoms, freedom of religion. The First Amendment was drafted and adopted to protect the segregated turfs of different religious communities in the early colonies: Congregationalism in New England, Quakerism in Pennsylvania, and Catholicism in Maryland. Over the years, these distinctions have become much less important, with "Christians" becoming a sort of religious melting pot for people of quite similar religious beliefs. Innumerable religions now exist in the United States.

In recent years, devil worship or Satanism has come to the attention of police departments in some areas. The First Amendment protects such practices. Police become concerned, however, when those engaged in Satanism desecrate churches, steal religious artifacts, or sacrifice their neighbor's dog.

Sometimes there is a very fine line between religious freedom and illegal activity. For example, the Supreme Court will consider whether a Florida city's ban on animal sacrifice in religious ceremonies violates the constitutional guarantee of religious freedom (*Star Tribune,* 3-24-92, p. 1A). In 1987 the city of Hialeah adopted an animal–sacrifice prohibition after members of Santeria, an ancient African religion which practices animal sacrifices, made plans to open a church there. In this case, *Church of the Lukumi Babalu Aye v. City of Hialeah,* those who challenge the ban argue that the law is specifically aimed at animal slaughter for religious purposes. The city has not made it a crime to kill animals, but rather a crime to kill animals in a religious ceremony.

Santeria has an estimated 50,000 to 60,000 followers in south Florida. Santerians sacrifice animals at rites celebrating birth, marriage, and death, and also during ceremonies to cure the sick. Opponents of the ban argue: "Hialeah has not interfered with the sale of lobsters to be boiled alive, and the record does not show that it has interfered with the practice of feeding live rats to pet snakes. . . . Religion is almost the only unacceptable reason for killing an animal in Florida."

In Oregon a similar situation existed when a group lobbied for an exception to the general drug laws to make it legal for American Indians to smoke peyote during their rituals. In this case, the Supreme Court ruled that such an exception need not be granted. Smoking peyote was illegal across the board; the American Indians were not a special group that had been singled out.

Socioeconomic Diversity

Even the casual observer recognizes that social and economic class factors create diversity in the United States. Sociologists typically divide individuals within the United States into three basic classes.

The three basic socioeconomic classes, based primarily on income and education, are the lower, middle, and upper classes. These basic classes may be further subdivided.

When considering the socioeconomic classes, do not forget the maxim that "Cow_1 is not Cow_2." Each person has unique, individual characteristics. Each socioeconomic class will also have members of all the diverse groups discussed in the previous section. Some groups, however, are more numerous in certain classes. As previously discussed, in their traditional role of crime fighter, the police interact most frequently with those from the lower socioeconomic class.

The Lower Socioeconomic Class

Certain races and ethnic groups are frequently equated with poverty and crime. Pace (1991, p. 102) describes the interaction of these factors as the *poverty syndrome.*

The **poverty syndrome** includes inadequate housing, inadequate education, inadequate jobs, and a resentment of those who control the social system.

Pace notes: "The poverty syndrome has a powerful psychological influence on how a person views society and how he views those who control society." He notes that poor people are in contact with the criminal justice system more frequently because they are on the streets and highly visible.

A poor person who drives an old car will get a repair ticket whereas a wealthier person is more likely to drive a newer car that does not require repairs. In addition, the repair ticket issued to the poor person is likely to be a much greater hardship for that person than a similar ticket would be to someone in the middle or upper classes.

Often members of the lower socioeconomic class live in ghettos. Pace (p. 44) notes: "Approximately 69% of the Black population lives in metropolitan areas, with about 56% of that number living in the inner city. . . . If society were to integrate totally, about 95% of all Blacks would have to relocate."

Indeed, getting out of the ghetto is difficult for many. Pace (1991, p. 45) notes that the **ghetto syndrome** is a vicious circle of failure: poverty, poor education, joblessness, low motivation to work, welfare, and poverty. . . . In addition, according to Pace (p. 43): "Since ghettos house more than 70% of racial or ethnic minorities, the ghetto, minorities, and crime become interrelated and are the focus for most of the anti-crime efforts of the criminal justice system." This accounts, in part, for charges of racism against some police departments, as discussed in Chapter 4.

Thirty years ago ghettos were more commonly referred to as *slums.* At that time internationally known scholar, scientist, educator, author, and former president of Harvard University, James B. Conant, wrote *Slums and Suburbs.* In this classic study of American education in the late fifties and early sixties, Conant (1961, p. 18) expressed a belief that

This grim street scene represents a small part of America's worst urban disaster areas, the South Bronx in New York. Here rubble-strewn lots extend for acres, thousands of people are on welfare, and thousands of buildings stand empty. Note the broken windows and the irony of the "Discover Yourself" poster.

de facto segregation, mixing Negro (the socially accepted term in the 1950s and 1960s) children into purely white schools, was not the solution to the problem of the inferior quality of the schools in the Negro slums: "I believe the evidence indicates that it is the socioeconomic situation, not the color of the children, which makes the Negro slum schools so difficult, the real issue is not racial integration but socioeconomic integration."

Conant (p. 3) noted that suburban schools spent $1,000 a year per student; the slum schools less than half that amount. Suburban schools were modern spacious facilities with seventy staff per 1,000 pupils; slum schools were unattractive dilapidated schools staffed by forty or fewer professionals per 1,000 pupils. Conant (p. 2) cautioned: "I am convinced we are allowing social dynamite to accumulate in our large cities." He (p. 18) also sent a warning:

> *What I should like to do is to create in the reader's mind a feeling of anxiety and concern. For without being an alarmist, I must say that when one considers the total situation that has been developing in the Negro city slums since World War II, one has reason to worry about the future. The building up of a mass of unemployed and frustrated Negro youth in congested areas of a city is a social phenomenon that may be compared to the piling up*

*of inflammable material in an empty building in a city block.
Potentialities for trouble—indeed possibilities of disaster—are
surely there.*

Not long after Conant wrote these words, riots occurred in the
same slums. Much of the rioting erupted out of a sense of frustration at
being denied the American Dream. Blacks trapped in the ghettos saw
no way of getting out. Whites who attended schools in the suburbs
seemed to have a fast track to college and a share of the Dream. In
many areas, the situation has not changed that much in the past
several decades.

Homelessness is a major problem for many in the lower socioeconomic class.

The Homeless

The police must interact with the three million homeless people sleeping
on our nation's streets. Among the homeless are women and children,
alcoholics and drug addicts, retarded and the mentally ill. Carrying their
worldly goods and camping everywhere from laundry rooms to train and
bus stations, the homeless pose a challenge for the police who often look
after their safety while attempting to minimize their public presence.
Grossman (pp. 39–40) describes the following groups making up the
homeless population, noting that the term "homeless" is almost meaningless because it fits so many different kinds of people:

Veterans—mainly from Vietnam, veterans in some cities comprise
fifty percent of the homeless male population.

Mentally ill—about two decades ago, an estimated
quarter million of today's homeless would have been
institutionalized. This problem is discussed in the next chapter.

Physically disabled or chronically ill—those who do not receive
any benefits or whose benefits cannot support permanent
shelter.

Elderly—the aged whose fixed incomes are inadequate to support
their needs.

Men, women, families—on the street after losing a job.

Single parents—usually women, without the resources or skills to
establish new lives.

Runaway children—often victims of abuse.

Alcoholics/drug abusers—the troubles of this group often stem
from extraneous conditions.

A homeless family settles in for the night.

> *Immigrants*—both legal and illegal, who often are not counted among the homeless because they constitute a "problem" in their own right.
>
> *Traditional tramps, hobos, transients*—those who have taken to the road for whatever reason, and prefer to be there—sometimes referred to as the "hard core homeless."

Although being homeless is not a crime, the average citizen is uncomfortable around and may feel threatened by those who are homeless. Whether motivated by guilt or fear, they want the homeless people "removed."

The police must somehow try to deal with the homeless, a problem that society has thus far been unable to solve. The needs of the homeless are as varied as the people who comprise the homeless population. To address the problems of and presented by the homeless, the police need to draw on many resources, from detoxification facilities to children's shelters, from hospital crisis units to county social services.

Further, as noted by Grossman (1987, p. 58): "In communities where sleeping on the streets is against the law, what begins as a social problem becomes a problem of criminal justice." The officer on the beat is, of course, the person expected to enforce the law. Finn (1988, p. 2) notes:

> *Police take action against street people for several reasons. First, this population frequently breaks the law. By camping in public*

places, panhandling, or trespassing on private property, they may violate local ordinances. Fights among street people are not uncommon. Street people sometimes shoplift, sell drugs, mug passersby, and break into buildings.

The presence of street people may give the impression that no one cares about a neighborhood, thus signaling to real criminals that they can enter the area and commit offenses with impunity. . . .

Even the most docile street people generate repulsion and fear among many residents, shoppers, and commuters.

The notice in Figure 5.1 illustrates how homelessness can, in effect, be made illegal. Such notices are being contested in court in some areas of the country. Miami has demonstrated a "malicious abuse" of the Constitution in arresting thousands of homeless people living in parks and under bridges, an attorney argued in the trial of a federal lawsuit. The central question "is whether the government can lock you up for being outside when you have no place to go," attorney Valerie Jonas said in her opening statement on behalf of the city's estimated 6,000 homeless (*Star Tribune*, 6-16-92, p. 7A).

In addition, according to Grossman (p. 58): "The homeless more often end up as victims of crime than as perpetrators." The homeless are robbed and assaulted and have no phone from which to call "911."

Sometimes when the police deal with homeless individuals both the homeless and the neighborhood can benefit. This was the case in a community where a group of homeless men were hanging around a business district, worrying the local merchants. When the business owners complained to the police, the officer on that particular beat talked to those involved and they worked out a solution. The homeless men swept the sidewalk and kept the area litter free in return for food and a place to sleep.

A New York City Police Officer, Fran Kimkowski, developed another innovative approach to the homeless problem for a particular group of homeless men in the Long Island City Section of Queens, New York. Assigned to calm the fears of residents when the Salvation Army opened a shelter for homeless veterans in the neighborhood, Kimkowski wanted to show the residents that the homeless men could and would contribute to the community if given a chance. She organized V-Cops in 1988 to help prevent crime in the neighborhood. Members of V-Cops, who volunteer their time, are all homeless veterans who volunteer "not only to help prevent crime in the neighborhoods, but also to aid in his [the veteran's] recovery from drug abuse or alcoholism and to regain a sense of self-esteem" (*Law Enforcement News,* September 30, 1991).

V-Cops use anticrime foot patrols to deter, detect, and report crimes to the police. About 200 homeless veterans have been members of the

NOTICE

The following is illegal in Minneapolis and you will be arrested for:

- Begging

- Trespassing on private property

- Trespassing on state property

- Drinking in public

- Urinating in public

- Unlawful assembly (gathering in groups of three or more)

- Interfering with pedestrians or vehicle traffic (touching, causing fear, etc.)

Parks are closed from 10:00 p.m. to 7:00 a.m.

FIGURE 5.1   Notice of Illegal Actions in Minneapolis City Parks

V-Cops since it began. In the first nine months of 1991, for example, twenty-seven men had donated 8,000 hours of patrol in the Queens, Bedford-Stuyvesant, and Brownsville sections of New York. The V-Cops patrol local banks, particularly when people cash social security and welfare checks. The number of robberies and scams against customers has fallen according to Officer Kimkowski, and V-Cops would like to believe they had something to do with that. Some banks are so pleased with the V-Cops that they provide free lunch for them on the days they patrol.

The V-Cops program has many other components, including crime prevention presentations to organizations, talks to high school students, and patrol of subways and "play streets" for neighborhood youth during the summer months. Beyond the obvious benefits to the community, the participating homeless veterans have an opportunity to make a contribution while getting their lives back on track. Simultaneously, the role of the police department in the program fosters good community relations. Tentative plans are being made for landlords in high-crime areas to offer V-Cops housing in exchange for patrol and other services.

The Privileged

At the opposite end of the socioeconomic scale are the privileged and celebrities. In the traditional role of crime-fighter the police seldom interact with the upper class, but when they must, problems can arise. With regard to community-policing, however, the personal and financial resources of those in the upper socioeconomic level can be invaluable.

When police officers share a common background and education with the citizens they serve, officers and citizens understand each other and good community relations are fairly easy to achieve.

Imagine for a moment a community where the majority of residents are better educated than the police. Or where they earn five or six times as much money as police officers. In that community, it may take a special effort to develop and maintain respect and confidence in the police department's credibility and expertise. There it would be important for the department to find ways to minimize the cynical or negative attitudes officers may develop toward the privileged class. Police officers may become bitter if powerful people misuse their political connections to obtain special privileges from the police or to circumvent the law.

How can police departments address such situations? Perhaps the most effective way is for citizens to be involved in some area of the police department. Many departments have crime prevention programs, reserve officer organizations, crime reward funds, all of which need citizen volunteers.

Some departments have educational incentive plans to pay the tuition of officers who go to college and give a salary increase to those who graduate. Educational achievement can be considered in the promotional process; officers with the most education should benefit.

Officers should also receive regular, up-to-date inservice training to help them maintain and update professional skills. Well-trained officers will have confidence in their own abilities, and that inspires confidence and respect in others.

Officers' equipment, uniforms, and physical condition all affect their image in the community and their own self-image. Departments with dirty and ill-equipped or damaged vehicles on the streets prevent officers from feeling professional, respected, or competent. Officers who are poorly equipped are less likely to act in a professional manner.

Boxer Mike Tyson enters the Indianapolis City-County Building with his attorney. Tyson was charged with rape in an incident involving a Miss Black America contestant in 1991.

Celebrities

Interacting with celebrities and other well-known citizens such as national politicians, especially if the interaction is a negative contact, can be very difficult for the police. Often media hounds will use a minor incident for publicity. On the other hand, they may try to exert undue influence on an officer by mentioning rich and powerful "close friends" who allegedly have the power to negatively affect the officer's career. Officers need some measure of assurance from their department that they can do their job professionally and not be subject to reprimand because they happen to take appropriate action against someone with powerful connections.

The manner in which the criminal justice system treats celebrities can also affect how the public views the police. The trials of Evangelist Jimmy Baker, and, more recently, that of Mike Tyson may have an impact on the public's perception of the police.

The privileged and celebrities are embodiments of the American Dream. They represent the promise America held in the past and continues to hold in the future. But is the American Dream truly available to all? And at what price?

AVAILABILITY OF THE
AMERICAN DREAM

The movement from one class to another is a cultural change that requires not only access to opportunities, but the willingness and ability to pursue them. Since the 1960s there has been debate over whether it is better for individuals from different cultures or ethnic groups to learn English, retain their own language, or become bilingual. The debate becomes especially heated when talking about "Black English." There are those who argue adamantly that black students should be allowed to speak and write their particular style of English without being penalized. Many black parents, however, insist that allowing their children to speak "Black English" is a ploy to keep them in the lower class—that their children will never succeed in the United States without good standard English skills.

Quite often entrance into colleges depends on test scores such as the Scholastic Aptitude Test. These tests assume facility with standard English. In addition, according to Hirsch (1988, p. xiii), to succeed, students must also be culturally literate:

> To be **culturally literate** is to possess the basic information needed to thrive in the modern world. The breadth of that information is great, extending over the major domains of human activity from sports to science. . . . Cultural literacy constitutes the only sure avenue of opportunity for disadvantaged children, the only reliable way of combating the social determinism that now condemns them to remain in the same social and educational condition as their parents.

Pace (1985, p. 66) warns about the dangers of what he calls the *multi-culturalism trap.*

The **multi-culturalism trap** occurs when people get so involved with their own cultural concerns they ignore the rest of the society in which they live.

This differs from ethnocentrism which views one's culture as superior to all others. The multi-culturalism trap, in contrast, is often encountered by minority groups who want to bring their culture "up to the level" of the mainstream culture. Pace (1991, p. 45) suggests that: "Multi-culturalism, while strengthening subgroup cohesiveness, can be deadly to the integration of the community at large."

> Groups that retain cultural ideals that are different or out of step with laws, mores, and customs, of the rest of society must change.

These groups must strike a balance between service to their own culture and a contribution to the services of the rest of the community. Unless this self-centeredness of the minority groups is rejected by the groups themselves, they will never foster public support from the rest of society nor will they develop rapport with the criminal justice system because this system represents the majority society (p. 67).

THE MAJORITY V. THE MINORITY WORLD-VIEW

Whenever cultural pluralism exists in a society, a majority and minorities will also exist. Which group one belongs to will greatly influence how one views the world.

The Majority World-View

The Minnesota Peace Officer Standards and Training (POST) Board (1991, p. 110) has identified the following as elements of the majority world-view:

- The majority view that its philosophy and ideas are most legitimate and valid.
- Minority viewpoints, while their expression may be tolerated, lack the force and power of the majority, therefore, are less valid than and secondary to the majority viewpoint.
- The minority members have the option of leaving the society if they cannot abide by majority rule.
- Alternative viewpoints are often considered disruptive or disloyal.
- Power, status, and wealth are the result of hard work and/or genetics.

Traditionally the majority culture in the United States has been defined and controlled by a white, male, European world-view.

Given current population trends, however, the majority culture is rapidly changing, as illustrated in Table 5.2.

Any groups which do not fall within the majority world-view can be considered a minority.

The Minority World-View

The POST Board (p. 110) identified the following elements as common to the minority world-view:

TABLE 5.2
Population Trends

	1990 Population	Percent Rise Since 1980
U.S. population	248,709,873	+10%
Whites	199,686,070	+6%
Blacks	29,986,060	+13%
Hispanics	22,354,059	+53%
Other races	9,804,847	+45%
Asians	7,273,662	+108%
Amer. Indians	1,959,234	+38%

SOURCE: U.S. Census Bureau, Hispanic Business, The Mingo Group

- Minorities must perform better to be accepted as average.
- Majority groups have the power and control major institutions.
- Minority groups lack power to control their own destiny.
- The minority views fairness as being more valid than power, status, and wealth.
- The minority views success as being achievable by working through the rules set by the majority.
- The minority world views the criminal justice system as biased against minorities.

Sometimes cultural conflicts between minority groups or between the majority and minority groups become so intense that they lead to racism, sexism, and bias crimes.

RACISM, SEXISM, AND BIAS CRIMES

Racism has been a problem almost since the beginning of the United States. Many people feel threatened by simply coming into contact with those who are culturally different. As noted by Bodinger-deUriarte (1991, p. 4): "Americans often are poorly informed and suspicious of cultures and lifestyles outside their own." What people do not understand they tend to fear, and what they fear, they tend to hate.

Racism

Racism has been likened to carbon monoxide. It may be silent, you may not see or hear it, but uncontrolled, it can kill. Monk (1991, p. 160) suggests: "Traditionally, America has been a racist society. Blacks, it is well known, were exploited and oppressed in virtually every aspect of social, economic, and political life. Today they are often not thought of as *victims* of crime but as criminals." Monk notes that some black sociologists and economists argue that blacks are economically deprived because of *class* rather than race—the same contention set forth by Conant in 1961. The fact remains, according to Monk that: "Crime and color are linked in both official statistics and public perceptions." Because this is the case, racism is common in our society.

Although our society has improved in several areas, it would appear from the statistics that racism is still a problem as described in the article, "Crime's Impact on Blacks Makes for a Bleak Picture."

- Blacks are both the victims and the perpetrators of violent crime in disproportionate numbers.
- The incarceration rate for black males in the United States is four times that of South Africa.
- While forty-one percent of those arrested on drug charges in 1989 were black, just fifteen percent of the drug-using population is black (1991, p. 1).

Sexism

Although women outnumber men in the United States, they are still often classified as a "minority." The reason for their minority status is that when it comes to having true power, women are still in the minority. Berglund (1992, p. 9) suggests that when dealing with bias: "We are dealing with deep-seated attitudes formulated in a culture dominated by white males."

Rosen (1992, p. 7) interviewed Houston Chief of Police, Elizabeth Watson, appointed by a female mayor who was defeated. Watson, about to be replaced by a male chief, noted: "Very often I would take a very hard stand on things that I believe in. Whereas in a man that might be called strength and determination, in me it was called arrogance and stubbornness." While testifying at a sexual harassment trial of a female sergeant, the former chief described the male officers in the department as "indefatigable sexual predators, libidinous in the extreme" (Hodges, 1992, p. 5B).

Sometimes racism, sexism, and other forms of prejudice are carried to the extreme and result in bias or hate crime.

Bias or Hate Crimes

"Wherever such statistics are kept across the United States," says Bodinger-deUriarte (1991, p. 2), "bigotry cases have become more common place.... The incidents have ranged from anonymous spray-painting of slurs to cross burnings to murder. What they have in common is their motivation: fury directed at those who are different because of their race, their religion, or their sexual orientation."

The Southwest Regional Laboratory (SWRL) defines hate crimes as follows.

A **hate** or **bias crime** is any act, or attempted act, to cause physical injury, emotional suffering, or property damage through intimidation, harassment, racial or ethnic slurs and bigoted epithets, vandalism, force, or the threat of force, motivated all or in part by hostility to the victim's real or perceived race, ethnicity, religion, or sexual orientation.

Homosexuals and lesbians are frequent targets of *gay-bashing,* a form of hate crime. Police officers should recognize when crimes might be the result of bigotry and seek the causes for a particular incident. Several states have passed mandatory reporting laws that require police departments to keep statistics on the occurrence of bias and hate crimes. In 1990 the Federal Hate Crime Statistics Act was passed mandating the justice department to secure data on crimes related to religion, race, sexual orientation, or ethnicity.

FACING THE CHALLENGE

Keeping the peace, "serving and protecting" in a society as diverse as the United States presents an extreme challenge to police officers. To meet the challenge, police might consider the following guidelines:

- Each person is, first and foremost, an individual.
- Each group, be it racial, ethnic, religious, or socioeconomic consists of individuals who share certain values. Knowing what these values are can contribute greatly to effective police-community interactions.
- Communication skills are vital. Empathy, listening, and overcoming language barriers are crucial to effective police-community interactions.
- An awareness of personal prejudices and biases can guard against discrimination.
- An awareness of the language used to talk about different groups is extremely important.

Hare (1991, p. 157) calls for a change in the terminology the public uses to refer to different cultures and ethnic groups of people. Although Hare is speaking of terminology used at American universities, police departments could benefit from Hare's guidelines:

The term "minority," for example, is laden with stereotypic images. The term fosters expectations of inability and pathology. . . .

We hold that in our multiethnic and multicultural university there are no minorities and there is only one race: the human race.

Hare suggests the following changes in terminology:

- Abandon the use of racial designations such as "black" and "white" in favor of continental, ethnic, and cultural heritage based identifiers such as African American, American Indian/Native American, Asian American, Latino-Hispanic American, and European American. Beyond gross "continental dividers," national identifiers such as Italian American, Polish American, Japanese American, Brazilian American, [and] Nigerian American, may also be used. When such designations prove too laborious, such phrases as "traditionally underrepresented groups" or "targeted populations" should be used when appropriate. In most instances, groups should be referred to respectfully—with the terms they prefer and not summarily put in a "minority" box. In addition, we should avoid the term "minorities," with its subtle secondary, if not caste status, that implies the antithesis to "majority," which is frequently polite code for "white." "People of color," given its antithetical relationship to "whiteness," should also be avoided. "Third world" should additionally be avoided as it is simply an international "non-European" and "non-white" euphemism. The continental, geographical, regional, or national areas of concern should simply be named.
- All publications, media, advertising, and reports should reflect a new sensitivity to terminology.
- All offices and programs in the university system that carry such labels as "Department of Minority Affairs" and "Office for the Disadvantaged" should be required to change their titles to more inclusive titles such as "Multicultural Affairs" or "Pluralistic Development" while enhancing their functions.

Whether you follow all of the preceding suggestions is not the main concern. It is important that officers consider the terms they use and how they might be perceived by those who are being "labeled." Of course, in an emergency when officers need to communicate with each other rapidly, a descriptive term such as *black* or *white* is appropriate and, indeed, necessary to rapid response. It is important for officers to know when to use certain terminology.

Himelfarb (1991, p. 53) suggests: "Few in policing today would dispute the important role that training must play in improving the relationship between police and the ethnocultural and visible minority communities they serve." He suggests six key principles that promote culturally sensitive, responsive policing:

- Respect for and sensitivity to the diverse communities served is essential for effective policing.
- Respect for and sensitivity to ethnocultural communities can best be achieved through a broad-based multicultural strategy.
- Training must be an essential element of such a strategy.
- Training must be ongoing and built into the experience of policing; that is, it must be more than a course or two on multiculturalism.
- A multicultural strategy and the training that supports it will be most effective if they are perceived as integrated aspects of the philosophy and operations of policing.
- A multicultural strategy and training program must be created in consultation with the ethnocultural communities served by the police.

Himelfarb (p. 55) concludes: "Multicultural training is only one element of multicultural policing, and multicultural policing is only one element—though a crucial one—of community-policing. While specialized courses may still be necessary to supplement such an integrated approach, they are more likely to achieve their objectives when they are seen as reflecting an overall philosophy of multicultural policing."

Summary

Ethnocentrism is the point of view that one's own way of life is better than all others. Assimilation theorists suggest that our society takes in or assimilates various cultures in what is common referred to as a "melting pot." Cultural pluralism suggests there are many melting pots. Some groups fuse into one pot, and other groups into another. The cultural conflict theory suggests that diverse cultures that share the same territory will compete with and attempt to exploit one another.

A major problem in police interactions with some ethnic/racial groups is the language barrier. Strategies to help improve communication with non-English speaking individuals include (1) learning the language or at least common words and phrases; (2) using a language guide; (3) having a list of local language teachers who could serve as interpreters; and (4) subscribing to the Language Line.

In addition to cultural diversity (including racial/ethnic diversity) the United States also has religious and socioeconomic diversity. The three basic socioeconomic classes, based primarily on income and education, are the lower, middle, and upper classes. These basic classes may be further subdivided. Those in the lower class are often trapped by the poverty syndrome. This syndrome includes inadequate housing, inadequate education, inadequate jobs, and a resentment of those who control the society.

The multi-culturalism trap occurs when people get so involved with their own cultural concerns they ignore the rest of the society in which they live.

Traditionally the majority culture in the United States has been defined and controlled by a white, male, European world view. A hate or bias crime is any act, or attempted act, to cause physical injury, emotional suffering, or property damage through intimidation, harassment, racial or ethnic slurs and bigoted epithets, vandalism, force, or the threat of force, motivated all or in part by hostility to the victim's real or perceived race, ethnicity, religion, or sexual orientation.

DISCUSSION QUESTIONS

1. What is your ethnic background? What is the background of your classmates?
2. How diverse is your community?
3. Have you ever tried to communicate with someone who does not speak English? What was it like?
4. How would you define the American culture?
5. Do you believe your generation can achieve the American Dream?
6. Have there been any instances of hate crimes in your community? Your state? Does your state have mandatory reporting laws for hate crimes?
7. Do you believe the "multi-culturalism trap" is a valid concern in the 1990s?
8. Would you favor eliminating the word *minority* when talking about diversity? If so, what term would you use instead?
9. Do you consider yourself "culturally literate"? Why or why not?
10. Have you encountered instances of ethnocentrism? Explain.

DEFINITIONS
Can you define the following terms: acculturation, assimilation, bias crime, cultural conflict, cultural pluralism, cultural window, culturally literate, culture, ethnocentrism, ghetto syndrome, hate crime, hyphenated American, multi-culturalism trap, poverty syndrome.

REFERENCES

Berglund, Judy. "Bias: Tearing the Fabric of Minnesota Nice?" *Advocate (Journal of the Minnesota Education Association).* (March 27, 1992): 8–9.

Bodinger-deUriarte, Cristina. *Research Bulletin: Hate Crime. The Rise of Hate Crime on School Campuses.* Bloomington: Phi Delta Kappa, December 1991.

Clement, Douglas. "Border Crossings: Refugees Travel Difficult Road to Health Care." *Minnesota Medicine.* (March 1992): 24–29.

Conant, James B. *Slums & Suburbs.* New York: McGraw-Hill, 1961.

"Crime's Impact on Blacks Makes for a Bleak Picture." *Law Enforcement News.* (February 14, 1991): 1, 9.

Day, Thomas W. "Cross-Cultural Medicine at Home." *Minnesota Medicine.* (March 1992): 15–17.

deFiebre, Conrad. "St. Paul Police Hope Focus on Asian Culture Will Help Communication." *Star Tribune.* (May 27, 1991): 1B.

deFiebre, Conrad. "Tradition of Trust Makes Hmong Targets of Scams." *Star Tribune.* (March 30, 1992): 1A, 6A.

Epstein, Kitty Kelly. "Oakland Moves to Create Its Own Multicultural Curriculum." *Phi Delta Kappan.* (April 1992): 635–38.

Finn, Peter. *Street People.* Washington: National Institute of Justice, 1988.

Grossman, Amy. "Homelessness in America." *Police.* (August 1987): 38–42, 58–60.

Gustafson, Paul and Prince, Pat. "Hmong Man Faces Charges for Marrying Underage Girl." *Star Tribune.* (May 16, 1991): 1A.

Hageman, Mary Jeanette. *Police-Community Relations.* Beverly Hills: Sage Publishing, 1985.

Hare, Bruce R. "Beyond 'Black' Students and 'White' Universities." *The NEA Higher Education Journal.* (Fall 1991): 157–59.

Himelfarb, Frum. "A Training Strategy for Policing in a Multicultural Society." *The Police Chief.* (November 1991): 53–55.

Hinkle, Douglas P. "Street Spanish." *Law Enforcement Technology.* (April 1990): 22–23, 44.

Hirsch, E. D., Jr. *Cultural Literacy: What Every American Needs to Know.* New York: Random House, 1988.

Hodges, Jill. "Was She Harassed or Not? Ex-Officer's Suit Leads to Trial." *Star Tribune.* (April 1, 1992): 5B.

Inkster, Norman D. "The Essence of Community Policing." *The Police Chief.* (March 1992): 28–31.

Learning Objectives for Professional Peace Officer Education. St. Paul: P.O.S.T. Board, July 1991.

Monk, Richard C. *Taking Sides: Clashing Views on Controversial Issues in Crime and Criminology.* 2nd rev. ed. Guilford: The Dushkin Publishing Group, Inc. 1991.

Pace, Denny F. *Community Relations Concepts.* Placerville: Custom Publications, 1985.

"Parlez-Vous Miranda Warnings?" *Law Enforcement News.* (September 30, 1990): 3.

Rachlin, Harvey. "Meeting the Demands of Foreign Languages in Small- and Medium-Sized Communities." *Law and Order.* (September 1992): 99–102.

"Religious Animal Sacrifice to Be Reviewed by Court." *Star Tribune.* (March 24, 1992): 1A, 6A.

Rosen, Marie Simonetti. "An Interview with Chief Elizabeth Watson of Houston, Tex." *Law Enforcement News.* (February 29, 1992): 6–7.

Sharp, Arthur G. "Are We All Speaking the Same Language?" *Law and Order.* (July 1991): 95–99.

RESOURCES

American Association of Retired Persons (AARP), Criminal Justice Services, 601 E. Street N.W. Washington, DC 20049 (202)434-2222

American Indian Movement (AIM), Peacemaker Center 2300, Cedar Ave. S., Minneapolis, MN (612) 724-3129

Anti-Defamation League of B'nai Brith, 823 United Nations Plaza, NY 10017

Bureau of Indian Affairs (BIA), 1849 C Street N.W., Washington, DC 20240; (301) 208-3711

Indian Human Development Services, 200 Independence Avenue S.W., Washington, DC 20201; (301) 245-2760

League of United Latin American Citizens (LULAC), 777 N. Capitol Street N.E., Washington, DC 20002; (301) 408-0060.

Mexican American Legal Defense and Education Fund (MALDEF), 634 S. Spring Street, 11th Floor, Los Angeles, CA 90014; (213) 629-2512.

Mexican Chancery, 1911 Pennsylvania Ave., N.W., Washington, DC 20007; (301) 728-1600.

National Association for the Advancement of Colored People (NAACP), 4805 Mount Hope Drive, Baltimore, MD 21215; (212) 481-4100.

National Association of Blacks in Criminal Justice (NABCJ), P.O. Box 66271, Washington, DC 20035; (215) 686-2961.

National Organization of Black Law Enforcement Executives (NOBLE), 908 Pennsylvania Avenue S.E., Washington, DC 20003; (202) 546-8811.

National Rehabilitation Information Center, 8455 Colesville Road, Suite 935, Silver Spring, MD 20910-3319; (301) 588-9284

National Urban League, 500 East 62nd Street, New York, NY 10021; (212) 310-9000

State Department of Human Rights—locate in phone book

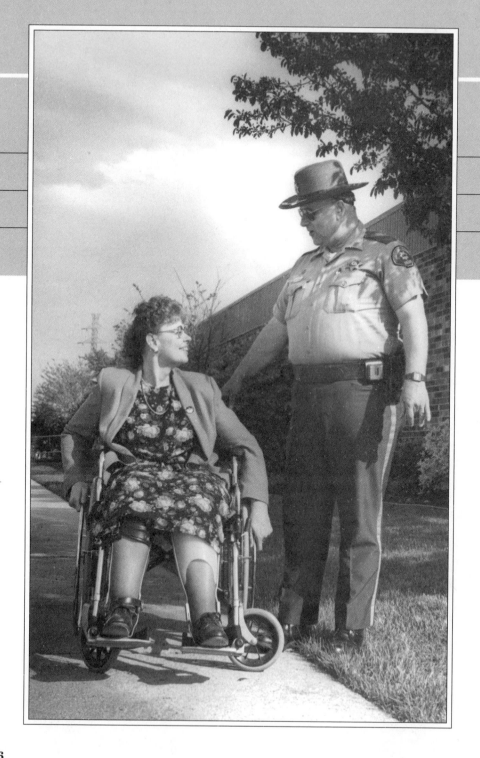

INTERACTING WITH THE
PHYSICALLY AND
MENTALLY DISABLED

*It is more important to know what sort of a patient
has a disease [or disability] than what sort of
disease [or disability] a patient has.*

—**Sir William Osler**

DO YOU KNOW

- How many people in the United States have disabilities?
- What *the* most important guideline is for interacting with an individual with disabilities?
- What disabilities police officers might frequently encounter?
- What method of communication most individuals who are deaf prefer?
- What effect deinstitutionalization of the mentally ill has had on communities?
- What behaviors police most frequently encounter in contacts with mentally disabled individuals?
- How serious the problem of suicide is in the United States?
- What mental health is? Mental illness?
- What the four common criteria for detainment and commitment of mentally ill individuals are?
- What dispositions are available when dealing with mental illness or mental retardation?
- How epilepsy can imitate intoxication or a drug high?

INTRODUCTION

A police officer asks an individual to perform some field sobriety tests and the person cannot do so even though she is not under the influence of any drug, including alcohol. Another person ignores the direct order of a police officer to step back on the sidewalk. Yet another person approaches an officer and attempts to ask directions, but his speech is so slurred he is unintelligible. Common occurrences for police officers that can often be misinterpreted. In each of the preceding instances, the individual interacting with the officer has a disability: a problem with balance, a hearing impairment, a speech disability.

A **disability** is a physical or mental impairment that substantially limits one or more of an individual's major life functions.

In the United States there are forty-three million people with disabilities.

The estimated number of disabled people in the United States is probably conservative. According to Burden (1991, p. 11): "Depending on how 'disabled' is defined, there are between 40 million and 70 million in the U.S.—easily the nation's biggest 'minority.'"

Concurring, Cushing (1992, p. 19A) suggests: "People with disabilities are the largest minority group in the United States. Just as with other minority groups, individuals are identified by stereotypes rather than ability, by how they are different rather than how they are like the able-bodied majority. They are identified as a what, rather than a who."

Greater recognition of this "minority" came on July 26, 1990, when President Bush signed into law the Americans with Disabilities Act **(ADA)**. President Bush called it "another Independence Day, one that is long overdue" (News Services, 1990, p. 1A). The ADA regulates bias against those with disabilities in the workplace. The law is likely to increase the number of disabled individuals who are "out and about" in the community. As stressed previously, and as aptly expressed by Burden (1991, p. 11):

> People with physical and mental disabilities are people first, disabled second. They have the same needs and desires of those (all the rest of us) they call **T.A.B**'s—the Temporarily Able–Bodied—but they have some special needs too. Often these needs are poorly understood by T.A.B.'s, including police officers.

How officers deal with the most vulnerable in our communities has a positive or negative affect on police-community relations. Many people in our communities have made the treatment of the disabled a priority and are available and willing to work with law enforcement agencies to ensure that people with disabilities are treated respectfully and protected from those who would victimize them. The outcome of increased awareness and service in this area will not only make police officers' jobs easier when they encounter disabled people, but will help reduce the disabled's fear and vulnerability. The focus on the disabled will make the community a better and safer place for everyone and help to build excellent police–community relations. To increase their comfort level when dealing with the disabled, officers should spend time with them, listen to them, and learn to see them as individuals.

FACTS ABOUT DISABILITY IN AMERICA IN THE 1990S

The National Institute on Disability and Rehabilitation Research has provided the following facts about disability in America today:

- More than one-sixth or seventeen percent of our population has a physical or mental disability—the largest minority in America.
- Disability knows no political, economic, educational, sexual, age, ethnic, religious, social, or geographic distinctions.
- An estimated one million Americans use wheelchairs.
- 2.5 million people are severely visually-impaired, and are unable to read a newspaper. Of those, 120,000 are totally blind and 600,000 are legally blind.
- 22 million Americans are hearing impaired. Two million of them are deaf.
- More than six million Americans are mentally retarded. Mental retardation affects more people than blindness, muscular dystrophy, polio, cerebral palsy, and rheumatic heart disease combined.
- Approximately two million people with disabilities reside in institutions, including nursing homes, mental hospitals, residential facilities, and mental retardation facilities.
- More than forty-six percent of all people over age sixty-five have chronic impairments. (The elderly are discussed in Chapter 7).
- On average, people with disabilities have less education, less income, fewer job opportunities, and fewer social contacts than others.
- People with disabilities are the most welfare-dependent minority in the United States.

- More than 25 million people with disabilities are registered voters, an emerging political force.

In addition to being victims of a particular accident or disease, disabled individuals are also frequently victims of crime.

VICTIMIZATION

The disabled are very frequent victims of crime. While the sex, race, and age of crime victims are known, generally no information is compiled on victims' disabilities. As noted by Burden (1991, p. 11): "The few limited studies that have been done by police and social scientists indicate that the disabled are frequent crime victims, which is not surprising since many are easy prey for muggers and some are patsies for con games."

Criminals often prey on the handicapped assuming they cannot readily protect themselves. The disabled may, like many of us, develop predictable patterns of activity that make them vulnerable to victimization. The disabled need the help of law enforcement personnel to feel safe and to learn means to protect themselves. Retarded individuals, for example, often use public transportation. They are often easily identified as vulnerable, and because of their dependency and often trusting nature, they are particularly prone to becoming victims.

The first steps a police department can take to better serve this segment of the community is to identify who the disabled are, what types of disabilities they have, and where and under what circumstances officers are likely to encounter them.

Police officers encounter disabled individuals in group homes, school special education programs, sheltered work programs, mental hospitals, detention facilities, private homes, apartments, trailer homes, or among the homeless. Disabled people can be average citizens, crime victims, or the perpetrators of crime. In other words, the disabled are not a homogeneous group. Some are obviously disabled, while others are not.

Most veteran officers can tell stories about criminals who have cruelly taken advantage of disabled people. Unfortunately, however, most officers are not aware of how much they can do to reduce the vulnerability of the disabled. Their vulnerability can be reduced through special programs in which police personnel effectively participate. These programs should include officers teaching disabled people what they can do to protect themselves.

GENERAL GUIDELINES FOR DEALING WITH THE DISABLED

The most important guideline for interacting with disabled people is to treat them as individuals with the same needs and desires as any other citizen.

In addition, the following guidelines apply to interactions with most individuals with disabilities:

- Do not shout.
- Be empathetic.
- Do not prejudge what a person with a disability can or cannot do. You do not know.
- Do not coddle individuals with disabilities. They need to be stretched and pushed, just like everyone else.

Disabilities police officers frequently encounter include mobility impairment, vision impairment, hearing impairment, mental or emotional impairment, and impairment as a result of epilepsy.

Now consider each of these disabilities and the recommended police response to each.

THE MOBILITY IMPAIRED

An estimated one million Americans use wheelchairs.

Not all people who are mobility disabled use wheelchairs. Also included within this group are those who are entirely dependent on walkers, canes, and other mobility aids. Many are victims of accidents. Many are victims of such diseases as muscular dystrophy or multiple sclerosis. Others were born with birth defects which make mobility difficult or impossible.

Sometimes the appearance of those with cerebral palsy or muscular dystrophy makes people believe they are mentally retarded. This is often *not* the case. Officers should not assume that a severely physically disabled individual in a wheelchair is also mentally disabled.

The Police Response

The following guidelines are suggested by an individual who was once able-bodied and is now disabled and in a wheelchair (Ehlert, 1991, p. 3E):

- Focus on the similarities you have with a disabled person, not on the differences.
- Don't lean on a disabled person's wheelchair. It's part of his/her space.
- Don't presume someone wants to tell you how they became disabled. Respect their privacy.
- Allow your kids to ask questions of disabled persons, though. Most disabled persons understand natural curiosity and don't mind explaining.
- Speak directly to disabled persons. Don't ask an able-bodied person present to intervene.
- Don't assume that disabled persons need to be "taken care of." Most can negotiate routine obstacles, such as getting in and out of their cars. If you think there is an unsurmountable barrier, ask them if they would like assistance—before you provide it.
- Get down at eye-level and converse with people in wheelchairs. Don't shout at them.
- Don't use words and phrases such as "a victim" of MS, "Confined" to a wheelchair. Wheelchairs actually liberate the disabled.
- Don't misuse the word "normal," which is a good way to describe objects, but not people.

If mobility is the only disability an individual has, you can communicate with the person as you would with any other individual.

In addition, police officers should be alert to physical conditions which might make access difficult for those with mobility impairments. Police can also make certain that handicapped parking spaces are provided and that nonhandicapped individuals who park in these places are either severely warned or ticketed.

Community relations programs which place mobile individuals, including business owners and police officers, in a wheelchair for a day are an excellent way to demonstrate the difficulties those with mobility impairments encounter.

THE VISION IMPAIRED

2.5 million people are severely visually impaired.

This figure represents only those who are *severely* visually impaired. According to the National Society to Prevent Blindness (Zehring, 1990, p. 33) over 11.5 million people in the United States are visually impaired.

Sometimes the visually impaired are very noticeable because of their white canes or their seeing-eye dogs. Other times, however, the

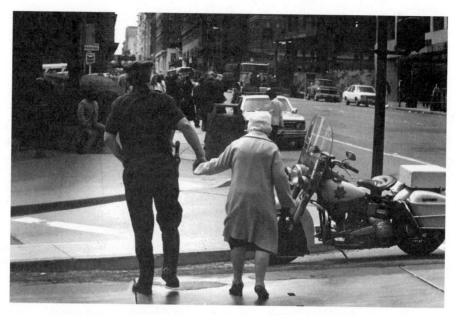

A San Francisco police officer helps a blind woman across the street.

disability is not readily apparent. Many people can see well enough to get around, but not well enough to read signs. Consequently, they may unknowingly break the law.

The Police Response

The natural tendency is to talk louder than usual to a visually impaired person. Refrain from doing this, unless, of course, you have determined they are also hearing impaired, a common combination.

When interacting with a blind or severely visually impaired person, allow the person to feel your badge or arm patch to establish your identity and authority.

The Mesa Public School District and the Mesa Police Department collaborated to adapt Stranger Danger and Officer Friendly programs to meet the needs of visually impaired elementary age students. The program helps children to recognize dangerous situations as well as to recognize police officers and their squad cars. As noted by Zehring (p. 34):

> *The design of the Mesa Police Department's patch allowed the children to feel three points at the top of the patch and the points in each of the lower corners. The children were not allowed to touch the officer's service revolver, but they happily settled for touching his handcuffs, portable radio, wallet badge, and other items on the officer's duty belt. The children also learned to*

identify the sounds of the police radio and specific items on the police car, such as door shields, overhead light bars, the cage between the seats, and the antenna on the trunk.

THE HEARING IMPAIRED

22 million Americans are hearing impaired. Two million are deaf.

The **hearing impaired,** commonly called *hard of hearing,* are those who have some residual hearing; that is, sounds may be audible, but not clear. For the hearing impaired, words are not just softer, they are garbled. **Deaf** people have such extreme hearing loss they cannot understand spoken words. They may respond to loud noises, but need visual communication clues. The deaf may or may not use sign language.

According to Dr. King, Director of Deaf Education at the University of Southern Mississippi (1990, p. 98):

Deaf people can do anything hearing people can—except hear. . . . It may be surprising to learn that deaf people are much more like hearing people than unlike them. . . . They are, however, cut off from both the spoken and written forms of the English language. . . .

To most deaf people, English is a second language, if not a foreign one; their first language is American Sign Language. . . . For this reason, the average deaf person has a difficult time interacting with the written form of English; in fact, the average reading level of the deaf is between third and fourth grade. This is the result of a linguistic deficit caused by not being able to hear the English language, not by a mental deficiency on the part of the deaf person.

Dr. King says that deaf people communicate differently depending on the age when they became deaf, the type of deafness, and the person's language skills, intelligence, personality, and education. Many hearing impaired individuals are undereducated.

Most deaf people cannot lip-read. According to Hageman (1985, p. 116) 60 percent of English words look exactly like some other word when formed with the lips.

Most deaf people prefer to communicate by means of sign language.

The sign language deaf people use most often is **Ameslan** (American Sign Language). Consequently, interpreters are often of great assistance for police to communicate with the hearing impaired, just as language interpreters assist police to communicate with non-English speaking people.

It is important to distinguish between an interpreter, that is, one who knows Ameslan, and a signer. Interpreters have special training and are registered. A list of interpreters can be obtained from the State Commission for the Hearing Impaired, the state chapter of the National Association of the Deaf (NAD), or the Registry itself.

Other people who can sign are considered "signers." Officers who are interested should consider taking "signing" classes so they can communicate more effectively with hearing impaired individuals. Signing skills can also be used in other aspects of police work, as noted by Gallo (1992, p. 54):

> *Officers who can sign can communicate over long distances when there is too much noise to use a radio, such as during a parade or demonstration. It is also useful if you do not wish a suspect to know what you are saying.*

An important consideration for police officers dealing with hearing impaired individuals who use signing is that sign language has a grammar and syntax all its own. Gallo (1992, p. 53) notes:

> *As a result, when officers try to communicate using notes passed between themselves and a deaf individual, they often experience messages that are more like baby talk than English. For example, in answer to an officer's written question "Where have you been tonight?" the answer might be, "I go there friends house finish, come here home sleep."*

> *Such an answer could, understandably, lead an officer to believe that he is dealing with a mentally deficient individual. But this may be far from the truth.*

Because sensitive or confidential information may be involved when dealing with hearing impaired individuals and interpreter/signers, it is important to use certified signers. Their code of ethics requires that they keep all information strictly confidential, use the appropriate mode of communication while conveying the full message, and not inject personal opinions into the situation.

Some police departments and some police officers have distinguished themselves in developing skills and services for the disabled. Dan Levin of the Chicago Police Department is one such officer. As the only known certified law enforcement sign language interpreter, he has a unique niche. He now works exclusively for the department's senior and disabled service division where he spends approximately 70 percent of his time assisting communications between deaf people and police officers. He teaches recruits how to deal with deaf individuals as well as other handicapped people, assists on cases involving deaf victims or suspects, and is also on cases which involve other types of disabled people. Levin sometimes gets called to assist a field unit who has a deaf victim or arrestee. Deaf people get arrested; they commit crimes as anybody does. He has been involved in everything from questions about parking tickets to murder.

Police officers who interact with hearing impaired individuals who are suspects must consider that if the individual needs to be handcuffed, the suspect will have no means of communication. Gallo (p. 54) suggests that: "This is synonymous with gagging a hearing person."

Technological advances have greatly improved communicating with the deaf. Telecommunications devices for the deaf (**TDD**) consist of a receiver and a keyboard used to transmit and receive written communication using the telephone. Often civic organizations such as the Lions or Rotary are willing to purchase such equipment for a police department and for the hearing impaired individuals residing in a community.

Another improvement in communications with the hearing impaired is close-captioned television whereby the words being spoken are displayed on specially equipped monitors for those who have impaired hearing.

When interacting with those who are hearing impaired, police should consider the potential for other difficulties in their lives. As noted by Hull (1985, p. 1):

> *Violence in deaf families is greater than it is for families without this limitation. Family violence may be more common among deaf people because of the many frustrations they encounter every day in their lives.*
>
> *Violence against deaf women is inflicted by deaf men as well as by hearing men. The rate of abuse among couples with only one deaf partner may be greater because of increased communication problems. However, 85–90% of hearing impaired women are married to hearing impaired men. It can be assumed that a higher number of abusers against deaf women are themselves deaf.*

The Police Response

King (1990, p. 98) suggests: "The key is to determine how that particular deaf person communicates and use whatever combination of techniques is necessary to facilitate communication." He recommends the following (pp. 98–100):

- Get the deaf person's attention. [Gently tap shoulder, wave]
- Make sure the deaf person understands the topic of discussion.

- Speak slowly and clearly, but do not over-enunciate or over-exaggerate words. Speak in short sentences.
- Look directly at the deaf person.
- Do not place anything in your mouth when speaking.
- Maintain eye contact.
- Avoid standing in front of a light source. [window, car's headlights, any other bright light]
- Don't hesitate to communicate by paper and pencil, but keep it simple. [third to fourth grade level]
- Use pantomime, body language, and facial expressions.
- If possible, learn sign language.
- Do not assume the deaf person has understood the message just because he nods his head in acknowledgement.

Other recommendations when dealing with deaf or hard of hearing individuals include the following:

- Use normal rate—not too fast nor so slow that the natural rhythm is lost. The thought should come as a whole.
- Change the wording if it is not understood. Do not keep repeating the same phrase over.
- Move away from noises such as TVs, radios, etc.
- Avoid statements such as, "Did you hear that?" "Did you understand that?"

If an interaction involves a group, arrange the chairs in a semicircle if possible. If tables are used, small tables are better than large ones. If there is a speaker or discussion, have all questions repeated from the front of the room.

When Using an Interpreter.   King (p. 100) suggests the following guidelines when using an interpreter to interact with a hearing impaired individual:

- Treat the interpreter as a professional.
- Provide good lighting.
- Speak directly to the deaf person, not the interpreter.
- Remember that the interpreter will be a few words behind the speaker.
- Permit only one person to speak at a time.
- Speak clearly and in a normal tone.

Sometimes written communication is most effective. When using written communication, write notes as you normally would, assuming the person can understand. Indications that the person does not understand include the following: an inappropriate or no response, quizzical or blank expression, smiling or nodding at inappropriate times. If any of these behaviors occur, rephrase your note.

King (p. 100) echoes a recurring theme of this textbook: "Perhaps the most important thing the officer can communicate is respect and dignity, remembering that deafness is not a defect, but a cultural difference, and that each deaf person is unique."

THE MENTALLY DISABLED

Historically society decided to institutionalize the mentally disabled, whether mentally ill or mentally retarded. In the mid-1960s however, institutionalization was replaced with treatment in the community. This was the result of several factors including the development of medications to control mental illness; research showing that institutionalized individuals did not receive adequate treatment and could do better in the community; federal programs to build and operate mental health centers; and patients' rights litigation and state legislation.

Deinstitutionalization refers to the release of thousands of mentally ill individuals into society to be cared for by family or a special network of support services.

Community-based mental health service rests on the premise that people have the right not to be isolated from the community simply because they are mentally ill. This premise works as long as a support system for them exists. Unfortunately, the network of support services has developed slowly. As a result, thousands of mentally ill people are on the street, homeless. Hundreds of others are in family situations where the family is totally ill-equipped to provide necessary care and assistance. In both such situations, the mentally ill individuals are likely to have encounters with the local police. This is usually as a result of some bizarre behavior rather than committing a crime. According to Finn and Sullivan (1988, p. 1): "Handling the mentally ill is perhaps the single most difficult type of call for law enforcement officers."

Mental Illness

The following discussion is a condensation of information Murphy presents in *Managing Persons with Mental Disabilities* (1989).

The Nature of The Problem.   One in ten people suffer from some type of mental illness. Between one and four million people are seriously mentally ill. They live in a variety of settings such as private residences with families or alone, halfway or group houses, bed and board homes, nursing homes, single room occupancy hotels, jails and prisons, homeless shelters, and on the street.

Factors Surrounding Police Responses. The police become involved with mentally ill people because they have the only twenty-four-hour, seven-days-a-week, mobile emergency response capacity. Also, police officers have the authority to detain, arrest, and use force if needed. Any citizen who feels threatened by the bizarre behavior or the mere presence of a mentally disabled person may call the police to "make the problem go away."

When police are called to manage mentally ill persons, the behaviors most frequently encountered include:

- Bizarre, unusual or strange behavior.
- Confused thoughts or action.
- Aggressive actions.
- Destructive, assaultive, or violent behavior.
- Attempted suicide.

Police most frequently encounter mentally ill individuals during the evening shift. Police also receive frequent calls regarding the mentally ill during weekends and holidays. The mentally ill individuals police encounter are frequently unattached and lack social support, they are difficult to manage, and may have complications such as alcohol or drug abuse.

Mental Health v. Mental Illness. Mental health is a relative term that means different things to different people. Generally speaking, those who are mentally healthy have a positive self-image and can successfully relate to others.

Mental health is the ability to integrate one's self with one's environment.
Mental illness is a severe disturbance in thinking, feeling, and relating that results in substantially diminished capacity to cope with the ordinary demands of life.

Basically, there are two broad categories of mental disabilities: disorders that cause a person to suffer from psychotic symptoms and those that do not. It is helpful for police officers to be familiar with the kinds of mental illnesses they may encounter and the terminology used by mental health professionals.

Psychotic symptoms demonstrate a significant loss of contact with reality and include illogical thought, incoherent speech, disorientation, extreme mood fluctuation, social withdrawal, hallucinations and delusions, and neglect of family and occupational obligations. These symptoms are beyond the person's control. Psychotic behavior may be a nuisance, a burden, or an outright danger. The public is generally threatened by such behavior.

The most chronic and disabling mental illness is **schizophrenia,** a deterioration in one's personality to the point where feelings, thoughts, and behavior are not coherent. This is *not* the same as a split personality. Common symptoms of schizophrenia include social isolation or withdrawal; bizarre, meaningless, inappropriate behavior; prominent hallucinations; peculiar behavior such as collecting garbage, talking to oneself in public, hoarding food; rapid shift in subject matter when speaking; confusion, and ambivalence.

Another mental illness with psychotic symptoms police commonly encounter is **delusional (paranoid) disorder**. This illness is characterized by nonbizarre delusions focused on a single theme or a series of connected themes. Common themes include persecution, jealousy, and grandiosity.

Mood disorders, severe depression, mania, or cycles of depression and mania, are also of concern to police officers. Suicide is the most serious complication associated with depression, although not all those who suffer from clinical depression are suicidal.

Three disorders do not cause psychotic symptoms: anxiety disorders, dissociative disorders, and personality disorders. There are three types of *anxiety disorders:* simple phobias (fears), panic disorders (characterized by sweating, dizziness, palpitations, trembling, nausea, and severe, frightening episodes of apprehension and feelings of impending doom), and obsessive compulsive disorders.

Dissociative disorders are also of three types: multiple personalities, psychogenic fugue (sudden, unexpected travel away from one's home, assumption of a new identity, and inability to recall previous identity), and amnesia.

Personality disorders are the form of mental illness most often encountered by police officers. This is because many habitual offenders have character or **personality disorders,** that is, inflexible and maladaptive personality traits and significant impairment of social and occupational functioning. Common elements of a personality disorder include lack of self-control, inability to learn from past experience, lack of good judgment, and lack of moral or ethical values. Individuals with personality disorders provoke trouble, think of themselves first, are prodigious liars, and are adept at manipulating others.

Police in one midwestern city shot and killed a suspect who had just robbed a gas station after a short foot chase through dark parking lots. The suspect turned out to be a mentally disturbed female whom they had dealt with often over the past year. After robbing the gas station, she ordered the clerk to call "911" and she stayed there until he had done so.

The confrontation and subsequent shooting seemed orchestrated, forced by the woman who was depressed and suicidal. She claimed to have a gun, threatened to shoot the officers, and advanced toward one with an object in her hand. The object turned out to be a comb. It is difficult to imagine a different outcome in this case; however, police should understand that motives of people, particularly of the mentally disturbed, may not be logical. Some suicidal people arrange to die at the hands of the police.

Mental Retardation

More than six million American children and adults have mental retardation.

Mental retardation is the nation's fourth ranking disabling condition, affecting three percent of the U.S. population. Essentially, **mental retardation** means that normal intellectual development fails to occur. Unlike mental illness, mental retardation is permanent. It is diagnosed when the following three criteria exist:

- Significant subaverage general intellectual functioning (as measured by IQ tests).
- Resulting in, or associated with, defects or impairments in adaptive behavior, such as personal independence and social responsibility.
- With onset by age 18.

Mental retardation can be caused by biological or environmental factors or a combination of both. Mental retardation may be mild, the most common level, with IQ just below that of average normal intellectual functioning; moderate; or severe and profound. The differences between mental illness and mental retardation are summarized in Table 6.1.

In addition to individuals who have mental illnesses or mental retardation, police officers may have to interact with individuals who have extreme emotional problems, including crisis behavior and suicidal behavior.

Crisis Behavior

Crisis behavior results when a person has a *temporary* breakdown in coping skills. Such people often fear they are going crazy and say such things as, "I must be losing my mind." Anyone can suffer from a crisis, and what may constitute a crisis for one person may not for another person.

Suicidal Behavior

Although the mentally ill may attempt to commit suicide, not all those who attempt suicide are mentally ill.

TABLE 6.1
Differences Between Mental Retardation and Mental Illness

Many people make the common mistake of confusing the mentally retarded with the mentally ill person. However, it is most important to understand that these disorders are separate and distinct conditions. The following chart compares the differences between the two.

Mental Retardation	differs from	Mental Illness
A. Retardation refers to subaverage intellectual functioning.		A. Mental illness has nothing to do with IQ. A person may be a genius or subaverage.
B. Retardation refers to impairment in social adaptation.		B. A mentally ill person may be very competent socially but may have a character disorder or other aberration.
C. Retardation usually occurs during the period of development or is present at birth. However, a brain injury or toxemia may cause retardation in anyone at any age.		C. Mental illness may strike at any time.
D. In mental retardation, the intellectual impairment is permanent, but can be compensated through education and development.		D. Mental illness is often temporary.
E. A retarded person can usually be expected to behave rationally at his operational level.		E. A mentally ill person may vacillate between normal and irrational behavior.
F. A retarded person will not be violent except in those situations that cause violence in non-retarded persons.		F. A mentally ill person may be erratic or even violent.
G. A mentally retarded person has a learning disability and uses the skills of educators, psychologists, and vocational rehabilitation therapists.		G. A mentally ill person uses the sevices of psychiatrists, psychotherapists, or psychologists.

SOURCE: Gerard R. Murphy. *Managing Persons with Mental Disabilities: A Curriculum Guide for Police Trainers.* Washington: Police Executive Research Forum, 1989. Reprinted by permission.

Suicide is the tenth leading cause of death among adults and the second leading cause of death among adolescents.

According to Wrobleski (1989, p. 20): "Suicide in North America is a white and male phenomenon. Two-thirds of all suicides each year are committed by white men over 35 years-old. White and minority men represent about 75% of all suicides." She further notes (p. 21): "Women attempt suicide three times more often than men, but men kill themselves four times more often than women."

For every "successful" suicide, there are eight to ten attempts that "fail," or about 300,000 attempts annually. Persons who attempt suicide *must* receive professional counseling—they must not be placed in a holding or jail cell.

In one study (Wrobleski, 1989, p. 49) 158 individuals who had a close friend or relative commit suicide were asked about the danger signs given by the 110 people who had killed themselves. The following table summarizes their answers:

Statements about hopelessness	72%
Statements about helplessness	68%
Statements about worthlessness	64%
Talk about suicide	57%
Preoccupation with death	51%
Were suddenly happier, calmer before death	41%
Lost interest in things they cared about	40%
Visited or called people they cared about	38%
Set their affairs in order	30%
Gave away prized possessions	15%

The following are some major indications of suicidal behavior: suicide plan, history of past attempts, internal and external resources, recent loss, physical illness, drinking and other substance abuse, physical isolation, dramatic changes in mood or behavior, mental illness, saying good-bye to loved ones, or taking steps to finalize plans by giving away possessions. A suicide can occur without these signs, but an officer should not hesitate to consider a person suicidal if only one or two of the signs are present.

Statutory Requirements and Implications

In handling calls involving mentally ill persons, officers often misinterpret civil criteria for detaining and committing those who are dangerous. This misinterpretation usually leads to unnecessary, time-consuming delays in disposition. With a solid understanding of the common civil criteria for detainment and commitment, officers will be better able to manage this population.

The four civil criteria for detainment and commitment of mentally ill individuals are:

- Mental illness.
- Dangerousness.
- Gravely disabled.
- In need of (mental health) treatment.

These criteria are quite subjective. Usually mental illness and one other criterion must be present for someone to be committed.

Mental illness is the undisputed first criterion for an involuntary civil commitment. None of the other criteria will be accepted as grounds for commitment unless the person is also mentally ill. *Dangerousness* may be in relation to oneself or to others.

The *commitment process* usually involves four steps: (1) the police officer determines a person needs a mental health examination; (2) a psychiatrist or mental health professional determines if the person needs to be examined—if not, the person is released; (3) a psychiatrist conducts the examination and may detain the person for seventy-two hours; (4) a civil hearing is conducted where both sides (the state and the individual) present arguments for or against short-term commitment.

Responding to the Call—On-Scene Management

When officers are called to a scene where an individual exhibits bizarre behavior, they must first try to assess whether the individual is mentally ill, mentally retarded, or suicidal. Himmelsbach established the following guidelines for handling such encounters.

Guidelines for Handling Frequently Encountered Situations*

1. Subject is Compulsive Talker.

Persons engaged in compulsive talking produce a stream of sometimes meaningless chatter at a rapid, almost non-stop rate. These are understandable communications, but bear little or no relation to the problem at hand. This behavior indicates high levels of anxiety. If your requests to slow down are not effective, you can interrupt the compulsive speech pattern by asking the individual specific concrete questions. For example, ask his birth date or address; ask him to give the full name of his children or his parents; or ask him where he works or goes to school. Your

*SOURCE: Himmelsbach, in Arnold P. Goldstein, *Police Crisis Intervention,* (Elmsford: Pergammon Press, 1979), reprinted in Gerard R. Murphy. *Managing Persons with Mental Disabilities: A Curriculum Guide for Police Trainers.* Washington: Police Executive Research Forum, 1989.

goal is to interrupt the speech in order to break its pattern and bring it somewhat under control.

2. Subject is Conscious but Non-responsive.

This happens in cases in which the person may be catatonic or severely depressed. You should never assume that because a person is not responding to your statement, he is not hearing what you say. In these situations, there is the temptation to begin acting and talking as if the subject were not present. This is a mistake. Mental illness does not render a person deaf. Therefore, you should make every effort to obtain a response from the individual. This can be done by quietly asking questions and being sensitive to any types of reply, such as a head nod.

If this is not successful, you should attempt to understand the person's thoughts or feelings and communicate that understanding to him. These "guesses" can be based on the information which you acquire at the scene, as well as on the body posture and emotion the individual may be displaying. By making this effort, you communicate to the subject that you wish to understand his situation. The subject may then feel less threatened about discussing his difficulties with you.

3. Subject is Hallucinatory.

Hallucinations are very frightening for the person who is experiencing them. Difficulties emerge when the person is actively hallucinating in the presence of the officer. The first response you must give is to validate the hallucinatory experience for the individual, but, at the same time, indicate that the hallucination does not (objectively) exist. If an individual is seeing or hearing things, you must indicate that you understand that those experiences are real and frightening for the subject, but that they do not exist in reality. Second, you must firmly and empathically indicate that those sensations are due to the extreme emotional stress that the person is experiencing, and that once the stress is lessened, the hallucinations will disappear. You may have to repeat this reassuring message many times before the individual can begin to respond to it.

4. Subject Exhibits Paranoid Tendencies.

Paranoia often involves very serious delusion. You must be very sensitive (both verbally and physically) when you respond to such individuals. Paranoid persons are marked by their extreme suspiciousness and tension. They can appear to be very frightening to others.

You must be acutely aware of any indications that the paranoid person is feeling threatened by you. If you detect this fear, you should become as non-threatening as possible, giving the person a feeling that he is in control of the situation. You should neither pick up on any verbal challenge, nor agree that you know anything more about the subject than he tells you. Many paranoid people may say things like, "You know what has been happening to me." Or, "You're a police officer, you have those secret records on me." You must not confirm that you have any special knowledge about the person.

When you're moving into or around a room in which a paranoid person is present, it is good practice to announce your actions before initiating them. Telling the subject that you are moving across the room to sit in a chair reduces the probability that he will think you are about to attack him. This telegraphing of your actions assumes that your goal is not to subdue the individual physically. Except in situations in which the person must be physically detained, avoid any physical contact with the person.

5. Subject is Psychotic and Aggressive.

This is probably the most troublesome situation for any police officer to respond to effectively. If the subject is in the act of attacking you or another individual, there is no question that you should respond with your police control skills. However, in many instances, the subject will not be acting out, but will be threatening someone. He may be waving his fists, or a knife, or yelling. If the situation is secure, and if no one can be accidently harmed by the individual, you should adopt a non-threatening, non-confrontative stance with the subject. You may point out that you do not like to get injured or beaten up, that there is no need for the individual to threaten you because you are going to "listen" to him, that getting into a pitched battle with you may cause more problems than it will solve.

You should then begin talking to the subject as outlined above, allowing the individual to vent some of his hostility. You can also indicate this low-threat, low-offensive style by sitting down, removing your hat, or otherwise trying to put the person at ease. Sit a comfortable distance from the subject, move the chair so that its back faces the subject, and straddle it. This permits you to use it as a protective block if the person suddenly charges you. It's essential that you appear relaxed and non-threatening, but you must also be on your guard.

6. Delusional Statements.

Delusions are unique ways of viewing the world, and delusional statements frequently come into conflict with the views of others. There are three possible responses to delusions:

- agree with them;
- dispute them; or
- defer the issue.

If you agree with the mentally disturbed person's delusion, you put yourself in a position of being ineffective in your attempts to provide the person with help. The individual could legitimately ask, "Why do you want me to go to the hospital, since you agree that what I say is true?" Such agreement can also have the effect of increasing the subject's upset state, since the delusion is only a means for him to reduce his anxiety. To have others begin to believe in "his world" may be more frightening than helpful.

The next option, disputing the delusions, is equally ineffective. A direct confrontation with the subject over his disordered thinking may well result in his withdrawing from the person making the attack. He will become inaccessible, or arguments may ensue. This might result in the individual's acting out aggressively due to the threat he experiences.

This leaves the third option, deferring the issue. In this response, you do not agree with or dispute the person's statement; rather, you acknowledge the person's view of the world, indicate that it is not your own, and follow with a statement of how you understand the person's feelings. An example of this type of response would be:

Subject: There are many people who want me dead. There is an organization on T.V. which had my name on T.V.

Officer: I can see you're worried about someone harming you. I don't know of anyone who wants to hurt you, but I really would like to assist you in any way I can to help you feel safer.

By this response, you neither confirm or dispute the person's view of the world. Rather, you give the person a message of the availability of help.

Recognizing and Handling Persons with Mental Illness.   Officers do not usually need to diagnose the type of mental disorder a mentally ill person has. In specific situations, however, such as a hostage situation or a barricaded subject, inappropriate remarks or gestures toward the mentally ill could prove tragic. For example, pointing out to a depressed person or one with a personality disorder that his or her behavior is an indication of personal failure could cause that person to kill hostages and/or commit suicide. For this reason, police hostage negotiators and others with certain crisis intervention training should learn the specific behavioral characteristics typical of mental

An agent with the Bureau of Alcohol, Tobacco and Firearms stands guard at a roadblock near the Branch Davidian compound near Waco, Texas, in April 1993. The 51-day standoff between the federal government and David Koresh's armed cult ended in a fiery, nationally televised spectacle.

illness. Police hostage negotiators should also know how to deal with each type of mental illness.

Most officers, however, need only determine whether there is a reason to believe the subject has a mental disorder. Depending on the severity of the disorder, mentally ill persons can be difficult to identify. They can be intelligent, perceptive, and articulate. The mentally ill can be employed and have strong family relationships. With the onset of a mental disorder, however, their thoughts and actions are not based in reality and their ability to think clearly is impaired.

General characteristics that indicate an individual has a mental illness include behavior and mood inappropriate to the setting, and inflexible or impulsive behavior. Specific indicators of mental illness can include sudden changes in lifestyle; major changes in behavior; extreme anxiety, panic, or fright; paranoia; hallucinations; delusions; depression; obsessions; unexplained loss of memory; confusion; and hypochondria.

Often people who suffer from mental illness are on medication to counteract a chemical imbalance. These medications, however, may cause side effects such as the following: minor stiffness, a rigid shuffling gait; an at rest, hand jerk; acute muscle spasms, tilted head; a constant, fine, fast tremor; blurry vision; rhythmic motion of the jaw or lips, a clucking of the tongue, smacking of the lips or—in severe cases—facial distortion.

The following questions will help officers assess whether an individual may have a mental health problem:

1.   Is the subject using or threatening to use violence?
2.   Is the subject threatening suicide?
3.   Is the subject acting dangerously towards himself or others?
4.   Has the subject neglected personal care or bodily functions?
     —Mutilated himself?
     —Neglected to bathe in the past few days?
     —Neglected to eat in the past few days?
     —Neglected to take prescribed medications in the past few days?
     —Been sleeping irregularly?
5.   Has the subject recently suffered a traumatic experience?
6.   Does the subject have a history of mental illness? If yes, specify illness.
7.   Does the subject feel that his behavior is controlled or influenced by outside forces?
8.   Does the subject claim to receive messages from strangers, radio, or television?
9.   Does the subject ever hear voices when others do not?
10. Does the subject ever see things when others do not?
11. Does the subject indicate that others are plotting against him or are after him?
12. Does the subject claim that others can read his thoughts?
13. Does the subject claim that he can read others' thoughts?
14. Is the subject overly concerned with religion or death?
15. Is the subject oriented to his environment, that is, time, place, and person?
16. Did the mood of the subject drastically change during the course of the interview or conversation?
17. Was the mood of the subject appropriate to the nature of the call?
18. Does it appear that the subject is under the influence of alcohol or illegal drugs?

If this assessment reveals that the person is likely to be mentally ill, the following guidelines are suggested.

General Guidelines.   When handling a mentally ill person, gather as much information as possible about him or her before arriving on the scene. In the presence of a mentally ill person, be discreet and avoid attracting attention. Be calm, avoid excitement, and have a take–charge attitude. Remove as many distractions from the scene as possible, including bystanders and disruptive friends or family members. Gather as much information as possible from helpful witnesses, family members, and friends.

Steps to Take when First Encountering a Mentally Ill Person.
The following steps are generally appropriate:

- Introduce yourself and explain the reason for your presence. Establish a helping and caring tone.
- Be aware that your uniform, gun, handcuffs, and nightstick may frighten the person. Explain how your equipment will keep away the person's enemies.
- Be aware of the potential for violence.
- If the person is acting dangerously, but not directly threatening any other person or himself, give the person time to calm down. Violent outbursts are usually short.

Keys to Successful Management. *Communication* is essential. It allows officers to gain valuable information. It also allows officers and the individual to understand each other and may reduce tensions. *Firm gentleness* is also effective. The person should be treated gently and with care. With a take-charge attitude and an insistence on your orders being followed, gently indicate that your only intention is to help the person. Remain *professional*. Empathize with the individual without sympathizing.

What Not to Do. Do not excite, confuse, or upset a mentally ill individual. Do not abuse, belittle, or threaten the individual either. Do not use inflammatory language when addressing the individual. Do not lie or deceive the person. Do not cross examine the person. Do not dispute, debate, or invalidate the person's claims. Do not rush the person or crowd his personal space. Avoid being a "tough guy." Do not let the person upset or trick you into an argument.

If the Person Must Be Restrained or Force Must Be Used. If the person is so dangerous or violent that he or another person is likely to be harmed, use the least amount of force necessary to restrain the person. If restraint is needed, two or more officers should be present. Such a show of force could dissuade the person from resisting. If not, however, increased adrenaline and insensitivity to pain enable mentally ill people to resist a "normal" amount of restraint.

Police should not always use handcuffs because they can injure the person or be broken. The ideal restraint would be a gurney with four-point restraints and body bands.

Handling Mentally Retarded Persons

The mentally retarded are usually aware of their condition and may be adept at concealing it. Thus, it may be more difficult for police officers to determine mental retardation than mental illness. Certain communication problems, interaction problems, inability to perform tasks, and personal history can help officers to make this determination.

Communication problems officers should look for that would indicate mental retardation include the following: an inability to communicate at the level of others of the same age; difficulty in understanding questions; difficulty in answering questions, for example, overreliance on "parroted" responses or offering standard responses; speech defects or impediments, including poor pronunciation; an inability to use abstract reasoning; and a limited vocabulary or limited grammatical skills.

Interaction problems that might indicate mental retardation include a preference by the person to associate with younger people; an excessive desire to please; reliance on a special person to provide help; behavior noticeably on a level below the person's age; crowding the personal space when interacting with others; a tendency to be easily persuaded or influenced by others.

Inability to perform tasks may also indicate mental retardation. Officers might ask the individual to read or write, identify money or make change, tell time, or use the telephone.

Personal history can also help the officer to identify someone as mentally retarded. Find out if the person has attended a vocational education center or a sheltered workshop. See if the person is listed in the telephone book.

Guidelines for Interacting if the Person Appears to Be Mentally Retarded.   If the person appears to be mentally retarded, avoid asking questions rapidly or attempts to unnerve or intimidate the person. Be aware of the person's reluctance to discuss the matter and that they are likely to attempt to please. If possible, use visual aids, pictures, or diagrams and be firm and purposeful.

Responding to Suicide Attempts

To effectively deal with a suicidal person use a calm, matter-of-fact tone; genuine concern for the person is best indicated through communication. Officers should insist, but not in a threatening manner, that the individual obtain some type of mental health help. Officers should talk about the finality of the act and use the terms *suicide, death,* and *kill yourself.* The belief that talking about suicide will prompt the person to do so is a myth. The best way officers can help a suicidal person is to discuss the person's problems, the suicide plan, and realistic alternatives. The following are suicide prevention guidelines:

- Obtain necessary personal data immediately.
- Bring the subject of suicide into the open. Also discuss the person's feelings of depression and that they are only temporary.
- Remove the means.

- Notify and meet with significant others.
- Offer realistic hope.
- Establish a specific plan of action.

Dispositions

After responding to the call and effectively interacting with the suicidal individual, officers must make a disposition.

The two formal dispositions are arrest or a civil commitment. Many informal dispositions are also available.

To determine an appropriate disposition, officers should continuously evaluate the person and the nature of the incident. Dispositions that *should* be available to officers include the following:

- Counsel, release, and refer the individual to a mental health center.
- Counsel, release to family, friends, or some other support network, and refer to a mental health center.
- Consult with a mental health professional.
- Obtain the person's agreement to seek voluntary examination.
- Detain for involuntary examination.
- Arrest.

Commitment criteria, by state, are summarized in Table 6.2.

Police officers protect and serve society and, in that capacity, serve as only one of the gatekeepers to the mental health system. Officers should be able to determine when someone needs referral to mental health professionals and should know how to gain access to those resources. They should be familiar with the resources available in the community, including the location of community mental health centers and hospitals that conduct mental health examinations, the services provided by those facilities, hours of operation, and staff to be contacted. They should also know the procedures to be followed at the facilities and what to do when the facilities are closed.

Programs for the Mentally Impaired

The Police Executive Research Forum undertook a study of treatment of the mentally ill in the community. During the course of this study they identified a number of elements that appear to be essential to the effectiveness of any program or involving the police in the handling of mentally disturbed individuals (Murphy, 1986, p. xiv):

- Each program maintains a 24-hour, on-site response capability, so there is less "slippage" in resolving cases involving the mentally ill.

TABLE 6.2
Commitment Criteria

State	Mentally Ill	Danger to Others by Recent Act	Danger to Self by Recent Act	Threat of Danger to Others	Threat of Danger to Self	Gravely Disabled	In Need of Treatment	Refused Voluntary Treatment	Danger to Property	Threat of Emotional Injury to Others	Hospital is Least Restrictive Alternative	Person Would Reasonably Benefit From Treatment
ALABAMA	YES	YES	YES	*	*							
ALASKA	YES			YES	YES	YES	YES					
ARIZONA	YES			YES	YES	YES						
ARKANSAS	YES	YES	YES	*	YES	YES						
CALIFORNIA	YES	YES	YES	YES	YES	YES						
COLORADO	YES			YES	YES	YES	YES+					
CONNECTICUT	YES			YES	YES	YES	YES+					
DELAWARE	YES			YES	YES		YES+−		YES			
DISTRICT OF COLUMBIA	YES			YES	YES							
FLORIDA	YES	YES	YES	*	*	YES	YES	YES				
GEORGIA	YES	YES	YES	*	*	YES						
HAWAII	YES	YES	YES	*	*		YES		YES	YES	YES	
IDAHO	YES	YES	YES	*	*	YES	YES+					
ILLINOIS	YES			YES	YES	YES						
INDIANA	YES			YES	YES	YES	YES					
IOWA	YES			YES	YES	YES	YES+			YES		
KANSAS	YES			YES	YES	YES	YES+		YES			
KENTUCKY	YES			YES	YES							YES
LOUISIANA	YES			YES	YES	YES	YES+					
MAINE	YES	YES	YES	*	*						YES	
MARYLAND	YES			YES	YES		YES+					
MASSACHUSETTS	YES	YES	YES	*	*	YES						
MICHIGAN	YES	YES	YES	*	*	YES	YES+					
MINNESOTA	YES	YES	YES	*	*	YES+						
MISSISSIPPI	YES			YES	YES	YES						
MISSOURI	YES			YES	YES							
MONTANA	YES	YES	YES	YES	YES	YES						
NEBRASKA	YES	YES	YES	*	*	YES						
NEVADA	YES			YES	YES	YES						
NEW HAMPSHIRE	YES			YES	YES							
NEW JERSEY	YES			YES	YES	YES	YES					
NEW MEXICO	YES	YES	YES	*	*	YES+	YES				YES	
NEW YORK	YES	YES	YES	*	*	YES	YES−					
NORTH CAROLINA	YES	YES	YES	*	*	YES						
NORTH DAKOTA	YES	YES	YES	*	*	YES+	YES					
OHIO	YES	YES	YES	*	*	YES	YES−					
OKLAHOMA	YES	YES	YES	*	*	YES	YES−					
OREGON	YES			YES	YES	YES						
PENNSYLVANIA	YES	YES	YES	*	*	YES	YES					
RHODE ISLAND	YES			YES	YES	YES	YES					
SOUTH CAROLINA	YES			YES	YES	YES	YES					
SOUTH DAKOTA	YES			YES	YES	YES						
TENNESSEE	YES	YES	YES	*	*	YES	YES					
TEXAS	YES			YES	YES	YES	YES−					
UTAH	YES			YES	YES	YES					YES	
VERMONT	YES	YES	YES	*	*	YES	YES					
VIRGINIA	YES			YES	YES	YES	YES				YES	
WASHINGTON	YES	YES	YES	*	*	YES				YES*		
WEST VIRGINIA	YES	YES	YES	*	*.	YES						
WISCONSIN	YES	YES	YES	*	*	YES	YES				YES	
WYOMING	YES			YES	YES	YES	YES					

[1]Adapted from Edward B. Beis, "Involuntary Civil Commitment Statutes." *Mental Disability Law Reporter,* 7 (July-August, 1983): 358–69.

*A threat of danger as a criterion is not specifically listed but is implied by a recent act of dangerousness.

+The criterion is not listed separately but is included in the definition of mental illness.

−Specifies hospitalization as the treatment necessary.

SOURCE: Gerard R. Murphy. *Special Care: Improving the Police Response to the Mentally Disabled.* Washington: Police Executive Research Forum, 1986. Reprinted by permission.

- Each program maintains a 24-hour access to the needed resources, which also forestalls delays in resolution.
- Each program either provides trained mental health professionals (police or civilian) or provides line officers with thorough and appropriate training, which is necessary for the expeditious and appropriate handling of cases.
- Each program clearly delineates the separation of duties and responsibilities among the key actors from different agencies.
- Each program has developed procedures that reduce the time officers need to spend handling mentally ill persons.
- Each program includes close and regular liaison between the participating agencies to ensure that operational information is shared, feedback is provided, and minor problems are addressed.

In Memphis, where officers respond to 4,000 calls a year involving "disturbed persons," a Crisis Intervention Team (CIT) of specially trained officers now responds around the clock to calls involving mentally disturbed people. Their primary objective, according to Crews and Cochran (1989, p. 67), is to: "minimize the use of force without relinquishing safety in potentially violent situations related to mentally disturbed persons."

The Memphis Police Department was concerned about the growing number of potentially violent confrontations officers were having with mentally ill individuals as a result of deinstitutionalization. The department was also concerned that the incidents might increase the potential for lawsuits alleging brutality, and result in negative press and a loss of community support. The department began to search for a better way to deal with the mentally ill and still provide for officer safety. Intensive training of the CIT officers has been crucial to the program's success. Officers learn how to use the Taser gun, a protective shield, and Velcro leg wraps, all important equipment in interacting with a potentially dangerous mentally ill person. Understanding that mental illness is a disease rather than a crime makes the crisis intervention approach a sensible alternative that often has a positive outcome for everyone involved.

During the first eight months of operation, there have been fewer serious injuries to individuals, and injuries to officers handling mental disturbance calls have decreased by 50 percent. Dr. Gilliland, a professor at Memphis State University, CIT instructor, and former FBI agent says: "The CIT concept saves lives and it saves the police a heck of a lot of bad press, embarrassment, and legal entanglement" (Crews and Cochran, 1989, p. 70).

Police officers are probably least trained in this area, yet they are likely to spend a great deal of time interacting with individuals who are mentally disabled.

INDIVIDUALS WITH EPILEPSY _____

Another population police officers should be prepared to interact with are individuals who have epilepsy. The following discussion is a condensation of the program *Epilepsy: A Positive ID,* developed by the University of Minnesota Epilepsy Foundation.

Epilepsy is a disorder of the central nervous system. Epilepsy is not contagious, and it is not an indication that a person is mentally retarded. Known causes of epilepsy include head injuries, infectious diseases such as meningitis, encephalitis, and brain abscesses. A person with epilepsy tends to have recurrent seizures.

A **seizure** is a sudden, uncontrolled event or episode of excessive electrical activity in the brain. It may alter behavior, consciousness, movement, perception and/or sensation. There are many types of seizures, and an individual's behavior differs according to the type of seizure.

Police officers need to be able to recognize seizures, administer the proper first aid procedures, and be responsive to the sensitivities and pride of people with epilepsy. Police officers' chances of encountering a seizure are probably greater than they may think.

The most common types of seizures are simple partial seizures, complex partial seizures, generalized tonic clonic seizures, and absence seizures.

A *simple partial seizure* consists of changes in a person's motor function or sensations *without* accompanying alteration of consciousness. It may be characterized by stiffening or jerking in one or more extremity, a strange feeling in the stomach, tingling, or an alteration of taste or smell. In some cases this type of seizure may progress to a generalized tonic clonic seizure.

A *complex partial seizure* impairs consciousness. The following behaviors may occur during a complex partial seizure: incoherent speech, glassy-eyed staring, aimless wandering, chewing or lip smacking motions, and picking at clothing. The person may be confused or need to rest after the seizure.

A complex partial epileptic seizure may be mistaken for a drug or alcohol-induced stupor because the person may have incoherent speech, glassy-eyed staring, and aimless wandering.

This type of seizure may last a few seconds to several minutes.

A *generalized tonic clonic seizure,* formerly called the grand mal seizure, is what most people commonly associate with epilepsy. *Tonic* means stiffening; *clonic* means jerking. In this type of seizure the following may occur: loss of consciousness, falling, stiffening and jerking, tongue biting and sometimes, drooling, loss of bowel and bladder control.

The *absence seizure,* formerly called the petit mal, is often mistaken for daydreaming or staring. Absence seizures can occur up to 100 times a day or more and are most common in children and adolescents.

The Police Response

It is important that police officers do not confuse the symptoms of an epileptic seizure with those of being high on drugs or alcohol. Table 6.3 summarizes the distinctions between an epileptic seizure and a drug reaction.

If the person is having a complex partial seizure it can last from thirty seconds to three minutes. The person may be confused or disoriented after the seizure. If possible, guide the person to a safe place to sit and let the seizure run its course. Keep the person calm, and do not restrain him or her in any way. Determine the person's level of consciousness by asking their name, where they are, and what day it is. Check for a medical-alert bracelet or tag. Do not leave the individual alone if they appear confused.

In the case of a generalized tonic clonic seizure: cushion the person's head, if they are wearing glasses remove them, loosen their collar and tie, and clear the area of any hard objects they may hit. Do NOT put anything in their mouth—this may damage their teeth or jaw. After the seizure has subsided, turn the person on his or her side, allow the saliva to flow from the mouth, and keep the airway open. Determine the individual's level of consciousness and check for a medical-alert bracelet or tag.

TABLE 6.3
Drug/Alcohol Abuse or Epileptic Seizure?

Complex Partial Seizure Symptoms	Drug/Alcohol Abuse Symptoms
▪ Chewing, lip smacking motions	not likely
▪ Picking at clothes	not likely
▪ Should regain consciousness in 30 seconds to 3 minutes, except in the rare case of a complex partial status (when seizure continues)	a drunk/high person will not recover in 3 minutes or less
▪ No breath odor	a drunk will smell like alcohol
▪ Possibly wearing an epilepsy I.D. bracelet/tag	not likely

Symptoms common to both

▪ Impaired consciousness ▪ Incoherent speech
▪ Glassy-eyed staring ▪ Aimless wandering

SOURCE: *Epilepsy: A Positive I.D.* Epilepsy Education, University of Minnesota. Reprinted by permission.

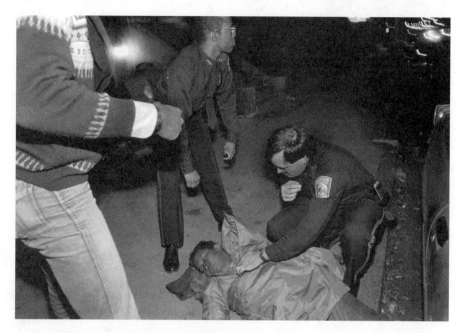

Police officers care for a seizure victim.

Call an ambulance if the person has hit his or her head, if you suspect injury, if there is no medical-alert bracelet or tag, if the seizure lasts between five to ten minutes, or if the seizures occur one after another. If the person has hit his or her head, it is a life-threatening situation that requires immediate action.

Police officers should also be familiar with the medications people with epilepsy may take so that they are not mistaken for illegal drugs. Figure 6.1 illustrates the most common antiepileptic medications.

CRIME PREVENTION FOR THE DISABLED

Disabled people, for the most part, can take responsibility for protecting themselves against crime once they are taught the correct responses to dangerous or suspicious circumstances. Programs should include community awareness, how to deal with strangers, shopping awareness, how to report crime, and resources available. Law enforcement can build positive relationships with the community by providing this vital assistance to some of our most vulnerable citizens.

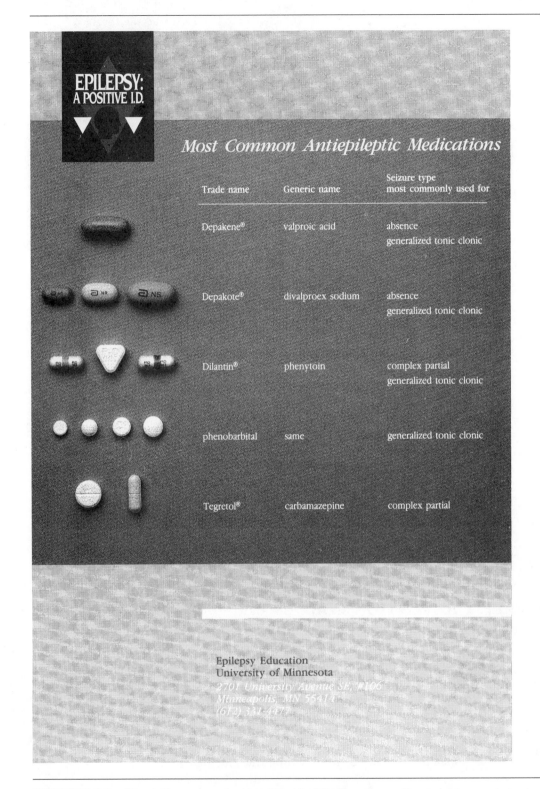

FIGURE 6.1 **Most Common Antiepileptic Medications** (Reprinted by permission.)
178

Crime Prevention Tips for the Disabled

Crime prevention programs geared toward the disabled should incorporate most of the following "tips" in some way:

- Consider your limitations and decide what you are prepared to do if an assailant confronts you.
- Use direct deposit for government payments to you.
- Know your neighbors and decide which ones you could rely on in an emergency.
- Let family or friends know where you are going and what time you expect to return home.
- Never let telephone callers know you are alone or disabled.
- When using public transportation, ride as near to the operator as possible.
- Travel with someone you know whenever possible.
- Be aware of body language. Transmit confidence and certainty.
- Carry enough money for telephone and emergency use, but never carry or display large amounts of cash.
- Be involved. Help your Neighborhood Watch with newsletters or telephone calls.
- Help a neighbor who has been a recent victim of crime. The more active you are, the safer you will be and the safer your neighborhood will be.

The basic premise to teach the disabled is that almost everyone can take responsibility for protecting themselves and their communities from crime. We all feel safer and *are* safer when we understand that we have some power over what happens to us. Of course, differences in disabilities require different approaches to crime prevention, but surprisingly, what works for most people will usually work for disabled people too.

Some law enforcement departments have developed programs specifically for disabled individuals. In addition, some existing programs developed for the general population work well for those who are disabled. Neighborhood Watch, for example, is a program that has a built-in component designed to enhance safety for the most vulnerable in the neighborhood. Block club members are encouraged to look after the elderly or disabled on their blocks, to be aware of suspicious activity around their residences, to check on them regularly, and to assist the disabled and elderly to participate in block activities. This might be described as old-fashioned neighborliness, but in some neighborhoods, it is a practice that needs to be renewed and encouraged.

Emergency ID for "Special Persons"

One program developed to fill a particular need of the disabled is the Emergency ID for "Special Persons," developed by Sheriff William M.

Lanzaro of Monmouth County, New Jersey. Sheriff Lanzaro became aware of the need in 1987 when the director of a school for handicapped children told him the children needed some form of identification in case they were off school grounds or suffered some medical emergency. Sheriff Lanzaro, working with the Monmouth County Department of Human Services, the Office of the Handicapped, and the Association for Retarded Citizens, developed the "Special Persons" ID card program for disabled and handicapped students. According to Freeman (1990, p. 91):

> *The blue card, which measures $2^1/_4 \times 3^1/_2$ inches, is available in two versions, one of which features the universal handicap logo for physically handicapped individuals. The card includes the individual's name, address, and telephone number, as well as the names and telephone numbers of three emergency contacts. The back of the card lists the doctor's name and phone number, social security number, a place for special remarks, and a photo of the individual. The cards are laminated at the presentation site and supplied with a 30-inch neck chain so that the cards may be worn and easily found in case of an emergency.*

As noted by Freeman (p. 91), the cards not only address the identification needs of the handicapped and disabled, the program also "provides high visibility for the police department or sheriff's office and creates an opportunity for community service presentations."

DEALING WITH INDIVIDUALS WITH DISABILITIES WHO BREAK THE LAW

It is natural for an officer to assume that individuals with disabilities are victims, not victimizers. This is not always true, however. The severely physically or mentally disabled are highly unlikely to be among those who break the law. Those with less limiting handicaps, however, are certainly represented among lawbreakers. When a handicapped individual violates the law, they should be treated as much like an able-bodied person as their disability will allow.

Do not make the mistake of thinking that physically disabled or mentally ill people cannot also violate the law. An individual's behavior, of course, will often be limited by his or her physical ability, but most officers encounter disabled offenders and must be prepared to recognize them as offenders when appropriate. Officers are acutely aware that the public will usually react critically toward any type of force used by police against a physically disabled person. As one officer noted:

Man, a whole career goes on the line when you deal with a mental person. Criticize . . . that's all they do. They don't understand what we have to do, but they criticize (Crews and Cochran, 1989, p. 67).

Nonetheless, it is imperative that officers never forget that disabled criminals can pose as much of a threat to safety as an able-bodied criminal can.

Consider the following scenario which happened in a midwestern city. The police were called to the courtyard of an apartment complex where a woman was being threatened by a man with a knife. When officers arrived, they encountered an hysterical female victim and a suspect who refused to drop the knife as ordered to at gunpoint. What the officers did not yet know was that this confrontation was between deaf spouses. The wife had just returned home to discover her husband had stabbed to death their young daughter, whose body lay in their nearby apartment. The confrontation ended with the arrest of the suspect and discovery of the child's body. Several different outcomes were possible because of the disabilities of the couple and the confusion they caused the officers.

A FINAL NOTE

Cushing (1992, p. 19A) recommends:

Just as the Americans with Disabilities Act requires us to build ramps, let our own commitment to inclusive communities require us to build attitudinal ramps. We can't really fight attitudes of discrimination and exclusion unless we do an end-run against ingrained beliefs.

Perhaps individuals with disabilities will eventually serve as the unifiers of society. People with disabilities come from all races, socioeconomic groups and religions. The smartest and the strongest can be laid low as easily as all others.

Perhaps if we begin to look at a disability as an equalizer, we'll understand that the greatest disability is what we do to our nation by preventing others from achieving their potential.

Adapting law enforcement duties and services to accommodate the millions of disabled Americans will not only help accomplish the law enforcement's objectives in a more efficient and safe manner, but will also help to provide the services all citizens need and deserve. When that happens, excellent police-community relations are a likely by-product.

Summary

The United States has 43 million people with disabilities. The most important guideline in interacting with people with disabilities is to treat them as individuals with the same needs and desires as you have. Disabilities police officers might frequently encounter include mobility impairment, vision impairment, hearing impairment, mental or emotional impairment, and impairment as a result of epilepsy. Most deaf people prefer to communicate by means of sign language.

Deinstitutionalization refers to the release of thousands of mentally ill individuals into society to be cared for by family or a special network of support services. When police are called to manage mentally ill persons, the behaviors most frequently encountered include bizarre, unusual, or strange behavior; confused thoughts or action; aggressive actions; destructive, assaultive, or violent behavior; and attempted suicide.

Mental health is the ability to integrate one's self with one's environment. Mental illness is a severe disturbance in thinking, feeling, and relating to other people that results in substantially diminished capacity to cope with the ordinary demands of life. Suicide is the tenth leading cause of death among adults and the second leading cause among adolescents.

The four civil criteria for detainment and commitment of mentally ill individuals are mental illness, dangerousness, being gravely disabled, and being in need of (mental health) treatment. The two formal dispositions are arrest or a civil commitment. Many informal dispositions are also available.

In addition to interacting with individuals with mental disabilities, police officers may also interact with individuals who have epilepsy and should know how to respond properly. A complex partial epileptic seizure may be mistaken for a drug or alcohol-induced stupor because the person may have incoherent speech, glassy-eyed staring, and aimless wandering.

DISCUSSION QUESTIONS _____

1. Do you know anyone with a physical disability? How do you feel around them?
2. Do you know anyone with a mental disability? How do you feel around them?
3. Do you support the deinstitutionalization movement of the late 1960s? Why or why not?
4. Has the local media covered any stories of individuals with mental disabilities coming into conflict with police officers? What was the outcome?

5. What are the criteria for commitment in your state? How do they compare to other states—are they more or less restrictive?
6. Are you aware of resources in your community available for the mentally ill? The physically handicapped?
7. What impact might the Americans with Disabilities Act have on the hiring of police officers?
8. Is it reasonable to require very small businesses to be handicap-accessible?
9. Which type of disability do you feel would pose the greatest challenge for effective police-community relations?
10. How might individuals with disabilities suffer from stereotyping?

DEFINITIONS

Can you define these terms: ADA, Ameslan, crisis behavior, deaf, deinstitutionalization, delusional (paranoid) disorders, disability, epilepsy, hearing impaired, mental health, mental illness, mental retardation, mood disorders, personality disorder, psychotic symptoms, schizophrenia, seizure, TAB, TDD.

REFERENCES

Burden, Ordway P. "Making a Difference in Police Response to the Disabled." *Law Enforcement News.* (July/August 1991): 11.

Crews, Walter and Cochran, Sam. "Memphis Police Department's Crisis Intervention Team." *Law and Order.* (August 1989): 66–70.

Cushing, Marty. "Attitudes about the Disabled Need Repair, Along with Buildings." *Star Tribune.* (October 10, 1992): 19A.

Ehlert, Bob. "Suggestions on How to Deal with Disabled." *Star Tribune.* (November 7, 1991): 3E.

Epilepsy: A Positive ID. Minneapolis: Epilepsy Education, University of Minnesota, 1991.

Finn, Peter E. and Sullivan, Monique. *Police Response to Special Populations: Handling the Mentally Ill, Public Inebriate, and the Homeless.* Washington: National Institute of Justice, January 1988.

Freeman, Ted. "Emergency ID for 'Special Persons.' " *The Police Chief.* (October 1990): 91.

Gallo, Francis J. "The Silent Community We Serve." *Law and Order.* (February 1992): 53–55.

Hageman, Mary Jeanette. *Police-Community Relations.* Beverly Hills: Sage Publications, 1985.

Hull, Bev. "Hearing Impaired Battered Women." *Minnesota Coalition for Battered Women News.* (February 1985): 1, 3.

King, J. Freeman. "The Law Officer and the Deaf." *The Police Chief.* (October 1990): 98–100.

Murphy, Gerard R. *Managing Persons with Mental Disabilities: A Curriculum Guide for Police Trainers.* Washington: Police Executive Research Forum, 1989.

Murphy, Gerard R. *Special Care: Improving the Police Response to the Mentally Disabled.* Washington: Police Executive Research Forum, 1986.

News Services. "Bush Signs Disabilities Act as 3,000 Cheer at Last." *Star Tribune.* (July 26, 1990): 1A.

Wrobleski, Adina. *Suicide: Why?* Minneapolis: Afterwords. 1989.

Zehring, Timothy. "New Insights for the Visually Impaired." *Law and Order.* (December 1990): 33–35.

RESOURCES

American Psychiatric Association, 1400 K Street, N.W., Washington, DC 20005; (202) 682-6000.

American Psychological Association, 1200 17th Street, N.W., Washington, DC 20036; (202) 955-7660.

Epilepsy Education, University of Minnesota, 5775 Wayzata Boulevard, Suite 255, Minneapolis, MN 55416; (612) 525-1160.

International Center for the Disabled (ICD), 340 East 24th Street, New York, NY 10010; (212) 679-0100; (212) 889-0372 TDD.

Muscular Dystrophy Association, 3300 E. Sunrise Drive, Tuscon, AZ 85718; (602) 529-2000.

National Alliance for the Mentally Ill, 1901 North Fort Meyer Drive, Suite 500, Arlington, VA 22209; (703) 524-7600.

National Association for Hearing and Speech Action (NAHSA), 10801 Rockville Pike, Rockville, MD 20852; (301) 897-8682; (800) 638-8255.

National Association of the Deaf, 814 Thayer Avenue, Silver Spring, MD 20910; (301) 587-1788.

National Council on the Handicapped (NCH), 800 Independence Avenue, S.W., Suite 814, Washington, DC 20591; (202) 267-3846; (202) 267-3232 TDD.

National Easter Seal Society, 2023 West Ogden Avenue, Chicago, IL 60612; (312) 243-8400; (312) 243-8880 TDD.

National Head Injury Foundation (NHIF), P.O. Box 567, Framingham, MA 01701; (617) 879-7473.

National Information Center for Handicapped Children and Youth (NICHCY), P.O. Box 1492, Washington, DC 20013; (703) 522-3332 (Voice/TDD).

National Institute of Mental Health, Public Inquiries Branch, 5600 Fishers Lane, Rockville, MD 21784; (301) 443-4515.

National Institute on Disability and Rehabilitation Research, National Rehabilitation Information Center, 8455 Colesville Road, Suite 935, Silver Spring, MD 20910; (301) 588-9284.

National Mental Health Association, 1021 Prince Street, Alexandria, VA 22314; (703) 684-7722.

National Society to Prevent Blindness (Formerly the National Society for the Prevention of Blindness), 500 E. Remington Road, Schaumburg, IL 60173 (708) 843-2020.

Registry of Interpreters for the Deaf, Inc., P.O. Box 1339, Washington, DC 20013.

"Tips for Disability Awareness." National Easter Seal Society, 2023 Ogden Avenue, Chicago, IL 60612; (312) 253-8400; (312) 243-8880 TDD.

"Together We Can Make A Difference." Pennsylvania Commission on Crime and Delinquency.

United Cerebral Palsy Fund, 1522 K Street, N.W., Suite 1112, Washington, DC 20005; 1-800-872-5827.

Local chapters of the organizations listed above.

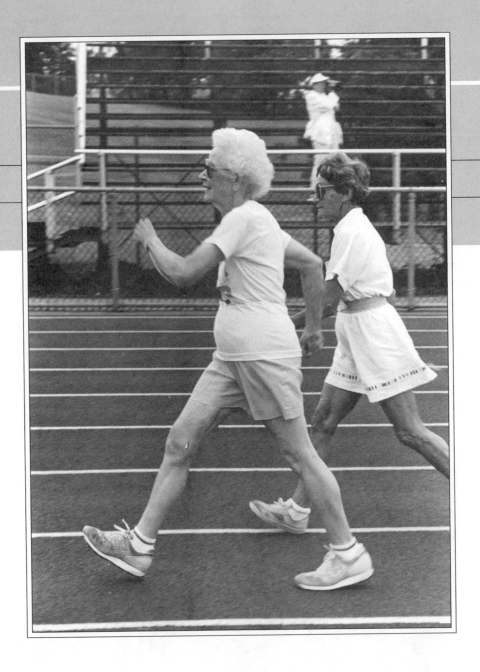

INTERACTING WITH THE ELDERLY

The first forty years of life give us the text; the next thirty supply the commentary on it.

—Schopenhauer

DO YOU KNOW

- What the "graying of America" refers to?
- What causes some older Americans to be prisoners in their own homes?
- How likely the elderly are to be crime victims?
- What effect the increasing age of our population is likely to have on crime?
- What elder abuse is? How prevalent it is?
- What the usual police response should be in cases of elder abuse?
- What Alzheimer's disease is? How prevalent it is? What its symptoms are?
- What behaviors Alzheimer's sufferers have that may bring them into contact with the police?
- How Alzheimer's disease can resemble intoxication?
- What the cardinal rule in dealing with an Alzheimer's victim is?
- How police departments can benefit from senior citizens?

INTRODUCTION

Older, retired people are one of the fastest growing segments of our population. Projections by the U.S. Census Bureau estimate that retired people will comprise more than 25 percent of the total population by the year 2025 (Enter, 1991, p. 67). During their careers, police officers have and will continue to have extensive contact with senior citizens. Police contact with older people rarely involves criminal activity; such contact usually arises from their vulnerability and the effects of the aging process.

Godwin (1992, p. 68) suggests that most gerontologists, those who study the elderly, do not focus solely upon age to determine who is "old." Rather, they consider the following factors:

1. Physical function—is the person able to get around easily and is still physically active;
2. employment status—is the person retired or still engaged in some business or work, even on a part-time basis;
3. life activities—how socially active is the person; and
4. self-perception—does the person view himself or herself as being old.

Some fifty-year-old individuals can seem as if they are eighty years old, and *vice versa*. To determine if someone is "elderly," police officers should consider the preceding factors and the individual's chronological age.

To have effective relationships with older citizens, officers must develop ways to serve their needs, reduce their victimization rate, and gain their cooperation. Older people are especially reluctant to report crime to the police. The elderly tend to admire and respect authority; they are often grateful for any assistance the police may offer them.

Older people are usually in contact with the police if they become victims of crime, are involved in an automobile accident, or are stopped for a traffic violation. Some elderly people do, however, suffer from Alzheimer's disease, a progressive, irreversible disease of the brain which adversely affects their behavior. Many elderly people have other serious medical problems for which they may require emergency medical assistance from a police officer. Older people may also have one or more of the disabilities discussed in the preceding chapter.

Statistics about the elderly make clear their relationship to the rest of society and some of the difficulties they face (Plotkin, 1988, p. F-15):

- There are 22.4 million Americans over sixty-five years of age.
- The elderly are the fastest growing minority.
- The elderly represent 25 percent of the nation's poor.
- The elderly are the most malnourished Americans.
- 33.5 percent of the elderly live in substandard housing.
- The elderly represent 25 percent of the nation's health costs.
- The elderly account for 66.5 percent of the national Medicare/Medicaid costs.
- 85 percent of the nation's elderly have chronic illness.
- 15 percent are ill enough to require some sort of care.
- 5 percent of the elderly are institutionalized and require long-term care.
- The minority elderly are the poorest, sickest, and most isolated of the older adult community.
- 20 percent of the urban elderly receive public assistance.
- 50 percent of the elderly live below the national poverty level.
- 25 percent of the elderly are from a minority racial or ethnic group.
- Between 60 to 80 percent of the long-term care needs of the elderly are met by family and/or friends.

These statistics highlight specific needs of the elderly, including health care, financial assistance, and housing. The statistics also indicate that the needs of the elderly will inevitably continue to grow. Police will have an ever increasing number of elderly people to "serve and protect" in the 1990s and beyond.

THE GRAYING OF AMERICA

Enter (1991, p. 67) notes: "America has traditionally been a youth-oriented nation. This tradition, however, is beginning to change. The maturation of the 'baby-boomers,' smaller nuclear families, and an extended life expectancy are contributing to that change."

The **graying of America** is a metaphor that reflects the fact that our population is aging. The average American is living longer, the general population is becoming older, and the percentage of elderly in the general population is increasing.

Table 7.1 illustrates the growth and decline of age categories within the U.S. population.

TABLE 7.1
U.S. Population Change, 1980–1987

Age	Percent Change
Under 5 years	+11.6
5 to 13 years	−1.1
14 to 17 years	−11.0
18 to 24 years	−9.7
25 to 34 years	+16.8
35 to 44 years	+33.8
45 to 54 years	+2.1
55 to 64 years	+1.5
65 to 74 years	+13.4
75 to 84 years	+20.3
85+ years	+28.0
All ages	+7.4

SOURCE: L. Miller. "First Baby Boomers Reach Age 40, Census Bureau Reports."
United States Department of Commerce News (Report No. CB88-53, April 8).
Washington: Bureau of the Census. 1988.

Square dancing provides a fun form of activity and an opportunity to socialize.

THE ELDERLY AND DRIVING PROBLEMS

"By the year 2020, 50 million people in the U.S., half of them over 75, will be eligible to drive. Many will still be driving" (Bowes, 1992, p. 13). Many states require people over a specific age to retake their driving test. More states are likely to follow as the number of elderly drivers increases.

Bowes (1992, p. 13) suggests that police officers should understand some of the problems the elderly have that can affect their driving:

- Slower reaction time—resulting in more rear-end collisions, a greater number of traffic signal and yield violations, and more pedestrian accidents.
- Decreased visual acuity—road direction signs are harder to read and the ability to judge speed and distance is reduced.
- Narrowed peripheral vision—resulting in accidents at intersections.
- Loss of strength—limits the ability to steer quickly, brake suddenly, or accelerate rapidly.
- Longer glare recovery time—an older person's glare recovery time can be as much as fifty percent longer than a younger person. Glare from automobile headlights can be fatal to an elderly driver.

Bowes also notes that elderly pedestrians with physical impairments such as arthritis can also pose problems to motorists because they walk slowly.

Driving represents independence to young and old alike.

THE ELDERLY AND VICTIMIZATION _____

According to Lindquist and Duke (1987, p. 55), the elderly fear crime more than any other segment of our population.

In some communities, the elderly's fear of crime makes them prisoners in their own homes.

Brunswick and Wolfe (1992, p. 16A) interviewed a sixty-seven year old woman who had not gone to church for the past two months, since three teenage boys harassed her while she was riding home on the bus:

> *I'm not some wishy-washy person. I take the bus all over. I have for years. But now only on weekdays. I never go out nights unless somebody picks me up at the door. I don't walk in strange neighborhoods. I don't open my door at night except for somebody I'm expecting. I have friends who have been bruised and pushed around by somebody grabbing a purse, and I just won't put myself in dangerous situations if I can help it.*

Although the elderly have a heightened fear of crime, they are less likely to be victims of crime than younger people, as shown in Table 7.2.

People aged sixty-five and older have the lowest rate of victimization in the United States both in violent and property crimes.

When elderly people *are* victimized, however, the crime tends to be violent. Older people are physically vulnerable and are likely to be hurt when they become victims of crime. According to the National Crime Prevention Council (1988):

> *Elderly violent crime victims are more likely to face offenders with guns, and are more likely to be attacked by strangers than younger victims. Violent crimes against the elderly are more likely to occur at or near their homes than offenses involving younger victims. About 45% of violent crimes against the elderly were robberies, compared with 17% of violent crimes against teenagers and young adults, and 18% of violent crimes against all victims under the age of 65.*

Many of the crimes perpetrated against the elderly are purse snatchings and street robberies. According to Lipman (1981, p. 132): "The typical purse theft involves grabbing the purse with one hand, shoving the victim down with the other and running away. Broken bones

TABLE 7.2

Victimization Rates for Persons Age 12 and Over, by Race, Sex, and Age of Victims and Type of Crime

Race, sex, and age	Total population	Rate per 1,000 persons in each age group	
		Crimes of violence	Crimes of theft
WHITE			
Male			
12-15	5,517,930	89.2	94.4
16-19	5,536,190	93.4	129.1
20-24	7,384,690	79.9	114.2
25-34	18,241,240	43.1	82.3
35-49	22,146,820	20.2	57.7
50-64	13,798,320	8.3	35.3
65 and over	11,270,280	3.1	21.1
Female			
12-15	5,294,550	42.5	98.5
16-19	5,454,340	51.3	111.7
20-24	7,546,290	49.8	108.3
25-34	17,992,570	28.0	72.2
35-49	22,339,560	17.4	59.0
50-64	14,895,250	5.9	37.0
65 and over	15,691,070	2.8	20.1
BLACK			
Male			
12-15	1,088,170	113.4	85.3
16-19	1,074,310	111.3	84.2
20-24	1,106,570	82.0	139.3
25-34	2,510,530	54.5	95.7
35-49	2,523,030	31.5	46.8
50-64	1,527,930	12.4*	56.1
65 and over	1,016,850	9.4*	17.7*
Female			
12-15	1,050,490	58.6	68.9
16-19	1,090,490	51.6	66.0
20-24	1,341,910	50.3	98.3
25-34	2,939,380	33.0	65.4
35-49	3,085,520	17.7	48.1
50-64	1,883,180	9.3*	26.7
65 and over	1,490,300	5.7*	35.1

* Estimate is based on about 10 or fewer sample cases.

SOURCE: *Criminal Victimization in the United States, 1990.* Bureau of Justice Statistics. (February, 1992): 29.

are common in this type of crime—often more serious than the loss of the contents of the purse."

As Brunswick and Wolfe note: "When older people are victims of crime, they present special problems. Many have frailties, such as poor eyesight or memory, which make testimony at a trial difficult. Others are fearful of retaliation and decline to help prosecute their assailants." In addition, the elderly may have frailties such as osteoporosis. If the elderly are pushed, fall, or are beaten, they may suffer broken bones and other serious injuries a younger person is not likely to sustain.

The Police Response

Police department crime prevention programs aimed specifically at the elderly can help immensely. The police need to remind the elderly:

- To have their social security checks deposited directly in their bank.
- Not to carry much cash or other valuables on their person.
- To let go of a purse if it is grabbed.

Too many senior citizens have tried to hold on to their purses and been dragged along, suffering broken bones and other injuries.

To help the elderly population, police officers might start a block or building watch, set up a daily telephone contact program, or enroll the elderly in Operation I.D. These programs will prevent crime and develop excellent police-community relations, not only among the elderly, but also the rest of the community who will appreciate the professional concern the police department shows for its elderly citizens.

Crime Trends and the Effect on the Elderly

According to Enter (1991, p. 72): "By the year 2025, more than one-quarter of the population will be 60 or older. Therefore, it would be logical to assume that victimization of this age group will substantially increase, simply because the elderly will represent the greatest target population for the criminally minded."

The increasing age of the population in the United States suggests that the elderly will be victimized more often simply because they will be a large target population, some very vulnerable, some very wealthy.

Although the elderly presently constitute only one-sixth of our population, they "own one–third of all household net worth and 40 percent of financial assets" (Naisbitt and Aburdene, 1990, p. 45).

Criminal activity has generally been attributed to the young; however, as our population ages, according to Enter (p. 71): "the incidence of the 'geriatric delinquent' will undoubtedly become a greater problem for the criminal justice system."

The number of elderly people who commit crimes will probably increase and present a great challenge to the criminal justice system, particularly corrections.

Enter (p. 71) suggests that:

One of the dilemmas that the criminal justice system will face concerns the processing of the older criminal through our present system. Arrest and detention policies, culpability issues, and sentencing options of today are limited in their ability to deal with the unique problems posed by elderly criminals. This gap will be especially apparent in issues concerning long-term incarceration of the elderly who will require extensive medical and psychological care beyond the present capabilities of most corrections institutions.

Another increase likely to result from the graying of America is an increase in what Enter (p. 72) calls **"granny bashing"** or domestic violence against the elderly.

ELDER ABUSE

One evening in March of 1992 television news programs included a story that involved a confused and helpless eighty-two year old man who had been abandoned in his wheelchair at a dog racing track. Viewers were saddened by images of him in a hospital bed clutching a teddy bear. He was wearing slippers and a sweatshirt that read "Proud to be an American" and was holding a bag of diapers. Pinned to his sweatshirt was a typewritten note that said he was "John King, an Alzheimer's patient in need of care." All labels had been removed from his new clothing, and all identifying marks had been removed from his wheelchair. Egan (1992, p. 4A) warns:

The face, that of an elderly person who does not even know his name and was left on society's doorstep, could become a face of the future. . . .

Increasingly, families pinched by the rising medical costs of aging parents and the strain of raising their own children are taking the radical step of abandoning the elderly. . . .

Although precise numbers are not available, the American College of Emergency Physicians surveyed hospitals and concluded that up to 70,000 elderly parents were abandoned last year by family members who were unable or unwilling to care for them any longer.

Such **granny dumping,** abandoning of the elderly, is only one form of elder abuse, however.

Elder abuse encompasses physical and emotional abuse, financial exploitation, and general neglect. The extent of elder abuse is unknown.

The American Association of Retired Persons **(AARP)** conducted a survey of 200 law enforcement agencies and received an 88 percent response rate (Plotkin, 1988). According to this survey, only 2 percent of the agencies saw elder abuse as a major problem; 54 percent considered it "somewhat" of a problem. The remaining 44 percent of the agencies saw it as "no problem." According to Plotkin (p. 19): "Police generally lack the data that suggest that the problem is of a magnitude significant to warrant the allocation of already scarce resources."

Most police agencies do not keep separate statistics on elder abuse. Agencies classify offenses by their traditional name, for example, assault, fraud, neglect, but not by age, so it is impossible to determine the extent of the problem. Further, many police officers believe elder abuse cases are "family matters" in which police should not interfere.

According to the AARP survey, in almost half the cases police did not know how the cases came to their attention, as illustrated in Table 7.3. As might be expected, a very low percentage of the reports came from family members.

TABLE 7.3
How Majority of Cases Are Brought to Police Attention

Don't know	43%
Call from concerned individual (e.g., neighbor)	12
Referred from social service agency or other organization	11
Call from elder victim	9
Discovered while investigating a complaint or disturbance	9
Call from family member	2
(Had no reported cases)	14

SOURCE: Martha R. Plotkin, *A Time for Dignity: Police and Domestic Abuse of the Elderly.* Washington: Police Executive Research Forum and the American Association of Retired Persons. 1988:22. Reprinted by permission.

The AARP survey also revealed that police officers are not often aware of relevant state statutes that govern elder abuse. According to Plotkin (p. 28): "Thirty-one percent of the departments reporting that they were unaware of specific statutes governing the police response to elder abuse actually had relevant state statutes. At a minimum, each of these departments was subject to mandatory reporting of suspected cases of elder abuse. The word had obviously not gotten down to police practitioners."

Because most states now have mandatory reporting laws regarding elderly abuse, it is important that police officers recognize the signs of physical abuse of the elderly, summarized in Table 7.4.

Police must also watch for signs of extortion or fraud and the other forms of elder abuse.

TABLE 7.4.
Signs of Physical Abuse of the Elderly

v Any injury incompatible with explanation.
v Burns (possibly caused by cigarettes, caustics, acids, friction from ropes or chains).
v Cuts, pinch marks, scratches, lacerations, or puncture wounds.
v Bruises, welts, or discolorations:
  v bilaterally on the upper arms;
  v clustered on trunk, but may be evident over any area of the body;
  v unexplained bruises/welts in various stages of healing;
  v presence of old and new bruises at the same time;
  v injury reflects shape of article used to inflict injury (electric cord, belt buckle).
v Dehydration and/or other malnourishment without illness-related cause; unexplained loss of weight.
v Poor skin hygiene; pallor; sunken eyes, cheeks.
v Eye injury.
v Absence of hair and/or hemorrhaging beneath the scalp.
v Soiled clothing or bedding.
v Lack of bandages on injuries or stitches where needed; or evidence of unset bone fractures.

Injuries are sometimes hidden under the breasts or on other areas of the body normally covered by clothing. Repeated skin or other bodily injuries should be noted and careful attention paid to their location and treatment.

Frequent use of the emergency room and/or hospital or health care "shopping" may also indicate physical abuse.

SOURCE: Martha R. Plotkin, *A Time for Dignity: Police and Domestic Abuse of the Elderly.* Washington: Police Executive Research Forum and the American Association of Retired Persons. 1988:F-24 © 1988, AARP. Reprinted with permission.

The Police Response

The issue of elder abuse is extremely sensitive. Often those who care for the elderly are ill equipped and lack resources themselves. Further, the arrest of the only caregiver could leave the elderly person in an even more precarious position. The victim of elder abuse may be extremely embarrassed by the treatment being given by "family." It is in the best interests of the elderly and the caregiver if the police can help work out a solution. Improving the care of the elderly does, however, involve more than just police intervention.

As noted by Plotkin (p. 65): "A proper response to domestic elder abuse must incorporate the resources and expertise of a myriad of professional groups, of which the police are just one." Table 7.5 summarizes the agencies that the AARP surveyed police departments currently work with.

The police response in cases of elder abuse should be one of concern and empathy for all involved. The solution should involve appropriate professional support services.

The AARP survey identified several model programs that deal with elderly abuse. Three such program, described by Plotkin (1988), are summarized below.

Charleston, South Carolina.   A specific elder abuse unit in the police department handles the casework, but all street supervisors are trained to handle complaints of elder abuse. The department uses a large network of agencies that assist with elder abuse cases: the Red Cross, home health agencies, nursing facilities, and churches. The department provides training for agencies that work with the elderly, as well as workshops and lectures for senior citizens' groups and other interested

TABLE 7.5
Coordination with Non-Police Agencies

Social workers	72%
Mental health workers	60
Victim services	58
Elder protective services	40
Hospital workers	35
Transportation services	14
Shelters for the elderly	13

SOURCE: Martha R. Plotkin, *A Time for Dignity: Police and Domestic Abuse of the Elderly.* Washington: Police Executive Research Forum and the American Association of Retired Persons. 1988:50. Reprinted by permission.

local and national organizations. They have an Elder Supportline, a telephone support project that provides the community with a direct contact for reporting cases of elder abuse and neglect.

Beaumont, Texas. A departmental policy requires police officers to leave their patrol cars for at least ten minutes every hour to meet the public. The policy provides officers with an opportunity to spend time checking on the safety and well–being of the elderly and homebound. To identify seniors interested in and in need of such police services, letters soliciting this information were sent to city churches and other organizations in contact with the elderly population. The beat officer visits each elderly participant in the program weekly and volunteers telephone the participant once a day except on the visitation day. If the participant does not answer the telephone or the officer finds no one home, the police investigate the situation.

New York City. New York City has a Crimes Against Senior Citizens Unit in each borough. These units emphasize preventing and investigating crimes against senior citizens, especially indoor robberies. The department produces an Older New Yorkers pamphlet which discusses city and police department assistance available to the elderly, crime prevention techniques, the courts and legal process, and provides a list of important telephone numbers.

In addition to being the victims of crime or of elder abuse, senior citizens are often the victims of disease. An especially devastating disease that affects the elderly is Alzheimer's disease.

ALZHEIMER'S DISEASE: A POLICE PROBLEM TOO

This discussion is a condensation of the information provided in *Victim, Not Criminal: The Alzheimer Sufferer,* and the Alzheimer's Association Police Training materials.

Imagine living in a world where every minute of your life is erased from memory as it passes. You can recall certain events from your childhood, school days, young adulthood, middle–age—but nothing from the past three years, five years, or five minutes. You are unable to recall things you have known most of your life: your neighborhood, home, children, friends, and spouse are all strange and foreign to you. This is the empty world of an Alzheimer's victim.

An estimated four million Americans have Alzheimer's disease (AD). AD afflicts about 10 percent of individuals over 65 and almost 50 percent of those over 85. AD also afflicts more women than men. One out of three families has a close relative or family member with Alzheimer's disease. More than 50 percent of all nursing home patients are victims of the disease or a related disorder.

As the population of the United States ages, the number of people afflicted with AD will grow—along with the likelihood that police officers will encounter AD victims in the line of duty.

Alzheimer's disease is a progressive, irreversible brain disease affecting four million elderly Americans. The classic symptom of Alzheimer's disease is loss of memory.

Pronounced *Altz'-hi-merz,* the disease affects individuals of all social, economic, and racial groups. It is the fourth leading cause of death in adults, causing 100,000 deaths per year. An estimated $40 to $50 billion is spent each year caring for Alzheimer's patients.

Alzheimer's victims may look perfectly healthy and may be well dressed. Those with Alzheimer's may be very adept at concealing their disease. Because police officers are likely to encounter individuals who suffer from Alzheimer's disease, and because there are no visible characteristics of the disease, officers should know the symptoms.

Symptoms of Alzheimer's disease include gradual memory loss, impairment of judgment, disorientation, personality change, decline in ability to perform routine tasks, behavior change, difficulty in learning, loss of language skills, and a decline in intellectual function.

AD patients forget, they forget that they have forgotten, and will not be able to recall what they have forgotten. It will not help to ask if they have AD because they will forget whether they have the disease.

The cause of Alzheimer's is not known, and it is a difficult disease to diagnose. In fact, medical confirmation of the disease is usually only possible by autopsy. Doctors diagnose AD by ruling out other diseases and by symptoms and family history. There is no cure for AD. The progress of the disease cannot be stopped. The course of the disease averages eight years from the time symptoms first appear, but individuals have lived as long as twenty years with the disease. Unfortunately, AD is always fatal. Although doctors cannot cure individuals with the disease, they can manage their symptoms.

Research has dispelled several *myths* associated with Alzheimer's. We now know that Alzheimer's disease:

- Is NOT a normal part of the aging process.
- Is NOT caused by hardening of the arteries or lack of oxygen.
- Is NOT contagious.

- Is NOT a mental illness or a form of insanity.
- Is NOT precipitated by alcoholism or malnutrition.

Behavior Patterns

A number of behavior patterns common to AD patients may bring them to the attention of police officers.

Alzheimer's victims may wander or become lost, engage in inappropriate sexual behavior, lose impulse control, shoplift, falsely accuse others, drive erratically, and appear intoxicated.

Any of these behaviors may cause the police to interact with an AD patient. The behaviors are the result of an individual's memory loss—the inability to make associations.

Wandering. Wandering is a common behavior of people with Alzheimer's that can occur any time, although it seems to be more common at night. An AD patient can become hopelessly lost, even when close to home and other familiar places. An officer may become frustrated when attempting to help because AD patients may not remember where they have been, where they are going, or where they live, even when driven past their homes. AD patients may make up a story rather than admit their confusion. They may be uncooperative or even hostile and combative.

Inappropriate Sexual Behavior. AD patients are fidgeters and often develop repetitive behaviors. They may fidget with their clothing, their buttons and zippers, usually without sexual intent. The AD victim who zips and unzips his pants or unbuttons her blouse in public may simply be fidgeting.

Loss of Impulse Control. AD patients also suffer the loss of impulse control and may do whatever occurs to them, regardless of whether it is appropriate or acceptable behavior. Loss of impulse control may lead the AD patient to remove clothing that is uncomfortable or too warm. It may also cause the patient to urinate or defecate when they feel the urge, wherever the patient may be.

Shoplifting. AD victims may forget to pay for things, forget they have picked up merchandise, or that they are even in a store. AD patients rarely steal. They will forget that they have not paid for an item and will sincerely believe they are being falsely accused.

Falsely Accusing Others. AD patients may also falsely accuse store personnel of stealing from them. AD patients forget their pocketbooks and wallets, how much money they had when entering a store, or how much money they have already spent. Unable to sort out the reality, they may become suspicious and accuse people around them.

AD patients may inaccurately believe they have been victimized by friends and family, as well as strangers. They may report crimes which did not occur.

In addition, neighbors may report that AD patients who live alone scream and yell at night. "Kidnap" or "adult abuse" reports may result from caregivers' attempts to limit an AD patient's behavior in public.

Appearance of Intoxication. AD victims may appear intoxicated because many symptoms of the disease are identical to those of drunkenness. Alcohol and AD both diminish brain function—alcohol temporarily, AD permanently.

Many of the symptoms of intoxication and AD are identical: confusion, disorientation, problems with short–term memory, problems with language, sight and coordination, combativeness and extreme reactions, and loss of contact with reality.

Victimization. People afflicted with AD are easy prey for con artists, robbers, and muggers. Police may become aware of AD patients as a result of legal actions such as evictions, repossessions, and termination of utility service due to the patients' forgetfulness or inability to make payments.

Poor Driving/Auto Accidents. AD victims are often physically able to drive a car long after the time when their memory, judgment, and problem–solving ability make it safe. Understandably, drivers who have Alzheimer's can have one or more of the following difficulties: "losing" their car and reporting it stolen; leaving the scene of an accident because they can actually forget it has happened; and "wandering" in the car because they are lost or have forgotten their destination. Sometimes drivers with AD are found several hundred miles from home. In such instances, the police should convince the AD patient to relinquish the car keys.

The Police Response

Police officers' encounters with AD patients usually fall into two categories: (1) those involving behavior due to the primary symptoms of AD such as loss of memory and communication skills or (2) behavior due to resulting symptoms of AD known as catastrophic reactions.

Problems Due to Memory Loss. Officers called to the scene of an incident such as shoplifting or indecent exposure may arrive to find that the AD sufferer has completely forgotten the incident. There may be a dozen witnesses of the incident, but the subject will deny it occurred. The implications of such memory impairment are tremendously complex for police officers. If the patient did, indeed, commit a serious crime, the officer must take legal action. Usually, however, it is a minor incident such as shoplifting, or misunderstood sexual behavior. If at all possible the officer should try to resolve the situation informally.

Problems with Communication. An AD patient who cannot remember or communicate what actually occurred may fabricate a story. Police officers could easily believe the subject is lying. The story may conflict so much with reality that the subject may appear to be taunting the officer.

Is It Alzheimer's?   The following signs can help police officers determine if the person they are dealing has Alzheimer's disease:

- Identification bracelet or other item indicating memory impairment (usually the bracelet will *not* indicate Alzheimer's disease, but will state memory impairment). Such a bracelet is the clearest way to identify an AD patient. Unfortunately, not all AD victims wear such identification.
- Confusion—an inability to grasp even the simplest sight, sound, or situation.
- Facial expressions that are blank or inappropriate to the situation.
- Inappropriate dress. (Heavy clothing on a hot day, for example, or no shoes or coat in the winter.)
- Forgetfulness, especially short-term memory loss.
- Communication problems—difficulty remembering and understanding the meaning of words, keeping thoughts clear, speaking logically and following simple instructions.
- Age (most are over the age of sixty-five, but the youngest documented AD patient was twenty-eight years old).

Catastrophic Reactions. Catastrophic reactions occur when a situation overloads the AD patient's ability to act rationally and the patient reverts to impulsive behavior. AD may short-circuit an individual's ability to think, and the result is like a blown fuse. Behavior resulting from a catastrophic reaction can be relatively mild such as sudden mood changes and restlessness, or rapidly deteriorate into suspiciousness, stubbornness, inconsolable crying, anger, and combativeness. During a catastrophic reaction, AD patients often lash out, verbally and/or physically, at people who try to help them.

Guidelines

Although Alzheimer's disease is quite complicated, police officers can follow certain guidelines when they suspect or know they are dealing with an AD patient.

The cardinal rule for police officers who deal with an Alzheimer's patient is to avoid the catastrophic reaction.

The following guidelines should help an officer interact with an AD patient.

- Look for an I.D. bracelet or other identification.
- Identify yourself and explain what you are or will be doing, even if it is obvious.
- Avoid lectures or confrontation. Not only will they be ineffective, they are likely to aggravate the situation.
- Speak softly and slowly in a low pitched voice. AD victims are not necessarily hard of hearing. Speaking loudly could be mistaken for anger and lead to a catastrophic reaction.
- Keep communication simple. Use short, familiar words and simple sentences.
- Use distraction to end inappropriate behavior; sometimes just your presence is sufficient.
- Maintain eye contact with the AD victim when speaking.
- Try to maintain a calm atmosphere. Any situation that may be mildly stressful for the average citizen can be extremely difficult for the AD victim. AD patients will often mimic your mood and respond more to the "climate" of an encounter than anything else. A nonaggressive posture and reassuring tones will help the officer to elicit the most helpful response from an AD patient.
- Do not overload the AD victim. When possible talk one-on-one, away from crowds and noise; ask simple questions one at a time.
- Avoid restraints, if possible. The use of handcuffs and physical restraint methods are almost certain to cause a catastrophic reaction, virtually eliminating chances of a simple solution to the situation.

The Alzheimer's Disease and Related Disorders Association (AD Association) suggests that, if at all possible, officers should avoid using handcuffs on an AD victim. Officers should, however, recognize that AD victims are unpredictable when frightened or upset, and they may need to be restrained for their own safety and the safety of others.

Additional Police Response

Police departments can prepare to deal more effectively with AD victims by educating officers about the disease and encouraging families to get hard-to-remove I.D. bracelets for AD patients.

The AD Association's *Police Training Kit* is an excellent resource containing a fifteen-minute video, *Innocent Offender,* a curriculum manual with objectives, suggested activities and sample presentation plans for training sessions of ten, thirty, or sixty minutes. The objectives of the training kit are that, through training, police officers will:

- Become sensitized to the physical and behavioral consequences of Alzheimer's disease.
- Identify situations where the person with Alzheimer's may be encountered.
- Learn specific intervention techniques for managing the Alzheimer person in crisis.
- Become familiar with the AD Association's resources for families in the community.

Included within the *Police Training Kit* is a Law Enforcement Officers Pocket Response Guide for Alzheimer's Victims. (See Figure 7–1, reproduced on the following pages by permission of Cain Consulting Associates, P.O. Box 545 Pewee Valley, KY 40056.) This double-sided, laminated guide summarizes the key training concepts.

The kit is endorsed by the Fraternal Order of Police and is available for a modest charge from your local AD Association. Training is also available from your local chapter of the AD Association.

A program started in 1991, the Helmsley Alzheimer's Alert program, provides information on missing patients to public safety agencies. When a person with Alzheimer's is reported missing, the Alzheimer's Association faxes an alert and identifying information to a fax service which transmits simultaneously to hundreds of locations, including police, hospital emergency rooms, and shelters. When the patient is found, another fax is sent to inform the agencies that the search is over. More than 275 patients have been assisted since the program began ("Alzheimer's Alert," 1993, p. 52).

SENILITY

Senility is another disabling condition often associated with aging. Godwin (1992, p. 70) notes: "Senile demential, organic brain syndrome (OBS), is the disorientation or change in the mental abilities and personality because of generalized brain damage." Factors commonly

LAW ENFORCEMENT OFFICERS POCKET RESPONSE GUIDE
FOR ALZHEIMER'S VICTIMS

Made possible through the generosity of . . .

KENTUCKY STATE LODGE
FRATERNAL ORDER OF POLICE

TO USE THIS GUIDE:

Review this side for general recommendations when you first encounter a potential Alzheimer's victim.

REVIEW SIDE 2:

For a brief description of the most common type of law enforcement encounters associated with individuals suffering from Alzheimer's Disease.

1. The primary symptoms of Alzheimer's Disease are memory loss, impaired judgment, carelessness in appearance especially with over/under dressing, disorientation, absent-mindedness, inability to communicate, and poor concentration abilities especially in response to the officer's kind of questioning. A neurological disorder, where the victim asks same questions over and over again, is quite common.

2. Since Alzheimer's Disease affects primarily the individual's mental functioning, there may not be any overt or recognizable physical characteristics of the disease.

3. Specific law enforcement encounters increase the likelihood that the individual may be suffering from Alzheimer's Disease. These encounters include wandering, auto accidents/traffic violations, indecent exposure, victimization/false reports, shoplifting, intoxication and homicide/suicide cases.

4. Bracelets indicating memory impairment, worn by the individual, may alert the officer that the subject is suffering from Alzheimer's Disease. Usually the words "memory impaired" distinguish this individual from other types of medic-alert categories. Some individuals will wear other forms of identification such as patches sewn to their clothing. If your area has a local Alzheimer's Chapter, it is recommended that it be contacted in case someone is missing, as well as to check with the Missing Persons Bureau.

5. When encountering a possible Alzheimer's victim, employ a non-threatening tone of voice. Maintain a calm environment and be cognizant of voice level so as to not give a false perception of anger or threat. Do not assume the individual is hearing impaired unless otherwise indicated.

6. Attempt to remove individual from noisy, stressful environmental situations. Excess stimuli may trigger a catastrophic reaction which is exhibited by increased symptoms of restlessness, pacing, agitation and anxiety. Sirens should be turned off, if possible, and radio volume and squelch turned down.

7. The ability to communicate (both sending and receiving messages) is greatly impaired with Alzheimer's victims.

   a) First, identify yourself as a law enforcement officer and state purpose of your being there no matter how obvious it may seem.

   b) Speak slowly — maintain low-pitched voice.

   c) Use short familiar words.

   d) Ask "yes" or "no" questions.

   e) Ask one question at a time allowing plenty of response time.

   f) If necessary, repeat question with exact previous wording. Victims may grasp only parts of initial question.

   g) Maintain good eye contact while communicating.

   h) Substitute non-verbal with verbal communication.

8. Avoid, if possible, the use of restraints or handcuffs. This action may trigger an increase in the victims' symptoms. Restraints should be used only as a last resort or when necessary for the safety of the individual and others.

In Memory of Mike Cain   ©1990 Cain Consulting Associates

FIGURE 7.1 Side 1 of the Pocket Response Guide

LAW ENFORCEMENT OFFICERS POCKET RESPONSE GUIDE
FOR ALZHEIMER'S VICTIMS

Typical behaviors associated with Alzheimer's Disease increase the likelihood of specific law enforcement encounters. Officers called to the scene, or who are confronted with a probable Alzheimer's victim, may very well find themselves dealing with a subject who has no recollection of an alleged incident.

Because Alzheimer's Disease affects that part of the brain where memory is stored, subjects may be unable to comprehend the seriousness of the issue and may be unable to effectively communicate and respond to the officers' line of questioning.

Officers may find themselves confronted with individuals who appear to be uncooperative and in denial of verifiable events.

WANDERING

Alzheimer's Disease destroys the victim's ability to associate and recognize familiar landmarks. The individual's ability to retrace directional road maps and recall familiar driving routes becomes diminished.

Wandering behavior often increases at night and may pose serious safety concerns, especially if the victim wanders off during inclement weather, into remote areas or into an area of high traffic intensity.

AUTO ACCIDENTS - TRAFFIC VIOLATIONS

Rules and regulations as they relate to highway safety are forgotten by Alzheimer's victims resulting in the failure to obey street signs, traffic lights and the maintenance of safe driving speeds. Individuals involved in accidents may even flee the scene unaware of any mishap.

SEXUAL BEHAVIOR - INDECENT EXPOSURE

Societal norms associated with dress and impulse control are erased or forgotten.

Repetitive behavior exhibited by Alzheimer's victims such as fidgeting with zippers or buttons may be misinterpreted as deviant behavior.

Because judgment is often impaired with Alzheimer's Disease victims, undressing in public or leaving one's household without proper attire are common occurrences. The officer should be alerted when individuals are dressed inappropriately for summer or winter.

SHOPLIFTING

Memory impairment will likely hinder the ability of Alzheimer's victims paying for merchandise. Victims may casually walk out of a store without paying, unaware of any wrongdoing.

Confrontation with the victim is not recommended and the officer is encouraged to work this out with the store owner if given the latitude to do so.

VICTIMIZATION - FALSE REPORTS

Alzheimer's victims fall easy prey to con artists; however, lost or misplaced items also may be reported stolen. Often burglary attempts or strange intruders turn out to be long-time spouses or family members whom the victim has forgotten.

INTOXICATION — D.U.I.

Erratic driving and failure to obey traffic signs may be caused by Alzheimer's Disease. Failure of the officer's assessment to identify any positive signs of alcohol or drug use may warrant the need to recognize the possibility of Alzheimer's Disease.

HOMICIDE - SUICIDE

Unfortunately, without a cure for Alzheimer's Disease, caregivers may find themselves unable to bear the burden of dealing with this devastating disease and may choose to take the law into their own hands.

Several cases of homicide/suicide involving Alzheimer's victims are reported each year.

FIGURE 7.1   (continued) Side 2 of the Pocket Response Guide

associated with the onset of senility include head injuries, infection, drug reactions, toxic chemicals, and other problems such as multiple sclerosis. Senility can also be caused by alcoholism, anemia, malnutrition, congestive heart failure, diabetes, and chemical reactions (Godwin, p. 70).

According to Godwin, common characteristics of OBS, include the following:

Disorientation of time, place or persons; memory loss; impairment of judgment with occasional auditory and visual hallucinations; and inappropriate behavior or emotional instability.

Godwin suggests:

When dealing with a confused person, an officer should ensure the person is receiving information. He should attempt to establish a familiar environment, communicate slowly, reinforce reality by not reacting to their delusions, and maintain a tolerant, calm, and unflustered manner.

CRIME PREVENTION AND COMMUNITY RELATIONS PROGRAMS

The older population's fear of crime, coupled with their unique vulnerabilities make them a logical target for crime prevention programs. The elderly are often cooperative and enthusiastic about participating in a police department's special efforts and programs.

Police departments across the United States have developed many effective programs for older citizens. Such programs can be easily adapted to other communities and are successful because they can reduce victimization, reduce the unrealistic fear of crime, and improve police-community relations.

Honolulu, for example, has a Senior Citizen Watch Program. Members of authorized programs are issued official Senior Citizen Watch Program Identification Pins and are encouraged to wear them when going to and from planned club functions and other activities. As noted in their brochure: "The concept of the program is to utilize members of organized senior citizen groups to assist the police by becoming the eyes and ears for the department." The opening statement by Gibbe, the Chief of Police, notes: "Senior citizens offer much in the way of crime prevention. They are mature, dependable, trustworthy, observant, and above all, enthusiastic."

Several similar programs are discussed in Section Three.

OLDER VOLUNTEERS WITH LAW ENFORCEMENT

The police are not solely responsible for or even capable of reducing or preventing crime. Crime prevention is a community responsibility shared by the young and the old. Recently, law enforcement executives have sought citizen involvement and support in programs designed to reduce and prevent crime. Volunteers are currently involved in neighborhood watch block clubs, anonymous reporting, and court watch programs.

Seniors make excellent volunteers. Police departments across the country staff innovative programs with elderly citizens.

Among the community volunteers are large numbers of older retired people who tend to be dependable, experienced, stable, available, trainable, committed, skilled, conscientious, and service oriented. In addition, older volunteers have fewer accidents, are more careful of equipment than younger volunteers, use good judgment, follow directions, like to avoid trouble, have good attendance records, and tend to be team players.

Benefits to the police department and the community that use older volunteers include:

- Increased service delivery.
- Increased cost-effectiveness.
- Improved public image.
- Relieving sworn personnel for other duties.
- Provision of new program opportunities.
- Increased political support.
- Restored community responsibility.
- Enhanced understanding of police functions.
- Reduced crime.
- Increased property values.

In addition, the volunteers may receive the following benefits:

- Reduced fear of crime.
- Use of their skills and expertise.
- The opportunity to help others.
- Enrichment of their daily lives.
- A greater sense of belonging and worth.

These lists, compiled by the AARP, are by no means exhaustive, but illustrate the many benefits to all involved in certain programs. Police sponsored programs that use elderly volunteers, have, however, raised some concerns.

Concerns about Using Seniors as Volunteers

One frequently expressed concern is that volunteers may accomplish police officers' duties, and thereby affect future departmental hiring decisions. Other concerns are that volunteers need to be supervised while working in the department or that they may come in contact with sensitive or confidential material.

Volunteer programs can be tailored to address most objections. Volunteers rarely perform actual police functions. Volunteers frequently work in programs the department could not otherwise afford to provide such as fingerprinting children, distributing literature, maintaining equipment, entering computer data, organizing block groups, conducting department tours, and translating.

Volunteers do, however, need supervision and recognition, and volunteer programs need a coordinator to handle those tasks. In some cases a member of the staff can act as coordinator. Where an extensive volunteer program is anticipated, a department may need to hire a volunteer coordinator.

Assistance and direction in managing seniors in volunteer programs is available from AARP. This organization has, for example, developed a checklist to use when implementing a program of volunteers in law enforcement, shown in Figure 7.2.

EXEMPLARY PROGRAMS

Several departments have developed programs focused on elderly concerns. The following are a few of the many exemplary programs.

Cleveland's Community Re-Entry Program.   Community Re-Entry is a church-sponsored, community-based corrections program that seeks to reintegrate ex-offenders into the community by entering into a contract with the Public Housing Authority to provide care to the elderly. Ex-offenders are hired by Community Re-Entry to serve as Care Team members. Sulton (1990, pp. 37–38) describes the responsibilities of the Care Teams:

> The Care Teams assist and protect the elderly who live in
> low-income, high-rise apartment buildings, and who are
> physically unable to complete basic tasks like cashing their checks,
> shopping for food and clothing, or traveling to doctors' offices.
> Because many of them are lonely, the Care Teams also provide

✓ **CHECKLIST**

_____ Is there executive level commitment?	_____ Will volunteers work specific shifts?
_____ Has a need been identified?	_____ Will you need back-up for occasional absenteeism?
_____ Are volunteers the answer?	_____ Do you plan group assignments?
_____ Have you prepared departmental personnel to accept this concept?	_____ What hours will you want them to work?
_____ Will there be Union objections?	_____ Will they log in and out on time sheets?
_____ What kind of unit is needed?	_____ Will you be able to keep backlogs from developing?
_____ Where will the unit be placed in the organization?	_____ Will there be adequate workspace?
_____ Who will supervise the unit?	_____ Comfort? Lighting?
_____ Are the supervisory lines clear?	_____ Will you have supplies available?
_____ Will you have a volunteer to coordinate the activites?	_____ Will you provide transportation?
_____ Who will set work schedules?	_____ Will you pay out-of-pocket expenses?
_____ How will you recruit the volunteers?	_____ Will volunteers be assigned parking spaces?
_____ Do you know how many you will need to start the program?	_____ What will be the direct costs?
_____ Will you develop screening criteria?	_____ Indirect costs?
_____ Who will interview volunteers?	_____ Have you considered liability?
_____ Will you prepare job descriptions?	_____ Will the department provide insurance?
_____ What kind of paperwork will be needed?	_____ Must the volunteer provide insurance?
_____ Can you identify specific tasks?	_____ How will you recognize their performance?
_____ Can the volunteers perform the tasks in the time offered?	_____ Will you have criteria for measuring their performance?
_____ What will be the training needs?	_____ What termination procedures would be necessary when service is completed?
_____ How much time for training?	_____ How will the public be informed about these activities?
_____ In the classroom? On-the-job?	

FIGURE 7.2   Volunteer Checklist

SOURCE: © 1988, American Association of Retired Persons. Reprinted with permission.

companionship. In addition, the teams have established a resident grocery-variety store for the elderly to facilitate their purchase of small items.

Security services are provided because the elderly requested it after several burglaries occurred. No elderly person has been victimized when a Care Team was on duty. The teams are effective, in part, because those most likely to cause disorder respect team members. . . .

According to Re-Entry staff, none of the ex-offenders who are Care Team members has returned to prison.

Detroit's Junior Police Cadet Section. Sulton (1990, p. 74) notes that this program's approach "is to intervene and restore an attitude of caring and sharing among youth, senior citizens, and public and private institutions." A pilot project to assist the elderly was established in 1979 and involved 200 youth. By 1980 over 1,600 high school students participated in the program. Cadets wear uniforms and provide escort services to the elderly. Says Sulton (p. 76): "The senior citizen escort service is designed to permit the elderly to move freely throughout the community without fear of being victimized. Cadets ride buses and walk with the elderly while they shop, bank, and visit physicians."

Triad—A Coordinated Approach. A joint resolution has been adopted by the AARP, the International Association of Chiefs of Police (IACP), and the National Sheriff's Association (NSA) (see Figure 7.3). As noted by Miller (1991, p. 96):

These organizations expressed concerns about criminal victimization of older people and agreed to work effectively together to bring about interjurisdictional approaches and programs designed to reduce the victimization of older persons, assist those who have been victimized, and generally enhance law enforcement services to older adults and the community at large.

This three-way partnership, called TRIAD, seeks to provide support, including specific information such as the following (Miller, p. 96):

- Crime prevention materials: brochures, program guides and audiovisual presentations on crime prevention and the elderly.
- Policies and exemplary projects relating to law enforcement response to the older community and the formation of senior advisory councils to advise departments on the needs of seniors.
- Training for police about aging, communication techniques with elderly citizens, victimization of the elderly, and management programs utilizing older volunteers.

Joint Resolution

WHEREAS,   the proportion of senior citizens in the population is increasing at a significant rate in Illinois and the entire United States, and

WHEREAS,   the State's rapidly increasing senior population has special needs, especially relating to certain types of crime and the resulting feelings of vulnerability and fear of victimization, directly affect their quality of life, and

WHEREAS,   older Americans present unique challenges, as well as an important source of support to the law enforcement community, and

WHEREAS,   in many communities the needs of the elderly are only partially being met by law enforcement agencies' policies and programs, and

WHEREAS,   it is incumbent upon law enforcement agencies to formulate and execute policies and programs to enhance the service and protection for the safety and welfare of the older citizens in their communities, and

WHEREAS,   the National Sheriff's Association, the International Association of Chiefs of Police, and the American Association of Retired Persons have agreed to undertake joint activity, renewing their emphasis on the needs and concerns of senior citizens, and have adopted a resolution encouraging the formation of senior advisory councils to be called S.A.L.T. (Seniors and Law Enforcement Together) groups

THEREFORE,   BE IT RESOLVED that the **Illinois Association of Chiefs of Police**, the **Illinois Sheriff's Association**, and the **Illinois State Leadership Council of the American Association of Retired Persons** agree to work jointly to develop and implement policies and programs to reduce criminal victimization of senior citizens, serve the special needs of older victims, and enhance the delivery of law enforcement services to the elderly.

ADOPTED,   this 11th day of July in the year of our Lord nineteen hundred and ninety at Chicago, Illinois.

_____
State Director, Illinois
American Association of Retired Persons

_____
President
Illinois Association of Chiefs of Police

_____
President
Illinois Sheriff's Association

FIGURE 7.3   Joint Resolution

As noted by Miller: "Concern for older people is neither radical or new. However, the idea that law enforcement leaders should form a partnership with leaders of the elderly in their communities is new and is a concrete example of community policing."

Leadership is provided by an advisory group of older persons and those providing services to the elderly. This group is called S.A.L.T. (Seniors and Lawmen Together). This group helps law enforcement departments determine the crime and public safety-related needs and concerns of the elderly and suggests services to meet those needs.

The organizational structure of S.A.L.T. is illustrated in Figure 7.4.

RECOMMENDATIONS OF THE POLICE FOUNDATION

The Police Foundation (Sulton, 1990, p. 104) has made the following recommendations for combatting crimes against the elderly:

- Programs similar to Cleveland's Community Re-Entry and the Detroit Police Department Junior Police Cadet Section should be adopted by inner-city communities. Such programs raise public awareness concerning crimes against the elderly; foster an attitude of help, safety, and caring toward the elderly; form partnerships and alliances to protect the elderly; and teach youth to appreciate and respect the elderly.
- Police should help reduce senior citizen fear of crime by providing them with information about the extent of crime in their neighborhoods.
- Senior citizen advisory councils should be established. These councils should: (a) provide support systems for the elderly; (b) encourage the elderly to participate in community activities; (c) operate programs that reduce the elderly's victimization and fear of crime; (d) match senior citizens with youth who will assist them with shopping, banking, letter writing, and other activities; and (e) advise service providers of the elderly's needs.
- Public agencies and private organizations should provide financial and personnel resources to help senior citizens develop programs to increase their participation in community life.

Summary

The *graying of America* is a metaphor that reflects the fact that our population is aging. The average American lives longer than previous generations, the general population is becoming older, and the percentage of elderly people in our society is increasing. The fear of crime among

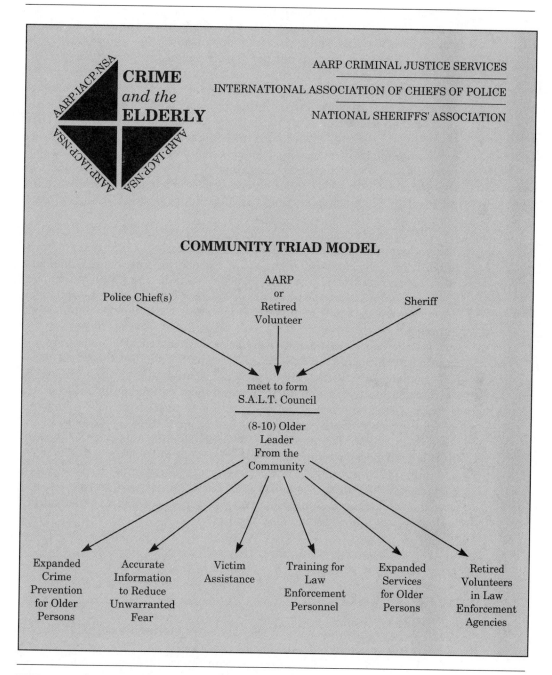

FIGURE 7.4   Community Triad Model

SOURCE: *Crime and the Elderly,* AARP Criminal Justice Services. Reprinted by permission.

the elderly in some communities makes them prisoners in their own homes. Yet people aged sixty-five and older have the lowest rate of victimization in this country both in violent and property crimes.

The increasing age of our population suggests that the elderly will be victimized more often simply because they will be a large target population, some very vulnerable, some very wealthy. The number of elderly people involved in committing crime is also likely to increase, presenting a great challenge to the criminal justice system, particularly corrections. Likewise, elder abuse may increase.

Elder abuse involves physical and emotional abuse, financial exploitation, and general neglect. The extent of elder abuse is unknown. In cases of elder abuse the police should express concern and empathy for all involved. The solution should involve appropriate professional support services.

The elderly may also be victims of Alzheimer's disease (AD), a progressive, irreversible brain disease affecting four million elderly Americans. Symptoms of Alzheimer's disease include gradual memory loss, impairment of judgment, disorientation, personality change, decline in ability to perform routine tasks, behavior change, difficulty in learning, loss of language skills, and a decline in intellectual function.

Alzheimer's victims may wander or become lost, engage in inappropriate sexual behavior, lose impulse control, shoplift, falsely accuse others, drive erratically, and appear intoxicated. Many of the symptoms of intoxication and Alzheimer's are identical: confusion, disorientation, problems with short-term memory, problems with language, sight and coordination, combativeness and in extreme reaction cases, loss of contact with reality. The cardinal rule police should follow when dealing with an AD patient is to avoid the catastrophic reaction.

The existence of a growing number of elderly individuals within a community has many benefits. One such benefit is that seniors are excellent volunteers. Police departments across the country use elderly volunteers to staff innovative programs.

DISCUSSION QUESTIONS _____

1. Do you know individuals who are caring for aging parents? How are they coping?
2. Have any cases of elder abuse been reported in your community recently? In your state?
3. What problems might police officers encounter when working with the staffs of nursing homes?
4. What resources does your community have for the elderly?

5. Do you know anyone who has Alzheimer's disease? What changes have they experienced?
6. Does your police department use elderly citizen volunteers? If so, how?
7. Does your police department provide support for retired officers?
8. In what specific ways might individual officers improve their interactions with the elderly?
9. Has the graying of America affected your community? If so, how?
10. What do you think your main concerns will be when you are a "senior citizen"?

DEFINITIONS
Can you define these terms: AARP, AD, Alzheimer's disease, catastrophic reaction, elder abuse, granny bashing, granny dumping, graying of America.

REFERENCES

"Alzheimer's Alert," *Law Enforcement Technology.* (January, 1993): 52.

Bowes, William B. "The Problems of Older Drivers." *Law and Order.* (May 1992): 13, 16.

Brunswick, Mark and Wolfe, Warren. "Reality of Crime Against Elderly Not as Great as Fear it Prompts." *Star Tribune.* (April 2, 1992): 1A, 16A.

Egan, Timothy. "Society's Doorstep Becomes Dumping Ground for Elderly." *Star Tribune,* citing *The New York Times.* (March 27, 1992): 4A.

Enter, Jack E. "Police Administration in the Future: Demographic Influences as they Relate to Management of the Internal and External Environment." *American Journal of Police.* Vol. X., No. 4, (1991): 65–81.

Godwin, David W. "Police Services and the Elderly." *Law and Order.* (June 1992): 68–71.

Lindquist, J. H. and Duke, J. M. "The Elderly Victim at Risk: Explaining the Fear-Victimization Paradox." 55–65 In *Exploring Crime: Readings in Criminology and Criminal Justice,* edited by J. F. Sheley. Belmont: Wadsworth, 1987.

Lipman, Ira A. *How to Protect Yourself from Crime.* New York: Avon Books, 1981.

Miller, William D. "The Graying of America: Implications Towards Policing." *Law and Order.* (October 1991): 96–97.

Naisbitt, J. and Aburdene, P. *Megatrends 2000: Ten New Directions for the 1990s.* New York: William Morrow and Company, 1990.

National Crime Prevention Council. *Topics in Crime Prevention.* October 1988.

Plotkin, Martha R. *A Time for Dignity. Police and Domestic Abuse of the Elderly.* Washington: Police Executive Research Forum, 1988.

Sulton, Anne Thomas. *Inner-City Crime Control: Can Community Institutions Contribute?* Washington: The Police Foundation, 1990.

"Victim, Not Criminal: The Alzheimer Sufferer." Chicago: The Alzheimer's Disease and Related Disorders Association, Inc., 1987.

RESOURCES

Alzheimer's Disease and Related Disorders Association, Inc., 70 E. Lake Street, Chicago, IL 60601-5997; (312) 853-3030, (800) 572-6037, (800) 372-3900.

American Association of Retired Persons (AARP), 601 E. Street N.W., Washington, D.C. 20049; (202) 434-2277.

INTERACTING WITH YOUTH: VICTIMS AND OFFENDERS

The moral test of government is how it treats those who are in the dawn of life, the children.

—**Hubert H. Humphrey**

DO YOU KNOW

- At what age most states consider an individual an adult?
- What *parens patriae* is?
- What three kinds of youth are combined into one "jurisdictional pot"?
- What status offenses are?
- What the *Big D*'s of juvenile justice are?
- How a welfare model and a justice model differ? Which is most often used in the 1990s?
- What street justice is?
- What crimes youth might be victims of?
- What a police officer's first concern is with an abused or neglected child?
- What youths with special needs police officers should be familiar with?

INTRODUCTION

A frequently overlooked segment of the population that is important to police-community relations is youth. Youth lack economic and political power; therefore, their problems may not command the attention they deserve. Many of our nation's youth are victimized; many others commit violent crimes. A community's youth poses significant challenges to law enforcement. The police should adopt a proactive approach toward the potential problems of the young.

> Of all minority groups, the most important one is the young. Their importance is emphasized because they represent all segments of society. The future of this nation depends upon the values they are forming. They obviously will be the future decision-makers of our society. . . .
>
> The law, to a young person, is often considered a "necessary evil." They do not understand the law, nor do they usually wish to learn about it. Rebellion against most laws, and especially those concerning the control of traffic, generates much hostility and animosity among the young.
>
> This hostility to law is naturally projected to police officers because they represent the negative forces that impose impossible sanctions. It is often said that the young do not like the police and the feeling is often mutual (Pace, 1991, pp. 108–9).

Frequently, the only contact police have with the young is with those who create problems or break the law. Consequently, police officers may stereotype youth, especially teenagers. Since the police do not interact with many preschool children, they are not considered a problem. Yet it is during the preschool years that many of our youth's problems begin.

According to Hodgkinson (1991, p. 10) the following examples illustrate the "spectacular changes" in our society that affect our youth and have implications for law enforcement:

- One-third are at risk of school failure even before they enter kindergarten.
- Since 1987, one-fourth of all pre-school children in the U.S. have been in poverty.

- Every year, about 350,000 children are born to mothers who were addicted to cocaine during pregnancy. Those who survive birth become children with strikingly short attention spans, poor coordination, and much worse.
- Today, 15 million children are being reared by single mothers, whose family income averages about $11,400 in 1988 dollars.
- Twenty percent of America's preschool children have not been vaccinated against polio.
- The **"Norman Rockwell"family**—a working father, a housewife mother, and two children of school age—constitutes only 6% of U.S. households today.
- One-fourth of pregnant mothers receive no physical care of any sort during the crucial first trimester of pregnancy. About 20% of handicapped children would not be impaired had their mothers had one physical exam during the first trimester, which could have detected potential problems.
- At least two million school-age children have no adult supervision at all after school. Two million are being reared by *neither* parent.
- On any given night, between 50,000 and 200,000 children have no home.
- In 1987, child protection agencies received 2.2 million reports of child abuse or neglect—triple the number received in 1976.
- Today, more than 80% of America's one million prisoners are high school dropouts (costing taxpayers upwards of $20,000 each per year).

Hodgkinson (p. 16) contends: "America's children are truly an 'endangered species,'" a fact society must address.

YOUTH DEFINED

Each state establishes its own age defining youth, ranging from sixteen to nineteen years.

> The most common age for an individual to legally become an adult is eighteen.

Table 8.1 summarizes the age at which young people are officially considered adults in each state.

Before addressing the specific challenges youth present to law enforcement, consider how the juvenile justice system affects the way police officers interact with youth.

TABLE 8.1
Age at Which U.S. Criminal Courts Gain Jurisdiction over Young Offenders

Age 16	Age 17	Age 18		Age 19
Connecticut	Georgia	Alabama	Nebraska	Wyoming
New York	Illinois	Alaska	Nevada	
N. Carolina	Louisiana	Arizona	New Hampshire	
	Massachusetts	Arkansas	New Jersey	
	Michigan	California	New Mexico	
	Missouri	Colorado	N. Dakota	
	S. Carolina	Delaware	Ohio	
	Texas	D. of Columbia	Oklahoma	
		Florida	Oregon	
		Hawaii	Pennsylvania	
		Idaho	Rhode Island	
		Indiana	S. Dakota	
		Iowa	Tennessee	
		Kansas	Utah	
		Kentucky	Vermont	
		Maine	Virginia	
		Maryland	Washington	
		Minnesota	W. Virginia	
		Mississippi	Wisconsin	
		Montana	Federal Districts	

SOURCE: Linda A. Szymanski. "Upper age of juvenile court jurisdiction statutes analysis." Washington: National Center for Juvenile Justice. (March 1987)

A Brief Overview of Juvenile Justice in the United States

For police officers to effectively interact with their community's youth, it is important for officers to understand how the juvenile justice system differs from the adult system and the implications such differences have.

The basic assumption upon which the juvenile justice system rests is that of *parens patriae*.

Parens patriae refers to the government's right to take care of minors and others who cannot legally take care of themselves.

The concept of *parens patriae* originated in thirteenth century England where common law established that the king was truly the "father of his country." As such the king was the guardian of all children. Children were considered wards of the state. The common law notion of

Youth in Austin, Texas receive anti-drug message from a police officer.

parens patriae is firmly entrenched in our system of juvenile justice. Krisberg (1991, p. 152) describes the evolution of the juvenile justice system:

> *Early reformers envisioned a special prison system for wayward youth that would emphasize education, industry, and moral training. . . . Throughout the nineteenth century, the practice of incarcerating wayward youth expanded. . . .*

Griffin and Griffin (1978, p. 20) outline the following significant events underlying our juvenile justice system:

- 1818 Juvenile delinquency defined.
- 1825 First House of Refuge established in the United States.
- 1847 State reform and industrial schools founded.
- 1869 First official use of probation (Massachusetts).
- 1870 First use of separate trials for juveniles (Massachusetts).
- 1877 Separate dockets and records established for juveniles (Massachusetts).
- 1880 First probation system applicable to juveniles instituted.
- 1898 Segregation of children under age sixteen awaiting trial (Rhode Island).
- 1899 First juvenile court established (Illinois).

In 1818 the term *juvenile delinquency* was first used. The term was equated with pauperism, that is, being poor. In 1825, delinquency was equated with poverty when the New York House of Refuge was opened to house juvenile delinquents. Its charter defined juvenile delinquents as "youths convicted of criminal offenses or found in vagrancy." The link between delinquency and poverty was strengthened by the first juvenile court act, passed in Illinois in 1899. The purpose of this act was to regulate the treatment and control of dependent, neglected, and delinquent children, again equating poor children and those in need of protection with children who committed crimes and treating them in essentially the same way.

Our juvenile justice system uses a **one-pot jurisdictional approach:** children who are abused or neglected, those who are status offenders, and those who are truly criminal are all treated the same way.

According to Springer (1986, p. 45):

One of the major failings in the juvenile court system is what can be referred to as the "one-pot" jurisdictional approach—putting poor, rebellious, and criminal children in the same jurisdictional pot. . . .

All three kinds of children were thought to be the products or victims of bad family and social environments; consequently, it was thought, they should be subject, as wards of the court, to the same kind of solicitous, helpful care.

At the end of the nineteenth century a group of reformers, mostly women, became known as the "child-savers." These reformers believed that "troublesome" youth could be "saved" by removing them from their homes and placing them in a "proper" environment. Their efforts led to legislation that authorized widespread governmental family intervention. This form of intervention continued for several decades.

By 1900 the juvenile justice system was very distinct from the adult system. Table 8.2 presents the current similarities and differences between the juvenile and adult justice systems.

Table 8.3 compares the different terminology used in juvenile and adult courts. The differences in terminology evidence a very basic difference in philosophy and approach.

An extremely important aspect of the juvenile justice system is its establishment of status offenses.

Status offenses are actions by a juvenile that would not be considered criminal acts if done by an adult, for example, truancy or smoking cigarettes.

TABLE 8.2
Similarities and Differences between the Juvenile and Adult Justice Systems

Similarities	Differences
1. Discretion in decision making is used by police officers, judges, and correctional personnel in both adult and juvenile systems.	1. The primary purpose of juvenile procedures is protection and treatment; with adults, the aim is punishment of the guilty.
2. Search and seizure law and the Fourth Amendment apply to juvenile and adult offenders.	2. The jurisdiction of the juvenile court is determined chiefly by age; in the adult system, jurisdiction is determined primarily by the nature of the offense.
3. The right to receive the *Miranda* warning applies to juveniles as well as to adults.	3. Juveniles can be held responsible for acts that would not be criminal if they were committed by an adult (status offenses).
4. Juveniles are protected, as are adults, from prejudicial lineups or other identification procedures.	4. Juvenile proceedings are not considered criminal, whereas adult proceedings are.
5. Procedural safeguards similar to those of adults protect juveniles when they make an admission of guilt.	5. Juvenile court procedures are generally informal and private; those of adult courts are more formal and open to the public.
6. Prosecutors and defense attorneys play an equally critical role in juvenile and adult advocacy.	6. Courts cannot release identifying information to the press concerning a juvenile, but must do so in cases involving adults.
7. Juveniles, like adults, have the right to counsel at most key stages of the court process.	7. Parents are highly involved in the juvenile process; with adults, this would not be the case.
8. Pretrial motions are available in juvenile and criminal court proceedings.	8. The standard of arrest is more stringent for adults than for juveniles.
9. Negotiations and plea bargaining are used with juvenile and adult offenders.	9. As a practical matter, juveniles are released into parental custody, whereas adults are generally given the opportunity for bail.
10. Children and adults have a right to a trial and appeal.	10. Plea bargaining is used in most adult cases, whereas most juvenile cases are settled by open admission of guilt.
11. The standard of evidence in juvenile delinquency adjudications, as in adult criminal trials, is that of proof beyond a reasonable doubt.	11. Juveniles have no constitutional right to a jury trial; adults do have this right.
12. Like adults, children waived from the juvenile court can receive the death penalty.	12. Juvenile dispositional decisions are ordinarily based on indeterminate terms, whereas adults' sentences include proportionality and definiteness.

TABLE 8.2 (Continued)
Similarities and Differences between the Juvenile and Adult Justice Systems

Similarities	Differences
	13. The procedural rights of juveniles are based on the concept of "fundamental fairness"; those of adults are based on the constitutional right to due process under the Bill of Rights and the Fourteenth Amendment.
	14. Juveniles have the right to treatment under the Fourteenth Amendment; adult offenders have no such recognized right.
	15. A juvenile's record is sealed when the age of majority is reached; the record of an adult is permanent.

SOURCE: Joseph J. Senna and Larry J. Siegel. *Introduction to Criminal Justice,* 5th rev. ed. St. Paul: West Publishing Company, 1990: 633. Reprinted by permission.

TABLE 8.3
The Language of Juvenile and Adult Courts

Juvenile Court Term	Adult Court Term
Adjudication: decision by the judge that a child has committed delinquent acts.	Conviction of guilt
Adjudicatory hearing: a hearing to determine whether the allegations of a petition are supported by the evidence beyond a reasonable doubt.	Trial
Adjustment: the settling of a matter so that parties agree without official intervention by the court.	Plea bargaining
Aftercare: the supervision given to a child for a limited period of time after he or she is released from training school but while he or she is still under the control of the juvenile court.	Parole
Commitment: a decision by the judge to send a child to training school.	Sentence to imprisonment
Delinquent act: an act that if committed by an adult would be called a crime. The term does not include such ambiguities and noncrimes as "being ungovernable," "truancy," "incorrigibility," and "disobedience."	Crime

TABLE 8.3 (Continued)
The Language of Juvenile and Adult Courts

Juvenile Court Term	Adult Court Term
Delinquent child: a child who is found to have committed an act that would be considered a crime if committed by an adult.	Criminal
Detention: temporary care of an allegedly delinquent child who requires secure custody in physically restricting facilities pending court disposition or execution of a court order.	Holding in jail
Dispositional hearing: a hearing held subsequent to the adjudicatory hearing to determine what order of disposition should be made for a child adjudicated as delinquent.	Sentencing hearing
Hearing: the presentation of evidence to the juvenile court judge, his or her consideration of it, and his or her decision on disposition of the case.	Trial
Juvenile court: the court that has jurisdiction over children who are alleged to be or found to be delinquent. Juvenile delinquency procedures should not be used for neglected children or for those who need supervision.	Court of record
Petition: an application for a court order or some other judicial action. Hence, a "delinquency petition" is an application for the court to act in a matter involving a juvenile apprehended for a delinquent act.	Accusation or indictment
Probation: the supervision of a delinquent child after the court hearing but without commitment to training school.	Probation (with the same meaning as the juvenile court term)
Residential child care facility: a dwelling (other than a detention or shelter care facility) that is licensed to provide living accommodations, care, treatment, and maintenance for children and youths. Such facilities include foster homes, group homes, and halfway houses.	Halfway house
Shelter: temporary care of a child in physically unrestricting facilities pending court disposition or execution of a court order for placement. Shelter care is used for dependent and neglected children and minors in need of supervision. Separate shelter care facilities are also used for children apprehended for delinquency who need temporary shelter but not secure detention.	Jail
Take into custody: the act of the police in securing the physical custody of a child engaged in delinquency. The term is used to avoid the stigma of the word "arrest."	Arrest

SOURCE: Reprinted by permission from Harold J. Vetter and Leonard Territo. *Crime and Justice in America: A Human Perspective*, St. Paul: West Publishing Company, 1984.

Status offenses are certain actions considered crimes if done by those under legal age. They are not crimes if committed by adults. In most states, status offenses include truancy, running away, curfew violations, smoking cigarettes, drinking alcoholic beverages, and "incorrigibility."

The philosophy of the first juvenile courts was to view children as basically good and in need of help—this approach is commonly referred to as the **welfare model.**

> *During the 1960s a series of major U.S. Supreme Court decisions fundamentally changed the Court's character. . . . A consensus emerged on behalf of limiting formal court intervention in children's lives. . . . From the late 1970s, a very different and more conservative political agenda dominated the juvenile justice policy arena. . . . As the juvenile court moves toward a punishment model, more attention must be paid to issues of due process, equal protection, and proportionality of sanctions (Krisberg, 1991, pp. 153–59).*

In the 1960s and early 1970s the national emphasis on civil rights greatly affected the juvenile justice system. The following milestone cases in juvenile justice continue to shape the manner in which law enforcement responds to youthful offenders:

- 1966—*Kent v. United States* established that if a juvenile court waives jurisdiction and transfers a case to adult court, it must follow the dictates of due process and fair treatment.
- 1967—*In re Gault* established that juveniles have the same constitutional rights as adults: notice of charges, right to counsel, right to cross-examine and to confront witnesses, and privilege against self-incrimination.
- 1970—*In re Winship* established that in a juvenile court hearing, the youth must be proven guilty beyond a reasonable doubt, just as in adult criminal court. (The former standards were preponderance of evidence, clear and convincing proof, and reasonable proof.)
- 1971—*McKeiver v. Pennsylvania* established that juveniles do *not* have the right to a jury trial in the juvenile court system.

The 1970s focused on the four Big D's as described by Drowns and Hess (1990, p. 192).

The **Big D's of juvenile justice** are diversion, decriminalization, deinstitutionalization, and due process.

Blomberg (1980, p. 572) explains the rationale underlying **diversion,** that is, finding alternatives to placing juveniles into detention facilities: "A major conceptual rationale underlying the diversion concept was that reducing offender insertion into the justice system would avoid the danger assumed to be associated with criminal stigmatization and criminal association, thereby reducing the likelihood of subsequent crime by the offender."

Decriminalization refers to the efforts to make status offenses noncriminal actions. **Deinstitutionalization,** as the name implies, refers to efforts to release incarcerated youth through parole and community programs. **Due process** suggests that the advances made in the rights of youth continued to be important considerations in the 1970s.

Another important case involving juveniles is *Schall v. Martin* (1984). This case established the state's right to place juveniles in preventive detention, to protect both the youth and society.

The 1980s brought reform in the juvenile justice system; a change from the welfare model to a justice model. As noted by Springer (1986, p. 2):

> *The first step in doing justice for juveniles is to revise juvenile court acts throughout the country so that when juvenile courts deal with delinquent children, they operate under a justice model rather than under the present treatment or child welfare model. By a justice model is meant a judicial process wherein young people who come in conflict with the law are held responsible and accountable for their behavior.*

A justice model views youth as responsible for their actions. Under the justice model, the good of society takes precedence over society's responsibility to take care of its children.

Springer (p. 2) contends that: "Except for certain mentally disabled and incompetent individuals, young law violators should not be considered by the juvenile courts as being 'sick' or as victims of their environment. Generally speaking, young criminals are more wrong than wronged, more the victimizers than the victims." Springer (p. 33) further notes: "It is time that we recognize the impossible double bind our juvenile judges are placed in when they, judicial officers, are commanded to diagnose the 'problem' of some young offender, when in most cases it is obvious that the criminal youth does not have a problem—he or she *is the problem.*"

This "get tough" attitude has been criticized by some, however, such as Brodt and Smith (1991, p. 176) who suggest:

> *In practice, getting tough means "let's get tough" with the following groups: (1) blacks; (2) Chicanos; (3) the poor; (4) the uneducated; (5) youth from single parent families; (6) the unemployed; (7) illegitimate youth; (8) welfare families; and (9) abused children.*

This criticism might be addressed, in part, by making the changes Springer proposes in the juvenile justice system. Springer (p. 40) calls for the juvenile justice system to be divided into two categories: civil and criminal. Two subcategories would be within the civil category: (1) children who are endangered, abused, or neglected; and (2) youth who commit status offenses. It is important for police officers to understand that the current juvenile justice system makes no such distinction. Consequently, police officers often use their discretionary powers and make the distinction themselves.

Street justice occurs when police officers use their discretionary powers to simply talk to or warn youthful offenders rather than taking them into custody.

Street justice may also involve talking to the youth's parents and/or making referrals to a social service agency.

THE CHALLENGE OF YOUTH WHO ARE VICTIMS

Police officers need to be informed about the various ways in which youth can be victimized. Officers should understand why young people may act as they do and the type of assistance they might need.

Youth may be victims of abuse, homelessness, or lead poisoning.

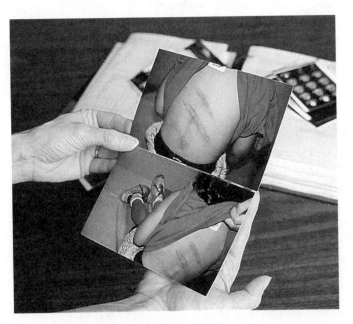

Photographs of a child abuse victim beaten with a broomstick by his father.

"Fourteen of 100 children between the ages of 3 and 17 experience family violence" (Straus and Kantor, 1988, p. 49). As noted by Craig (1992, p. 67): "For some children, family violence is so severe that it results in intervention by public authorities. For many other youngsters, it remains a secret destroyer that slowly permeates the fabric of self and distorts the content of all relationships."

The primary responsibility of police officers who deal with abused or neglected children is to protect the child, remove him or her from the home if necessary, and collaborate with social service agencies to assure that the needs of the child are met.

The dedication in *Deprived Children: A Judicial Response* notes: "The efforts of skilled and committed judges, legislators, law enforcement officers, health and child care workers, doctors, teachers, attorneys, volunteers and others involved in the lives of deprived children can do little without a rekindled national awareness that the family is the foundation for the protection, care and training of our children."

There is a correlation between children who have been abused and those who commit criminal acts. A national expert on child abuse and neglect, Robert ten Bensel, has gathered a large body of evidence linking child abuse and neglect to later violent criminality (Springer, 1986, p. 76):

> *Studies have shown that virtually all violent juvenile delinquents have been abused children, that all criminals at San Quentin prison . . . studied had violent upbringings as children, and that all assassins . . . in the United States during the past twenty years had been victims of child abuse.*

Another group of youthful victims are those who are homeless, either because they are runaways, throwaways (their family has kicked them out), or their entire family is homeless. Stevens and Price (1992, p. 18) note that more than 300,000 school-age children are homeless each year.

Stevens and Price also note that three to four million children have been exposed to damaging levels of lead. The seriousness of this problem is reflected in the declaration of the Public Health Service that "lead poisoning remains the most common and societally devastating environmental disease of young children" (Needleman, 1992, p. 35). Needleman notes that:

> *Being poor increases a child's risk radically. The ATSDR [Agency for Toxic Substances and Disease Registry] estimates that 7% of well-off white children have elevated blood lead levels; for poor whites, the proportion is 25%. Of poor African-American children,*

55% have elevated levels. More than half of African-American children who live in poverty begin their education with this potentially handicapping condition. Lead exposure may be one of the most important—and least acknowledged—causes of school failure and learning disorders.

YOUTH WITH SPECIAL NEEDS AND THE POLICE OFFICER

Police officers may have to deal with children who have very special needs.

Children with special needs include those who are emotionally/behaviorally disturbed, who have learning disabilities, who have an attention deficit hyperactivity disorder, or who have behavior problems resulting from prenatal exposure to drugs, including alcohol or to HIV.

Emotionally/Behaviorally Disturbed Children

One group of young people police will encounter are emotionally/behaviorally disturbed children, often referred to as **EBD.** Usually EBD youth exhibit one or more of the following behavioral patterns:

- Severely aggressive or impulsive behavior.
- Severely withdrawn or anxious behavior such as pervasive unhappiness, depression, or wide mood swings.
- Severely disordered thought processes that are reflected in unusual behavior patterns, atypical communication styles, and distorted interpersonal relationships.

Parents and teachers in some communities have expressed concerns that children labeled as EBD have less coping skills to deal with police contacts than other children and may be traumatized by such contacts. Suggestions that police not interview or contact such children unless an EBD specialist is present have, for the most part, not been implemented because it is usually impossible for the police to know who is EBD and who is not.

Police may assume that a large percentage of children who are suspects in crimes are EBD and that condition is one of the causes of their unlawful behavior. It is not possible, however, to arrange for an EBD specialist to be present at all police contacts because a majority of contacts are unplanned, unscheduled events that occur on the street.

Youth with Attention Deficit Hyperactivity Disorder

Attention deficit hyperactivity disorder (ADHD) is one of the most common disruptive behavior disorders in children. It is estimated that five to ten percent of all children have the disorder; boys are four times more likely than girls to be diagnosed with it. This disorder is characterized by the following behaviors:

- Heightened motor activity (fidgeting and squirming).
- Short attention span.
- Distractibility.
- Impulsiveness.
- Lack of self-control.

Such behaviors are likely to be very unnerving for parents, teachers, and other adults who must deal with children who have this disorder.

The *Washington Post* (1993, p. 7A) notes: "Children with ADHD . . . often do poorly in school, have low self-esteem, and try the patience of parents and friends. The condition is treated with behavior modification and often with a drug called Ritalin." Although the condition often disappears by adulthood, by then former ADHD children often have other behavior problems including drug abuse, alcoholism, or personality disorders.

Youth with Learning Disabilities

An estimated five to ten million children suffer from some form of learning disability in the United States. The Association for Children with Learning Disabilities (ACLD) (p. 4) describes a learning disabled child in the following way.

A person with a **learning disability** is an individual who has one or more significant deficits in the essential learning processes.

The federal government, in The Education of All Handicapped Children Act, defines a learning disability as follows:

Specific learning disability means a disorder in one or more of the basic psychological processes involved in understanding or in using language, spoken or written, which may manifest itself in an imperfect ability to listen, think, speak, read, write, spell, or to do mathematical calculations. The term includes such conditions as perceptual handicaps, brain injury, minimal brain dysfunction, dyslexia, and developmental aphasia. The term does not include children who have learning problems which are primarily the result of visual, hearing or motor handicaps, of mental retardation, of emotional disturbance or of environmental, cultural, or economic disadvantage.

According to the ACLD (p. 3): "The most frequently displayed symptoms are short attention span, poor memory, difficulty following directions, inadequate ability to discriminate between and among letters, numerals, or sounds, poor reading ability, eye-hand coordination problems, difficulties with sequencing, disorganization and numerous other problems." Such children are often discipline problems, are labeled "underachievers," and are at great risk of becoming dropouts.

Although learning disabilities are usually discussed in an educational context, as noted by the ACLD (p. 8): "The consequences are rarely confined to school or work." Characteristics which may bring a learning disabled youth into conflict with the law include the following:

- Responds inappropriately in many instances.
- Says one thing, means another.
- Forgets easily.
- Is impulsive.
- Needs immediate gratification.
- Has an overabundance of frustration resulting in disruptive behavior.

Other behaviors which are common to youth with learning disabilities include the following (ACLD, p. 8):

- Inability to read and interpret environment and people.
- Inability to adequately interpret their problems and needs.
- Little thought about the consequences of their actions—poor judgment.
- Inability to set realistic priorities and goals.
- Inappropriate conclusions due to deficient reasoning ability.
- Illogical reasons for their actions—sometimes even contradicting what was previously stated.
- Inability to develop meaningful social relationships with others; usually these children are loners.
- Inability to draw appropriate conclusions due to poor reasoning.
- Childish and bossy behavior.

Those who interact with such children need to be patient and communicate effectively. Youth with learning disabilities look like their peers. Inwardly, however, most are very frustrated, have experienced failure after failure, and have extremely low self-esteem.

Youth Exposed to Drugs or HIV Prenatally

Noted pediatrician T. Berry Brazelton (1990, p. 1) suggests: "Intrauterine exposure to drugs is the epidemic of the 1990s. Drug abuse is not new. . . . But the threat today is like a tidal wave." Sautter (1992, p. K2) cites the following statistics from the National Institute on Drug Abuse:

- The number of drug-exposed children born each year ranges from 375,000 to 739,000—possibly 18% of all newborns in the United States.
- Nearly 5% have been exposed to cocaine, from which crack is derived.
- Nearly 17% have been exposed to marijuana.
- Nearly 73% have been exposed to alcohol.
- By the year 2000 as many as *four million* drug-exposed children will be attending school.

The term **crack children** is sometimes used to refer to children who were exposed to cocaine while in the womb. They may exhibit social, emotional, and cognitive problems. As noted by Downing (1990, p. 9):

> *These children, exposed to the damaging effects of cocaine (commonly in its less expensive and highly-addictive crystalized form: crack) while still in the womb, are already showing up in significant numbers in kindergarten classes and preschool programs in New York and Los Angeles. . . .*
>
> *They may over-react to—or fail to respond to—the stimuli of a classroom. They may have difficulty forming attachments. They may not be capable of structuring their own play or playing with other children.*
>
> *Typically, these kids do not socialize well, do not work well in groups, and stimulate too easily or do not respond at all—they can be either hyperactive or lethargic.*

Griffith (1992, p. 30) cautions against stereotyping such children, however, noting that: "[T]he media have sensationalized the problems these children present and have shown worst-case scenarios as if they were the norm."

Another pressing problem is that of **fetal alcohol syndrome (FAS)**. Burgess and Streissguth (1992, p. 24) suggest: "Fetal alcohol syndrome (FAS) is now recognized as the leading known cause of mental retardation in the western world." They estimate that approximately one in 500 to 600 children is born with FAS and one in 300 to 350 children has FAS effects, including the following:

- Impulsivity and poor communication skills.
- Inability to predict consequences or to use appropriate judgment in daily life.
- Small children may exhibit a high level of activity and distractibility.
- Adolescents may suffer frustration and depression.

Tyler (1992, p. 711) cites the following "classic symptoms of drug–damaged children":

- Attention deficit disorder (the child has difficulty concentrating and is easily distracted).
- Hyperactivity (the child is unable to sit still, to be quiet, or to control movement).
- Poor coordination (the child is clumsy, unable to control crayons or scissors).
- Low tolerance level (the child is easily frustrated by tasks and gives up quickly).
- Unpredictability (the child has mood swings, temper tantrums).
- Poor memory (the child has trouble following three-step directions).
- Indications of drug use in the home.

Police officers should be aware of these classic symptoms and recognize that they reflect a condition over which the youth has limited or no control.

Yet another group of children at risk and presenting special problems to law enforcement are children who were prenatally exposed to HIV. Scott et al. (1989, p. 1791) notes: "Today, a disproportionate number of children with HIV infection come from low-income, minority families in our inner cities and acquire the virus from maternal transmission." Such children may experience the following difficulties (Seidel (1992, p. 39):

- Deficits in both gross and fine motor skills.
- Reduced flexibility and muscle strength.
- Cognitive impairment including decreased intellectual levels, specific learning disabilities, mental retardation, visual/spatial deficits, and decreased alertness.
- Language delays.

Youth with special needs are entering grade schools in the early part of 1990, and will be adolescents in the latter part of the decade. Many are likely to be in contact with the police long before then and many may become status offenders. Others may become more serious offenders. Many youth with special needs are likely to join gangs.

STATUS OFFENDERS AND THE LAW _____

For centuries a double standard has existed for that which is expected of youth and of adults. Consider the "offenses" described in the following quote:

> *The children now love luxury. They have bad manners, contempt for authority, they show disrespect for elders, love chatter in place of exercise. They no longer rise when their elders enter the room. They contradict their parents, chatter before company, gobble up their dainties at the table, cross their legs, and tyrannize over their teachers.*

Some behavior by youth is illegal only by virtue of age. Youth may feel guilty about such "illegal" actions as smoking, or they may view them as a way to flaunt the rules.

Many readers may nod in agreement. This quote, however, is not about the youth of today. It was written by Socrates in 500 B.C.

The Police Response

Between eighty and ninety percent of children under eighteen commit some offense for which they could be arrested, yet only about three percent of them ever are (*Criminal Justice* 88/89, p. 159). The reason for the low percentage of arrests is police discretion. Of those who do come into the juvenile justice system, eighty-four percent are from law enforcement referrals. Police most commonly release minor offenders, with or without a warning, and without making an official record or taking further action. This is called **station adjustment.** These children, many of whom desperately need help of some kind, are not referred on to the proper social agency in the community where such help is available.

The police response usually is based on two factors: the specific incident and the "demeanor" of the youthful offender. If the incident is minor and the offender is respectful and appears contrite, the police will usually drop the matter. The older the offender, the more likely the police will be to take official action.

Senna and Siegel (1990, p. 655), in discussing what to do with status offenders, state:

> *Since its inception, the DSO [deinstitutionalization of status offenders] approach has been hotly debated. Some have argued that early intervention is society's best hope of forestalling future delinquent behavior and reducing victimization. Others have argued that legal control over status offenders is a violation of youth's rights. Still others have viewed status-offending behavior as a symptom of some larger trauma or problem that requires attention. These diverse opinions still exist today.*

YOUTH WHO COMMIT SERIOUS CRIMES AND THE LAW

According to Regnery (1991, p. 165): "Juveniles do commit crimes at a rate significantly higher than the rest of the population. In fact, 16-year old boys commit crimes at a higher rate than any other single age group. These are criminals who happen to be young, not children who happen to commit crimes."

The scene pictured in "Kids Who Kill" (Witkin, 1991, p. 181–82) graphically portrays the deadliness of some youth:

The datelines change daily, but the stories are chillingly similar.
In Washington D.C., 15-year-old Jermaine Daniel is shot to death
by his best friend. In New Haven, Conn., Markiest Alexander, 14,
is killed in a drive-by shooting. In St. Louis, Leo Wilson, 16, is
robbed of his tennis shoes and Raiders jacket and then shot dead.
In New York, a 14-year-old boy opens up with a semiautomatic
pistol in a Bronx schoolyard, wounding one youngster and
narrowly missing another, apparently in a dispute over a girl. . . .

During every 100 hours on our streets we lose more young men
than were killed in 100 hours of ground war in the Persian
Gulf. . . . Where are the yellow ribbons of hope and remembrance
for our youth dying in the streets?

The reasons for the increase in serious crimes committed by youth
are complex. Eitzen (1992, p. 585) states: "Some children are angry,
alienated, and apathetic. A few are uncooperative, rude, abrasive, threatening, and even violent. Some abuse drugs. Some are sexually promiscu-
ous. Some belong to gangs. Some are sociopaths." Eitzen goes on to state:
"My strong conviction is that children are *not* born with sociopathic
tendencies; problem children are socially created."

The theory that environment has the most effect on a child's
development is, however, becoming increasingly controversial. Recent
studies conducted at the University of Minnesota of identical twins
separated at birth and raised apart seem to indicate that heredity plays
a larger role than previously thought in temperament and behavior. This
view is also supported by some studies of adopted children. It would seem
that criminals are made *and* born. This view is supported by Harvard
Professor James Q. Wilson (1983, p. 86):

[W]e now have available an impressive number of studies that,
taken together, support the following view: Some combination of
constitutional traits and early family experiences account for more
of the variation among young persons in their serious criminality
than any other factors, and serious misconduct that appears
relatively early in life tends to persist into adulthood. What
happens on the street corner, in the school, or in the job market
can still make a difference, but it will not be as influential as what
has gone before.

Eitzen (1992, p. 584) notes: "Some young people act in antisocial
ways because they have lost their dreams." He contends that families
and the youth within those families are shaped by their economic
situation and that our economy has changed dramatically. Eitzen uses
the analogy of a boat and the traditional argument about the economy
that "a rising tide lifts all boats." This was true from 1950 to 1973 when

the average standard of living rose steadily. In the past twenty years, however, the "rising tide" analogy has not been accurate.

Eitzen notes: "But since 1973 the water level was not the same for all boats, some boats leaked severely, and some people had no boat at all." The American Dream is fading for many. A home and a college education, things formerly taken for granted, are now out of reach for millions of Americans. In addition, says Eitzen (p. 587): "Children, so dependent on peer approval, often find the increasing gap in material differences between themselves and their peers intolerable. This may explain why some try to become 'somebody' by acting tough, joining a gang, rejecting authority, experimenting with drugs and sex, or running away from home."

An unfortunate result of our changing economy is the rise in poverty in our country. According to Eitzen (p. 587): "A significant proportion of people—13.5% in 1990 and rising—are officially poor." He notes:

> Poverty is especially damaging to children. Poor children are more likely to weigh less at birth, to receive little or no health care, to live in substandard housing, to be malnourished, and to be exposed to the health dangers of pollution. . . . Poor children are much more likely than others to be exposed to lead from old paint and old plumbing fixtures and from the lead in household dust. Sixteen percent of white children and 55% of black children have high levels of lead in their blood, a condition that leads to irreversible learning disabilities and other problems.

Eitzen (p. 588) also notes the changes that have occurred in American families: "These trends indicate widespread family instability in American society—and that instability has increased dramatically in a single generation."

Further, the cultural milieu of America greatly affects our youth. Eitzen (p. 588) suggests:

> The highly valued individual in American society is the self-made person—that is, one who has achieved money, position, and privilege through his or her own efforts in a highly competitive system. Economic success, as evidenced by material possessions, is the most common indicator of who is and who is not successful. Moreover, economic success has come to be the common measure of self-worth.

> Competition is pervasive in American society, and we glorify the winners. . . . What about the losers in that competition? How do they respond to failure? How do we respond to them? How do they respond to ridicule? How do they react to the shame of being poor?

> *. . . They may respond by working harder to succeed, which is the great American myth. Alternatively, they may become apathetic, drop out, tune out with drugs, join others who are also "failures" in a fight against the system that has rejected them, or engage in various forms of social deviance to obtain the material manifestations of success.*
>
> *The other aspect of culture that has special relevance here is the influence of the media, particularly the messages purveyed by television, by the movies, and by advertising. These media outlets glamorize—among other things—materialism, violence, drug and alcohol use, hedonistic lifestyles, and easy sex.*

Witkin (p. 181) echoes this theme: "Today's kids are desensitized to violence as never before, surrounded by gunfire and stuffed with media images of Rambos who kill at will." Witkin notes another significant change in the cultural milieu: "By far the biggest difference in today's atmosphere is that the no-problem availability of guns in every nook of the nation has turned record numbers of everyday encounters into deadly ones."

This is *not* to suggest that society is completely to blame for our wayward youth. It is to suggest that for police and the community to deal effectively with delinquency mandates that they deal with underlying causes, a recurrent theme throughout this text. Specific programs aimed at youth are discussed in detail in Chapter 14. Unless police and the community effectively deal with juveniles and make them feel a part of the community, the problem of gangs is likely to grow. This is the focus of the next chapter.

Summary

The most common age for legally becoming an adult is eighteen. *Parens patriae* refers to the government's right to take care of minors and others who cannot legally take care of themselves. Our juvenile justice system uses a one-pot jurisdictional approach, treating abused or neglected children, those who are status offenders, and those who are truly criminal in the same way. Status offenses are actions by a juvenile that would not be a crime if committed by an adult, for example, truancy or smoking cigarettes.

The Big D's of juvenile justice are diversion, decriminalization, deinstitutionalization, and due process. A justice model views youth as responsible for their own acts. Under the justice model, the good of society takes precedence over society's responsibility to take care of its children. Street justice occurs when police officers use their discretionary powers to simply talk to youth who are status offenders rather than taking them into custody.

Youth may be victims of abuse, homelessness, or lead poisoning. The primary responsibility of police officers who deal with abused or neglected children is to protect the child, remove him or her from the home if necessary, and to collaborate with social service agencies to assure that the child's needs are met.

Children with special needs include those who are emotionally/ behaviorally disturbed, who have learning disabilities, who have an attention deficit hyperactivity disorder, or who have behavior problems resulting from prenatal exposure to drugs, including alcohol or to HIV.

DISCUSSION QUESTIONS

1. At what age do individuals become adults in your state?
2. When you were a teenager, did you get into any trouble with the law?
3. Do you feel the juvenile justice system should change from a welfare model to a justice model?
4. Do you agree with Springer's proposals to revamp the juvenile court?
5. What examples of street justice have you witnessed? Do you think street justice is fair?
6. Do you know anyone with a learning disability? How has it affected their lives?
7. At what age did you feel you should be considered an adult?
8. Do you feel youth are becoming more violent?
9. Have youth committed any violent crimes in your community within the last few months?
10. Do you feel status offenses should be decriminalized?

DEFINITIONS
Can you define these terms: attention deficit hyperactivity disorder, "Big D's" of juvenile justice, crack children, decriminalization, deinstitutionalization, diversion, due process, fetal alcohol syndrome (FAS), justice model, learning disability, "Norman Rockwell" family, one pot jurisdictional approach, *parens patriae*, status offenses, street justice, welfare model.

REFERENCES

Association for Children with Learning Disabilities. "Taking the First Step to Solving Learning Problems." Pittsburgh: Association for Children with Learning Disabilities.

Blomberg, Thomas G. "Widening the Net: An Anomaly in the Evaluation of Diversion Programs." In *Handbook of Criminal Justice Evaluation.* edited by Malcolm W. Klein and Katherine S. Tielmann. Beverly Hills: Sage Publications, 1980.

Brazelton, T. Berry. In *Identifying the Needs of Drug-Affected Children:* 1990 Issue Forum. Washington: Office for Substance Abuse Prevention, U.S. Department of Health and Human Services, 1990.

Brodt, Stephen J. and Smith, J. Steve. "Public Policy and the Serious Juvenile Offender." In *Taking Sides: Clashing Views on Controversial Issues in Crime and Criminology,* 2nd rev. ed. edited by Richard C. Monk, 171–80. Guilford: The Dushkin Publishing Group, Inc., 1991.

Burgess, Donna M. and Streissguth, Ann P. "Fetal Alcohol Syndrome and Fetal Alcohol Effects: Principles for Educators." *Phi Delta Kappan.* (September 1992): 24–30.

Craig, Susan E. "The Educational Needs of Children Living with Violence." *Phi Delta Kappan.* (September 1992): 67–71.

Downing, David. "Coming Soon to a Classroom Near You: 'Crack Kids.' " *Advocate.* (October 5, 1990): 9.

Drowns, Robert W. and Hess, Kären M. *Juvenile Justice.* St. Paul: West Publishing Company, 1990.

Eitzen, Stanley. "Problem Students: The Sociocultural Roots." *Phi Delta Kappan.* (April 1992): 584–90.

Griffin, Brenda S. and Griffin, Charles T. *Juvenile Delinquency in Perspective.* New York: Harper and Row, 1978.

Griffith, Dan R. "Prenatal Exposure to Cocaine and Other Drugs: Developmental and Educational Prognoses." *Phi Delta Kappan.* (September 1992): 30-34.

Hodgkinson, Harold. "Reform versus Reality." *Phi Delta Kappan.* (September 1991): 9–16.

Krisberg, Barry. "The Evolution of the Juvenile Justice System." In *Criminal Justice 92/93,* 152–59. Guilford: The Dushkin Publishing Group, Inc., 1992.

Needleman, Herbert L. "Childhood Exposure to Lead: A Common Cause of School Failure." *Phi Delta Kappan.* (September 1992): 35–37.

Pace, Denny F. *Community Relations Concept.* Placerville: Custom Publishing Company, 1991.

Regnery, Alfred S. "Getting Away with Murder: Why the Juvenile Justice System Needs an Overhaul." In *Taking Sides: Clashing Views on Controversial Issues in Crime and Criminology.* 2nd rev. ed. edited by Richard C. Monk, 164–70. Guilford: The Dushkin Publishing Group, Inc. 1991.

Sautter, R. Craig. "Crack: Healing the Children." *Phi Delta Kappan Special Report.* (November 1992): K1–K12.

Scott, Gwendolyn B. "Survival of Children with Prenatally Acquired Human Immunodeficiency Virus Type I Infection." *New England Journal of Medicine.* Vol. 321, (1989): 1791–96.

Seidel, John F. "Children with HIV-Related Developmental Difficulties." *Phi Delta Kappan.* (September 1992): 38–56.

Senna, Joseph J. and Siegel, Larry J. *Introduction to Criminal Justice.* 5th rev. ed., St. Paul: West Publishing Company, 1990.

Springer, Charles E. *Justice for Juveniles*. Washington: U.S. Department of Justice, Office of Juvenile Justice and Delinquency Prevention, 1986.

Stevens, Linda J. and Price, Marianne. "Meeting the Challenge of Educating Children at Risk." *Phi Delta Kappan*. (September 1992): 18–23.

Straus, Murray A. and Kantor, Glenda K. "Stress and Child Abuse." In *The Battered Child*, 4th rev. ed. edited by Ray E. Helfer and Ruth S. Kempe. Chicago: University of Chicago Press, 1988.

Tyler, Rachelle. "Prenatal Drug Exposure: An Overview of Associated Problems and Intervention Strategies." *Phi Delta Kappan*. (May 1992): 705–10.

Washington Post. "Attention Deficit-Hyperactivity Caused by Gene Defect, Study Says," *Star Tribune*. (April 8, 1993): 7A.

Wilson, James Q. "Thinking About Crime." *The Atlantic*. (September 1983): 86.

Witkin, Gordon et al. "Kids Who Kill." *Criminal Justice 92/93*, 181–85. Guilford: The Dushkin Publishing Group, Inc., 1992.

RESOURCES

Association for Children with Learning Disabilities (ACLD), 4156 Library Road, Pittsburgh, PA 15234. (412) 341-1515

Office of Juvenile Delinquency Prevention (OJDP), 633 Indiana Avenue N.W., Washington, DC 20531. (202) 724-7782

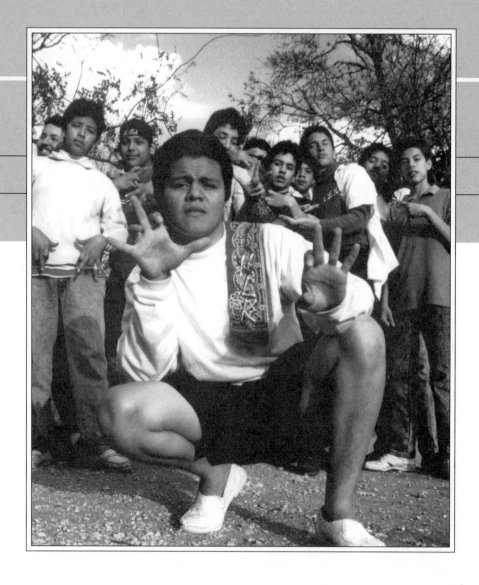

INTERACTING WITH GANGS AND GANG MEMBERS

Street gangs prey upon their neighborhood much like a malignant growth which continues to spread through its host until only a wasted shell remains.

—**"Street Gangs of Los Angeles County"**

DO YOU KNOW

- What the difference is between a gang, a street gang, and a youth gang?
- Which term is preferred by most local law enforcement agencies?
- What two basic functions are served by youth gangs?
- How gang activity can be identified?
- How contemporary gangs can be classified?
- What approaches have been used with youth gangs in the past forty years?
- What five strategies for gang intervention were identified by the OJJDP?
- Which strategy best predicted a decline in the gang problem?
- What are keys to successful gang-reduction programs?

Gangs are now spreading through our society like a violent plague. Daily, countless news stories depict the tragedy of gang violence. The following excerpts document only the tip of the problem:

> *Item . . . "A gang fight at a crowded park resulted in a seven year old girl being shot in the head, while picnicking with her family.*
>
> *Item . . . "Shot gun blasts from a passing car, intended for a rival gang member, strike a child on a tricycle."*
>
> *Item . . . "A shoot-out between rival gangs claimed the life of a high school track star as he jogged around the school track"* (Harris, 1985, p. 2).

GANGS, STREET GANGS, AND YOUTH GANGS

The definitions of gangs, street gangs, and youth gangs provided by Spergel, Chance, and Curry (1990) are central to the following discussion.

A **gang** is a somewhat organized group of people for some duration with a special interest in violence for status-providing purposes.

Gangs are identified by turf concerns, symbols, special dress, and colors. A gang is recognized by both its members and by others.

A **street gang** is a group of people who form an allegiance based on various social needs and engage in acts injurious to public health and public morals. This is the preferred term of most local law enforcement agencies.

Members of street gangs engage in (or have engaged in) gang-focused criminal activity either individually or collectively. Gangs create an atmosphere of fear and intimidation in a community. Most local law enforcement agencies prefer the term *street gang* because it includes juveniles and adults and designates the location of the gang and most of its criminal behavior.

For criminal justice policy purposes, the **youth gang** is a subgroup of a street gang.

Miller (1980, p. 121) defines a youth gang as follows: "A youth gang is a self-formed association of peers, bound together by mutual interests, with identifiable leadership, well-developed lines of authority, and other organizational features, who act in concert to achieve a specific purpose or purposes which generally include the conduct of illegal activity and control over a particular territory, facility, or type of enterprise."

Spergel, Chance and Curry (1990, p. 3) suggest:

> *The notion of* youth gang *incorporates two concepts: often a more amorphous "delinquent group" (e.g., a juvenile clique within a gang), and the better organized and sophisticated "criminal organization." The latter may be an independent group or clique of the gang and usually comprises older youth and young adults primarily engaged in criminal income-producing activity, most commonly drug trafficking.*

They also note that youth gangs fulfill "socialization and survival functions for youths in low-income, socially isolated ghetto or barrio communities and increasingly in transitional areas with newly settled populations."

Youth gangs provide their members with a feeling of belonging as well as protection from other youth.

THE EXPANSION OF GANGS

Street gangs have operated in the United States since the 1820s. Irish Americans in five point districts of New York City organized the Forty Thieves and engaged in murder, robbery, and street muggings. These gang members came from overcrowded areas with substandard housing, poor or nonexistent health care, broken homes, and few opportunities to improve their situation. Despite all of the social and economic advances made since 1820, many of the same conditions still exist today and explain the continued existence of street gangs.

TABLE 9.1
Type of Gang Problem by Area (City, County, Site)

Chronic Problem Cities/Areas	Emerging Problem Cities/Areas
Albuquerque, NM	Atlanta, GA
Chicago, IL	Benton Harbor, MI
Chino, CA	Cicero, IL
Detroit, MI	Columbus, OH
East Los Angeles, CA	Evanston, IL
El Monte, CA	Flint, MI
Inglewood, CA	Fort Wayne, IN
Long Beach, CA	Fort Worth, TX
Los Angeles City, CA	Hialeah, FL
Los Angeles County, CA	Indianapolis, IN
New York, NY	Jackson, MS
Oakland, CA	Louisville, KY
Pomona, CA	Madison, WI
Philadelphia, PA	Miami, FL
Phoenix, AZ	Milwaukee, WI
San Diego, CA	Minneapolis, MN
San Francisco, CA	Reno, NV
San Jose, CA	Rockford, IL
Santa Ana, CA	Sacramento, CA
Stockton, CA	Salt Lake City, UT
Tucson, AZ	Seattle, WA
	Shreveport, LA
	Sterling, IL
	Tallahassee, FL

Chronic Problem- Institutional Sites	Emerging Problem- Institutional Sites
California Youth Authority[a]	Ethan Allen School (WI)
Sunrise House (CA)	Glen Mills School (PA)
	McClaren School (OR)
	Paramount School (CA)

a. In much of the analysis, only the California Youth Authority is included as an area along with cities or county areas. It has also dealt with the youth gang problem since before 1980.

SOURCE: C. Ronald Huff. *Gangs in America*. Newbury Park: Sage Publications, Inc. 1990:292. Reprinted by permission.

Street gangs now exist across the United States. Originating on the East Coast, they have flourished in California, particularly the Los Angeles area, Chicago, and other major cities in the United States. Not content to confine their activities to the crime-ridden areas of the large cities and searching to expand their drug trade, the Los Angeles and Chicago gangs have invaded other previously untouched areas of the United States. As noted by Taylor (1991, p. 103): "The increase and spread of youth gangs in today's United States constitute a movement that must be recognized and understood. Gangs can no longer be defined in traditional, preconceived terms. Social and economic factors have redefined them, and their imperialistic spread is a multidimensional movement."

Miller (1991, p. 263) suggests: "Youth gangs in the 1980s and 1990s are more numerous, more prevalent, and more violent than in the 1950s, probably more so than at any time in the country's history." Table 9.1 indicates where gangs were a chronic problem and where they were an emerging problem as of 1990.

Minneapolis, with an estimated 3,000 gang members and Des Moines, Iowa, now have to cope with drive-by shootings, cocaine babies, and the violence and crime that accompanies gangs.

INDICATORS OF GANG ACTIVITY

There are many signs of gang activity.

Indicators of gang activity include graffiti, drive-by shootings, intimidation assaults, murders, and the open sale of drugs.

Graffiti may appear on neighborhood buildings and walls to mark gang turf. Drive-by shootings, intimidation assaults, and murders are among the criminal activities of gangs. Gangs declare entire streets and neighborhoods as their turf. Gangs sell drugs openly. Children as young as eleven or twelve are identified by pagers they carry constantly and become drug runners for gangs. Residents of neighborhoods in which gangs flourish become filled with fear. Some citizens become virtual prisoners in their own homes, afraid to get caught in the crossfire of a gang gun battle.

Police-community relations in a gang-infested area are affected by the way local authorities respond to the threats posed by gangs. Typically, police chiefs in cities where gangs have recently arrived are slow to recognize the threat gangs pose to the community. If police chiefs deny the existence of a gang problem, despite mounting evidence to the contrary, the gang problem often grows to unmanageable proportions.

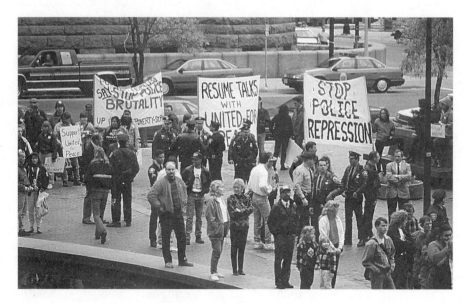

United for Peace March in Minneapolis, Minnesota

To effectively respond to gangs, police officers need to understand what gangs are and how they work. To some, gangs are merely a group of individuals in conflict with the establishment. The constant publicity of gangs on television and in the newspapers adds to their "Robin Hood Mystique." There is, however, nothing romantic about gangs. A youth who cannot break away from a gang is likely to have a future filled with continued criminal behavior, repeated arrests, and ultimately prison—if he or she lives that long. Gang life is violent and dangerous for gang members and the rest of society.

Street gangs consist of individuals who group together in secret enclaves, yet defiantly identify themselves by signs, symbols, and clothing. Gang members have a code of personal honor, yet as their major activity, they engage in a wide range of criminal activities.

GANG STRUCTURE

The internal structure of gangs tends to be formal, similar to any corporate structure. Because of their structure, gangs tend to be mirror images of each other. Usually led by small groups of hard-core members (approximately 10 to 15 percent of the membership), the structure is usually as follows:

President

Vice President

War Lord

  Gestapo or Goon Squad

  Armorer

Spokesman

Peacemaker

Advisor

The *president,* (prez, king, general, prince) is the supreme leader of the gang and has unlimited authority. Usually the president is older and smarter than other members of the gang, shrewd, articulate, charismatic, and, for some reason, often of small stature. The president must retain the gang's respect by warding off rivals for the position, resolving internal problems, successfully confronting rival gangs, and demonstrating leadership through critical periods or crisis situations.

The *vice president* is a close, trusted follower of the president and supports him in all decisions. The vice president is in charge of gang rituals and sometimes of discipline.

The *war lord or war counselor* is usually the most aggressive member. When the gang is in conflict, the war lord may actually assume control of the gang until the situation is resolved.

The *gestapo or goon squad* work for the war lord. These hard-core members enforce the war lord's will, correcting internal and external problems by force. The *armorer* also works for the war lord and is responsible for securing the gang's weaponry and keeping it in working order. Only the armorer and a few trusted gang members know where the weapons are stored.

The *spokesman* (statesman or intelligence officer) often acts on behalf of the president. The spokesman knows all the details of the gang's activities, alliances, treaties, territorial boundaries, and disputes.

The *peacemaker* position exists in large gangs and is usually held by an older member. The peacemaker has proven skill in dealing with other gangs to establish alliances and settle gang disputes inside and outside the group.

An *advisor* to the gang is an older, often "retired" gang member who may or may not have a direct affiliation with the group. The gang consults with the advisor out of respect for his beneficial advice in previous matters.

The hard-core members who hold these leadership positions pose a threat to the community and the police because (1) they typically possess guns and other weapons, and (2) they tend to be aggressively anti-social and are encouraged to be so by the gang as long as their behavior does not violate gang rules or discipline.

The *marginal membership* is a much larger group that surrounds the hard-core members. The marginal members are not privy to the inner activity of the gang and are relegated to follower roles. Hard-core members are recruited from the marginal membership.

Gangs use children ages nine to fifteen, called *Peewees,* to commit crimes such as shoplifting, burglaries, armed robberies, and drug sales in schools. Their youthful appearance is used to advantage because they often do not arouse suspicion. If caught, the criminal justice system deals more leniently with juveniles than adults.

Females are used by gangs in a variety of ways. They may:

- Serve as lookouts for crimes in progress.
- Conceal stolen property or tools used to commit crimes.
- Carry weapons for males who do not want to be caught with them.
- Carry information in and out of prison.
- Provide sexual favors (they are often drug dependent and are physically abused).

Like juveniles, females arouse less suspicion than male adults.

PROFILE OF A GANG MEMBER

A typical gang member is usually poor and often has a need for protection and a need to belong. A gang member often develops into an anti-social, aggressive, hostile person who rebels against society and who gets support for his feelings of anger and frustration from the gang structure.

Gang members are usually between the ages of nine and thirty. The majority are between thirteen and twenty-three.

The typical gang member is also male. Gangs are overwhelmingly male organizations; the male-female ratio is approximately twenty to one.

The ethnic/racial makeup of gangs has changed over the past few decades from predominantly white gangs to the majority of gangs now being African-American, Hispanic, and Asian. Some Native American gangs also exist in certain parts of the country. There seems to be a correlation between the racial makeup of gangs and the racial makeup of our society at or near the poverty level.

The lifestyle of a gang member is narrow and limited primarily to the gang and its activities. The typical gang member is a school dropout, unemployed, and in trouble with the police. The gang provides its members with an identity and status. Members develop fierce loyalty to their respective gang and become locked into the gang's lifestyle, values, attitudes, and behavior. It eventually becomes quite difficult for a member to break away from a gang.

OUTWARD TRAPPINGS OF THE GANG

Gangs establish **turf,** territorial boundaries, within which they operate and which they protect at all costs from invasion by rival gangs. Turf begins at the meeting place which is the center of gang activity. This can be any place such as the backroom of a grocery store, the basement of a neighbor's home, or a room in an abandoned building. The meeting place provides a sanctuary when a gang member is in trouble, a refuge when home life is intolerable, a hideout from the police, a hiding place for weapons, a place to plot future gang activities, a retreat, and a safe haven.

A gang's turf is centered at its meeting place and spreads out through the community. Gangs are very territorial. Boundaries are well defined, and it is not unusual for boundaries to be clearly specified among gangs in written pacts. Rival gangs should never infringe upon these boundaries. If a gang does cross into another gang's territory it is understood that the response may be violent.

GANG SYMBOLS

Like corporations, gangs use symbols or logos to identify themselves. In addition, a gang's choice of colors is important. The symbols and colors indicate whether the gang is an independent organization or a branch or affiliation of an already established group.

Common gang symbols include the following:

- Pyramid.
- Ring of fire.
- Five- and six-pointed stars.
- All-seeing eye.
- Crossed pitchforks.
- Crown.
- Variations of the "Playboy" bunny.
- Champagne glass.

Gangs use graffiti to define their boundaries and mark their turf. Graffiti consists of painting gang symbols on walls, buildings, bridges, bus stops, and any other available public surface. Graffiti has very specific meanings to gangs. (See Figure 9.1.)

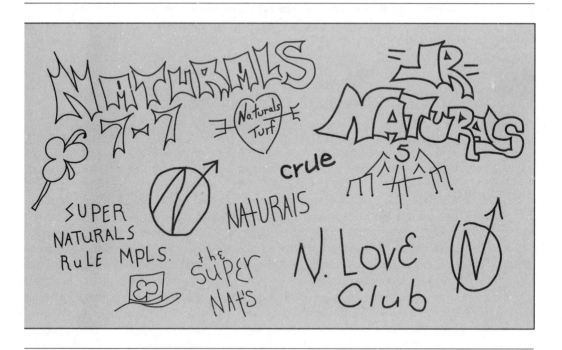

FIGURE 9.1   Typical Graffiti of the Naturals

Any misrepresentation or destruction of the gang's unique symbols could bring violent retribution against the offender, whether he knows the meaning of the symbols. Painting over graffiti on a building can result in dire consequences.

In addition to marking territory, gangs use graffiti to show opposition or contempt for rival gangs. Contempt is shown by displaying a rival gang's symbols upside down, backwards, or crossed out. This is a very serious insult to the rival.

Hand signs are a means of showing allegiance or opposition to another group. Most hand signs duplicate or modify the sign language used by the deaf and hearing impaired. Occasionally, legitimate use of hand signs has jeopardized the safety of the users. For example, two deaf women signing to each other on a street corner were shot and killed by gang members who thought they were members of a rival gang.

Representing, like hand signs, is used to show allegiance or opposition to a gang. It is based on a manner of dress which uses an imaginary line drawn vertically through the human body. Anything to the left of the line represents left or "dress left," and *vice versa.* An example of right dress would be a hat cocked to the right side, right pants leg rolled up, and a cloth or bandana tied around the right arm.

Gang members at a national gang summit held in Kansas City in May 1993 displaying two fingers held together as a symbol of togetherness.

Other important symbols are tattoos, certain hair styles, including cutting gang designs in the hair, gold jewelry in gang symbols, and certain cars.

The following symbols, used by the Disciples gang, create a snapshot of gang symbols:

- Refer to themselves as "folk."
- Major insignia is the six-pointed star.
- Dress to the right.
- Colors are black and blue.
- Earrings, if worn, are in the right ear.
- One glove may be worn on the right hand.
- One pocket, right side, is turned inside out, sometimes dyed one of the gang's colors.
- Right pant leg rolled up.
- Two fingernails on right hand painted gang colors.
- Hoods of sweatshirts dyed gang colors.
- Shoes or laces of right shoe are gang colors.
- Belt buckle worn loose on the right side.
- Bandana in gang colors worn on right side.

The Disciple nation includes affiliates of the Simon City Royals, Ambrosse, Harrison Gents, Imperial Gangsters, Spanish Cobras, Latin Disciples, Latin Eagles, Satan Disciples, Latin Jivers, Two-Six Boys, etc.

Their major rival, the Vice Lords, have a similar way of representing their gang symbols and also have many affiliates. Appendix A contains a brief history and description of the symbols, colors, and affiliates of the B-Boys, the Disciples, the Latin Kings, the Naturals, the Vice Lords, and cult-oriented gangs.

The primary problem with gangs is noted in *Street Gangs of Los Angeles County:* "Street gangs prey upon their neighborhood much like a malignant growth which continues to spread through its host until only a wasted shell remains." The largest of the Los Angeles gangs are the Bloods and the Crips. Offshoots of these gangs have penetrated most large cities west of the Mississippi.

GANG DIVERSITY

According to Huff (1991), gang membership and activity is quite diverse. He notes (p. 28) that "new generation" research on gang activity documents the increasing diffusion and diversity of gangs as well as the relationship between gangs and drug use. In fact, drugs "represent a unifying economic force for gangs just as alcohol did for organized crime during Prohibition."

Contemporary gangs can generally be classified as one of three types.

Contemporary gangs may be classified as scavenger, territorial, or corporate.

Taylor (1991, p. 105) describes the three types of gangs.

Scavenger Gangs. *Members of these gangs often have no common bond beyond their impulsive behavior and their need to belong. Leadership changes daily and weekly. They are urban survivors who prey on the weak of the inner city. Their crimes are usually petty, senseless, and spontaneous. Often acts of violence are perpetrated just for fun. They have no particular goals, no purpose, no substantial camaraderies. Scavenger gang members generally have the characteristics of being low achievers and illiterates with short attention spans who are prone to violent, erratic behavior. The majority come from the lower class and the underclass.*

Territorial Gangs. *A territorial gang, crew, group, or individual designates something, someplace, or someone as belonging exclusively to the gang. The traditional designation of territory as it relates to gangs is better known as turf.*

When scavenger gangs become serious about organizing for a specific purpose, they enter the territorial stage. During this stage, gangs define themselves and someone assumes a leadership role. . . .

Gangs defend their territories in order to protect their particular business. The word is out on the street to everyone: "This is gang territory—stay away." . . .

Mobility through financial power is the distinguishing factor between the traditional definition of territory and the nontraditional concept of territory. . . . Prior to the windfall of illegal drug profits, territory as a concept was limited to the immediate neighborhood. Today, with the power of organized crime, technology, and escalating wages, territory can be intrastate, interstate, or international.

Organized/Corporate Gangs.   *These well-organized groups have very strong leaders or managers. The main focus of their organization is participation in illegal money-making ventures. . . . Discipline is comparable to that of the military, and goals resemble those of Fortune 500 corporations.*

Spergel and Curry (1991) contend that the key problem components of gang formation are economic deprivation, lack of opportunities, social disorganization, and the failure of community institutions.

STRATEGIES FOR DEALING WITH THE GANG PROBLEM

The Office of Juvenile Justice and Delinquency Prevention (OJJDP) undertook a study to determine what has historically been done to address the problem of youth gangs as well as what is currently being done. The OJJDP study found a distinct difference in the approach used in the 1950s and 1960s compared to that used in the 1970s and 1980s.

In the 1950s and 1960s law enforcement used a social services approach toward youth gangs. During the 1970s and 1980s law enforcement focused on a suppression approach.

Neither approach to youth gangs is clearly superior. Some communities adopted a comprehensive approach that combines social services intervention and suppression strategies.

The OJJDP also surveyed 254 experts from forty-five cities and six special programs as to what strategies they were currently using. Those who were surveyed identified five strategies.

The five strategies law enforcement currently uses to address the gang problem are as follows:

- Suppression.
- Social intervention.
- Social opportunities.
- Community mobilization.
- Organizational development or change.

Suppression includes tactics such as prevention, arrest, imprisonment, supervision, and surveillance. *Social intervention* includes crisis intervention, treatment for the youths and their families, outreach, and referral to social services. *Social opportunities* include providing basic or remedial education, training, work incentives, and jobs for gang members. *Community mobilization* includes improved communication and joint policy and program development among justice, community-based, and grassroots organizations. Finally, *organizational development* or change includes special police units and special youth agency crisis programs.

According to the OJJDP survey, law enforcement most frequently used suppression as a strategy to address the gang problem; forty-four percent of those reporting used it. This was followed by social intervention (31.5 percent), organizational development (10.9 percent), community mobilization (8.9 percent), and social opportunities (4.8 percent).

Although only a small percent of the reporting agencies used community mobilization, according to the OJJDP (p. 3): "Community mobilization was the factor that most powerfully predicted a decline in the gang problem."

Community mobilization is the most effective strategy to address the gang problem.

The OJJDP survey also found that providing gang members with basic social opportunities, including education and employment, were also important in combatting the gang problem.

PROGRAMS SPECIFICALLY DESIGNED TO COMBAT GANG PROBLEMS

Spergel and Curry (1991, p. 295) list the following community organization strategies for dealing with gang problems:

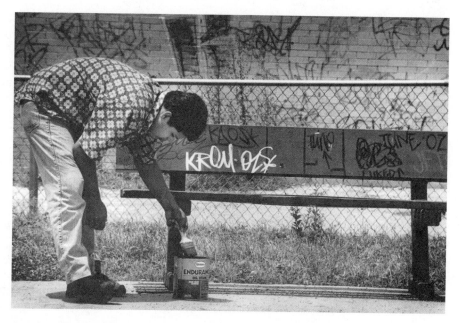

A teen participant in a neighborhood cleanup project prepares to paint over gang-related graffiti on a bench in an inner-city park.

- Cleaning up graffiti in the community.
- Involving the schools.
- Mobilizing the community.
- Building community trust.
- Involving parent groups in community programs.
- Educating the community.
- Changing the community.

Spergel and Curry conducted a survey of forty-five cities or urban areas to determine the scope of the youth gang problem. They also examined the response of different types of agencies and cities to the problem. Their findings are as follows (p. 309):

> More resources alone for police or even human service programs would not contribute much to dealing effectively with the youth gang problem. It is more likely that community mobilization and more resources for and reform of the educational system and the job market, targeted at gang youth or clearly at-risk youth, would be more cost-effective as well as more effective in the reduction of the problem.

> Police recommendations emanating from these findings would not necessarily require a renewed war on poverty, but rather a series of programs targeted specifically at the youth gang problem addressing not only issues of economic deprivation and lack of

opportunities but social disorganization and the mobilization of community institutions in a concerted attack on the problem.

Furst (1991, p. 1A, 3A) describes a community project where eleven teenagers, most gang members, and two adult artists made ninety wooden lawn chairs for a neighborhood "plagued by crime and fear and crack." The two artists obtained funding from a local foundation and other sources to pay the neighborhood youth $4.50 an hour to build the chairs. To most of them, it was not the money, but the chance to do something positive that was important. As one gang member said: "It gave me something to do. . . . If there isn't anything to do, people walk up and down the street messing with people." Said another youth who claimed membership in two gangs, the Four Corner Hustlers and the Vice Lords: "It's cool. We did something for the block, and it was kind of fun. Everybody worked together."

Benson (1990) describes a program developed in Austin, Texas by the police department and concerned citizens to combat an onslaught of graffiti and violence caused by gangs. They formed a group called Citizens Helping Austin Neighborhood Gang Environment (CHANGE). As noted by Benson (p. 66):

CHANGE is a gang diversion program which uses a varied approach involving juveniles, their parents, churches and community-based organizations in an attempt to contain further gang violence and graffiti. A unique goal of CHANGE is to encourage the gangs to call a truce among themselves long enough to meet and discuss their differences. . . .

Since inception of the program, gang members have filed charges, appeared as witnesses, and signed statements if they have been victimized instead of resorting to violence. . . .

CHANGE approached area businesses with the idea of letting the gangs use their walls for murals instead of for random defacement. Officers are challenging the youths to make their community more attractive than a rivals' by getting rid of neighborhood refuse or helping older residents maintain their homes by helping them mow their lawns.

CHANGE is also channeling the hostility the gangs have for one another into competitive sports [sponsoring a double elimination softball tournament twice a month]. . . . "It was a lot harder to shoot at somebody that you have tried to put out at second base." . . .

The city council was so impressed with the volunteer efforts of the people involved with CHANGE and their remarkable results that they added an additional $240,000 in unsolicited funds to the police budget for the express use of the prevention of juvenile crime.

Philadelphia has developed a boystown called House of UMOJA which seeks to prevent youngsters from joining gangs. It works with youngsters who have gang affiliations or who are at risk of such affiliations. According to Sulton (1990, pp. 17-18), the House of UMOJA provides the following resources and services: a surrogate family, food, shelter, emotional and spiritual support, life skills and job training, job placement, employment opportunities, counseling, reintegration planning, stress and aggression control training, values clarification and problem solving skills, remedial reading, remedial math, GED preparation, vocational education, conflict resolution and communication skills, and recreational activities. Sulton notes (p. 18): "The house of UMOJA builds upon the *positive* characteristics of gangs—loyalty, trust, sharing, and mutual respect among members."

Another exemplary program is Los Angeles' Community Youth Gang Services Project. According to Sulton (1990, p. 61): "Police estimate that 70,000 children and young adults belong to over 600 gangs [in Los Angeles]. Unofficial estimates indicate that over 100,000 young people belong to gangs and that 150,000 more are at risk of joining gangs." The Los Angeles Community Youth Gang Services Project (YGSP) is a grassroots community-based program aimed at reducing youth gang violence at the individual level through education, employment, and involvement in positive activities.

Keys to successful gang reduction programs are education, employment, and involvement in positive activities.

The YGSP program includes the following projects: crisis intervention teams, career guidance programs that served over 10,000 youth last year, parent-teacher education, graffiti removal, a college mentor project, and a series of "town hall meetings." Ex-gang members are hired for many YGSP staff positions. Over 30,000 youth were served by program projects in the past year.

RECOMMENDATIONS

Recommendations of the National Symposium on Community Institutions and Inner City Crime related to youth gang problems include the following (Sulton, pp. 100-01):

1. Parents should be held accountable for their children's behavior and required to participate, with their children, in programs designed to prevent or discourage youth gang membership.

2. Schools and educational programs should develop curricula that discourages youth (grades 3 through 6) from joining gangs.

These curricula should use a model similar to that employed by the community Youth Gang Services Project in Los Angeles.

3. Inner-city communities should be encouraged to establish urban boystowns similar to the model developed by the House of UMOJA in Philadelphia. In addition to providing housing, these boystowns should offer a variety of education, employment, and recreational services and maintain cooperative working relationships with juvenile justice agencies, businesses, and human service agencies.

4. Newspapers should exercise caution when publishing stories about youth gang violence. Gang members regularly read newspapers and often perceive articles concerning their violent activities as certificates of notoriety and success.

5. Federal, state, and local governments should expand summer youth employment programs and establish year-round job programs emphasizing community service and neighborhood improvement projects such as graffiti removal. These programs should employ gang members and youth at risk of becoming gang members. Ample supervisory positions also should be allocated.

6. A national task force on gangs should be established by a consortium of community-based organizations working to reduce youth gang violence. It should be funded by private foundations and corporations, and work with federal and local government agencies. It should a.) analyze youth gang violence, b.) develop a comprehensive plan to eliminate youth gang violence and gang warfare, and c.) provide technical assistance to public and private agencies working to eliminate these problems. The task force should consist of representatives of various community institutions and operate under the direction of a national coalition of community-based organizations.

7. A national research and training institute on gang violence and membership reduction should be established and operated under the auspices of a national coalition of community-based organizations. The institute should study the issue of conflict resolution without violence, and collect and analyze data pertaining to gangs, gang-related crime, and gang violence prevention programs. It also should periodically survey gang violence reduction programs, which should in turn submit questions for inclusion in the survey instruments. The institute should disseminate the findings to public and private agencies through publications and formal training programs. Juvenile and criminal justice officials should be encouraged to attend these training programs.

Other programs geared specifically for youth are discussed in Chapter 14.

Summary

A gang is a somewhat organized group of people with a special interest in violence for status-providing purposes. A street gang (the preferred term for local law enforcement agencies) is a group of people that form an allegiance based on various social needs and engage in acts injurious to public health and public morals. A youth gang is a subgroup of a street gang.

Indicators of gang activity in a neighborhood include graffiti, drive-by shootings, intimidation assaults, murders, and open sale of drugs.

Contemporary gangs may be classified as scavenger, territorial, or corporate. In the 1950s and 1960s law enforcement used a social services approach to address the problems of youth gangs. In the 1970s and 1980s law enforcement efforts focused on a suppression approach. The five strategies currently being used to address the gang problem are suppression, social intervention, social opportunities, community mobilization, and organizational development or change. Community mobilization has the most positive impact on the gang problem.

Keys to successful gang reduction programs are education, employment, and involvement of gang members in positive activities.

DISCUSSION QUESTIONS _____

1. Are there gangs in your community? If so, do they cause problems for the police?
2. Have you seen any movies or television programs about gangs? How are gang activities depicted?
3. What do you think are the main reasons individuals join gangs?
4. How does a youth gang differ from a group such as a Boy Scout troop or a school club?
5. How does a youth gang member differ from other juvenile delinquents?
6. Should convicted youth gang members be treated like other juvenile delinquents, including status offenders?
7. What factors might influence you to become a gang member? To not become a gang member?
8. If you were to try to infiltrate a gang as an undercover agent, what factors would be important to you?
9. Are there efforts in your community to combat the gang problem?
10. Do you think the gang problem will increase or decrease during the 1990s?

DEFINITIONS

Can you define these terms: gang, graffiti, representing, street gang, turf, youth gang.

REFERENCES

Benson, Carol. "Gang Diversion." *Law and Order.* (August 1990): 66-68.

Furst, Randy. "2 Artists + 11 Kids = Something of Value." *Star Tribune.* (August 24, 1991): 1A, 3A.

Harris, Sidney J. "Gangs Make Martyrs of Losers." In Robert K. Jackson and Wesley D. McBride, *Understanding Street Gangs.* Sacramento: Custom Publishing, 1985.

Huff, C. Ronald. *Gangs in America.* Newbury Park: Sage Publications, Inc., 1991.

Miller, Walter B. "Gangs, Groups and Serious Youth Crime." In *Critical Issues In Juvenile Delinquency,* edited by D. Chichor and D. Kelly. Lexington: Lexington, 1980.

Miller, Walter B. "Why the United States Has Failed to Solve its Youth Gang Problem." In *Gangs in America,* edited by C. Ronald Huff, 263-87. Newbury Park: Sage Publications, Inc., 1991.

Spergel, Irving A.; Chance, Ronald L.; and Curry, G. David. "National Youth Gang Suppression and Intervention Program." *Juvenile Justice Bulletin.* June 1990.

Spergel, Irving A. and Curry, G. David. "Strategies and Perceived Agency Effectiveness in Dealing with the Youth Gang Problem." In *Gangs in America,* edited by C. Ronald Huff, 288-309. Newbury Park: Sage Publications, Inc., 1991.

Sulton, Anne Thomas. *Inner-City Crime Control: Can Community Institutions Contribute?* Washington: The Police Foundation, 1990.

Taylor, Carl S. "Gang Imperialism." In *Gangs in America,* edited by C. Ronald Huff, 103-15. Newbury Park: Sage Publications, Inc., 1991.

RESOURCE

Office of Juvenile Delinquency Prevention (OJDP), 633 Indiana Avenue N.W., Washington, DC 20531; (202) 724-7782.

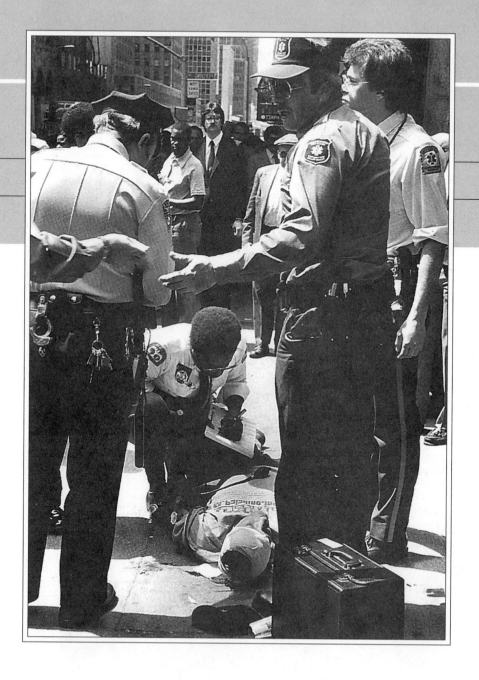

INTERACTING WITH
VICTIMS

In the Nation's ongoing fight against crime, statistics tell only part of the story. More than a violation of the law, every crime is a violation of the rights, property, person, or trust of another human being. Thus, behind every tally of offenses ranging from misdemeanors to aggravated felonies are innocent victims—individuals and families who must be recognized in the administration of justice.

—President George Bush, April 22, 1991,
  Proclamation of National Crime Victims Rights Week

DO YOU KNOW

- How extensive victimization is?
- How victims may be affected?
- What a secondary victim is and who might become one?
- What victimology is and what it includes?
- Who is at most risk of being victimized?
- What "second injury" victims may suffer?
- What national organizations exist to help victims?
- What major legislation regarding victims has been passed?
- What a victim impact statement is?
- What two types of programs have been established to help victims? What services are most commonly provided in each program?
- What rights victims have in most states?
- What special populations have been targeted for additional needs if victimized?

If you haven't been there, you don't know the feelings of emptiness and fear, and how it changes your life. I was in a state of shock. I walked around in a daze for weeks. I wasn't functioning. No one really understood how I felt.—Sherry Price, rape victim.

"No one really understood how I felt." This sentiment, vividly expressed by Sherry Price, currently regional coordinator of the Sunny Von Bulow National Victim Advocacy Center, Manhattan Office, and former president of the New York chapter of Victims for Victims, underscores the need of victims to be understood, to not be further victimized by the criminal justice systems.

As noted by Roberts (1990b, p. 13): "After decades of neglect, crime victims are finally being recognized as a vulnerable and forgotten group of people who have rights and are in need of services." Victimization is a much more extensive problem than is often realized. According to Monk (1991, p. 336): "Almost every American family contains one or more members who have been or will be victims of a serious crime.... Recently, the Bureau of Justice Statistics reported that 7 out of 8 Americans will be victims of personal theft three or more times within their lifetimes. Most Americans over the course of their lives will be victims of at least one assault."

National Crime Survey statistics estimate that 34.4 million victimizations were committed in the United States in 1990.

Table 10.1 summarizes the types of victimizations that occurred in 1990.

FBI statistics (1988, p. 152) suggest that victims lose approximately $8 billion dollars annually, but this figure reflects only the value of lost property. Cohen (1988, p. 538) estimates the other "real" costs such as victims' pain and suffering and risk of death to be $92.6 billion annually.

In addition to dealing with victims of crime, police officers also frequently deal with victims of accidents and natural disasters. Law enforcement officials should be trained to assist victims of violent crimes, accidents, and natural disasters.

TABLE 10.1
Estimated Percent Distribution of Personal and Household Victimizations
By type of victimization and reporting to police, United States, 1990[a]

| Type of Victimization | Number of Victimizations | Reported to Police | | | |
		Total	Yes[b]	No	Not Known and Not Available
All crimes	34,403,610	100%	37.7 %	61.3%	1.1 %
All personal crimes	18,984,120	100	34.7	63.9	1.3
Crimes of violence	6,008,790	100	48.0	50.8	1.2
Completed	2,421,530	100	60.6	38.1	1.3
Attempted	3,587,260	100	39.6	59.3	1.1
Rape	130,260	100	53.9	46.1	0.0[c]
Completed	62,830	100	62.7	37.3	0.0[c]
Attempted	67,430	100	45.7	54.3	0.0[c]
Robbery	1,149,710	100	50.1	49.2	0.8[c]
Completed	800,510	100	57.1	42.3	0.6[c]
With injury	286,020	100	67.7	32.3	0.0[c]
From serious assault	123,740	100	78.5	21.5	0.0[c]
From minor assault	162,280	100	59.5	40.5	0.0[c]
Without injury	514,480	100	51.1	47.9	1.0[c]
Attempted	349,190	100	34.1	64.8	1.1[c]
With injury	110,380	100	53.6	46.4	0.0[c]
From serious assault	43,930	100	46.5	53.5	0.0[c]
From minor assault	66,440	100	58.3	41.7	0.0[c]
Without injury	238,810	100	25.1	73.3	1.6[c]
Assault	4,728,810	100	47.4	51.3	1.3
Aggravated	1,600,670	100	58.7	39.8	1.5
Completed with injury	627,000	100	71.1	28.0	0.9[c]
Attempted with weapon	973,660	100	50.7	47.3	2.0[c]
Simple	3,128,130	100	41.6	57.2	1.2
Completed with injury	931,170	100	56.3	41.3	2.4
Attempted without weapon	2,196,960	100	35.4	63.9	0.7[c]
Crimes of theft	12,975,320	100	28.6	70.0	1.4
Completed	12,154,550	100	28.9	69.7	1.4
Attempted	820,760	100	23.1	75.1	1.9[c]
Personal larceny with contact	637,010	100	37.2	61.9	0.9[c]
Purse snatching	165,490	100	52.1	47.9	0.0[c]
Completed	124,010	100	59.5	40.5	0.0[c]
Attempted	41,470	100	30.2[c]	69.8	0.0[c]
Pocket picking	471,520	100	32.0	66.8	1.2[c]

(continued)

TABLE 10.1 (Continued)
Compensation Programs to Help Victims of Violent Crimes

Type of Victimization	Number of Victimizations	Total	Reported to Police		
			Yes[b]	No	Not Known and Not Available
Personal larceny without contact	12,338,310	100	28.1	70.5	1.4
Completed	11,559,010	100	28.5	70.1	1.4
Less than $50	4,592,470	100	13.3	85.6	1.1
$50 or more	6,452,940	100	39.5	59.1	1.4
Amount not available	513,590	100	25.3	70.4	4.4
Attempted	779,290	100	22.7	75.3	2.0[c]
All household crimes	15,419,490	100	41.3	58.0	0.7
Completed	13,072,490	100	42.4	57.0	0.6
Attempted	2,346,990	100	35.1	63.3	1.6
Burglary	5,147,740	100	51.4	47.5	1.0
Completed	4,076,210	100	56.6	42.7	0.7
Forcible entry	1,816,130	100	74.8	24.3	0.9[c]
Unlawful entry without force	2,260,080	100	42.0	57.4	0.6[c]
Attempted forcible entry	1,071,530	100	31.9	65.9	2.2
Household larceny	8,304,190	100	27.0	72.3	0.7
Completed	7,769,280	100	26.7	72.7	0.6
Less than $50	3,144,290	100	13.1	86.3	0.6[c]
$50 or more	4,205,830	100	36.6	62.8	0.6
Amount not available	419,160	100	29.7	69.4	0.9[c]
Attempted	534,900	100	31.4	67.0	1.6[c]
Motor vehicle theft	1,967,540	100	75.1	24.6	0.2[c]
Completed	1,226,990	100	94.8	5.2	0.0[c]
Attempted	740,550	100	42.5	56.8	0.6[c]

[a]Subcategories may not sum to total because of rounding.
[b]Represents the rates at which victimizations were reported to the police, or "police reporting rates."
[c]Estimate is based on about 10 or fewer sample cases.
SOURCE: *Criminal Victimization in the United States, 1990.* U.S. Department of Justice, Bureau of Justice Statistics, Washington: U.S. Department of Justice. (1992): 102.

RESULTS OF BEING VICTIMIZED

The director of the Office for Victims of Crime, U.S. Department of Justice, Jane Nady Burnley (1990, p. 10) suggests: "As we begin the decade of the nineties, a growing and critical rediscovery of the impact of

Assault victims can be of any age. Especially vulnerable are our nation's young children.

crime and the trauma of crime victims is in full stride in the United States." The results of victimization vary depending on the specific crime committed and the individual who is victimized.

Victims of crime may suffer physical injury, financial and property losses, emotional distress, and psychological trauma. Some suffer from **post traumatic stress disorder (PTSD),** a persistent re-experiencing of a traumatic event through intrusive memories, dreams, and a variety of anxiety-related symptoms.

According to Frederick, Hawkins, and Abajian (1990, p. 106): "PTSD is nonselective, affecting professionals and nonprofessionals, males and females, and people of all races and socioeconomic backgrounds. The American Psychiatric Association (1985) presents the following diagnostic criteria for PTSD:

- Existence of a recognizable stressor that would evoke significant symptoms of distress in almost anyone.
- Re-experiencing of the trauma as evidenced by at least one of the following:
  –Recurrent and intrusive recollection of the event.
  –Recurrent dreams of the event.
  –Sudden acting or feeling as if the traumatic event were reoccurring, because of an association with an environmental or ideational (mental) stimulus.

- Numbing of responsiveness to or reduced involvement with the external world, beginning some time after the trauma, as shown by at least one of the following:
  –Markedly diminished interest in one or more significant activities.
  –Feeling of detachment or estrangement from others.
  –Constricted affect.
- At least two of the following symptoms that were not present before the trauma:
  –Hyperalertness or exaggerated startle response.
  –Sleep disturbance.
  –Guilt about surviving when others have not, or about behavior required for survival.
  –Memory impairment or trouble concentrating.
  –Avoidance of activities that arouse recollection of the traumatic event.
  –Intensification of symptoms by exposure to events that symbolize or resemble the traumatic event.

Frederick, Hawkins, and Abajian (p. 106) note that PTSD occurs in phases. Table 10.2 summarizes the phases victims are likely to experience, as the result of a natural disaster, sexual abuse, physical assault, or a hostage-taking situation. The table includes the psychological and physical symptoms of each phase.

Police officers may also experience these symptoms, including PTSD, after responding to shooting incidents or other especially grisly crimes. As noted by Conroy and Hess (1991, p. 65): "Frequently officers involved in shootings have recurrent nightmares. You may dream about a bullet leaving your gun in slow motion and falling ineffectively to the ground or about shooting a person repeatedly without effect." They cite the statement of one officer after a shooting incident:

> *In some of the dreams I had been shot, people were holding me and stabbing me. I was being chased by crowds of people. I am being held and then shot by other parties. It is always a group. It is never one person just chasing me.*

> *In some of the dreams I shoot back, and the crowd keeps coming at me. It's like nothing is happening. And they just come up to me and grab me and stab me. The bullets don't seem to stop them. They just keep coming.*

Waller (1990, p. 146) notes that: "The emotional trauma, or 'invisible wound' is the least evident and understood, but it is often the most brutal effect of crime, not only on the direct victim, but on the victim's dependents and friends."

TABLE 10.2
Phases and Symptoms of Victimization

	Phases	Psychological Symptoms	Physical Symptoms
Natural Disaster	Impact/shock	Anxiety, depression	Insomnia
	Heroic	Depression	Nightmares
	Honeymoon	Phobias	Anorexia
	Disappointment	Hostility, resentment	Hypertension/hyper-alertness
	Reorganization	Loss of concentration, marital discord	Startle reaction, sexual inhibition
Sexual Abuse	Impact/shock	Fear of perpetrator, blunted emotions	Nightmares, stomach-aches
	Withdrawal	Shame, guilt, isolation	Diarrhea, startle reactions
	Regression	Depression, marital discord	Sexual inhibition, fast heart
	Compliance/anger	Intrusive thoughts, sexual confusion	Loss of appetite, urinary problems
	Recovery	Irritability, anger, substance abuse	Increased blood pressure
Physical Assault	Impact/shock	Denial, disbelief, anxiety, muscle tension	Fast heart, dry mouth, enlarged pupils
	Submission/ withdrawal	Fear of perpetrator, depression, isolation	Sleeplessness, headaches
		Fear, momentary anger	
	Ambivalence/anger	Periodic fear, making mistakes	Sexual inhibition, chest pains, pale skin
		Guilt, isolation, fear	Increased blood pressure
	Dependent aggression		Loss of sexual interest, increased blood pressure
	Recovery		
Hostage Taking	Impact/shock	Denial/disbelief, anxiety, muscle tension	Loss of appetite, dry mouth, fidgety, clammy palms
		Anxiety, phobias	
	Interaction	Helplessness, depression, intrusive thoughts	Tension, pacing
	Acceptance/ acquiescence		Fitful sleep, nightmares
		Phobias, loss of concentration	
	Ambivalence/anger		Diarrhea, fast heart, trembling, weight loss
		Tension, irritability	
	Recovery		Stomach problems, skin disorders, increased blood pressure, startle reactions

SOURCE: Reprinted by permission. Calvin J. Frederick, Karen L. Hawkins, and Wendy E. Abajian, "Beyond the Call of Duty? Victim/Witness Intervention Techniques."*The Police Chief.* (October 1990): 110. Copyright © International Association of Chiefs of Police, Inc. Further reproduction without express written permission from IACP is strictly prohibited.

Primary v. Secondary Victims

Two types of victims usually result from natural disasters and violent crime:

A **primary victim** is a person actually harmed by an incident. A **secondary victim** is one indirectly affected by the trauma.

In a rape, for example, the woman is, obviously, the primary victim. Her husband may be a secondary victim who also suffers from the trauma. A secondary victim includes anyone who is close to the primary victim and can truly empathize with that victim. Riggs and Kilpatrick (1990, p. 133) state:

Data suggest that individuals who are emotionally close to crime victims, particularly those of violent crime, should be assessed for psychological problems and counseled about the difficulties they may face.

Police officers may also be victims. This police officer was riding on routine patrol in Canton, Massachusetts when a drunk driver sped down the road and struck the hourse and officer. The impact crushed the horse's rear leg. The mortally injured horse was given a lethal injection.

The development of the psychological problems that are likely to appear among indirect victims of crime may exacerbate the symptoms of direct victims. For example, a husband faced with the news that his wife has been raped may respond with feelings of guilt, anger, and desire for revenge. These feelings are likely to make it more difficult for him to provide the emotional support that his wife needs to deal with her own response to the rape.

Riggs and Kilpatrick (p. 135) conclude: "It is important for the criminal justice system to recognize the difficulties faced by the friends and family members of crime victims. Those involved in the criminal justice system should help indirect victims find legal and psychological assistance and prepare them for the stress that might result from contact with the criminal justice system."

In the case of police officers, as noted by Conroy and Hess (pp. 39–40):

The most obvious way officers become primary victims *is through the physical dangers associated with the job. You may be assaulted, shot at, stabbed, or even killed in the line of duty. A much more subtle, more insidious way you become a primary victim, however, is through the psychological effects of your work. This type of victimization is far less obvious, frequently contrary to established self-image, and until recently, denied to even exist by both officers and management. . . .*

For the most part, however, officers seem to become secondary victims. *You deal constantly with other people's victimization while the pain and blood are fresh and real.*

Lurigio and Resick (1990, pp. 50–63) describe correlates of victim recovery following a traumatic incident. *Previctimization factors* include the following:

- Age—younger victims cope more effectively than older victims.
- Sex—women have been shown generally to be more distressed by crime than men.
- Education and income—victims with little formal education and low incomes are more traumatized than victims from higher socioeconomic and educational groups.
- Previctimization adjustment—a history of prior victimizations is associated generally with poorer adjustment.

Among the *victimization factors* are the following:

- Seriousness of the crime—severity of victim symptoms is related directly to the degree of violence or injury occuring in the incident.

- Relationship between victim and offender—some studies find no difference between victims of stranger and non-stranger offenders. Other studies indicate that women sexually assaulted by strangers were more anxious and depressed than those sexually assaulted by acquaintances.

Post-victimization factors that affect recovery include the victim's perception of the event and whether self-blame can be avoided. A victim's recovery is also affected by the ability to cognitively restructure what happened. As noted by Lurigio and Resick (1990, p. 59):

> **Cognitive restructuring** *is a coping mechanism in which victims reinterpret their experience to ameliorate the adverse effects of the incident. It can take several forms, such as finding meaning in the episode, engaging in downward comparisons (i.e., thinking about themselves as being better off than other real or imagined victims), comparing themselves to a hypothetical "worst world scenario" in that they are harmed to a much greater extent than in reality, and evaluating the event as occasioning personal growth or some other benefit.*

The way individuals react to victimization is related to whether they report the incident to the police. As noted by Waller (1990, p. 139): "Given the importance of the victim to the police, one would expect police leaders to have ensured that victims are treated as 'privileged clients.' "

Nonreporting of Being Victimized

Waller (1990, p. 141) notes that victims are the source of sixty percent of the common crime information known to police. He also notes that more than one-third of the robberies, aggravated assaults, burglaries, and rapes reported in the National Crime Survey were *not* reported to the police. He lists the following reasons victims do not report crime (pp. 142–43):

- They believe the police will be unable to do anything. Statistics confirm the victim's view: 75 percent of robberies and 85 percent of burglaries will not be cleared.
- They consider the matter private.
- They fear reprisals and threats.
- They delay while discussing what action to take with a family member or neighbor.
- They fear the reception they might be given by the police.

Criminal Victimization in the United States, 1990 (1992, p. 100) reports:

- Females were more likely to report violent victimizations than males. This was also likely to be the case for crimes of theft as well.
- White victims were somewhat more likely than black victims to report thefts to the police. Reporting rates for violent crimes committed against whites and blacks were similar.

Kelly (1990, p. 173) says: "A major reason for nonreporting was victims' apprehension as to how they would be treated and whether they would be believed." Waller (p. 144) notes that two out of five victims report crimes because they want to recover their property or file an insurance claim. One in three victims files a report to keep the crime from reoccurring. Less than ten percent of victims report the crime to see the offender punished. Waller concludes: "The police could aid victims by giving greater emphasis on returning property to its owners and to crime prevention."

VICTIMOLOGY

In the 1940s scholars became interested in the relationship between criminals and their victims. Benjamin Mendelsohn coined the term *victimology* and proposed that this be a new field of study, not simply a branch of criminology. Researchers in the 1940s and 1950s postulated that in a large percentage of cases, victims were partially responsible for their victimization. In *The Criminal and His Victim,* for example, von Hentig (1948) concludes that personality characteristics of some crime victims contributed to their victimization and that others became victims because of the community in which they lived.

Victimology, the study of crime victims, includes the concepts of victims' vulnerability and culpability.

Vulnerability suggests that certain groups of people are more susceptible to being victimized because of demographics rather than any unique, individual attributes. For example, are females or the elderly more likely to become victims than males or the young? Are people who live in certain neighborhoods or cities more vulnerable than those who live in other neighborhoods or cities? What about the victimization rate of children? Or teenagers, who some studies show are victimized far more than the elderly. Does race make a person more likely to be a target? Or does socioeconomic status influence the probability of being victimized? Table 10.3 summarizes answers to such questions for the year 1990.

TABLE 10.3
Characteristics of Victims

	Victimizations per 1,000 Persons Age 12 or Older						
	Crimes of Violence						
				Assault			Crimes of Theft
	Total	Total*	Robbery	Total	Aggravated	Simple	
Sex							
Male	105.1	37.5	7.5	29.8	11.5	18.3	67.5
Female	82.6	22.2	3.9	17.2	4.5	12.7	60.4
Age							
12–15	160.3	68.8	13.6	53.3	13.9	39.4	91.5
16–19	187.8	74.4	9.5	63.5	26.2	37.2	113.4
20–24	174.8	63.1	12.3	48.9	16.8	32.1	111.6
25–34	114.0	36.4	7.6	28.2	9.9	18.3	77.5
35–49	76.6	19.2	3.2	15.6	4.7	10.9	57.5
50–64	44.0	7.5	2.2	5.3	1.4	3.9	36.5
65 or older	24.6	3.5	1.5	1.9	1.1	.8	21.2
Race							
White	91.9	28.2	4.5	23.0	7.4	15.7	63.6
Black	103.7	39.7	13.0	26.0	12.2	13.9	64.0
Other	96.7	28.1	8.4	18.9	5.3	13.6	68.6
Ethnicity							
Hispanic	97.2	37.3	13.9	23.1	10.1	13.0	59.9
Non-Hispanic	92.9	28.8	5.0	23.2	7.6	15.6	64.0
Family income							
Less than $7,500	118.3	51.2	11.4	38.5	13.9	24.7	67.1
$7,500–$9,999	89.2	37.0	8.8	27.9	10.2	17.7	52.2
$10,000–$14,999	96.6	37.7	7.9	28.7	12.4	16.2	58.9
$15,000–$24,999	91.2	29.8	5.6	23.4	7.8	15.6	61.4
$25,000–$29,999	85.4	25.0	3.4	21.2	6.3	14.8	60.4
$30,000–$49,999	85.2	23.1	3.4	19.3	5.9	13.4	62.0
$50,000 or more	94.5	20.9	3.2	17.2	4.2	13.0	73.6
Residence							
Central city	122.8	41.3	11.1	29.2	11.0	18.2	81.5
Suburban	89.1	25.2	3.9	20.8	6.3	14.5	64.0
Nonmetropolitan areas	66.6	23.2	2.2	20.5	6.8	13.7	43.4

*Includes data on rape not shown separately.

SOURCE: *Criminal Victimization 1990: A National Crime Victimization Survey Report.* U.S. Department of Justice, Bureau of Justice Statistics. Washington: U.S. Government Printing Office. (October 1991): 6.

> Bureau of Justice statistics show that those most at risk of being victimized are young, black males with low incomes who live in urban areas.

Laub (1990, pp. 29–32) notes the following correlates of victimization:

- As age increases, the risk of victimization decreases.
- Males are victimized at twice the rate of females.
- The rate of violent victimization—especially aggravated assaults and robberies—is greater for blacks than whites.
- As income goes up, the risk of personal victimization goes down.
- Those who live in urban areas suffer more victimizations than residents of suburban or rural areas.

In addition to vulnerability, victimology also examines culpability. **Culpability** refers to any action of the victim that may in some measure contribute to their victimization. Do victims of auto theft share responsibility for theft if they left the keys in the ignition and the car unlocked? What about the person who continues to live with a violent spouse? Or the rape victim who was walking alone after dark when attacked? The concept of victim culpability is controversial because "blaming the victim" shifts some responsibility from the criminal onto the injured party.

SOCIETY AND VICTIMS

The "blame-the-victim" syndrome is explained by Teresa Saldana, an actress who received nearly fatal stab wounds from a demented fan (Newton, p. 60): "They said I had no business walking alone like that, or that actresses have to expect these things. It was unbelievably painful for me."

This sentiment is echoed by Colleen Davis, who says that becoming a victim "is like becoming a leper" (Newton, p. 60):

> *Victims report being dropped by friends, who no longer invite them to parties for fear they'll cast a cloud of doom. Others have been fired by employers who became intolerant of time lost to medical or psychiatric care or time spent at court proceedings.*

> *When crime victims look for comfort, they report, friends advise them to just snap out of it, to brush themselves off and get back in the race.*

Why does society treat victims badly? According to Martin Symonds, director of the Victim Treatment Center at the Karen Horney

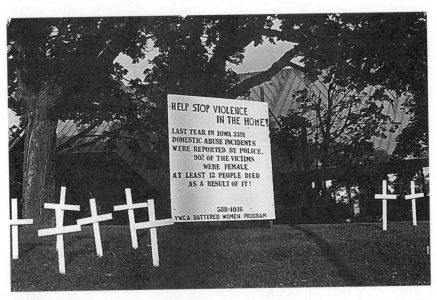

A shelter for battered women in Iowa. Such shelters often also provide care for children and for abused husbands.

Clinic in New York: "People want to distance themselves from victims. It's a way of saying, 'If this can happen to you, I'm vulnerable.' That makes us uncomfortable." This may also partially explain why people do not want to get involved and, in fact, may not come to the aid of someone in distress.

Often police officers and the entire criminal justice system add "insult to injury" rather than assisting those who have been victimized.

POLICE OFFICERS, THE CRIMINAL JUSTICE SYSTEM, AND VICTIMS

During their careers, police officers deal with many more crime victims than criminals. Most officers feel some frustration, even exasperation with victims because their level of trauma, fear, anger, or injury makes it difficult for them to be as cooperative as the officer needs them to be to obtain the maximum amount of information and evidence.

According to Karmen (1992, p. 48): "A relatively small percentage of privileged people harmed by street criminals might enjoy 'first class,' 'red carpet,' or 'VIP' treatment—their rights are scrupulously observed—while socially disadvantaged persons experience mistreatment as 'second-class complainants.' " Victims are often hurt by the physicians, nurses, and police officers who interact with them immediately following their victimization. Victims often expect more warmth and assurance from these professionals than they can give. Professionals often assume businesslike attitudes to protect themselves emotionally and to function effectively in crises.

As noted by Waller (1990, p. 146): "Police officers may have difficulty in being sensitive to emotional reaction. In the course of their duties, they deal routinely with crimes and severe accidents in which victims have been physically injured and must handle such situations with professional detachment."

When victims interpret this necessary emotional detachment as a personal rejection, they receive what is commonly referred to as the "second injury."

The **second injury** often occurs to victims when they are treated badly by professionals who should assist them, including police officers.

According to Skogan, Lurigio, and Davis (1990, p. 9): "Crime victims are the 'forgotten persons' of the criminal justice system, valued only for their capacity to report crimes and to appear in court as witnesses." People who have just been victimized may have to endure any or all of the following (Finn, 1981, p. 1):

- The police may question the victim insensitively.
- There may be innuendos or suspicion that the victim was somehow at fault.
- The victim may have difficulty learning what is going on in the case.
- Property is often kept for a long time as evidence and may never be returned.
- Wages may be lost for time spent testifying in court.
- Time may be wasted when a victim appears in court only to have the case postponed or dismissed.
- Victims may find that the authorities are indifferent to their fear of retaliation if they cooperate in the criminal's prosecution.
- Victims may be fearful of testifying in court and being embarrassed by defense attorneys.

According to Newton (1988, p. 57): "For victims, the hazards and humiliations begin as early as the moment they are led dazed and limping into a busy police station. There they discover the brutal truth—that their case is just one of many. . . ."

He cautions that victims must "be prepared to be treated brusquely by jaded, overworked officers even at the scene of the crime." As an example Newton describes the initial contact of relatives of a homicide victim with law enforcement as "the first terrible moment in what becomes an ongoing nightmare."

One distraught California woman received a late night phone call from a police officer, who dispassionately directed her to call a number for information about her missing husband. "When the phone was answered, the first words she heard were 'Coroner's Office,'" says the woman's sister. "She fell apart even before saying a word."

Another victim, a man whose son was brutally murdered, pleaded: "All I ask is that I be treated with the same concern as a criminal" (Newton, 1988, p. 57).

CRIMINAL RIGHTS

Newton (1988, p. 59) notes:

"Innocent until proven guilty" is the principle that is at the very heart of our criminal justice system. In fact, the rights of defendants—those accused of crimes—have been so extensively spelled out in American jurisprudence that police officers need special training for just a minimal understanding of them. From the moment the "suspect" is arrested, fairness is so scrupulously adhered to that battered and grieving victims and their families have begun to eye the array of defendants' rights with downright envy.

Siegal (1983, p. 1271) graphically describes this inequity as follows: "Vulnerable, angry, insecure, selfless, the victim who survives observes a criminal who is fed, housed, given legal, medical, psychological, and psychiatric aid—even education and vocational training. The victim . . . suffers alone."

According to Newton (p. 57): "Criminals have all the rights. Once a crime has been committed, muggers and murderers have more rights than their innocent victims." Newton cites the following examples:

Criminals have the right to . . .	but victims . . .
v Be informed of their rights when arrested.	v Are given no warning before being selected as victims.
v Be represented by counsel—free of charge if they can't afford to pay.	v Are represented as "the people" in a case, not as individuals.
v Free food, clothing and medical care while in custody.	v May face financial ruin due to medical costs, time lost from work.

v Psychological counseling.

v Plea-bargain to a lesser charge in exchange for a guilty plea.

v A speedy trial (though they can ask for postponements).

v Be present at proceedings and confront their accusers in court.

v Appeal to a higher court to overturn a ruling or lighten a sentence.

v Are counseled free only when limited state funds are available.

v Have no legal power to object to victimizers' plea bargain.

v Are subject to delays in court proceedings, sometimes as long as several years.

v May be excluded from trial; can confront their victimizers only if called as witnesses.

v Cannot appeal the acquittal of the victimizers.

The disparity between how criminals and victims are treated by the criminal justice system forces some victims to join together in support groups. The disparity also prompts others to try to better understand the victims of crime.

PROGRESS IN ASSISTING VICTIMS

Society has made progress in assisting victims of crime. In 1981 President Ronald Reagan proclaimed National Victims of Crime Week, putting the full weight and influence of his office behind the victims' movement. In 1982 President Reagan created a Task Force on Victims of Crime to do an extensive study on crime victimization (Burnley, 1990, p. 11):

> *The Task Force found that crime victims were often victimized twice—first by the crime itself, and then by the criminal justice system. Innocent victims were ignored, mistreated or even blamed for what happened. Traumatized by criminal and judicial proceedings they did not understand and relegated to serving as evidence at the convenience of the courts, the experience left victims unwilling to become involved again in the criminal justice system.*

The Task Force's finding that more emphasis was put on the defendant's rights than on the rights of victims prompted it to call for a balancing of the rights of defendants and victims. The Task Force examined the Sixth Amendment clearly establishing the rights of suspects to a trial, to confront witnesses, and to have an attorney present:

> *In all criminal prosecutions, the accused shall enjoy the right to a speedy and public trial, by an impartial jury of the state and District wherein the crime shall have been committed, which districts shall have been previously ascertained by law, and to be*

informed of the nature and cause of the accusation; to be confronted with the witnesses against him; to have compulsory process for obtaining witnesses in his favor, and to have the assistance of counsel for his defense.

The Task Force recommended that the Sixth Amendment of the Constitution be changed to include the following statement: "In every criminal prosecution, the victim shall have the right to be present and to be heard at all critical stages of the judicial proceedings" (U.S. Department of Justice, 1983, p. 115). The Task Force made other recommendations, including developing guidelines for the fair treatment of crime victims and witnesses and expanding programs of victim compensation.

In addition, victims of crime and those concerned about victims have become advocates for changes in the criminal justice system's response to victims. Grass roots victim organizations have been formed including such groups as Mothers against Drunk Driving, Parents of Murdered Children, the National Organization of Victim Assistance, and Victims for Victims. In addition, victim compensation laws and victim advocacy and protection programs attempt to address what is widely perceived as the system's protection of the accused's rights to the victim's detriment.

Organizations

According to Burnley (1990, p. 10): "The notion of providing help to crime victims is a rather recent phenomenon. It originated in grassroots efforts in the 1960s and 1970s to assist victims of sexual assault and battered women."

The first national organization to support victims' rights was the National Organization for Victim Assistance (NOVA), founded in 1976 in Fresno, California, by a small group of victim advocates.

The National Organization for Victim Assistance (NOVA) was founded in 1976.

NOVA has accomplished the following (Carrington and Nicholson, 1991, p. 342):

(1) Assistance in formulating and passing the Victims of Crime Act, the Victim and Witness Protection Act, the Justice Assistance Act, and bills of rights for victims; (2) providing through its advocates, crisis counseling, information, referral, and assistance; and (3) providing local victim assistance programs with updated information on how to serve the victims with whom they have contact.

Grassroots organizations that have developed to support victims and survivors include Parents of Murdered Children (POMC) and Mothers Against Drunk Driving (MADD)

The emergence of citizen groups concerned with victims' rights is well illustrated by the formation of the Stephanie Roper Committee. In 1982, Stephanie Roper, honors college student and daughter of Roberta and Vince Roper, was kidnapped, raped, tortured, then shot in the forehead and set aflame. During the trial of the two men accused of the atrocities, the Ropers were barred from the courtroom after they gave their testimony. They were allowed back into the courtroom when the accused were sentenced, but the court did not permit them to make a statement about how the crime had affected them. Outraged at the light sentence the two men received, the Ropers founded the Stephanie Roper Committee. Thousands of people joined and lobbied for tougher sentencing laws and better treatment of victims. In 1983 Maryland legislators passed the "Stephanie Roper legislation" which:

- Permits the use of written victim-impact statements to be submitted to the judge or at the sentencing hearing, which allow crime victims or their families to describe how the crime affected their lives.
- Increases the time before the convicted are eligible for parole in life sentences.
- Ensures the victim's right to remain in the courtroom after being called as a witness.
- Ensures the victim's right to be notified of parole release hearings and to give an updated impact statement.
- Gives victims the right to withhold their addresses and phone numbers to protect them from intimidation by defendants.

A second national organization for victims, the National Victim Center, was founded in 1985.

The National Victim Center was formerly the Sunny von Bulow National Victim Advocacy Center. This Center's broad-ranging programs include the following (Carrington and Nicholson, 1991, p. 342):

(1) Seminar training across the country of direct-line victim service personnel involved in such areas as rape crisis counselling, child protection activities, assistance with domestic violence cases, and counselling survivors of homicide victims; (2) work for constitutional amendments creating "Victims' Bills of Rights" in the several states; (3) information referral to individual crime victim service agencies; (4) maintaining a data base of some 13,000 pieces of legislation that concern victims' rights, directly or indirectly; and (5) maintaining another data base of the names

and addresses of, and key individuals involved with, over 7000 victim assistance agencies nationwide.

In 1986 NOVA established a Crisis Response Team (CRT) to assist communities that experienced disasters such as plane crashes, forest fires, and shootings. As noted by Davis and Henley (1990, p. 164):

> The CRT is a nationwide network of volunteers who have attended NOVA-sponsored training sessions throughout the country.
>
> When a community requests help, NOVA staff members contact network members in the vicinity of the stricken community. Typically a specific team consists of a NOVA coordinator, member of the clergy, mental health professional, law enforcement representative, medical specialist, and press liaison.

Again, the cooperation of various professionals and community organizations is critical to the success of each CRT. In addition to the growth of grassroots organizations and national organizations to help victims, Congress and various states have passed legislation to assist victims.

Legislation

In 1982 Congress passed the Federal Victim and Witness Protection Act. Through this act, as noted by Kelly (1990, p. 174): "The Congress finds and declares that . . . without the cooperation of victims . . . the criminal justice system would cease to function."

The Federal Victim and Witness Protection Act of 1982 (WPA) established the victim impact statement (VIS) as a formal part of the presentence report.

The WPA suggests that law enforcement officials should:

> [E]nsure that the appropriate U.S. probation officer is fully advised of any information pertinent to the preparation of the victim impact statement . . . so that the report will fully reflect the effects of the crime upon the victims as well as the appropriateness and amount of restitution. The victim should be apprised that the probation officer is required to prepare a VIS that includes a provision on restitution. The victim should be advised as to how to communicate directly with the probation officer if he so desires.

The **victim impact statement (VIS)** is a written report describing in detail the full effect of a crime on the victim. A VIS may influence the sentence passed by the judge.

According to Wells (1991, p. 45): "The VIS can significantly benefit both the victim and the officer—it is the principle means for communicating with the court on issues such as emotional impact and financial loss; it helps to ensure that restitution amounts are accurate and reflect the total loss sustained by the victim; and it may influence final sentences imposed by the court. But perhaps its greatest benefit is the one most often overlooked; *it may promote psychological recovery of victims.*"

Other legislation attempts to reduce the financial hardships of victims. In 1984 Congress passed the Comprehensive Crime Control Act and the Victims of Crime Act, establishing a fund of up to $100 million for victims of crimes and the agencies that serve them.

The Victims of Crime Act (VOCA), passed in 1984, established a fund making state grants available for victims compensation, victim assistance programs, and child abuse prevention and treatment.

As noted by Muraskin (1992, p. 13), in 1988 Congress reauthorized VOCA for another six years and appropriated $150 million for the VOCA fund.

Forty-five states and Washington, D.C., have established compensation programs to be eligible to receive VOCA funds and help crime victims recover financial losses incurred through medical bills. Table 10.4 summarizes the victim compensation programs and procedures in forty-two states. The dollar amounts of crime victims compensation awards and victim assistance allocations from 1986 through 1990 are contained in Appendix B.

According to Carrington and Nicholson (1991, p. 339):

Legislatures of every state continued to respond enthusiastically to the victims' movement. Major initiatives were seen in such areas as victim impact statements, victims' rights to allocution at sentencing (and in some cases even at the plea bargaining stage), rape shield laws, extension of statutes of limitations in child sexual abuse cases, and other areas as well.

Programs Implemented

Financial compensation is not the only type of assistance available from programs for victims. The most frequent services provided by victim/witness programs are summarized in Table 10.5.

In 1985 Albert R. Roberts undertook a nationwide survey of the organizational structure and functions of 312 victim/witness assistance programs that were identified at the time. He received 184 responses (60

TABLE 10.4
Compensation Programs to Help Victims of Violent Crimes

State	Use to Inform Victim						Reporting Deadline (days)	Filing Deadline (days)	Processing Time (weeks) (avg. claim)	Processing Time (days) (emergency award)	Time Limit—Appeals (days)	Payment Method		
	Police	Hospital/Emergency	Victim Assistance Programs	Prosecutor	Poster/Brochure	Public Service Announcements						Lump Sum	Installments	Pay Vendors Directly?
Alabama	2	3	1	1	4	5	3	365	16	2	30	x		x
Alaska	1	3	5	2	4		5	730	16	3	30	x	x	
Arizona	1	2	3	4	5	6	3	365	9	1		x	x	x
Arkansas							3	365	10	22	30	x	x	x
California	2	3	1		4			365	40	30	45	x		x
Connecticut	1	3	2		4	5	5	730	13	1	30	x		x
Delaware	1	4	2	3	5		3	365	13	12	30	x		
Florida							3	365	16	15	60	x	x	x
Hawaii			1					548	40		30	x		x
Idaho	1	2	3	5	6		3	365	9	10	145		x	x
Indiana	3	2	1	4	6		2	730	7	2	30	x	x	
Iowa	1	2	3	4	5		1	180	16	42	30	x		
Kansas	1	4	3	2			3	365	12		30	x	x	x
Kentucky	4	3	1	2	5	6	2	365	20	30	30	x	x	x
Louisiana	1							365	45	6	5		x	
Maryland	2	3	1	4	5		2	180	10	10	30	x	x	x
Massachusetts	2		3	1			2	365	32		15	x		x
Michigan	2	4	3	1	5		2	365	22	30	30	x	x	x
Minnesota	1		2	3	4		5	365	14	12	30	x		
Missouri	1	3	4	2			2	365	30	30	30	x		
Montana	1	2	3	5	9	6	3	365	7	7	30	x	x	x
Nebraska	1	5	2	3	6	4	3	730	6		30	x	x	
Nevada	2	1	3	3			5	365A	12	20	15	x	x	x
New Jersey	1	2	4	3	9	6	90	730	26	5	20	x	x	x
New Mexico							30	365				x	x	
New York	1	2	4	5	3		7	365	16	1	30	x	x	
N. Carolina	3	1	2				3	365	13	3	60	x	x	
N. Dakota			1				3	365	10		30	x	x	
Oklahoma	2	3	5	1	4	7	3	365	15	12	30	x	x	
Oregon	1	2	1	2	3		3	365	18	7	60	x	x	
Pennsylvania	2	4	1	3	3		72	365	20	28	20	x		
Rhode Island		3	2	1	4	5	10	1,095	104		20	x		
S. Carolina	3	4	1	2	9	5	2	180	9	2	30	x	x	
Tennessee	1	3	1	4	7		2	365	12	15	30	x		
Texas	2	1	3	4	9	5	3	365	22	3	20	x	x	
Utah	1		4	2			7	365	4	4	20	x	x	
Virgin Islands	1	2	4	3	5		1	730	27			x		
Virginia	2	3	1	4			5	180	8	30	20	x	x	x
Washington	4	2	1	3	5		3	365	4		60	x	x	
W. Virginia	1	3		2			3	730	4		21	x		
Wisconsin	1	2	3	4	3		5	365	14		30	x	x	x
Wyoming	2	5	4	3	1	6		365	5	5		x		x

A—Minor sexual assault victims have until age 21 to apply.

SOURCE: Dale G. Parent, Barbara Auerbach, and Kenneth Carlson. *Compensating Crime Victim: A Summary of Policies and Practices.* U.S. Department of Justice, National Institute of Justice. Washington: U.S. Government Printing Office. (January 1992.)

TABLE 10.5
Victim-Witness Program Services

Emergency Services
Medical care
Shelter or food
Security repair
Financial assistance
On-scene comfort

Counseling
24-hour hotline
Crisis intervention
Follow-up counseling
Mediation

Advocacy and Support Services
Personal advocacy
Employer intervention
Landlord intervention
Property return
Intimidation protection
Legal/paralegal counsel
Referral

Claims Assistance
Insurance claims aid
Restitution assistance
Compensation assistance
Witness fee assistance

Court-related Services
Witness reception
Court orientation
Notification
Witness alert
Transportation
Child care
Escort to court
Victim impact reports

Systemwide Services
Public education
Legislative advocacy
Training

SOURCE: Reprinted by permission. Peter Finn and Beverly Lee. *Establishing and Expanding Victim-Witness Assistance Programs.* Washington: National Institute of Justice. (1988).

percent). According to his survey (1990b) the great majority of programs (84.7 percent) were separate components or relatively autonomous units of larger agencies. Over half operated under the auspices of the city or county prosecutor, while only seven percent were under the auspices of the police department, as indicated in Table 10.6.

According to Roberts' survey (1990b, p. 47) the great majority of programs indicated that they provided five or more of the eleven services listed in the questionnaire, as summarized in Table 10.7.

> The two main types of programs provided for victims are **victim service programs** that provide crisis counseling, shelter, and other specialized treatment and **victim/witness assistance programs** that seek to provide assistance to victims and witnesses as their case moves through the judicial process.

Programs should be based on identified needs of victims and witnesses. According to McClenahan (1990, p. 104):

TABLE 10.6
Auspices of Responding Programs

	Number of Programs	Percentage
City or county prosecutor	107	58
State's attorney	21	11
Nonprofit social service agency	20	11
Police department	13	7
County probation department	8	4
County criminal justice or social service agency	5	3
Hospital	3	2
Nonprofit criminal justice agency	3	2
U.S. Attorney's Office	1	0.5
Miscellaneous	2	1
No information given	1	0.5
Total	184	100

SOURCE: Reprinted by permission. Albert R. Roberts. *Helping Crime Victims: Research, Policy, and Practice.* Newbury Park: Sage Publications. (1990): 41.

TABLE 10.7
Services Provided by Programs

Type of Service	Number of Programs	Percentage
Explain court process	131	71
Make referrals	126	69
Provide court escort	120	65
Help with victim compensation applications	118	64
Public education	112	61
Assist with employers	111	60
Provide transportation to court	109	59
Provide crisis intervention	99	54
Provide child care	69	38
Provide emergency money	45	25
Repair locks	22	12

NOTE: 184 respondents supplied 1,063 responses.
SOURCE: Reprinted by permission. Albert R. Roberts. *Helping Crime Victims: Research, Policy, and Practice.* Newbury Park: Sage Publications. (1990): 47.

The most common needs among victims are access to case progress information, assistance with their safety concerns, compensation for losses, crime prevention information and feedback on how their feelings compare to those of others in similar situations.

There are often many practical needs, as well. These include being in a safe environment, having funds to meet immediate expenses (E.G., bus fare, money for a meal) and having someone to talk to who is interested not only in their recollection of facts, but also in their experience and its emotional impact.

In addition to the formation of victims' organizations and the passage of legislation to provide funding and services for victims, progress has also been made in formalizing the rights of victims.

Victims' Bill of Rights

"The struggle to gain formal, legal rights has been a powerful moving force throughout history. . . . The most well-known include civil rights, workers' rights, students' rights, children's rights, women's rights, gay rights and prisoners' rights. The victims' rights movement of the late 1970s and 1980s falls within this tradition" (Karmen, 1992, p. 46).

Thirty-six states have enacted victims' bills of rights, omnibus bills that, according to Newton (p. 61):

> [D]epending on the state, assert the right to be protected from intimidation, the right to access to information about a case, the right to submit a statement prior to sentencing, and the right to be consulted during plea bargaining.

Senna and Siegel (1990, p. 178) note that comprehensive victims' bills of rights laws may also:

- Ensure the victim's right to continued employment.
- Provide medical or social support services.
- Require the appointment of an "ombudsman" to protect the rights of the victim during the trial period.

Most victims' bills of rights include both informational and participatory rights.

According to Karmen (1992, pp. 46–47) the most widely enacted *informational rights*, gained at the expense of criminal justice agencies and officials, include the following:

- To be read one's "rights": to reimbursement of losses—from state compensation funds, court ordered offender restitution, insurance coverage, civil lawsuits, or tax deductions; to referrals—to counseling programs, self-help support groups, shelters for battered women, rape crisis centers, and other types of assistance; and to be told of one's obligations—to attend line-ups, appear in court, be cross-examined under oath, and to be publicly identified and the subject of media coverage.

- To be informed of the whereabouts of the "accused" offender: at large; or in custody (jail or prison); escaped from confinement; or released back to the community (on bail, or due to dropped and dismissed charges, or because of acquittal after a trial, or out on appeal, probation, furlough, parole, or after an expired sentence).
- To be kept posted about key decisions: arrests, the granting of bail, rulings at evidentiary hearings, negotiated pleas, verdicts at trials, sentences, and parole board deliberations.
- To receive assistance in the form of intercession by an official on behalf of a victim with an employer or creditor; advance notification and facilitation of court appearances; and expeditious return of recovered stolen property.

Karmen (p. 47) lists the following *participatory rights,* gained at the expense either of offenders or agencies and officials:

- To be consulted when the terms and conditions of bail are being determined (as a protection against harassment and reprisals for cooperating with the prosecution).
- To be consulted about the offers made during plea negotiations.
- To be permitted to submit a victim impact statement, detailing how the crime caused physical, emotional, and/or financial harm, as part of the presentence report, and to submit a statement of opinion suggesting remedies, for the judge's consideration.
- To be permitted to exercise **allocation** rights in person, in court, detailing the harm caused by the offender and suggesting an appropriate remedy, before the judge imposes a sentence.
- To be permitted to bring to the attention of the parole board, either in writing or in person, information about the harm caused by the offender and an opinion about an appropriate remedy.

Victims' rights bills commonly require the victim to be informed about available financial aid and social services; advised of case status and scheduling; protected from harassment and intimidation; provided with separate waiting areas during the trial; and a speedy return of property held as evidence.

The International Association of Police (IACP, 1983) has defined the "incontrovertible rights of all crime victims" as follows:

1. To be free from intimidation;
2. To be told of financial assistance and social services available and how to apply for them;
3. To be provided a secure area during interviews and court proceedings, and to be notified if presence in court is needed;
4. To be provided a quick return of stolen or other personal property when no longer needed as evidence.
5. To a speedy disposition of the case, and to be periodically informed of case status and final disposition; and, wherever personnel and resource capabilities allow, to be notified in felony cases whenever the perpetrator is released from custody;
6. To be interviewed by a female official in the case of rape and other sexual offenses, wherever personnel and resource capabilities allow.

More Remains to Be Done

As noted by Elias (1991, p. 44):

> *Victims have progressed significantly in the last quarter century, but they have not yet shaken their second-class status. When victimized, they lack confidence in receiving the aid they need, and for good reason—they often must tolerate inadequate services, cultural insensitivity, political insignificance, and official maltreatment.*

One critical area in which to deter "official maltreatment" mandates that police improve their response to those who have been victimized.

THE POLICE RESPONSE

Talking to victims and witnesses requires police to use specific skills to ensure that the victim or witness provides all available information for successful investigation, apprehension, and prosecution of the perpetrator. At the same time, officers must treat victims and witnesses respectfully and take care of their immediate needs. Victims are frequently traumatized or injured. Crime victims might be frightened, injured, in shock, angry, and confused when police expect them to submit to questioning and provide minute details of the crime and suspect. Occasionally a victim may have reason to lie about the events. The following interview skills will help to gain the victim's cooperation:

1. Take care of the victim's safety and medical needs first. Frightened people need to be assured that they are safe and

that you will keep them safe. Any injuries or pain need to be attended to before they can be expected to provide any meaningful information.

2. Victims and witnesses need to be interviewed individually so they will not alter their recollections to match each other's. Victims sometimes trust another victim's memory more than their own.

3. Let the victim or witness know that what they tell you is very important and that you need their help. Try to calm fears they may have of retaliation or of testifying in court.

4. Provide the individual with resources that will help them to deal with the problems that result from being a victim or in some cases, a witness. They may need transportation, a place to stay, assistance in security for their house or business, the use of a telephone, a referral to counseling, or an advocate to help them.

The manner in which police officers interact with victims and witnesses makes a difference in how the officers and the department are perceived by the public, if you can develop informants, how many criminals the department can apprehend, how effectively they are prosecuted, how many complaints are lodged against officers and/or the department, and how far officers are able to advance in their careers. It is critical that officers interact effectively with victims and witnesses.

According to Frederick, Hawkins, and Abajian (1990, p. 106): "The outcome of effective police-victim interviewing can have a positive dual effect, aiding police in retrieving pertinent evidence and factual data relevant to the case, while protecting the immediate and potential future mental well-being of the victim." The first few moments of police contact with a victim or witness are critical. Frederick, Hawkins and Abajian (pp. 106–09) offer police officers the following victim/witness intervention techniques:

1. Display composure.
2. Try to put the victim at ease. ("I'm here with you and I want to help you.")
3. Give honest and accurate information (without being brutally frank or alarming).
4. Remove the victim temporarily from a stressful situation.
5. Begin interviewing and questioning the victim only after establishing psychological and physical equilibrium. (Lack of support and understanding from an official has been reported by some victims to be worse than the initial trauma.)
6. Proceed with a clear and unambiguous plan.
7. Contact and meet with available relatives and friends.

   8. Make use of the victim's personal resources.
   9. Encourage physical activity. (Simply suggesting that the individual get up and get a drink of water or accomplish some other useful act can be invaluable.)
   10. Supply suitable advice and direction. (Every victim should be encouraged to seek psychological assistance from a skilled professional.)
   11. Adapt to the needs of the victim, taking into account verbal facility, social background, age, sex, and the like.

Waller (1990, p. 151) emphasizes:

> *The police are well situated to initiate crisis support to victims. Because they are often the first officials to talk to the crime victim, they are able to reassure and refer the victim to appropriate services in the community. . . .*
>
> *The police could improve their support for crime victims by requiring the responding officer to provide the victim with a card that identifies the key telephone numbers of such services as the local distress center, locksmiths, criminal injuries compensation, the crime prevention unit, and a service that could help or refer the victim to other community services. Ideally, this card would identify both the file number of the case as well as the name of the police officer.*

One important area in which police officers can help victims is in preparation of the victim impact statement (VIS). Wells (1991, pp. 45–46) suggests these steps for law enforcement officers:

   1. Let victims know that the opportunity to provide such a statement exists, and that they have the right to become active in the court case process. Remember, victims' rights are like offenders' rights were before the *Miranda* decision—if victims don't know these rights exist then, in effect, they do not exist.
   2. Let victims know what procedures and policies are in place regarding the administration of the VIS program in your area. Do they simply send a letter to the judge? Do they complete a VIS form sent by the police department, the prosecutor, a victim advocate or the probation department? Do they talk directly to probation about the impact?
   3. Encourage the victims' participation. Let them know that the information they have to offer can make a difference.
   4. Let them know that you can answer their questions or concerns about the process and help them prepare their statements.

Wells (p. 46) notes that most of the forms used for VIS are directed "primarily toward meeting the needs of the system rather than the needs of victims." He suggests that police departments that use such forms should review them and ask the following questions (pp. 46–47):

- Do the forms match victim and crime, or are they "one size fits all"? [Suggestion: develop separate forms and cover letters for violent, property, and white-collar crime.]
- Do the forms enable the victim to express the crime's impact? [Suggestion: start the form with a simple, open-ended question such as "How are you and members of your family being affected by this crime?" and leave one page for the response.]
- Do the forms or cover letters use terms unfamiliar to many victims? [Suggestion: avoid such terms as "restitution," "deposition," "preliminary hearing," or "crime compensation," or explain them fully if they must be used.]
- Avoid using impersonal opening sentences such as: "We have been advised that a member of your family is deceased as a result of a crime." [Suggestion: say something like, "We are aware that you have been victimized by a crime and would like to know how you and members of your family have been affected by this crime."]

Many police departments are becoming more aware of the problem of officer insensitivity to victims and witnesses and are providing "consciousness-raising courses" to help officers understand and deal with victims empathetically.

SPECIAL POPULATIONS

Interacting effectively with victims is a critical part of police officers' jobs that requires extreme skill and sensitivity. Some victims have additional medical and psychological needs that require officers to be quite sensitive. Officers should be aware of resources available for these "special" victims.

"Special" crime victims who require additional services include battered or sexually assaulted women, abused children, and elderly victims of crime or abuse.

Battered or Sexually Assaulted Women

Traditionally, police have not treated domestic violence as a crime except in extremely brutal cases. Police often considered domestic violence to be a "family matter." Wives had to press charges before the police could intervene. This requirement has been eliminated in most states. As noted by Friedman and Shulman (1990, p. 89): as the result of womens' rights advocates' lobbying efforts and the grave consequences to women in cases where they had been denied police protection after being assaulted, police departments now treat domestic violence as a crime.

In addition: "Only the state of West Virginia has failed to pass legislation that authorizes the police to make warrantless, probable-cause arrests and file complaints in domestic violence cases." No longer must the victim press charges, which in effect, has shifted the burden of stopping the violence away from the victim. Friedman and Shulman (p. 91) stress: "Police departments have begun to develop policies on family violence that are guided by two principles: (1) domestic violence is a crime; and (2) victims of domestic violence require special considerations." They conclude (p. 100): "The staggering, but probably conservative statistics that indicate 2.1 million women are beaten each year, 3,000 die, and 20% of homicides are committed within the family demand that law enforcement and criminal justice agencies develop special responses to domestic violence cases to counteract years of reverse practices."

The Domestic Abuse Intervention Project is a national training project which includes seminars for law enforcement officers and trainers, prosecutors, legal advocates, and police administrators. The seminars introduce two key wheels that can drive a relationship, the power and control wheel and the equality wheel, shown in Figure 10.1 and Figure 10.2.

In addition to explaining the dynamics of domestic violence, the seminars teach:

- State law and department policy regarding domestic violence.
- Establishing probable cause in domestic violence cases.
- Distinguishing between mutual assaults and self-defense.
- Making the decision to arrest, mediate between, or separate spouses.
- Gathering evidence effectively and writing reports.
- Enforcing civil protection orders.
- Interviewing child witnesses.
- Maintaining officer safety and awareness of liability issues.
- Understanding the psychological dynamics of battering in relationships.

Such programs illustrate the progress that is being made to educate officers about domestic violence.

According to Roberts (1990a) recognition of the need for and establishment of crisis intervention for victims has increased dramatically since the mid-1970s when there were only seven emergency shelters for

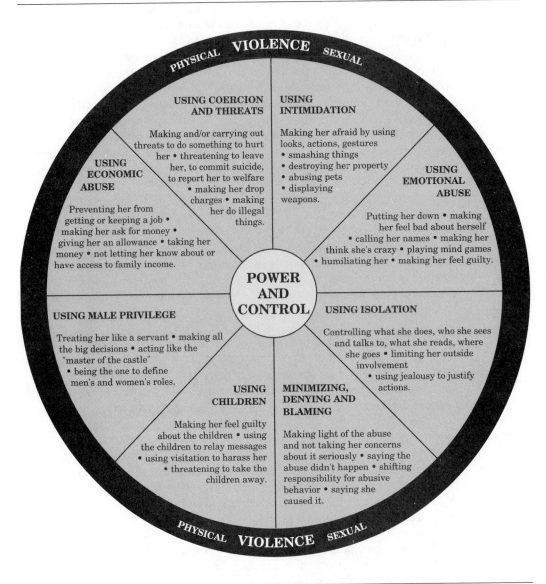

FIGURE 10.1   The Wheel of Power and Control

SOURCE: Reprinted by permission. **Domestic Abuse Intervention Project,** 206 West Fourth Street, Duluth, Minnesota 55806

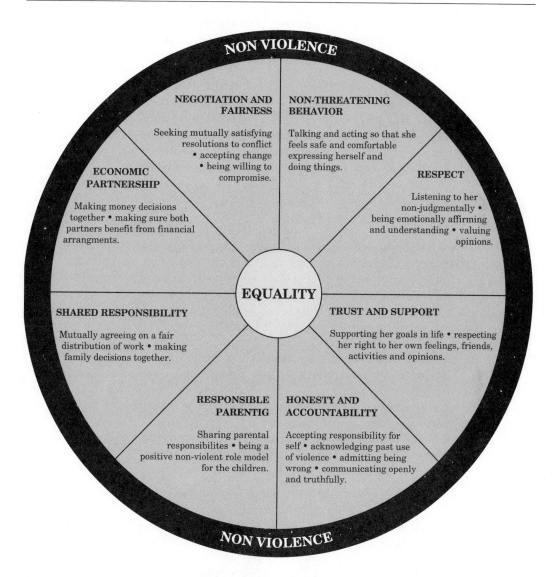

FIGURE 10.2   The Wheel of Equality

SOURCE: Reprinted by permission. **Domestic Abuse Intervention Project,** 206 West Fourth Street, Duluth, Minnesota 55806 battered women and four police-based crisis intervention programs nationwide. He notes that by 1987 there were more than 1,250 such emergency shelters and crisis services for battered women and their children.

According to Roberts and Roberts (1990b, p. 188) the most common precipitating events that lead battered women to seek help from a domestic violence program are: "(a) an acute battering incident resulting in a serious physical injury, (b) a serious abusive injury inflicted on the woman's child, and (c) a temporary impairment of hearing, sight, or thought process as a direct result of severe batterment."

Roberts and Roberts emphasize that it is essential for police to be familiar with referral sources that go beyond the immediate crisis. Such sources may include job training and placement, low-cost housing, and child care needs. According to Roberts and Roberts (p. 202): "The most frequently used referral sources involved legal aid, medical care, Careers for Homemakers, Job Bank, day-care programs, Women in Need (WIN, an agency concerned with long-term housing for single women), Alcoholics Anonymous, Women's Self-Help Center (providing counseling and support groups), and St. Pat's (a Catholic social service agency that finds low-cost housing and provides classes in budgeting money and other life skills)."

As noted by Elias (1990, p. 230), progress has been made in legislation regarding battered women: "Better record-keeping, like monthly police reports are required to track abuse patterns. Other laws provide protective orders, assign possession of the residence, get the defendant to pay support, and set custody and visitation rights. Thirty states authorize warrantless arrests for misdemeanor assaults; ten require it upon probable cause."

Women who have been sexually assaulted also have unique needs. Resick (1990, pp. 70–81) suggests the following:

> With very little effort on their parts, practitioners in the criminal justice system are in the position to help rape victims recover. . . . Although the police who investigate cases may disagree with the victims' appraisal of the imminent danger posed by the situation based on their experience, they should not disregard the victims' perceptions. . . . Investigators and other criminal justice system personnel should make a special effort to refer victims to counseling who describe the crime as an imminent death situation or who describe themselves as being terrified during the crime. . . .
>
> How a victim is treated by criminal justice practitioners may affect how the rape victim psychologically processes the event. Investigations can and should be conducted without implying that the victim brought on the crime . . . even when the investigator feels that the victim put herself at risk by her own behavior. . . . Teenagers are particularly naive and cannot always discriminate

safe from potentially unsafe situations. Poor judgment is not an offense punishable by rape. . . .

Police . . . need to be careful in their phrasing of questions. For example, "What happened next?" or "What did you do then?" are neutral questions, whereas, "Why did you . . . ?" implies blame and puts the victim on the defensive. . . .

A few judicious statements by the criminal justice practitioner may help greatly in a victim's recovery. Statements about the normal course of recovery (months, not days or weeks) and normal symptoms, such as flashbacks, nightmares, intrusive memories, the desire to avoid reminders, sleeping problems, and roller-coaster emotions, may help victims know that their reactions are normal and that they are not crazy. Rape victims should be advised to take things one step at a time but to return to normal activities as soon as they are able rather than avoid non-dangerous "danger" cues that were conditioned during the crime. They should be encouraged to mobilize their social support network and tell their loved ones what they need . . . . Most often, families and friends want to be supportive but do not know what to do or say. . . .

Finally, . . . they should be warned that they may be given bad advice from well-meaning but uninformed people . . . to subscribe to the "stiff-upper-lip school of psychology," to disregard their emotions, . . . put the event behind them, and get on with their lives.

According to Elias (1990, p. 230): "Sexual assault victims also receive special attention, with laws for services, such as hotlines and counseling, crime prevention and prosecution, and medical attention. At least one state requires sexual assault victims to be given information about AIDS."

Abused Children

Dealing with abused children, especially those who have been sexually abused, is another very sensitive type of case and one which often involves considerable media attention. According to Smith (1990, p. 108): "It is important to emphasize that no arrest was made in nearly half of the cases in which the police believed sexual abuse had occurred." This statistic highlights the difficulty of investigating and prosecuting child sexual abuse cases.

According to Elias (1990, p. 229): "All but nine [states] try to make child testimony less traumatic, permitting a videotaped statement either alone (unsworn interrogatory) or under oath and cross-examination (deposition), or live testimony through closed-circuit television. . . . Nine states require everyone, and all states at least require professionals, to report suspected child abuse, backed by civil damages, or even criminal penalties."

Often child sexual abuse cases are jointly investigated by a child protection service agency and the police department. Smith (1990, pp. 114–55) suggests the following guidelines to make cooperative efforts successful:

- Maintain open communication.
- Conduct joint training.
- Conduct interagency staff retreats.
- Conduct regular interagency meetings.
- Establish specialized units.
- Balance the number of staff among the coordinated agencies.
- Exercise patience.

Professionals must receive extensive training to learn how to prevent and investigate child abuse. Abuse against children is one of the most underreported crimes in the United States. Serious attempts to reduce crime and violence in our society require that children be protected from abuse. Child abuse is a cyclical crime: those who have been abused tend to abuse others when they become adults. Many serious criminals were abused as children. The link between abuse as a child and adult criminal behavior was discussed in Chapter 8.

Elderly Victims

A special report conducted by the Bureau of Justice Statistics (Whitaker, 1987, p. 1) reported the following major findings:

- Elderly violent crime victims were more likely than younger victims to face offenders armed with guns.
- Elderly violent crime victims were more likely than younger victims to report that the offenders were total strangers.
- The elderly were more likely than victims under age 65 to be victimized by a violent crime at or near their own homes.
- Among the elderly, certain groups were more vulnerable to crime than others: Males, blacks, separated or divorced persons, and urban residents generally had the highest victimization rates.

Elderly victims of violent crimes often have unique problems and often are more drastically affected than younger victims. The elderly often live on a fixed limited income, so financial losses can be especially devastating. In addition, the elderly are frail, can be easily injured, and take a long time to heal. The elderly may also be less emotionally able to cope with victimization.

Among services that a community might provide for the elderly are the following suggested by Roberts (1990b, p. 78):

- Transportation and escort to stores, public health clinics, hospitals, and banks.
- Provision of a special police unit that responds to cases of senior burglaries, robberies, purse snatchings, and assaults.
- Training youth to help elderly victims.
- Establishment of neighborhood block watch programs and neighborhood building patrols.
- Arrangement for new locks on doors and windows of elderly burglary victims.
- Provision of 24-hour hotlines and daily telephone reassurance.
- Making information and referral services available.
- Installation of video monitors in elevators and corridors of large apartment buildings.

Roberts (p. 81) emphasizes: "The protection and provision of services for victims of elder abuse and neglect should be the joint responsibility of a network of community agencies, including victim assistance programs, family violence programs and shelters, police departments, visiting nurses' associations, in-home respite care programs, hospital senior care programs, and senior community centers."

According to Elias (1990, p. 230):

> *Elderly victims have elicited laws allowing the victim's age to be used in determining sentences, producing tougher penalties and probation denial. Some states criminalize the abuse or neglect of the elderly. Many states require elderly-abuse reporting, especially by professionals, with 25 states protecting all vulnerable adults and 22 protecting older adults over a certain age. Some states mandate ombudsmen, speedy trials, abuser registries, hotlines, food, clothing, shelter, medical care, and other social services.*

Police officers must be sensitive to victims and understand the reasons they behave as they do. During the 1990s police departments will emphasize victimology studies in police recruit training and continue to develop victim assistance programs.

THE RESPONSE OF THE CRIMINAL JUSTICE SYSTEM

The entire criminal justice system should be sensitive to the needs of victims. According to Kelly (1990, p. 175): "Studies revealed that a sense of participation was more critical to victims' satisfaction with the criminal justice system than how severely the defendant was punished." Victim participation can occur in several ways.

Plea Bargaining

Kelly (p. 176) notes that between 83 and 90 percent of all cases that remain in the criminal justice system are plea bargained. She also notes that the Victim Witness Protection Act of 1982 states that prosecutors should consult victims about the terms of a plea. Further, twenty-three states now allow or mandate some form of victim participation in plea bargaining.

Victim Involvement in Sentencing

Kelly (p. 178) notes that 96 percent of the states allow some form of victim involvement in sentencing, with the two most common forms being the VIS and the **victim statement of opinion (VSO).** According to Kelly:

> The VIS allows victims to detail the medical, financial, and emotional injuries that resulted from the crime. . . .

> In contrast, the VSO is considered more subjective. VSO allows the victim to tell the court their opinion on what sentence the defendant should receive.

Hillenbrand (1990, p. 193) notes: "Virtually every state now also provides for some sort of victim impact statement prior to sentencing."

Court Attendance

The Sixth Amendment to the Constitution establishes the right of the defendant to be in the courtroom, but crime victims often have no such rights. As noted by Kelly (1990, p. 180): "For many victims, to be relegated to a hallway or waiting room represents both the ultimate insult and the ultimate loss of control."

According to Elias (1990, p. 228): "Fifteen states allow victims in the courtroom (waiving sequestration rules) at the judge's discretion, and one state makes court attendance a victim right." In 1987 a national movement, the Victims Constitutional Amendment Network (VCAN), was organized to lobby for constitutional amendments to allow victims to be present and heard at all stages of the criminal justice process.

Probation and Parole

According to Hillenbrand (1990, p. 193): "By the end of 1987, restitution was authorized or required in virtually every state as a condition of probation. In addition, at least 23 states authorized it as a condition of parole, 14 as a condition of suspended sentence, and 10 as a condition of work release. At least 26 states provided for restitution in addition to, or in lieu of, other sentences."

RECOMMENDATIONS

The National District Attorneys Association (p. 8) recommends that the following types of agencies be included in a victim/witness assistance referral network: community groups, day-care centers, domestic violence programs, food stamp distribution centers, job counseling and training programs, mental health care programs, physical health care programs, private sector allies, private and community emergency organizations, rape crisis centers, unemployment services, victim assistance or advocacy organizations, victim compensation boards, volunteer groups, and welfare agencies.

Summary

National Crime Survey statistics estimate that 34.4 million victimizations were committed in the United States in 1990. Victims of crime may suffer physical injury, financial and property losses, emotional distress, and psychological trauma. Some suffer from post traumatic stress disorder (PTSD), a persistent re-experiencing of a traumatic event through intrusive memories and dreams and a variety of anxiety-related symptoms. A primary victim is a person actually harmed by an incident. A secondary victim is one indirectly affected by the trauma.

Victimology, the study of crime victims, includes the concepts of vulnerability and culpability. Bureau of Justice statistics show that those most at risk of being victimized are young, black males with low incomes living in urban areas. A "second injury" often occurs to victims when they are treated badly by the professionals who should be helping them, including police officers and the criminal justice system.

Our society has made progress in helping crime victims. The National Organization for Victim Assistance (NOVA) was founded in 1976. A second national organization, the National Victim Center, was founded in 1985. Congress and many states have passed legislation to assist crime victims. The Federal Victim and Witness Protection Act of 1982 established the victim impact statement (VIS) as a formal part of the presentence report. The victim impact statement is a report written by the victim that describes in detail the full effect of the crime. The VIS may influence the sentence passed by the judge. The Victims of Crime Act (VOCA), passed in 1984, established a fund making state grants available for victims' compensation, victim assistance programs, and child abuse prevention and treatment.

The two main types of programs provided for victims are victim service programs that provide crisis counseling, shelter, and other specialized treatment and victim and witness assistance programs that seek to provide assistance to victims and witnesses as they move through the judicial process.

Most victims' bills of rights include both informational and participatory rights. Victims' rights bills commonly require victims to be informed about available financial aid and social services, notification of case status and scheduling, protection from harassment and intimidation, separate waiting areas, and a speedy return of property held as evidence. Victims who require additional services include battered and sexually abused women, abused children, and elderly victims of crime or abuse.

DISCUSSION QUESTIONS

1. Have you ever been victimized? How were you treated by those who "assisted" you?
2. How large a role do you believe culpability plays in victimization?
3. Did the "blame the victim" syndrome play a role in the Anita Hill—Clarence Thomas hearings?
4. Do police and other professionals who assist victims treat those victims who are wealthy differently than those who are poor?
5. How do you balance professional detachment and the need for empathy?
6. How large a role should victim impact statements play in sentencing?
7. What victim services are available in your community?
8. What services that are not currently available should be available in your community?
9. In what ways do police officers become victims?
10. What differences exist between assisting victims of crime and victims of accidents or natural disasters?

DEFINITIONS

Can you define these terms: allocution, cognitive restructuring, culpability, post traumatic stress disorder (PTSD), primary victim, "second injury," secondary victim, victim impact statement (VIS), victim service programs, victim statement of opinion (VSO), victimization, victimology, victim/witness assistance programs, vulnerability.

REFERENCES

American Psychiatric Association. *Diagnostic and Statistical Manual of Mental Disorders.* 3rd rev. ed. Washington: American Psychiatric Association, 1985.

Burnley, Jane Nady. "Foreword." In *Helping Crime Victims: Research, Policy, and Practice,* edited by Albert R. Roberts, 10–12. Newbury Park: Sage Publications, 1990.

Carrington, Frank and Nicholson, George. "Victim's Rights? An Idea Whose Time Has Come—Five Years Later: The Maturing of an Idea." In *Taking Sides: Clashing Views on Controversial Issues in Crime and Criminology.* 2nd rev. ed., edited by Richard C. Monk, 338–43. Guilford: The Dushkin Publishing Group, Inc., 1991.

Cohen, Mark, "Pain, Suffering, and Cost Jury Awards: A Study of the Cost of Crime to Victims." *Law and Society Review 22.* (1988): 537–55.

Conroy, Dennis L. and Hess, Kären M. *Officers at Risk: How to Identify and Cope with Stress.* Placerville: Custom Publishing Company, 1991.

Criminal Victimization in the United States, 1990. U.S. Department of Justice, Bureau of Justice Statistics. Washington: U.S. Government Printing Office, 1992.

Davis, Robert C. and Henley, Madeline. "Victim Service Programs." In *Victims of Crime: Problems, Policies, and Programs,* edited by Arthur J. Lurigio, Wesley G. Skogan, and Robert C. Davis, 157–71. Newbury Park: Sage Publications, 1990.

Elias, Robert. "The Politics of Victimization." In *Taking Sides: Clashing Views on Controversial Issues in Crime and Criminology.* 2nd rev. ed., edited by Richard C. Monk, 344–50. Guilford: The Dushkin Publishing Group, Inc., 1991.

Elias, Robert. "Which Victim Movement? The Politics of Victim Policy." In *Victims of Crime: Problems, Policies, and Programs,* edited by Arthur J. Lurigio, Wesley G. Skogan, and Robert C. Davis, 226–50. Newbury Park: Sage Publications, 1990.

Federal Bureau of Investigation. *Crime in the United States, 1987.* Washington: U.S. Government Printing Office, 1988.

Finn, Peter. *Victims.* Washington: Bureau of Justice Statistics, 1988.

Frederick, Calvin J.; Hawkins, Karen L; and Abajian, Wendy E. "Beyond the Call of Duty? Victim/Witness Intervention Techniques." *The Police Chief.* (October 1990): 106–10.

Friedman, Lucy N. and Shulman, Minna. "Domestic Violence: The Criminal Justice Response." In *Victims of Crime: Problems, Policies, and Programs,* edited by Arthur J. Lurigio, Wesley G. Skogan, and Robert C. Davis, 87–103. Newbury Park: Sage Publications, 1990.

Hillenbrand, Susan. "Restitution and Victim Rights in the 1980s." In *Victims of Crime: Problems, Policies, and Programs,* edited by Arthur J. Lurigio, Wesley G. Skogan, and Robert C. Davis, 188–204. Newbury Park: Sage Publications, 1990.

International Association of Chiefs of Police. *Crime Victims Bills of Rights. Board of Officers.* Arlington: Policy Center, 1983.

Karmen, Andrew. "The Implementation of Victims' Rights: A Challenge for Criminal Justice Professionals." In *Annual Editions: Criminal Justice 92/93.* 16th ed., 46–49. Guilford: The Dushkin Publishing Group, Inc., 1992.

Kelly, Deborah. "Victim Participation in the Criminal Justice System." In *Victims of Crime: Problems, Policies, and Programs,* edited by Arthur J. Lurigio, Wesley G. Skogan, and Robert C. Davis, 172–87. Newbury Park: Sage Publications, 1990.

Laub, John H. "Patterns of Criminal Victimization in the United States." In *Victims of Crime: Problems, Policies, and Programs,* edited by Arthur J. Lurigio, Wesley G. Skogan, and Robert C. Davis, 23–49. Newbury Park: Sage Publications, 1990.

Lurigio, Arthur J. and Resick, Patricia A. "Healing the Psychological Wounds of Criminal Victimization: Predicting Postcrime Distress and Recovery." In *Victims of Crime: Problems, Policies, and Programs,* edited by Arthur J. Lurigio, Wesley G. Skogan, and Robert C. Davis, 50–68. Newbury Park: Sage Publications, 1990.

Lurigio, Arthur J.; Skogan, Wesley G.; and Davis, Robert C. eds. *Victims of Crime: Problems, Policies, and Programs.* Newbury Park: Sage Publications, 1990.

McClenahan, Carol A. "Victim Services—A Positive Police-Community Effort." *The Police Chief.* (October 1990): 104.

Monk, Richard C. *Taking Sides: Clashing Views on Controversial Issues in Crime and Criminology.* 2nd rev. ed. Guilford: The Dushkin Publishing Group, Inc., 1991.

Muraskin, Roslyn. "The Growth Industry of Victim Services." *Law Enforcement News.* (March 15, 1992): 13.

National District Attorneys Association. *A Prosecutor's Guide to Victim Witness Assistance.* Alexandria: National District Attorneys Association, n.d.

Newton, Edmund. "Criminals Have All the Rights." In *Criminal Justice 87/88,* edited by John J. Sullivan and Joseph L. Victor, 57–61. Guilford: The Dushkin Publishing Group, Inc., 1988.

Resick, Patricia A. "Victims of Sexual Assault," In *Victims of Crime: Problems, Policies, and Programs,* edited by Arthur J. Lurigio, Wesley G. Skogan, and Robert C. Davis, 69–86. Newbury Park: Sage Publications, 1990.

Riggs, David S. and Kilpatrick, Dean G. "Families and Friends: Indirect Victimization by Crime." In *Victims of Crime: Problems, Policies, and Programs,* edited by Arthur J. Lurigio, Wesley G. Skogan, and Robert C. Davis, 120–38. Newbury Park: Sage Publications, 1990.

Roberts, Albert R. *Crisis Intervention Handbook: Assessment, Treatment and Research.* Belmont: Wadsworth, 1990a.

Roberts, Albert R. *Helping Crime Victims: Research, Policy, and Practice.* Newbury Park: Sage Publications, 1990b.

Roberts, Albert R. and Roberts, Beverly Schenkman. "A Model for Crisis Intervention with Battered Women and Their Children." In *Helping Crime Victims: Research, Policy, and Practices,* edited by Albert R. Roberts, 186–205. Newbury Park: Sage Publications, 1990.

Senna, Joseph J. and Siegel, Larry J. *Introduction to Criminal Justice.* 5th rev. ed. St. Paul: West Publishing Company, 1990.

Siegal, M. "Crime and Violence in America: The Victims." *American Psychologist,* 38. (1983): 1267–73.

Skogan, Wesley G.; Lurigio, Arthur J.; and Davis, Robert C. "Criminal Victimization." In *Victims of Crime: Problems, Policies, and Programs,* edited by Arthur J. Lurigio, Wesley G. Skogan, and Robert C. Davis, 7–21. Newbury Park: Sage Publications, 1990.

Smith, Barbara E. "The Adjudication of Child Sexual Abuse Cases," In *Victims of Crime: Problems, Policies, and Programs,* edited by Arthur J. Lurigio, Wesley G. Skogan, and Robert C. Davis, 104–19. Newbury Park: Sage Publications, 1990.

U.S. Department of Justice. *Report of the President's Task Force on Victims of Crime.* Washington: U.S. Government Printing Office, 1983.

"Victimology." *Criminal Justice 87/88,* pp. 46–47. Guilford: The Dushkin Publishing Group, Inc.

von Hentig, H. *The Criminal and His Victim: Studies in the Sociology of Crime.* New Haven: Yale University Press, 1948.

Waller, Irvin. "The Police: First in Aid?" In *Victims of Crime: Problems, Policies, and Programs,* edited by Arthur J. Lurigio, Wesley G. Skogan, and Robert C. Davis, 139–56. Newbury Park: Sage Publications, 1990.

Wells, Robert C. "Victim Impact: How Much Consideration Is it Really Given?" *The Police Chief.* (February 1991): 44–47.

Whitaker, Catherine J. *Elderly Victims: Special Report.* U.S. Department of Justice, Bureau of Justice Statistics. Washington: U.S. Government Printing Office, 1987.

RESOURCES

National Center for Missing and Exploited Children, 1835 K Street, N.W., Suite 700, Washington, D.C. 20006; (202) 634–9821. Hotline: (1–800) 843–5678.

National Organization for Victim Assistance (NOVA), P.O. Box 11000, Washington, D.C. 20008; (202) 232–NOVA.

National Victims Resource Center, Box 6000, Rockville, MD 20850; (800) 627–6872.

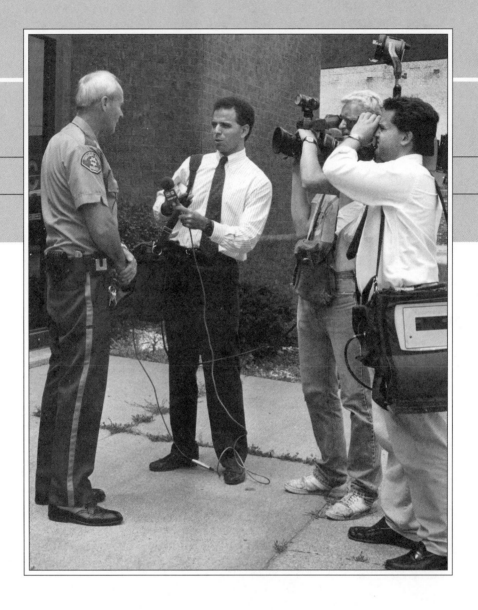

INTERACTING WITH THE MEDIA

The police work is very much an "us-and-them" kind of thing. They are the beleaguered minority who are out there protecting the citizens from themselves and the citizens are not smart enough to appreciate them. And the newsies are out there lying in wait, and the moment they screw up, we're there to jump their throats and tell the world.

—**Kevin Diaz.**

DO YOU KNOW

- What organizations the "media" includes?
- What is the common goal of the police and the media?
- Why the police-media relationship can be called symbiotic?
- What amendment protects "freedom of the press"?
- What amendment guides the police in their relationship with the media?
- What conflicts exist between the media and the police?
- What are legitimate reasons for not giving information to the press?
- What "off the record" really means?
- How to enhance the safety of members of the media during explosive situations?
- How reporters and police generally differ in decision making?
- Whether conflict between the police and the press must be dysfunctional?
- Why reporters may louse up stories? What implications this has for law enforcement?

INTRODUCTION

"On any given day on any given newscast in any given city, law enforcement-related news—misdemeanors, felonies, traffic accidents—consumes approximately 30% of the available air time" (Gleick, 1991, p. 98). In addition: "The image of the entire criminal justice system is dependent upon what is said in the media about each of its components" (Pace, 1991, p. 244). Pace notes that: "Good publicity is the life blood of a police agency."

Conversely, negative publicity can be extremely damaging, as evidenced by the "Rodney King Affair" aired internationally by CNN.

The media includes newspapers, radio, and television.

The police beat reporter and police officers have much in common (Kiernan, 1987, p. 670):

> *Both are powerful, visible institutions, are highly structured, and assign personnel specific "beats" for which they are responsible. Individuals are expected to have a highly defined sense of civic responsibility, fairness and compassion. Ingenuity, individual effort and investigative skills are prized as well as good writing or verbal skills. Both rely on the use of anonymous sources, and must work quickly under pressure when routine activities are suddenly interrupted by bursts of Pandemonium.*

The police and members of the media share the common goal of serving the public.

In addition to sharing a common goal, they also rely heavily upon each other.

MUTUAL RELIANCE OF THE POLICE AND THE MEDIA

Police departments and individual officers need the press. The press can shape public opinion, and most police agencies are concerned about their public image. Administrators know that crime and police activities are covered by the media regardless of whether the police provide reporters with information. Most police departments understand that the level of police cooperation will ultimately affect how the public views the police. As noted by Guffey (1992, p. 33):

> *The police and the media are two organizations that interact regularly. The relationship can be described as symbiotic. The media need the police to supply them with information about crime and crime patterns that are of interest to their readers, listeners, or viewers. The police need the media to improve their image within the community, to publicize major crimes or crime patterns, to publicize wanted persons, and to seek witnesses from the community.*

The police and the media share a **symbiotic** relationship; they are mutually dependent upon each other.

The symbiotic nature of the relationship between the police and the media is described by news director Penny Parrish (pers. com. 1992) who formed special bonds of friendship and respect with some officers. She was able to get extra information from the officers, and they "used" her when they needed to have information made public: "We both used each other, and we both knew it. I got some scoops. And the officers I worked with let it be known in the department that I was trustworthy, and it helped to open doors." Such relationships can be advantageous to all parties.

Unfortunately, relations between the police and the media are often strained. Weinblatt (1992, p. 32) asks: "Why would modern day police officers rather meet a hulking bad guy in a back alley than face a white-collar professional person armed with only a pen and note pad? . . . The trepidation and distrust comes from a lack of communication and a failure to understand just what each party's responsibilities are."

To understand the relationship between the police and the media, officers should be aware of what rights the media has, what their mission is, and why law enforcement does not always appear in a positive light in the media.

THE FIRST AMENDMENT AND FREEDOM OF THE PRESS

The First Amendment to our Constitution states: "Congress shall make no law . . . abridging the freedom of speech or of the press."

The First Amendment to the Constitution guarantees the public's right to know, that is, freedom of the press.

Our society deems the public's right to know so important that the media operates without censorship, but is subject to legal action if it publishes untruths.

Police reporters are often eager and aggressive in carrying out their duty to inform the public. Traditionally, police beat reporters are anxious to do well, to be the first with information and, therefore, they gather and publicize police and crime news as much as they can. According to Parrish (pers. com. 1992):

> *Although traditionally green reporters were assigned to the police beat, more recently, the police beat is the prestige beat sought by the experienced, hungry, aggressive reporters. It has become the sexy beat, the way to get your face (or byline) on record just about every day. TV and movies have made cops big news and big box office fodder. The police beat has become the high visibility beat. Viewers and readers remember the reporters assigned to these stories. They never remember who did a story on the financial status of a school district.*

As noted by Dunphy and Garner (1992, p. 47): "Most news media representatives are honest, up-front, hardworking types. They, too, are interested in seeing that an accurate accounting is given to the public."

Every state has a public records law that specifies what information a law enforcement agency must release, what information must not be released, and what is up to the discretion of the particular agency. Such laws are enacted to protect the rights of citizens under suspicion of breaking the law.

THE SIXTH AMENDMENT, SUSPECT'S RIGHTS, AND INVESTIGATING CRIMES

The Sixth Amendment of our Constitution establishes that "in all criminal prosecutions, the accused shall enjoy the right to a speedy and public trial, by an impartial jury of the state and district wherein the crime shall have been committed. . . ."

The Sixth Amendment guarantees suspects the right to a fair trial.

In addition to assuring these rights, police officers are also responsible for investigating the crimes suspects are accused of committing.

Law enforcement officers sometimes view reporters as an impediment to fulfilling their duties to the public. Law enforcement officers often try to protect information they deem imperative to keep out of the media and may, therefore, be at odds with reporters. Such conflicts arise when police try to prevent public disclosure of information that may tip off a criminal of impending arrest, make prosecution of a particular crime impossible, or compromise privacy rights or safety of a victim or witness. Reporters are anxious to do well on their assignments while officers try to avoid weakening their case and reprimands for being too open with the press. The parties' conflicting interests may result in antagonism.

CONFLICT BETWEEN THE PRESS AND THE POLICE

The press and the police are two powerful forces in our society that depend on one another but are often hostile towards and mistrust each other. According to Kobel (1988, p. 95):

> *In police jurisdictions throughout the United States, police become angry, adversarial and uncooperative with the press for a variety of reasons, including press criticism of the police agency, inaccurate reporting, publication of sensitive information, lack of press sensitivity, or the betrayal of an officer's trust.*

Kobel goes on to note: "Whatever the reasons, the resulting anger and cynicism impedes the work of both groups and, more subtly, can compromise the flow of important information to the public." A basic source of the conflict is the competing objectives of the press and the police.

A Conflict in Objectives

As noted by Pace (1991, p. 244): "The objectives of the police and the news services may not be compatible because their roles are different. . . . There is even an incongruity between constitutional guarantees."

The First Amendment guarantees freedom of the press, yet the Sixth and Fourteenth Amendments guarantee the right to a fair trial and protect the defendant's rights.

Kobel (1988, p. 96) summarizes the conflict as follows:

> *The situation is one that pits the administration of justice against the public's right to know, fair trial and privacy against a free*

press, the Sixth Amendment against the First. At its simplest, the police-press standoff is a legitimate, necessary, constitutionally recognized and protected conflict of interests between two groups whose missions are to serve the public good.

Weinblatt (1992, p. 32) suggests some other internal conflicts that result from these differences:

Police officials with an active investigation in progress are very conscious of the dichotomy which exists in their mandate. On the one hand, cases are solved with information from the public. The police need the press to get to the masses. On the other, police concerns regarding next of kin notification, family suffering and investigation impairment are also bona fide *issues and need to be addressed.*

Police may need to withhold information from the press until next of kin are notified, in the interest of public safety, or to protect the integrity of an investigation.

Although many police officers are keenly aware of the conflict between themselves and the press, they often do not understand how the need to withhold information contributes to the conflict and the resulting negative coverage and what officers can do to alleviate the problem.

Complaints of the Press

To do their job, members of the media need information from the police. Press people say they have problems obtaining information they are entitled to because the police refuse to provide it. In some cases, reporters believe they have been singled out by the police for "punishment" in response to a negative story about the police. Police support each other regarding negative media attention:

You write a story saying a cop screwed up, a cop died of a drug overdose, a cop was murdered trying to buy drugs, and a lot of police take it personally. It's part of the police mentality, I guess. Maybe it's the military mentality of oneness. Maybe it's the us-against-them attitude that you'll always find among cops. David Krajicek, Police Bureau Chief, New York Daily News (Kobel, 1988, p. 6).

Reporters tell of police who restrict information, refuse requests for interviews, disregard reporters' deadlines, hang up the telephone on reporters, provide inaccurate information, play dumb, or even blackball a particular reporter in retaliation for a story they did not like.

Guffey (1992, p. 40) reports the following frequent media complaints about the police:

- They are not forthcoming.
- They cannot accept legitimate criticism.
- They withhold important information.
- They hide behind the shield of the Sixth Amendment too often.
- They are often uncooperative.
- They cannot accept that the media are a legitimate "check" on possible abuses of authority.

The police have a similar list of complaints about the press.

Complaints of the Police

Complaints of the police regarding the press include the following (Guffey, 1992, p. 38):

- Interference with ongoing investigations.
- Insensitivity to legitimate privacy interests of victims.
- Insensitivity to the impact of their report on the police.
- Penchant for sensationalism even at the expense of accuracy.

Some police agencies or officers, who have had negative experiences with the media or believe they have been tricked into releasing information, react by becoming uncooperative, not giving information to which the press is entitled, playing favorites among reporters, and even lying. The behavior of the police aggravates a difficult relationship.

Consider, for example, the "off the record" comments some public officials are inclined to make to reporters. Many have been unpleasantly surprised to be quoted in the next edition of the newspaper. Officers must learn to say only that which they can accept attribution for and are prepared to read or hear reported in the media.

To speak to a reporter "off the record" does not guarantee that the information will not be reported. It may, in fact, make it more likely to be reported.

In some cases, reporters promise to keep information "off the record" when they have no authority to do so.

Motivated by a desire to protect their case and the privacy of those involved, police complain that the press is critical and biased against the police, that reporting is often inaccurate, that reporters lack sensitivity especially towards victims, that the press releases sensitive material and betrays the trust of officers. As noted by Cook (1991, p. 88): "A sensitive

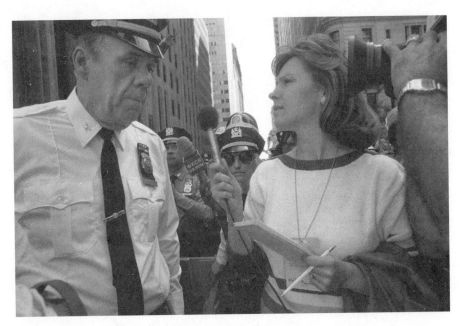

WKCR radio in New York interviews a police supervisor.

investigation is a tough job. But often the toughest part is the confrontation from a pack of reporters bent on yanking something 'newsworthy' (i.e., 'controversial') out of your mouth." Cook contends: "Important cases are going to be tried in the press, with or without you." Often press coverage of important cases is sensationalist.

The way the public views crime depends in large part on what the media prints. Wright (1991, p. 114) suggests that the media presents a distorted, sensationalized view:

> *Overdramatization is the norm rather than the exception in modern crime reporting.*

> *The media distorts its presentation of crime patterns by selecting particular incidents to report. Unusual, bizarre, violent, and macabre incidents receive more media attention. A recent review of research about patterns of crime reporting found that "without exception, violent individual crimes—particularly murders—are represented disproportionately in news media presentations."*

Officers must remember, however, that the media consists of businesses, in fierce competition with each other for readers, listeners, and viewers. What officers may consider sensationalism, reports might consider the competitive edge.

Another source of conflict between law enforcement and the media is the danger members of the press may expose themselves to in getting a story and the police's obligation to protect them. A reviewer of this chapter, Penny Parrish, wrote: "When I saw you on 5/6, I had no idea that the next night my news crew would be attacked during the riot in North Minneapolis. Julia, my reporter, is a patient at Sister Kinney and is still unable to walk because of her head injuries. It's been very scary." Parrish discussed the suggestion that this text address the issue of media safety:

> *Maybe I'm a little sensitive right now, but the safety of the media at crime scenes or riots or potentially dangerous situations is important. Generally reporters and photographers will not cross yellow lines of police tape. But what about situations which are unfolding and the police and the media are both on the scene.*
>
> *Cops should* not *tell journalists to stay away. That is a red flag to most reporters who will run headlong into the area to get their story. But cops are better trained at reading dangerous situations. I would suggest that they urge reporters and photographers to leave an area if they deem it unsafe and tell them why. Don't just bark, "Get out of here."*
>
> *Since the KMSP incident, I have talked to cops who said they knew their first responsibility was to secure the area and calm things down, but they also felt a responsibility for the safety of the media. That angered them . . . that the media was "stupid" enough to be in the middle of the riot. My crew was told to leave and was doing so when attacked. But despite their supposed hatred of the media, the cops in North Minneapolis didn't want to see my people hurt, and they felt bad when they were.*
>
> *Police should meet with local media representatives to explain about rules of safety. And this should be done before an incident arises. It might boil down to telling journalists that they have the right to make decisions about their own well-being, but that as officers, they will issue warnings to try and ensure the safety of news crews. I think that, with the ugly mood in this country right now, the matter of safety of news crews—and whether or not the police are responsible for that safety—will become a big issue.*

To help assure the safety of media personnel at explosive situations, police should meet with media representatives to explain the safety rules *before* an incident arises.

One Possible Factor Underlying the Conflict Between the Press and the Police

Fundamental differences in personality type may be one reason for the conflict that sometimes exists between the police and the press.

Hennessy studied the personalities of police compared to those of the population at large and specific groups, including editors and reporters. Hennessy used the Myers-Briggs test which divides individuals into four basic types, depending on how they make decisions and interact with others.

Individuals may prefer to rely upon how they *feel* about a situation or what they *think* about the situation. Some people are more emotional or more logical in their decision making process. In addition, individuals may prefer to rely upon their senses (*sensing*) or on their *intuition* when making decisions. These preferences result in the following possible combinations:

ST Sensing/Thinking

SF Sensing/Feeling

NT Intuitive/Thinking

NF Intuitive/Feeling

Hennessy gave a sample of 23,557 individuals the Myers-Briggs test to establish what is "normal" for Americans. The same test was given to over 3,000 police officers and to over 100 editors and reporters. The test results of the three groups are summarized in Table 11.1.

Note that while the majority (58 percent) of citizens and reporters relied upon feeling in making decisions, the majority of police officers (80 percent) relied on thinking. Another very obvious difference between the

TABLE 11.1
Preferred Cognitive Styles by Group

		Citizens (N=23,557)	Editors/ Reporters (N=113)	Police Officers (N=3,101)
		Percent	Percent	Percent
Intuitive-Feeling	NF	28.32	41.71	6.3
Sensing-Feeling	SF	29.34	16.82	14.0
Intuitive-Thinking	NT	17.56	27.43	16.6
Sensing-Thinking	ST	24.78	15.04	64.1
Totals		100.00	100.00	100.0

DATE SOURCE: G. P. Macdaid, M. H. McCaulley, and R. I. Kainz, *Myers-Briggs Type Indicator Atlas.* Gainesville: Center for Applications of Psychological Type, Inc., 1986, and Stephen M. Hennessy, *Thinking Cop/Feeling Cop: A Study in Police Personalities,* Scottsdale: Leadership, Incorporated of Scottsdale, 1992.

TABLE 11.2
**Comparison of Citizens, Reporters, and Police Officers
on the Myers-Briggs Test**

	Citizen	Editors/ Reporters	Police Officers
Feeling	58%	58%	20%
Thinking	41%	42%	80%
Intuition	46%	69%	23%
Sensing	54%	32%	78%

two personality types is the reliance of police officers on sensing in contrast to reporters who rely heavily on intuition.

Police tend to rely on thinking and their senses in decision making, in contrast to editors and reporters who tend to rely on feeling and intuition.

The specific percentages for each of the four ways to approach decisions are summarized in Table 11.2.

It is interesting to note that social workers had results within seven percentage points of the editors and reporters which may explain some of the communication problems police have with these professionals.

POLICE OFFICERS AND REPORTERS AS INDIVIDUALS

Chapter 4 discussed the need for police to avoid stereotypes. Stereotypes can greatly impede good working relationships between law enforcement and members of the press. Penny Parrish wrote a letter that was published in a law enforcement agency's union newsletter. Her letter illustrates the position held by many members of the media:

> As police, you despise being lumped together in a bad light. So do we. Not all journalists are out to get you. You are out to find justice; we are out to seek truth. If we find a story regarding questionable behavior by an officer, we cover it. But we also do stories on community meetings, the COP program, and DARE classes. We show you receiving medals for acts of heroism. We ride along with officers to get a better feel for the difficult job you do. We air composites when you need our help in finding a suspect.

And we cover the funerals of your comrades who fall in the line of duty.

You ask for more respect from us. I respond by saying you should give some respect in return. Be more open and honest with us when we are trying to get information on a story. . . . hiding facts just makes us suspicious. And it's hard to do a "balanced" story when no one at [a law enforcement agency] will talk to you. We understand your need to keep some information confidential so it doesn't jeopardize your case. We work to report what you are doing, not to thwart it.

Stereotyping is a dangerous habit these days. It is happening to you, and it is happening to us. We both work under the cloak of the U.S. Constitution. I firmly believe we could do more to open up the lines of good communication between our two groups and work together for the public good.

Understanding differences in personality can be a significant step toward changing a dysfunctional conflict into a healthy, beneficial conflict:

[To] the police and the media, functional, or healthy, conflict is necessary. The media must avoid a close, bonding relationship with the police and vice versa. Each must remain distant enough to be able to criticize the other when necessary, but not to allow the criticism to end communication (Guffey, 1992, p. 35).

Conflict need not be dysfunctional. In fact, healthy conflict between the press and the police is necessary and beneficial.

Conflict can stimulate people to grow and change. It can diffuse defensiveness if those in conflict recognize that their roles are, by definition, conflicting yet complementary. Better understanding of each other may lead to a cooperative effort to serve the public. Most large law enforcement agencies recognize that a cooperative relationship with the media is to their benefit. Many have developed media policies which set forth for officers exactly what may and may not be released to the press, how information will be released, and by whom.

GENERAL POLICIES
FOR MEDIA RELATIONS

As noted by Couper (1983, p. 23): "Officers should have some guidance about when they may talk to the press and what they are allowed to disclose. . . . The agency should work with the media to develop policies about the nature and scope of information to be released in all sensational cases such as hostage situations, murders, and kidnappings. These policies should balance the media's need for immediate information with the operational needs of the police."

Most agencies have developed written policies governing release of information to the press. These policies recognize the right of reporters to gather information and often direct officers to cooperate with the media. Lying to the press is always a bad idea. So is making promises that you cannot keep or misleading the reporter. Such actions usually haunt the individual or their agency in the form of negative press or lack of media cooperation when the police need help. It is better to honor commitments to the press and be straightforward when information is to be released.

Garner (1989, p. 34) suggests the following guidelines for police when working with the media:

- You protect your credibility with the news media by telling the truth.
- If you tell a reporter you will get back to him with additional facts, do so without fail.
- If there are things you must withhold, and often there will be, give the reporter an explanation.
- Do not play favorites. Equal treatment of all your reporter contacts is the best policy.
- Your best response to the occasional "bad news" item is to avoid overreacting to it. . . . Let short-lived bad news die a natural death.

Additional guidelines are suggested by Dunphy and Garner (1992, pp. 46–47):

- Practice your presentation in advance. Anticipate questions and prepare responses.
- Treat every microphone as "live" and every camera as "on."
- Establish and maintain control.
- Make sure you understand the question.
- Defuse volatile questions by rephrasing them in softer, less emotional terms.
- Do your homework. Know your topic and your interviewer. . . . Never try to bluff your way through; admit that you do not have the answer and promise to get it if possible.
- Tell the truth. Never lie, even by omission.
- Know the reporters and their deadlines.
- Emphasize your interest to serve the public.

POLICIES REGARDING PHOTOGRAPHING AND VIDEOTAPING AT CRIME SCENES

Police departments vary in whether they allow news cameras in or around crime scenes. According to Sharp (1991, p. 90): "To prohibit

Interviews with police officers are often featured on local television programs.

pictures gives a perception that cops have something to hide in their activities." Nonetheless, it is imperative that individuals not involved in an investigation *not* be allowed to contaminate the crime scene, as noted by one chief of police: "I feel the First Amendment right does not guarantee an individual the right to photograph or otherwise record a police scene at will. To the contrary, such activities must be controlled to preserve the scene's integrity. To do otherwise could compromise the criminal investigation beyond a salvageable point" (Sharp, 1991, p. 91).

Another chief of police noted a different type of problem with photographing crime or accident scenes: "I perceive problems not from our standpoint, but from that of the victim or complainant, who might not want to be on someone's video, documentary or TV series and might not want cameras in his or her home" (Sharp, p. 92).

In addition, says Sharp (p. 92): "Training bulletins should include warnings to [police to] always be on their best behavior, lest they unwittingly star in a videotape shown on a local television or international network. . . . It never hurts to remind them to 'Smile, they may be on candid camera.'"

Finally, police officers should be aware of the news system called "file video" or "file photos" where pictures are kept indefinitely and can be reused at any time. Parrish (pers. com. 1992) cites an example of how video taken during a ride with a police officer intended to promote police-community relations can also be used differently. In this case a photographer arranged to go with a squad on a high-risk entry into a crack house. The police department let the reporter come along to get some video of how they are working to curb drug traffic in the city. The reporter did the story, and the police were pleased with the resulting public image. Two years later, one officer involved in the high-risk entry unit faced an indictment by a federal grand jury for police brutality. The reporter mentioned to his boss that they had video of this officer breaking into the home of some poor black citizens on the north side. The editors decided that was just what they needed for the story. Video the police had at one time encouraged the media to take was used against an officer.

IMPROVING RELATIONS WITH THE MEDIA

As an important first step to improve relations with the media, Cook (1991, p. 88) suggests that police officers be aware of three basic reasons why reporters often "louse up" a story.

> Reporters may bungle a story due to ignorance, time constraints, or oversimplification.

- Ignorance—Reporters may be ignorant of law enforcement procedures.
- Time constraints—Reporters work under severe deadline pressure.
- The need to simplify—Police deal in complex realities. . . . A reporter must turn a complicated investigation into a paragraph-long news story or a fifteen-twenty second story at the top of the hour.

If officers are aware of these three common problems they can more effectively deal with reporters.

> To improve police-media relations, inform the press of your department's procedures, respect reporter's deadlines, and simplify your information.

- Be a teacher—Provide background information to reporters.
- Respect the reporter's deadlines—Release information in a timely manner so that the press has a chance to fully understand the situation.
- Simplify—Present complex matter in its simplest terms. Avoid police jargon and technical terminology.

BEING PROFESSIONAL
WHEN INTERVIEWED

Officers who know in advance that the press will interview them should prepare carefully. Garner (1989, pp. 35–36) suggests the following:

- Find out in advance from the reporter the purpose of the interview.
- Have your facts straight.
- Anticipate questions.
- Find out some background about your interviewer. If you are to be interviewed on a radio or television show, catch a program or two in advance and plan your strategy accordingly.
- Recognize stage fright as a normal response.
- Dress so you look your best.
- When the interview starts, remember you are talking with, not at, the reporter. Maintain a normal, comfortable, conversational style of speaking and good eye contact.
- Insist on the right to reply to an obviously biased remark, but don't get nasty or pout.
- Avoid jargon and law enforcement slang.

Garner warns that officers should be aware of the "dead air" ploy in which reporters remain silent, waiting for the officer to say something. It is the reporter's responsibility to keep the conversation going. Garner also warns of the "interrupter" or "speechmaker" who cuts you off to ask another question or make his own statement. Garner (p. 37) suggests: "Keep talking over the interruption. . . . The reporter is being discourteous, not you. Keep at it until you have said your piece." Other guidelines offered by Garner (p. 37) include the following:

- Speak only for yourself or your agency. Do not attempt to represent the position of the whole law enforcement profession or criminal justice field.
- Listen very carefully to each question. Ask that it be repeated if you are uncertain of its meaning. Answer only one question at a time.
- Multi-part questions are confusing and dangerous. Have these "laundry list" queries broken down into single questions, if possible. Repeat a question aloud, if necessary, to be sure that you and everyone else knows what you are responding to.
- Resist any attempt to put words in your mouth. Disagree and clarify immediately if your words are being paraphrased or otherwise reported inaccurately.
- Don't try to think of cute replies or be evasive.
- Remain calm, composed, and in charge of the session.

THE NEWS CONFERENCE

News conferences can keep the public informed and build positive relations with the media. Dunphy and Garner (1992, p. 45) offer the following guidelines for effective news conferences:

- Help select the site for the conference, preferably one with an exit near the speaker.
- Maintain good eye contact with the audience. Keep your gaze moving.
- Limit the opening statement to about 10 minutes maximum. Then answer questions.
- Repeat each question to the audience.
- Keep your responses short and to the point.
- Remain responsive and open to your audience, but be aware that every word you speak is now part of the public domain.
- Shift your attention. Try to involve the whole audience in the conference.
- Keep the conference on subject.
- Let your audience know that prepared copies of your statement or news release will be available at the conclusion of the conference.
- Provide an after conference contact. Someone "in the know" should remain accessible by telephone for several hours after the news conference ends to field any questions reporters might have as they write up their stories.

PRESS INFORMATION OFFICERS

Some police departments feel comfortable allowing any member to talk to the press and provide information. The former chief of the Minneapolis Police Department, Tony Bouza, did not have press officers during his administration: "Every member of the department serves as a spokesperson. Reporters are free to call any member of the department and ask them any questions they want. And you will get an answer, regardless of the rank of the officer you speak to." Bouza was fond of saying that the Minneapolis Police Department had 714 public information officers.

Journalists complain that although any officer could speak on behalf of the police department in many cases the police usually release far less information than such an open policy permits.

Some departments have press information officers (PIOs) who disseminate all information to the press and discourage individual officers from providing information to reporters. PIOs try to provide accurate information in a consistent manner while controlling leaks of confidential or inaccurate information.

As noted by Hageman (1985, p. 139): "Their [information officers'] task is to cooperate with reporters, and they also serve as 'gatekeepers' for the information needed to complete investigations. . . . This process of coordinating police and news media coverage by trained officers produces a working relationship which honors the limitations and the professionalism of both occupations."

Press officers are trained in public relations and are professionals in managing controversial or negative situations to the department's benefit. Pace (1991, pp. 244–45) lists the following responsibilities of most press relations officers:

- The officer speaks for the chief of police and for all persons throughout the department.
- The designated press relations officer will always be available to the press.
- Information about major cases will be made available to the media on a timely basis.
- Withholding information about a critical case is asked for by the police and is a voluntary act on the part of the news media.
- The officer provides all news media with facilities and holds press conferences as requested.
- The officer makes available data on the internal processes and procedures in a department and keeps the press informed about personnel investigations and any plans it may have for major operations.

The PIO has a significant amount of responsibility. When PIOs properly carry out their responsibilities they can improve police-media relations. In addition, Kelsey (1992, p. 35) offers the following suggestions for PIOs:

1. When notified respond directly to the scene, unless ordered otherwise. That is where you will be most effective.
2. Know who the incident commander is and take direction only from him.
3. If more than five media representatives are present, insist that a uniformed officer be assigned to assist you. You cannot control the movements of more than five individuals and do your job at the same time.
4. At your initial media briefing, introduce yourself and inform them that you will be the sole source of official information. (Members of your agency must accept that you are the only spokesman.) This will insure that conflicting information is not issued.

5. Your main responsibility is to maintain order to insure that the media representatives know that you are in charge. A fair but firm attitude will allow for mutual respect to be fostered.
6. Do not address any questions that you don't know the answer to and don't speak on any subject that would be better dealt with by another responding agency. If you don't know an answer, inform the questioner that you will get an answer and report back to them. THEN FOLLOW THROUGH. Don't promise anything that you can't deliver.
7. Inform the media representatives as to the time that you will hold your next briefing and then make sure you appear as scheduled.

Kelsey (p. 35) notes: "There is no faster way to reach the public than by way of the media and it is to your advantage to be in control as the situation unfolds. As Parrish warns:

> *Any Chief or PIO who thinks all the information will flow from that one mouthpiece is sadly mistaken. A good reporter will not stop with the official line. He or she will try to talk to investigators to get more on the story. If journalists all wrote their pieces based on the press conference or press release, all stories would sound the same. They don't because other avenues are explored. PIOs should be regarded as funnels or starting points, not the be-all and end-all for journalists. And Chiefs had better know that.*

The press needs the police to provide them with necessary information. The press knows that bad relations between the media and the police can result in limited access to police information. Cooperation and mutual trust benefit both the press and the police.

ESTABLISHING COOPERATIVE RELATIONSHIPS WITH THE MEDIA

Gerald Garner (1989, p. 34), Lakewood Colorado Police Department, claims "a police administrator can gain as much benefit from the media as they can from you. What they have to offer, in many instances, is publicity for your agency and, to a lesser extent, yourself. With a little understanding, that publicity can be positive and make your organization look good."

This sentiment is echoed by South Brunswick Police Captain Thompson: "Police haven't learned to market themselves. We will be better cops if the public sees what we do and knows how to assist us in our service to the community" (Weinblatt, 1992, p. 38).

Training is one way to improve relationships and enhance the media's understanding of what police work involves. Lakewood Colorado Police Department, for example, invited the local newspaper and broadcast reporters to enroll in a citizens' police academy. The reporters were given laser guns and acted out different scenarios to demonstrate the difficult decisions police must make. Inviting members of the media to ride in squad cars is also an effective way to enhance the media's understanding of policing. Conversely, police officers could benefit from learning more about the media and its mission and responsibilities. Officers must remember that reporting is a highly competitive *business*.

In addition to improving community relations, a good rapport with the media can also help the police department accomplish its mission. Comments from police chiefs from across the country underscore this point (Weinblatt, 1992, p. 32):

> *We need goodwill to be efficient. Without the press, we won't get witnesses. We won't get people dialing 911.*

> *We view the media as a messenger. We can't reach our residents without them.*

One outstanding example of the police and media working together is described by Wolfgang (1992). In 1988 press information officers from the Albany Police Department, the New York State Police, and other area law enforcement agencies as well as representatives from the media formed the Capital District Law Enforcement/Media Group. This group, representing eighty different agencies as well as print and electronic media, meets bimonthly to discuss areas of mutual concern. One problem the group tackled was the need to get information to all the media rapidly. Most members of the media believed the practice of PIOs calling down through a media list was very inequitable. It also required a great deal of the PIOs' time. The group found a mutually acceptable solution to the problem: a Pager Information Network (PIN).

Pagers can display full text messages and also have printing capability. One phone call from a law enforcement agency can simultaneously notify all the media. The PIOs can call from the department, home, or a pay or cellular telephone. The system is kept secure through use of passwords and identification codes. According to Wolfgang (1992, p. 30):

> *A department can relay information to all the media in the Albany area by simply dialing an unpublished phone number. An operator employed by Airpage is on duty 24 hours a day. . . .*

> *Messages entered into the Airpage computer are time and date stamped, and transmitted within 30 seconds to the more than 50 pagers now assigned to the network. . . .*

*Since the system began operating in May 1990, it has been used to
warn people of major traffic obstructions on highways, announced
hazardous conditions, notified reporters of shams and cons being
carried out, described bank robberies, announced newsworthy
arrests and arraignments, announced press conferences and
countless other items of interest to the media.*

The media can also be of assistance in public education programs.
For example, an agency in California wanted to increase the accuracy of
citizens' reports of suspicious and criminal activities. They enlisted the
aid of the local newspaper to run a public announcement about what to
include in suspect and vehicle descriptions.

In Chicago, the police use the media in their crime prevention
efforts. Hageman (1985, p. 145) notes that: "As a requirement of the
Federal Communications Commission (FCC), all media are required to
set aside airtime or publication space for community projects." This is
another excellent avenue for law enforcement agencies to convey educational messages to the residents of their communities.

Hageman (pp. 146–47) also suggests: "Other media possibilities include talk shows, in which an agency spokesperson can discuss a controversy or a trend. Sometimes the editor of a local newspaper or publication
will permit an organization a regular column. Letters to the editors may be
written in response to other letters sent in to the editorial page."

RECOMMENDATIONS

The National Symposium on Community Institutions and Inner City
Crime (Sulton, 1990, p. 107) makes the following recommendations
regarding the news media:

- News media should exercise caution when covering crime-related
  incidents. When publishing stories about victims and children who
  are runaways, news media should refrain from using their names
  and faces. The filing of criminal complaints and indictments should
  not be characterized as evidence of guilt. The media should report
  acquittals as well as indictments.
- News media should cover positive aspects of inner-city
  neighborhoods.

Police should work to establish a positive, mutually beneficial
relationship with the media. Cook (1991, p. 93) suggests the following
three-pronged, proactive plan for positive publicity from the media:

1. *Create a master calendar.* You're probably doing a lot of good
    work that never gets reported. How about those talks at the

local elementary schools? The ride-along program? The
baseball card give-aways? What about some of the community
projects individual officers are involved in? Make a calendar
of events and story ideas you'd like covered.

2. *Inventory the local media.* Are you overlooking any media?
   Company newsletters enjoy a loyal readership. So do
   supermarket bulletin boards. These are media, too.

3. *Develop an announcements/events plan.* Call reporters on a
   regular basis to provide story ideas. Draft an occasional press
   release. For a really big event, plan an open house or press
   conference. You can create positive news.

As noted by Weinblatt (1992, p. 32): "A host of police media experts
underscored one clear principle—a working, proactive relationship with the
press is an essential component in the success or failure of an agency in its
service to the community. Communication is of paramount importance."

MODEL POLICE DEPARTMENT PROGRAM

The results of a survey conducted in the San Francisco Bay Area as well
as a national survey mailed to the police departments in the fifty largest
cities in the United States led to the development of a proposed model
police department program for dealing with the media (Guffey, 1992,
pp. 45–48):

1. The model department should designate a public information
   officer (or someone designated to serve as such), including a
   part-time assignment in smaller departments.

2. "Ride-alongs" of reporters with patrol officers should be
   encouraged.

3. There should be training at all levels on proper police-media
   contacts.

4. A thorough media relations policy that has been reviewed by
   at least one local newspaper and, if available, one radio and
   one television station should be implemented.

5. Consider implementing one or more programs such as Secret
   Witness, Crime Stoppers, Green Light, and Media Hotline.

6. Ideally, reporters should be allowed to read offense reports
   and traffic accident reports under supervised conditions.

7. Reporters should be allowed to use departmental telephones
   to call in news stories to their agencies.

8. Reporters should be allowed to talk with any police
   personnel having a part in the news story they are
   preparing.

9. Communication channels should be kept open constantly by telephone or by monthly meetings at neutral, congenial settings such as police-media breakfasts.

10. Chiefs and PIOs should actively seek to appear on radio newstalk programs to discuss current events and issues and to answer live questions from the listening public.

11. The PIO should be trained in use of conflict resolution techniques.

12. The department should issue press identification cards after a careful background investigation of reporters.

Although every component of this model program may be unrealistic for some agencies, police departments should consider those which are feasible.

Summary

One important group with which the police interact is the media. The media includes newspapers, radio, and television. The police and members of the media share the common goal of serving the public. They share a symbiotic relationship in that they are mutually dependent upon each other.

The press are guided by the First Amendment to the Constitution which guarantees the public's right to know, that is, freedom of the press. The police are guided by the Sixth Amendment which guarantees the right to a fair trial. The objectives of these amendments are sometimes in conflict. The First Amendment right to know must be balanced against the Sixth Amendment's guarantee of the right to a fair trial and the protection of the defendant's rights.

Police may need to withhold information from the press until next of kin are notified, in the interest of public safety, or to protect the integrity of an investigation. When police do give information to the press, they should be aware that to ask to speak "off the record" does not guarantee that the information will not be reported. It may, in fact, make it more likely to be reported.

Another source of conflict between the press and the police is the danger members of the press may place themselves in trying to obtain a story. To help assure the safety of media personnel at dangerous situations, police should meet with media representatives to explain the rules of safety *before* an incident arises.

One possible explanation for the conflict between police and the press may be the different ways in which they tend to approach decisions. Police tend to rely on thinking and their senses in decision making, in contrast to editors and reporters who tend to rely on feeling and intuition.

Conflict between the police and the press need not be dysfunctional. In fact, healthy conflict between the press and the police is necessary and beneficial. A step toward mutual understanding is to recognize why reporters may louse up a story. Reporters may bungle a story because of ignorance, time constraints, or oversimplification. To remedy this situation police need to be teachers, respect reporter's deadlines, and simplify the information they provide to the press.

DISCUSSION QUESTIONS

1. Why should the police never lie to the press?
2. Does your police department have a press information officer?
3. How fairly do you feel the media in your community reports crime and violence?
4. How fairly do you feel national media (radio, televisions, magazines, newspapers) cover crime and violence?
5. What might make good topics for PIOs during crime prevention week?
6. Have you ever conducted a news conference or issued a press release? If so, what went well? What was difficult?
7. Why is it important to remember that the media is a for-profit business?
8. Do you feel the media is sometimes insensitive to victims and could also be part of the "second wound" of victimization? If so, can you give examples?
9. What media are available in your community to inform the public of police department operations?
10. Which media do you feel has most impact on the public?

DEFINITIONS
Can you define these terms: PIN, PIOs, and symbiotic.

REFERENCES

Cook, Marshall J. "How to Handle the Press." *Law and Order.* (September 1991): 88–94.

Couper, David C. *How to Rate Your Local Police.* Washington: Police Executive Research Forum, 1983.

Dunphy, Francis R. and Garner, Gerald W. "A Guide to Effective Interaction with the News Media." *The Police Chief.* (April 1922): 45–48.

Garner, Gerald. "Working with the Media: Winning at the Interview Game." *Law and Order.* (May 1989): 34–37.

Gleick, Richard H. "Public Information Officers: Trained to Deal with the Media." *Law and Order.* (August 1991): 98.

Guffey, James E. "The Police and the Media: Proposal for Managing Conflict Productively." *American Journal of Police,* Vol. XI, No. 1. (1992): 33–51.

Hageman, Mary Jeanette. *Police-Community Relations.* Beverly Hills: Sage Publications, 1985.

Hennessy, Stephen M. *Thinking Cop / Feeling Cop: A Study in Police Personalities.* Scottsdale: Leadership, Incorporated of Scottsdale, 1992.

Kelsey, Dean R. "The Crash of Flight 585: Working with the Media." *Law and Order.* (February 1992): 33–35.

Kiernan, M. "Police vs. the Press: There's Always Tension." In *Police and the Media: Bridging Troubled Waters,* edited by P. Kelly. Springfield: Charles C. Thomas, 1987.

Kobel, Richard, "Do Police Determine the Rules and Tone of Press Relations?" *Law Enforcement News.* (July 31, 1988): 1, 6, 13.

Pace, Denny F. *Community Relations Concepts.* Placerville: Custom Publishing Company, 1991.

Parrish, Penny. Letter to author, October 7, 1991.

Parrish, Penny. Letter to author, May 26, 1992.

Sharp, Arthur M. "Picture This." *Law and Order.* (September 1991): 89–92.

Sulton, Anne Thomas. *Inner-City Crime Control: Can Community Institutions Contribute?* Washington: The Police Foundation, 1990.

Weinblatt, Richard. "The Police and the Media." *Law and Order.* (February 1992) 32, 36–38.

Wolfgang, Robert. "Working Together, Police and the Media." *Law and Order.* (February 1992): 29–30.

Wright, Kevin N. "The Overdramatization of Crime in America." In *Taking Sides: Clashing Views on Controversial Issues in Crime and Criminology.* 2nd rev. ed., edited by Richard C. Monk, 111–17 Guilford: The Dushkin Publishing Group, Inc., 1991.

RESOURCES

Parrish Institute for Law Enforcement and Media, 4900 Kingsdale Drive, Bloomington, MN 55437; (612) 835-0582.

Radio Television News Director's Association, 1000 Connecticut Avenue N.W., Suite 615, Washington, DC 20036; (202) 659-6510.

PROJECTS AND PROGRAMS: COORDINATED EFFORTS

Communities consist of individuals, organizations, businesses, agencies, citizen groups, schools, churches, and police departments. Effective interactions with the members of ethnic and cultural minorities, the disabled, the elderly, the young, victims, and members of the media are critical to developing projects and programs to meet a community's needs.

This section begins by describing experiments in community policing and crime prevention (Chapter 12). Among the most common programs are those by which law enforcement agencies attempt to improve communication between the police and the public. Law enforcement is part of the criminal justice system. The other two components of this system, courts and corrections, also sponsor programs that may directly affect the image of the police. These programs also affect how well the entire criminal justice system serves the community, including those who break the law (Chapter 13).

Programs focused on youth are prevalent (Chapter 14). Community-based programs geared at crime prevention have been in existence for decades. The programs may be organized and operated by citizen groups, volunteers, businesses, churches, social service agencies, or a combination of these organizations. They may focus on crime prevention in general or eradicating a specific type of crime such as the sale of drugs (Chapter 15).

The section concludes with a discussion of problem-oriented policing, which emphasizes not only approaches to reducing or preventing specific crimes but also identifying the underlying causes of those crimes and means to address the causes (Chapter 16).

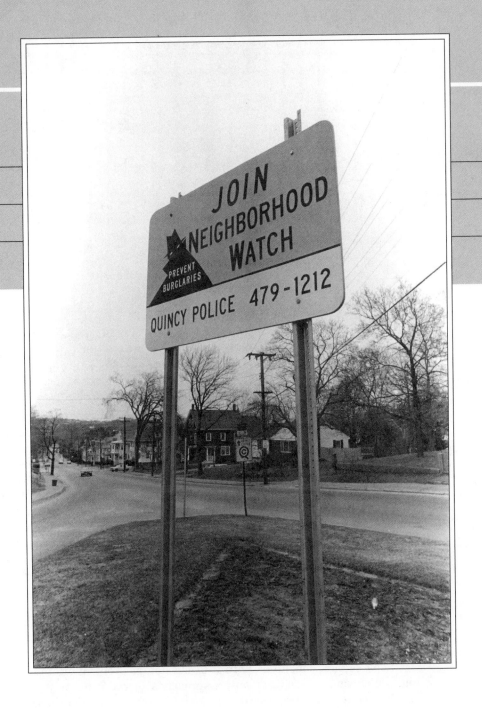

EXPERIMENTS IN COMMUNITY POLICING AND CRIME PREVENTION

Don't be afraid to take a big step if one is indicated.
You can't cross a chasm in two small jumps.

—David Lloyd George,
former prime minister of England.

DO YOU KNOW

- What was demonstrated in studies of community policing in Flint? Newark? Oakland? San Diego? Houston? Boston? Baltimore County?
- What the most common components of community policing have been?
- What was demonstrated in studies of community crime prevention programs in Seattle, Portland, and Hartford?
- What the CPTED Commercial Demonstration Project in Portland found?
- How successful the McGruff national campaign was?
- How successful crime prevention newsletters are?
- What are characteristics of several exemplary police-community programs?
- What impediments might hinder implementing community policing?

"It is probably premature to pronounce community policing the wave of the future," says Ordway P. Burden (1992, p. 5), president of the Law Enforcement Assistance Foundation and chairman of the National Law Enforcement Council. "However, were I a betting man, I would give hefty odds that it is."

Community involvement with and assistance in accomplishing the mission of law enforcement is becoming widely accepted. The change toward community involvement is illustrated in a change in the Portland Police Department's mission statement. The old mission statement proclaimed:

> *The Bureau of Police is responsible for the preservation of the public peace, protection of the rights of persons and property, the prevention of crime, and the enforcement of all Federal laws, Oregon state statutes and city ordinances within the boundaries of the City of Portland.*

The new mission, in contrast, is:

> *to work with all citizens to preserve life, maintain human rights, protect property and promote individual responsibility and community commitment.*

The change from traditional policing to community involvement does require many chiefs of police and their officers to take risks. Are the results of the shift toward community policing worth the risks? This chapter reviews experiments conducted across the country to answer this question.

EMPIRICAL STUDIES OF COMMUNITY POLICING

An **empirical study** is based on observation or practical experience. Greene and Taylor (1991, pp. 206–21) describe eight studies of community policing in major cities throughout the country, including Flint, Newark, Oakland, San Diego, Houston, Boston, and Baltimore.

Flint, Michigan

The *Neighborhood Foot Patrol Program* of Flint, Michigan was conducted from January 1979 to January 1982. It focused on fourteen experimental neighborhoods to which twenty-two police officers and three supervisors were assigned. The officers were given great discretion in what they could do while on foot patrol, but communication with citizens was a primary objective.

The Flint Neighborhood Foot Patrol Program appeared to decrease crime, increase general citizen satisfaction with the foot patrol program, reduce citizens' fear of crime, and create a positive perception of the foot patrol officers.

Mastrofski (1992) explains that the Flint study tried to document what police did on foot patrol and how that differed from motorized patrol. He notes (p. 24):

Looking at the department's daily report forms, the researchers found that foot officers reported many more self-initiated activities—such as home and business visits and security checks—than police in cars. Officers on foot averaged much higher levels of productivity across most of the standard performance measures: arrests, investigations, stopping of suspicious persons, parking citations, and value of recovered property. The only category in which motor patrol officers clearly outproduced their foot patrol counterparts was in providing miscellaneous services to citizens.

According to citizen surveys (Trojanowicz, 1986, pp. 165–67), 64 percent were satisfied with the project and 68 percent felt safer. When asked to compare foot patrol and motorized patrol officers, citizens rated the foot patrol officers higher by large margins on four of the six areas: preventing crime, encouraging citizen self-protection, working with juveniles, and following up on complaints. Motorized patrol officers were rated superior only in responding to complaints. In addition, in the foot patrol neighborhoods crime rates were down markedly and calls for service were down more than 40 percent.

No statistical tests were done, however, and results across the fourteen neighborhoods varied greatly. Therefore, the results should be interpreted with caution. In addition, problems were encountered in the Flint Foot Patrol Program. For example, because the program was loosely structured some officers were not accountable and their job performance was poor.

Nonetheless, according to Skolnick and Bayley (1986, p. 216): "Foot patrol . . . appears from our observations and other studies to generate four meritorious effects:

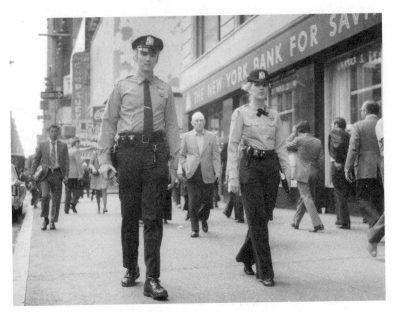

Two officers walk their beat in the Times Square area of New York.

1. *Since there is a concerned human presence on the street, foot patrol is more adaptable to street happenings, and thus may prevent crime before it begins.*
2. *Foot patrolmen may make arrests, but they are also around to give warnings either directly or indirectly, merely through their presence.*
3. *Properly carried out, foot patrol generates goodwill in the neighborhood, which has the derivative consequence of making other crime prevention tactics more effective. This effectiveness in turn tends to raise citizen morale and reduce their fear of crime.*
4. *Foot patrol seems to raise officer morale.*

Newark 1

The original Newark Foot Patrol Experiment was done between 1978 and 1979 and addressed the issues of untended property and untended behavior. This experiment used twelve patrol beats. Eight of the beats, identified as using foot patrol, were divided into pairs, matched by the number of residential and nonresidential units in each. One beat in each pair dropped foot patrol. An additional four beats which had not previously used foot patrol, added foot patrol officers. As in the Flint experiment, officers had great flexibility in their job responsibilities while on foot patrol.

In the first Newark Foot Patrol Experiment, residents reported positive results, while business owners reported negative results.

In areas where foot patrol was added, residents reported a decrease in the severity of crime and evaluated police performance more positively. Business owners, however, believed that street disorder and publicly visible crime increased and reported that the neighborhood had become worse. Pate (1986, p. 155) summarizes the results of the first experiment:

> *The* addition *of intensive foot patrol coverage to relatively short (8 - 16 block) commercial / residential strips during five evenings per week over a one-year period can have considerable effects on the perceptions of residents concerning disorder problems, crime problems, the likelihood of crime, safety, and police service. Such additional patrol, however, appears to have no significant effect on victimization, recorded crime, or the likelihood of reporting a crime.*
>
> *The* elimination *of foot patrol after years of maintenance, however, appears to produce few notable negative effects. Similarly, the* retention of foot patrol does not prove to have notable beneficial effects.

Newark 2

A second foot patrol experiment was conducted in Newark in 1983 and 1984. This experiment used three neighborhoods and a control group (which received no "treatment"). The foot patrol officers in the experimental neighborhoods engaged in one of three "treatments": coordinated foot patrol, which included conducting radar checks, bus checks, road checks, and enforcement of disorderly conduct ordinances; coordinating a cleanup campaign; or distributing a neighborhood newsletter.

The second Newark Foot Patrol Experiment included a coordinated foot patrol, a cleanup campaign, and distribution of a newsletter. Only the coordinated foot patrol was perceived to reduce perception of property crime and improve assessments of the police.

The cleanup effort and newsletter programs did not affect any of the outcome measures studied. In addition, the cleanup effort and newsletter programs did not reduce crime rates. Nonetheless, as noted by the Police Foundation (1981, p. 118): "If vulnerable and weak people feel safe as a result of specific police activity and if that feeling improves the quality of their life, that is terribly important."

Oakland

In 1983 Oakland assigned 28 officers to foot patrol in Oakland's central business district. In addition, a Report Incidents Directly program was established whereby local business people could talk directly to the patrol officers about any matters that concerned them. Mounted patrol and small vehicle patrols were also used in the Oakland program.

The Oakland program, using foot patrol, mounted patrol, small vehicle patrol, and a Report Incidents Directly program, resulted in a substantial drop in the rate of crime against individuals and their property.

The crime rate dropped in the Oakland treatment area more than citywide declines, but again, no statistical tests were reported for this experiment.

San Diego

San Diego conducted a community profile project from 1973 to 1974 designed to improve police-community interactions. Twenty-four patrol officers and three supervisors were given sixty hours of community-orientation training. The performance of these officers was compared with twenty-four other patrol officers who did not receive the training.

The San Diego Community Profile Project provided patrol officers with extensive community-orientation training. These officers became more service oriented, increased their non-law-enforcement contacts with citizens, and had a more positive attitude toward police-community relations.

The project did not consider the effect of community profiling on crime or on citizens' fear of crime.

Houston

Like the second Newark experiment, Houston conducted a fear-reduction experiment between 1983 and 1984, testing five strategies: a victim recontact program following victimization, a community newsletter, a citizen contact patrol program, a police storefront office, and a program aimed to organize the community's interest in crime prevention.

The victim recontact program and the newsletter of the Houston Fear Reduction Project did not have positive results. The citizen contact patrol and the police storefront office did, however, result in decreases in perceptions of social disorder, fear of personal victimization, and the level of personal and property crime.

As noted by Skogan and Wycoff (1986, pp. 182–83) the police storefront officers developed several programs, including monthly meetings, school programs, a fingerprinting program, a blood pressure program, a ride-along program, a park program, and an anticrime newsletter. A comparison of these results to those achieved in the Newark experiment is made on pp. 352–53.

Boston

In 1983 Boston changed from predominantly two-officer motorized patrol to foot patrol. The Boston police department also shifted the responsibilities of the foot patrol and motorized one-officer patrol to less serious crimes and noncrime service calls. The experiment studied 105 beats to determine if high, medium, low, unstaffed, or no change in foot patrol made a difference in calls for service by priority.

The Boston Foot Patrol Project found no statistically significant relationship between changes in the level of foot patrol provided and number of calls for service or the seriousness of the calls.

Violent crimes were not affected by increased or decreased foot patrol staffing. After the department shifted to foot patrol, the number of street robberies dropped, but the number of commercial robberies rose.

Baltimore County

The Baltimore Citizen Oriented Police Enforcement (COPE) Project, started in 1981, focused on the reduction of citizens' fear of crime. This problem-oriented project focused on solving the community problems of fear and disorder that lead to crime. According to Taft (1986, p. 10): " 'Citizen Oriented Police Enforcement' officers would engage in intensive patrol, develop close contacts with citizens, conduct 'fear surveys' (door-to-door canvassing to identify concerns) and use any means within their power to quell fear."

Baltimore County's COPE Project reduced fear of crime by 10 percent in target neighborhoods. It also reduced calls for service, and increased citizen awareness of and satisfaction with the police.

A study conducted in 1985 indicated that the COPE Project "passed its first statistical test with flying colors" (Taft, p. 20). The results of the study are summarized in Table 12.1.

TABLE 12.1
COPE Effects

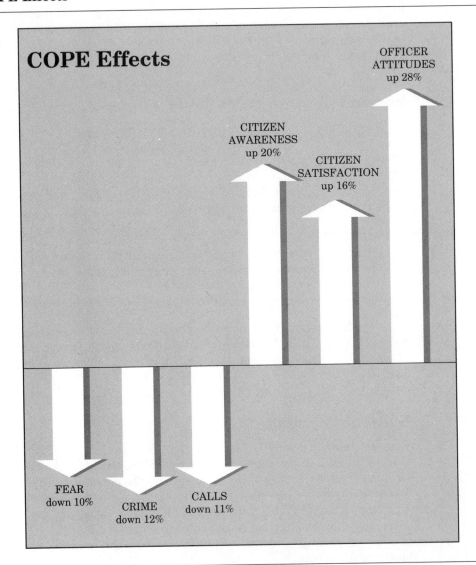

SOURCE: Reprinted with permission of PERF. Philip B. Taft, Jr. *Fighting Fear: The Baltimore County COPE Project.* © The Police Executive Research Forum, 20. Washington: 1986.

Summary and Implications of the Experiments

Greene and Taylor (1991, p. 215) note that "there is not much consistency in findings across studies." Regarding *fear of crime,* Newark 1 observed a reduction; Newark 2 observed a reduction in the **panel analysis** (where the data was analyzed by individuals responding). It did not show a reduction in the **cross-sectional analysis** (where the data was analyzed by area rather than by individuals responding). The Houston study had the opposite results: a reduction in fear in the cross-sectional analysis, but not in the panel analysis. In the Flint study, citizen perceptions of the seriousness of crime problems increased. In Baltimore County it declined slightly. The San Diego, Oakland, and Boston programs did not consider fear of crime. Greene and Taylor (p. 216) conclude: "Based on the problems associated with the evaluation of each of these programs, there is at present no consistent evidence that foot patrol reduces fear of crime."

Greene and Taylor also note inconsistent findings regarding crime rates. The Oakland study was the only one to demonstrate a reduction, but no statistical treatment was done. Again they conclude (p. 216): "Clearly, these studies do not point to decreases in crime or disorder as a consequence of community policing or foot patrol."

Table 12.2 summarizes the critical features of the eight studies, including the specific target of each study, the number of "units" within this target, the elements in the program, the research design, and the desired outcome in each.

The most common components of community policing are foot patrol, newsletters, and community organizing.

Greene and Taylor discuss several problems with the research designs of the eight studies of community policing and suggest ways to improve the designs. This is *not* the view taken by Wycoff (1991, p. 103), however, who states that the fear-reduction studies conducted in Houston and Newark: "provide evidence of the efficacy of what the authors referred to as 'community-oriented' policing strategies for reducing citizen fear, improving citizens' attitudes toward their neighborhoods and toward the police and reducing crime."

FEAR-REDUCTION STRATEGIES
EXPERIMENTS COMPARED

Wycoff (pp. 107–108) summarizes the seven strategies tested in the Newark and Houston experiments as follows:

> Newsletters *(Houston and Newark). These were tested with and without crime statistics. They were police-produced and provided residents of the test area with information about crime prevention*

TABLE 12.2
Critical Features of Community Policing Studies

Study	Unit of Analysis	Number of Experimental Units	Elements in Proposed Program	Research Design	Outcomes
Flint	Foot Patrol Areas of Varied Size and Composition	14	Foot Patrol Unspecified Treatment	Case Study	Crime Rate Fear Satisfaction with Police
Newark 1	Police Beats Matched by Residential/ Nonresidential	12	Foot Patrol Unspecified Treatment	Non-Equivalent Comparison Pre-Post	Fear Crime Rate Perception of Safety
Newark 2	Treatment "Neighborhoods" Matched on Unspecified Criteria	3	Foot Patrol Radar Checks Bus Checks Enforcement of Disorderly Conduct Laws Road (Driver) Checks	Non-Equivalent Comparison Pre-Post	Perceptions of Disorder, Crime, and Victimization Satisfaction with Area, and Police
Oakland	Portion of CBD (6-7 City Blocks)	1	Foot Patrol RID Program Other Patrols	One-Group Pre-Post	Crime Rate
San Diego	Northern Police District	22	Community Profile	Untreated Control Pre-Post	Police Values and Behavior, Organizational Change

TABLE 12.2 (continued)
Critical Features of Community Policing Studies

Study	Unit of Analysis	Number of Experimental Units	Elements in Proposed Program	Research Design	Outcomes
Houston	Program and Control Areas	4	Newsletter Victim Recontact Station Contact Patrol Community Organizing	Non-Equivalent Comparison[1] Pre-Post[2]	Perceptions of Disorder, Crime, and Victimization
Boston	Police Beats and Reporting Areas	105/296	More or Less Foot Patrol	Non-Equivalent Comparison Pre-Post	% Share of Calls for Service, Crime, Maintenance
Baltimore	Targeted "Neighborhoods"	24	Problem-Oriented Policing	One-Group Pre-Post	Fear, Awareness of Police, Satisfaction with Police, Reported Crime

Reprinted with permission of the Publisher Jack R. Greene and Ralph B. Taylor, "Community-Based Policing and Foot Patrol." In *Community Policing: Rhetoric or Reality* edited by Jack R. Green and Stephen D. Mastrofski, 208–09. Westport: Praeger 1988. © 1988 by Jack R. Greene and Stephen D. Mastrofski.

[1]"Non-equivalent comparison" means that no attempt was made to assure that the "experimental" group—the group who implemented the program—and the "control" group—the group who did nothing differently—had the same characteristics.

[2]"Pre-post" means that the items listed under "outcomes" were measured before the program was implemented and after it had been in effect for a specific time period.

steps they could take, the police department, and police programs in their area.

Victim Recontact *(Houston). Patrol officers made telephone contact with victims to inform them of the status of their case, inquire whether they needed assistance, offer to send crime prevention information, and ask whether victims could provide additional information.*

Police Community Station *(Houston). A neighborhood storefront operation was conducted by patrol officers. The station provided a variety of services for the area.*

Citizen Contact Patrol *(Houston). Officers concentrated their patrol time within the target area where they made door-to-door contacts, introducing themselves to residents and business people, and asking whether there were any neighborhood problems citizens wished brought to the attention of the police.*

Community Organizing *(Houston). Officers from the Community Services Division worked to organize block meetings attended by area patrol officers. They organized a neighborhood committee that met monthly with the district captain and developed special projects ("safe" houses for children, identifying property, and a clean-up campaign) for the area.*

Signs of Crime *(Newark). This program focused on social disorder and conducted "random intensified enforcement and order maintenance operations" (e.g., foot patrol to enforce laws and maintain order on sidewalks and street corners; radar checks; bus checks to enforce ordinances and order; enforcement of disorderly conduct laws to move groups off the street corners, road checks for DWI, improper licenses, stolen vehicles). Addressing physical deterioration involved an intensification of city services and the use of juvenile offenders to conduct clean-up work in the target areas.*

Coordinated Community Policing *(Newark). This was the "kitchen sink" project that included a neighborhood community police center, a directed police-citizen contact program, a neighborhood police newsletter, intensified law enforcement and order maintenance, and a neighborhood clean-up.*

Two types of samples were used: (1) cross-sectional analysis which gave data for each area and (2) panel respondents which gave data for individuals. The results of the testing are summarized in Tables 12.3 and 12.4. The checks in the table indicate that the results were **statistically significant** at the .05 level. This measurement means that the results would occur by chance only five times in one hundred. This level is most

TABLE 12.3
Effects of Fear-Reduction Programs (cross-sectional results) (area results)

Programs	Reduce Perceived Area Physical Deterioration	Reduce Perceived Area Social Disorder	Reduce Fear of Personal Victimization	Reduce Worry About Property Crime	Reduce Perceived Area Personal Crime	Reduce Perceived Area Property Crime	Improve Evaluation Of Police	Increase Satisfaction With Area
Houston Newsletters With and Without Statistics	n.a.	n.a.						
Newark Newsletters With and Without Statistics	n.a.	n.a.						
Houston Victim Recontact Program	n.a.	n.a.						
Houston Police Community Station	n.a.	✔	✔		✔	✔		
Houston Citizen Contact Patrol	n.a.	✔	✔		✔	✔		✔
Houston Community Organizing Response Team	n.a.	✔					✔	
Newark "Signs of Crime" Program				✔				
Newark Coordinated Community Policing		✔				✔	✔	

✔ = Desired goal achieved; significant at .05 level

n.a. = Not applicable

SOURCE: Reprinted by permission. A. M. Pate, W. G. Skogan, M. A. Wycoff, and L. W. Sherman. *Reducing the "Signs of Crime": The Newark Experience.* Washington: The Police Foundation, 1986. © The Police Foundation.

355

TABLE 12.4
Effects of Fear-Reduction Programs (panel results) (individual results)

Programs	Reduce Perceived Area Physical Deterioration	Reduce Perceived Area Social Disorder	Reduce Fear of Personal Victimization	Reduce Worry About Property Crime	Reduce Perceived Area Personal Crime	Reduce Perceived Area Property Crime	Improve Evaluation Of Police	Increase Satisfaction With Area
Houston Newsletters With and Without Statistics	n.a.							
Newark Newsletters With and Without Statistics	n.a.							
Houston Victim Recontact Program	n.a.							
Houston Police Community Station	n.a.		✓		✓			
Houston Citizen Contact Patrol	n.a.	✓					✓	✓
Houston Community Organizing Response Team	n.a.	✓			✓	✓	✓	
Newark "Signs of Crime" Program			✓	✓				
Newark Coordinated Community Policing		✓	✓			✓	✓	✓

✓ = Desired goal achieved; significant at .05 level

n.a. = Not applicable

SOURCE: Reprinted by permission. A. M. Pate, W. G. Skogan, M. A. Wycoff, and L. W. Sherman. *Reducing the "Signs of Crime": The Newark Experience.* 28. Washington: The Police Foundation, 1986. © The Police Foundation.

frequently used in such studies. A statistically significant finding at the .01 level means the results would occur by chance only one time in one hundred.

The programs were least effective reducing concerns about property crime and most effective reducing perceived social disorder. According to the data provided by individuals, the Newark Coordinated Community Policing study met the greatest number of goals.

CRIME PREVENTION PROGRAM STUDIES _____

Several communities have conducted crime prevention studies. Studies in Seattle, Portland, and Hartford focus on citizen efforts to prevent residential crime; the study in Portland also focuses on preventing crime in and around commercial establishments. Two studies examine the media and crime prevention: the McGruff national media campaign, and the effectiveness of anticrime newsletters.

According to Heinzelmann (1986, p. 7): "In general, the results of these evaluations are favorable, indicating that community crime prevention programs can serve to reduce crime and fear, and at the same time improve the quality of life and the economic viability of urban neighborhoods and commercial settings."

The Seattle Program

The Citywide Crime Prevention Program (CCPP) of Seattle, described by Lindsay and McGillis (1986, pp. 46–67), focused on residential burglaries and included three primary police services: property identification, home security checks, and organizing neighborhood block watch programs.

The Seattle Citywide Crime Prevention Program used property identification, home security checks, and neighborhood block watches to significantly reduce the residential burglary rate as well as the number of burglary-in-progress calls.

Fleissner, Fedan, and Klinger (1992, p. 9) note:

When citizens and police in South Seattle banded together to fight crime, quarterly crime statistics showed dramatic improvements in the quality of life. Citizen activity spread in the city's other three police precincts; now community policing is a going concern throughout Seattle—a citywide success.

According to Lindsay and McGillis (p. 65), not only did the burglary rate drop significantly, "burglary-in-progress calls as a proportion of all burglary calls to police increased significantly in treated areas and their quality was relatively high as measured by presentation of suspect information and the occurrence of subsequent arrests."

The Portland Program

Portland also instituted a burglary prevention program, described by Schneider (1986, pp. 68–86), which included providing citizens with information about locks, alarms, outside lighting around entrances, removal or trimming of hedges, and precautions to take while on vacation. The program also encouraged citizens to mark property with identification numbers. Door-to-door canvassing and a heavy emphasis on neighborhood rather than individual protection were important components of the program.

The Portland antiburglary program succeeded in reducing the burglary rate for those who participated.

As noted by Schneider (p. 84): "In the high crime areas of Portland more than 20% of the homes could expect to be burglarized at least once a year. This was reduced to about 8% for participating households in those areas." Schneider (p. 85) also points out a class bias in this study: "Those attending meetings, engraving their property, and displaying the decals tended to be in the higher socioeconomic groups."

The Hartford Experiment

The Hartford Experiment, described by Fowler and Mangione (1986, pp. 87–108), used a three-pronged approach to reduce crime and the fear of crime: changing the physical environment, changing the delivery of police services, and organizing the citizens to improve their neighborhoods. This experiment centered on the interdependence of citizens, the police, and the environment. As noted by Fowler and Mangione (p. 89): "The approach focuses on the interaction between human behavior and the (physically) built environment. It was hypothesized that the *proper design and effective* use of the built environment can lead to a reduction in crime and fear."

The program was based on four previous research efforts. First was that of Jacobs (1961) which found that neighborhoods which were relatively crime free had a mix of commercial and residential properties, resulting in many people on the streets and a great opportunity for police surveillance. In addition, a community with such mixed use property tended to have residents who cared about the neighborhood and watched out for each other.

Angel (1968) described similar findings in his concept of "critical density," which states that if quite a few people are present on the most frequently used streets, they will serve as deterrents to burglary. In addition, Newman's classic work (1972) suggests that crime can be reduced by redesigning buildings to increase the number of doorways and other spaces that could be easily observed. Finally, Repetto (1974), like Newman, found that opportunities for surveillance could reduce crime, and, like Jacobs, that neighborhood cohesiveness could have the same result.

Based on this research the Hartford Experiment focused on Asylum Hill, a residential area a few blocks from the central business district of Hartford that was rapidly deteriorating. It was found that due to the high rate of traffic, residents did not use their yards and felt no ties to the neighborhood. The physical design of the neighborhood was changed to restrict traffic through and visually define the boundaries of the neighborhood. Cul-de-sacs were built at a few critical intersections, and some streets were made one-way.

A second change in the neighborhood involved the assignments of patrol officers. Instead of using rotating assignments within a centralized department, Hartford began using a decentralized team of officers assigned permanently to the Asylum Hill area.

Finally, the Hartford Experiment caused the neighborhood to organize. Organization included setting up block watch programs, recreational programs for youth, and improvements for a large neighborhood park.

As a result of these changes, according to Fowler and Mangione (p. 96): "Residents used their neighborhood more, walked more often both during the day and evening hours, used the nearby park more often, and spent more days per week outside in front of their homes."

The Hartford Experiment restructured the neighborhood's physical environment, changed how patrol officers were assigned, and organized the neighborhood in an effort to reduce crime and the fear of crime.

Fowler and Mangione (p. 106) caution: "A crime control program such as this must be custom fit to a particular set of circumstances. What one would want to derive from the Hartford project is not a program design, but rather an approach to problem analysis and strategies to affect them."

The Portland Commercial Demonstration Project

The Crime Prevention through Environmental Design **(CPTED)** Commercial Demonstration Project implemented in Portland from 1974 to 1979, described by Lavrakas and Kushmuk (pp. 202–27), also built upon the research of Jacobs (1961) and Newman (1972) and the concept of "defensible space."

MOTIVATION REINFORCEMENT

Design and Construction: Design, build, and/or repair buildings and building sites to enhance security and improve quality.

Owner/Management Action: Encourage owners and managements to implement safeguards to make businesses and commercial property less vulnerable to crime.

Territorial Identity: Differentiate private areas from public spaces to discourage trespass by potential offenders.

Neighborhood Image: Develop positive image of the commercial area to encourage user and investor confidence and increase the economic vitality of the area.

ACTIVITY SUPPORT

Land Use: Establish policies to prevent ill-advised land and building uses that have negative impact.

User Protection: Implement safeguards to make shoppers less vulnerable to crime.

Social Interaction: Encourage interaction among businessmen, users, and residents of commercial neighborhoods to foster social cohesion and control.

Police/Community Relations: Improve police/community relations to involve citizens in cooperative efforts with police to prevent and report crime.

Community Awareness: Create community crime prevention awareness to aid in combating crime in commercial areas.

SURVEILLANCE

Surveillance Through Physical Design: Improve opportunities for surveillance by physical design mechanisms that serve to increase the risk of detection for offenders, enable evasive actions by potential victims, and facilitate intervention by police.

Mechanical Surveillance Devices: Provide businesses with security devices to detect and signal illegal entry attempts.

Private Security Services: Determine necessary and appropriate services to enhance commercial security.

Police Services: Improve police services in order to efficiently and effectively respond to crime problems and to enhance citizen cooperation in reporting crimes.

ACCESS CONTROL

Access Control: Provide secure barriers to prevent unauthorized access to building grounds, buildings, and/or restricted building interior areas.

FIGURE 12.1 Commercial Environment Objectives of CPTED

NOTE: The four key hypotheses are not mutually exclusive. Surveillance objectives also serve to control access; activity support involves surveillance; and motivation reinforcement provides support for the other three hypotheses.

SOURCE: Reprinted by permission. H. Kaplan, K. O'Kane, P. J. Lavrakas, and S. Hoover. *CPTED Final Report on Commercial Demonsteration in Portland Oregon.* Arlington: Westinghouse Electric Corporation, 1978. © Westinghouse Electric Corporation.

The CPTED Project incorporated four major strategies: motivation reinforcement, activity support, surveillance, and access control, as described in Figure 12.1.

The CPTED project developed seven specific strategies (Lavrakas and Kushmuk, pp. 206–207):

1. Creation of a "Safe Streets for People" component.
2. Creation of a Residential Activity Center and miniplazas along Union Avenue Corridor (UAC).
3. General promotion of UAC.
4. Improved transportation both into and out of UAC.
5. Security services provided by a UAC security advisor.
6. Increased law enforcement support throughout UAC.
7. Development of a "Cash Off the Streets" program.

The first two strategies of the CPTED Project involved redesigning some streets, improving roads, adding street lighting, and generally making the area more attractive.

The Portland CPTED Commercial Demonstration Project found that the most successful strategies were security services, organization and support of the business community, and the street lighting program.

According to Lavrakas and Kushmuk (p. 223): "Of moderate success were the economic development activities. Large-scale and comprehensive improvements in the physical environment (with the exception of the redesign of Union Avenue itself), promotional events, and residential social cohesion were judged to have achieved, at best, low levels of success." The results are summarized in Figure 12.2.

Lavrakas and Kushmuk (pp. 223–24) suggest three important lessons learned from this project. First, it is essential to have a realistic time frame and strong political support. Second, the more groups that are involved, the more complicated and difficult the project will become. And third, changes in the social environment of a community are much more difficult to make than those in the physical environment.

USING THE MEDIA IN CRIME PREVENTION EFFORTS

Two different approaches to using the media have also been extensively studied: the "McGruff" media campaign and the use of police-community anticrime newsletters.

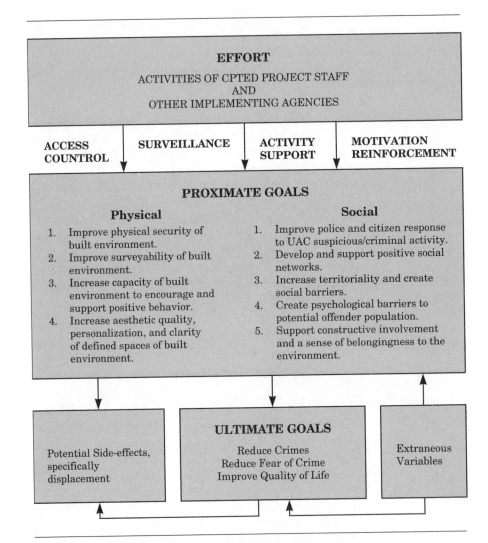

FIGURE 12.2   CPTED Evaluation Design

SOURCE: Reprinted by permission. P. J. Lavrakas, J. Normoyle, and J. Wagener. *CPTED Commercian Demonstration Evaluation Report.* Evanston: Westinghouse Electric Corporation, 1978. © Westinghouse Electric Corporation.

The "McGruff" National Media Campaign

McGruff, the crime dog, is to law enforcement what Smokey the Bear is to the fire service. A press release from the National Crime Prevention Council describes the creation of McGruff and the campaign:

> *The concept of a national public education campaign to teach Americans that they could prevent crime (and how to do so) was*

Send now for the only book on crime ever written by a dog!

Get hot tips on crime prevention from the Crime Dog himself! Me! Send for my book. It's got all the hot topics, like how to make your home safer, your neighborhood better, and more! So write to me, McGruff, P.O. Box 362, Washington, D.C. 20044, and help me take a bite out of crime.

TAKE A BITE OUT OF CRIME

A message from the Crime Prevention Coalition, the U.S. Department of Justice, and the Advertising Council. © 1989 National Crime Prevention Council.

CRIME PREVENTION CAMPAIGN
NEWSPAPER AD NO. CP-89-1465—2 COL.

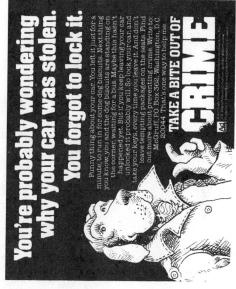

You're probably wondering why your car was stolen. You forgot to lock it.

Funny thing about your car. You left it, just for a minute, to run in for some dog biscuits. Next thing you know, you and the dog biscuits are standing on the corner, waiting for a bus. Maybe this hasn't happened yet. But if you keep leaving your car unlocked it probably will. So lock your car and take your keys, every time you leave it. And don't leave tempting packages on the seats. Find out more about preventing crime. Write to McGruff, P.O. Box 362, Washington, D.C. 20044. That's one way to help me.

TAKE A BITE OUT OF CRIME

A message from the Crime Prevention Coalition, the U.S. Department of Justice, and the Advertising Council.

CRIME PREVENTION CAMPAIGN
NEWSPAPER AD NO. CP-89-1470—2 COL.

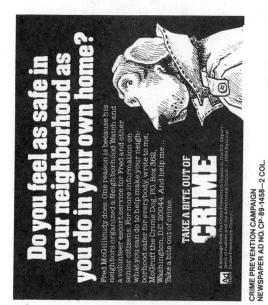

Do you feel as safe in your neighborhood as you do in your own home?

Fred McGillicudy does. One reason is because his neighbors organized a Neighborhood Watch and a volunteer escort service for Fred and other senior citizens. For more information on what you can do to help make your neighborhood safer for everybody, write to me, McGruff the Crime Dog, P.O. Box 362, Washington, D.C. 20044. And help me... Take a bite out of crime.

TAKE A BITE OUT OF CRIME

A message from the Crime Prevention Coalition, the U.S. Department of Justice, and the Advertising Council. © 1989 National Crime Prevention Council.

CRIME PREVENTION CAMPAIGN
NEWSPAPER AD NO. CP-89-1458—2 COL.

McGRUFF WANTS YOU

To get involved. Because you're the ones that make a difference, you and your neighbors.

So take an active part in making your community a safer and better place to live. Teach your children how to avoid drugs, take a neighborhood teen under your paw, work with the police on crime prevention. And watch crime drop. Get going, I'll show you how. Write to me, McGruff, P.O. Box 362, Washington, D.C. 20044. And help me...

TAKE A BITE OUT OF CRIME

A message from the Crime Prevention Coalition, the U.S. Department of Justice, and the Advertising Council.

CRIME PREVENTION CAMPAIGN
NEWSPAPER AD NO. CP-89-1463—2 COL.

McGruff crime prevention posters cover a variety of areas.

A young girl holds the paw of a McGruff crime dog robot during an anti-drug rally at the Texas State Capitol building.

first conceived in 1978. The Department of Justice supported the plan, as did distinguished civic leaders and such organizations as the AFL-CIO, the International Association of Chiefs of Police, and the National Sheriffs' Association. The Advertising Council, Inc. agreed to support the campaign. Research and program development advisory groups helped formulate a strategy. With the creative aid of the volunteer ad agency then known as Dancer Fitzgerald Sample (now Saatchi & Saatchi), the first McGruff public service ads were developed in 1979 and premiered in February 1980. . . .

The Campaign's objectives were clear:

1. To change unwarranted feelings and attitudes about crime and the criminal justice system.

2. *To generate an individual sense of responsibility for crime prevention.*
3. *To initiate individual action toward preventing crime.*
4. *To mobilize additional resources for crime prevention efforts.*
5. *To enhance existing crime prevention programs and projects conducted by national, state, and local organizations.*

This campaign, also known as the "Take a Bite Out of Crime" campaign, as described by O'Keefe (1986, pp. 252–68), was aimed at promoting citizen involvement in crime prevention activities through public service announcements **(PSAs).**

The public has favorably received the "McGruff" format and content. The "McGruff" campaign has had a sizeable impact on what people know and do about crime prevention.

As noted by O'Keefe (p. 259): "Most said they thought the ads were effective in conveying the message, that they liked the McGruff character, and that they felt the information in the ads was worth passing on to other people." In addition, people indicated that they felt more confident about their own ability to protect themselves from crime. Most importantly, almost one-fourth of the people took preventive action after exposure to the PSA, particularly to improve their own household security and work with neighbors in cooperative efforts—the two main themes of the McGruff promotions.

Police-Community AntiCrime Newsletters

Lavrakas (1986, pp. 269–91) reviews the results of three studies on a relatively new crime-prevention strategy, the police-community anti-crime newsletter. Included in Lavrakas' review are *ALERT,* the Evanston Illinois Police Department newsletter; the *Community Policing Exchange* newsletter of the Houston Police Department; and *ACT I,* the newsletter of the Newark Police Department.

One important finding of these three studies was that although readers were much more aware of crime, at a statistically significant level, their fear of crime did *not* increase. According to Lavrakas (p. 286): "In each of the cities, results indicated that residents were overwhelmingly positive in their assessments of the newsletters, especially the versions that included crime statistics. Not only was exposure greater to the version with crime statistics, but it was rated as significantly more interesting and more informative."

Studies of three police-community anticrime newsletters found them to be highly effective, especially if crime statistics were included.

Lavrakas (pp. 289–90) concludes that the three tests "suggest that such newsletters merit consideration elsewhere as one strategy in the arsenal in the fight against crime."

LESSONS LEARNED

Yin (1986, pp. 294–308) analyzes eleven research studies of community policing/crime prevention and suggests that they "point to the desirability of joint police-citizen initiatives in successful community crime prevention efforts" (p. 304). Table 12.5 summarizes the research studies Yin analyzed and the results of each.

A key finding, according to Yin, is that any crime prevention strategy, taken singly, is likely to be ineffective. A second finding points to the importance of improving the police-community relationship. Yin (p. 306) suggests that the results of these studies provide a general pattern and a major lesson about crime prevention:

Successful crime prevention efforts require joint activities by the residents and police and the presumed improvement of relationships between these groups.

Skolnick and Bayley (1986, p. 212) describe this as police-community **reciprocity:** "Police-community reciprocity means that police must genuinely feel, and genuinely communicate a feeling, that the public they are serving has something to contribute to the enterprise of policing." Both parties can benefit from working together.

In addition to these relatively formal evaluations, other less quantitative evaluations have been conducted.

QUALITATIVE EVALUATIONS AND SALIENT PROGRAM FEATURES

Qualitative evaluations are more descriptive and less statistical. One large-scale qualitative evaluation, undertaken by the National Symposium on Community Institutions and Inner-City Crime Project, sought to identify model programs for reduction of inner-city crime. According to Sulton (1990, p. 8) almost 3,500 national organizations, criminal justice scholars, and federal, state, and local government agencies were asked to recommend outstanding local programs. This resulted in the identification of approximately 1,300 programs. Each was sent a request for detailed information, and 350 (27 percent) responded. From these, eighteen were selected for site visits.

TABLE 12.5
Summary of Eleven Evaluation Studies

Description of Intervention	Study Author(s)	Intervention Sites and Period	Type of Crime Addressed	Type of Outcomes Examined	Nature of Outcomes	Analytic Criteria Used to Test Outcomes
Hartford Project: physical redesign, police redeployment, and community organizing	Fowler & Mangione	Hartford, Connecticut 1973–1979	residential	informal social control; burglary and robbery victimization rates; fear of crime	crime reduction when whole intervention in place	statistical significance
Crime Newsletters: distribution of community newsletters in target neighborhoods	Lavrakas	Evanston, Illinois, 1981 Houston, Texas, 1983 Newark, New Jersey, 1983	residential	awareness of newsletter; perceived crime problem; fear of crime	positive changes at one of three sites	statistical significance
Portland Project: physical redesign, police assistance, and business organizing	Lavrakas & Kushmuk	Portland, Oregon 1974–1980	commercial	reported burglaries; fear of crime; quality of life	burglary reduction	statistical significance
Seattle Community Crime Prevention Program: block watch, security inspections, and property engraving	Lindsay & McGillis	Seattle, Washington 1974–1975	residential	burglary victimization rate	burglary reduction	statistical significance
McGruff National Media Campaign: information used in mass media and in pamphlets	O'Keefe	Nationwide campaign, 1979	residential	awareness of announcements; reported learning; reported preventive actions	reported learning and actions increase	data in supplemental report
Newark Foot Patrol: foot patrols from 4 p.m. to midnight	Pate	Newark, New Jersey 1973–1979	residential	reported crime victimization rates; perceived crime, safety, and satisfaction with police	no crime reduction; changed perceptions	statistical significance
Urban Crime Prevention Program: block watches and related neighborhood meetings	Rosenbaum, et al.	Chicago, Illinois 1983–1984	residential	victimization rates; perceived crime; fear of crime; perceived efficacy; social disorder; physical deterioration	crime reduction at only one of four sites; increases at others	statistical significance
Portland Anti-Burglary Program: street lighting, property engraving, and community education	Schneider	Portland, Oregon 1973–1974	residential	reported burglaries; victimization rates	burglary reduction	statistical significance
Commercial Security Field Test: security surveys undertaken by business proprietors	Tien & Cahn	Denver, Colorado, 1981 Long Beach, California, 1981 St. Louis, Missouri, 1981	commercial	burglary victimization rates; fear of crime	burglary reduction at one of three sites	statistical significance
Neighborhood Foot Patrol: foot patrol and community organizing	Trojanowicz	Flint, Michigan 1979–1982	residential	reported crime; satisfaction with police	crime reduction increase in satisfaction	descriptive data only
Storefront Police Office: location of storefront office, staffed by police, in local neighborhood	Wycoff & Skogan	Houston, Texas 1983–1984	residential	fear of crime; perceived crime, safety, and satisfaction with police	fear reduction improved perceptions	statistical significance

SOURCE: Reprinted by permission. "Community Crime Prevention, A Synthesis of Eleven Evaluations." In *Community Crime Prevention: Does It Work?* 297–99, edited by Dennis P. Rosenbaum. Beverly Hills: Sage Publications, 1986. © Sage Publications.

Sulton (p. 10) notes that although each program was unique, they shared some common characteristics.

Eighteen model programs shared the following characteristics. The program:

- Focused on causes of crime.
- Built on community strengths.
- Incorporated natural support systems.
- Had an identifiable group of clients.
- Targeted those who were less affluent.
- Had clearly stated goals and well-defined procedures.
- Had sufficient resources.
- Had a strong leader.

Sulton (p. 10) notes that many of the problems focus on specific social problems of inner-city residents "identified as correlates with, if not causes of, inner-city crime, such as emotional or family instability, lack of education, absence of vocational skills, unemployment, drug and alcohol abuse, juvenile gangs, and sexual abuse and exploitation." The programs have a clear focus, a clear audience, and a clear idea of how to proceed. Several of these programs will be described in the chapters that follow.

On a much smaller scale, but equally instructional, is the Newport News Police Department's reliance on data to identify a problem and to evaluate their solution (Guyot, 1992, p. 321):

The problem was that local hunters and other gun owners were doing target practice at a large pit where dirt had been excavated for I-64. Officer Ron Hendrickson found out that between April and September 1987, the department had been called 45 times to chase away shooters and that the problem had existed for at least 15 years. Most of the calls had come from a couple whose nearby home was bullet-riddled and who thought the police were doing a good job because each time they chased away the shooters.

When Officer Hendrickson decided, with the support of his sergeant, to end the problem, he interviewed shooters and learned that most were soldiers from nearby Ft. Eustis and that many others were sent to the pit by gun shop owners. The officer determined that the pit was close enough to I-64 to make any firearms discharge illegal there. Deciding to use education backed by legal sanctions, he first took photographs of damage and other evidence. These he used to persuade a judge to give anyone convicted of illegal shooting a suspended sentence and a small fine, with a warning that a second appearance would result in confiscation of the weapon and a jail sentence. The officer obtained from the property owners permission to arrest on their property and the same from the C & O Railroad for shooters crossing the tracks to reach the pit. In a crucial step, he wrote a pamphlet which defined the problem and the department's intended enforcement action. He distributed the pamphlet to the military base and to all gun shops in the area. Finally, he had no parking—tow zone signs erected on the shoulder where most shooters were parking.

The statistics on the results were simple. Officers issued 35 summonses to shooters in September, only 15 in October, and the last on November 12, 1987. The pit soon became so overgrown that it was uninviting for target practice.

Success in the preceding incident and others might indicate that community-oriented and problem-solving policing would be readily accepted by law enforcement officials and the communities they serve. Such acceptance is not, however, always the case.

IMPEDIMENTS TO COMMUNITY-ORIENTED POLICING

Resistance to change is common, especially in a tradition-oriented profession such as law enforcement. Skolnick and Bayley (1986, pp. 225–26) describe six impediments to implementing innovative community-oriented policing.

Impediments to implementing innovative community-oriented policing include the following:

- The powerful pull of tradition.
- Substantial segments of the public do not want the police to change.
- Unions will continue to be skeptical of innovation.
- Innovation may prove costly.
- Lack of vision on the part of police executives.
- Police departments' inability to evaluate their own effectiveness.

Despite these impediments, community-oriented policing appears to offer a realistic approach to reducing violence, crime, and the drug problem. The remaining chapters discuss specific programs that use community-oriented policing to address these problems.

Summary

Several studies have assessed the effectiveness of community policing efforts. The Flint Neighborhood Foot Patrol Program appeared to produce a decrease in crime, general citizen satisfaction with the foot patrol program, a decline in the public's fear of crime, and a positive evaluation of the foot patrol officers.

In the first Newark Foot Patrol Experiment, residents reported positive results, while business owners reported negative results. The second Newark Foot Patrol Experiment used coordinated foot patrol, a cleanup campaign, and distribution of a newsletter. Only the coordinated foot patrol was perceived to reduce perception of property crime and improve assessments of the police.

The Oakland program, using foot patrol, mounted patrol, small vehicle patrol, and a Report Incidents Directly program, resulted in a substantial drop in the rate of crime against individuals and their property.

The San Diego Community Profile Project provided patrol officers with extensive community-orientation training. These officers became more service oriented, increased their non-law-enforcement contacts with citizens, and had a more positive attitude toward police-community relations.

The Houston Fear Reduction Project did not achieve desired results from the victim recontact program or the newsletter. Citizen contact and the police storefront operation did, however, result in decreases in the public's perception of social disorder, fear of personal victimization, and the level of personal and property crime.

Baltimore County's COPE Project reduced fear of crime by 10 percent in target neighborhoods. It also reduced calls for service and increased citizen awareness of and satisfaction with the police.

The most common components of community policing experiments have been foot patrol, newsletters, and community organizing.

Other studies have reviewed the effectiveness of community crime prevention efforts. The Seattle Citywide Crime Prevention Program, using property identification, home security checks, and neighborhood block watches, significantly reduced the residential burglary rate as well as the number of burglary-in-progress calls. The Portland antiburglary program also succeeded in reducing the burglary rate for the participants. The Hartford Experiment restructured the physical environment, changed how patrol officers were assigned, and organized the neighborhood in an effort to reduce crime and the fear of crime.

The Portland CPTED Commercial Demonstration Project found that the most successful strategies were security services, organization and support of the business community, and the street lighting program.

The effectiveness of the media in assisting crime prevention efforts is another evaluation focus. The public has favorably received the

"McGruff" format and content. The "McGruff" campaign has had a sizeable impact on what the public knows and does about crime prevention. Studies of three police-community anticrime newsletters found them to be highly effective, especially if they included crime statistics.

Some general conclusions can be drawn from the preceding studies, including the finding that successful crime prevention efforts require joint activities by the residents and police and the presumed improvement of relationships between these groups.

Eighteen model programs identified by the National Symposium on Community Institutions and Inner-City Crime project shared the following characteristics: The programs (1) were focused on causes of crime; (2) built on community strengths; (3) incorporated natural support systems; (4) had an identifiable group of clients; (5) targeted those who were less affluent; (6) had clearly stated goals and well-defined procedures; (7) had sufficient resources; and (8) had a strong leader.

The implementation of community-oriented policing must be weighed against several impediments including the powerful pull of tradition; substantial segments of the public do not want the police to change; unions are skeptical of innovation; innovation may be costly; lack of vision on the part of police executives; and the incapacity of police departments to evaluate their own effectiveness.

DISCUSSION QUESTIONS

1. Why is it difficult to conduct research on the effectiveness of community-oriented policing?
2. Which studies do you think have the most value for policing in the 1990s? Which studies have the most promise?
3. Why would a police department want to reduce fear of crime rather than crime itself?
4. Which of the fear reduction strategies do you believe holds the most promise?
5. What do you think are the most reasonable aspects of the crime prevention through environmental design (CPTED) approach?
6. If you believe in the CPTED approach and see individuals ignoring its potential to reduce crime, do you think that if they are victimized the concept of culpability should be considered?
7. Has your police department conducted any research on community policing or crime prevention efforts? If so, what were the results?
8. Does your police department have its own McGruff? If so, how does the department use him?

9. What do you think are the most important questions related to police-community relations that should be researched in the next few years?

10. How much of a police department's budget should be devoted to research? Which areas should be of highest priority?

DEFINITIONS
Can you define these terms: CPTED, cross-sectional analysis, empirical study, panel analysis, PSA, qualitative evaluation, reciprocity, statistically significant.

REFERENCES

Angel, S. *Discouraging Crime through City Planning.* Berkeley: University of California Press, 1968.

Burden, Ordway P. "Citizens Spur Community-Based Policing." *Law Enforcement News.* (March 15, 1992): 5.

Fleissner, Dan; Fedan, Nicholas; and Klinger, David. "Community Policing in Seattle: A Model Partnership Between Citizens and Police." *National Institute of Justice Journal.* (August 1992): 9–18.

Fowler, Floyd J., Jr. and Mangione, Thomas W. "A Three-Pronged Effort to Reduce Crime and Fear of Crime: The Hartford Experiment." In *Community Crime Prevention: Does It Work?* edited by Dennis P. Rosenbaum, 87–108. Beverly Hills: Sage Publications, 1986.

Greene, Jack R. and Taylor, Ralph B. "Community-Based Policing and Foot Patrol: Issues of Theory and Evaluation." In *Community Policing: Rhetoric or Reality,* edited by Jack R. Greene and Stephen D. Mastrofski, 195–223. New York: Praeger Publishers, 1991.

Guyot, Dorothy. "Problem-Oriented Policing Shines in the Stats." In *Source Book: Community-Oriented Policing: An Alternative Strategy,* 317–21. Bernard L. Garmire, Washington: ICMA, May 1992.

Heinzelmann, Fred. "Foreword." *Community Crime Prevention: Does It Work?* edited by Dennis P. Rosenbaum, 7–8. Newbury Park: Sage Publications, 1986.

Jacobs, J. *The Death and Life of Great American Cities.* New York: Vintage, 1961.

Lavrakas, Paul J. "Evaluating Police-Community Anticrime Newsletters: The Evanston, Houston, and Newark Field Studies." In *Community Crime Prevention: Does It Work?* edited by Dennis P. Rosenbaum, 269–91. Beverly Hills: Sage Publications, 1986.

Lavrakas, Paul J. and Kushmuk, James W. "Evaluating Crime Prevention through Environmental Design: The Portland Commercial Demonstration Project." In *Community Crime Prevention: Does It Work?* edited by Dennis P. Rosenbaum, 202–27. Beverly Hills: Sage Publications, 1986.

Lindsay, Betsy and McGillis, Daniel. "Citywide Community Crime Prevention: An Assessment of the Seattle Program." In *Community Crime Prevention: Does It Work?* edited by Dennis P. Rosenbaum, 46–67. Beverly Hills: Sage Publications, 1986.

Mastrofski, Stephen D. "What Does Community Policing Mean for Daily Police Work?" *National Institute of Justice Journal.* (August 1992): 23–27.

Newman, O. *Defensible Space: Crime Prevention through Urban Design.* New York: Macmillan, 1972.

O'Keefe, Garrett J. "The 'McGruff' National Media Campaign: Its Public Impact and Future Implications." In *Community Crime Prevention: Does It Work?* edited by Dennis P. Rosenbaum, 252–68. Beverly Hills: Sage Publications, 1986.

Pate, Antony M. "Experimenting with Foot Patrol: The Newark Experience." In *Community Crime Prevention: Does It Work?* edited by Dennis P. Rosenbaum, 137–56. Beverly Hills: Sage Publications, 1986.

Police Foundation. *The Newark Foot Patrol Experiment.* Washington: The Police Foundation, 1981.

Reppetto, T. A. *Residential Crime.* Cambridge: Ballinger, 1974.

Schneider, Anne L. "Neighborhood-Based Antiburglary Strategies: An Analysis of Public and Private Benefits from the Portland Program." In *Community Crime Prevention: Does It Work?* edited by Dennis P. Rosenbaum, 68–86. Beverly Hills: Sage Publications, 1986.

Skogan, Wesley G. and Wycoff, Mary Ann. "Storefront Police Offices: The Houston Field Test." In *Community Crime Prevention: Does It Work?* edited by Dennis P. Rosenbaum, 179–99. Beverly Hills: Sage Publications, 1986.

Skolnick, Jerome H. and Bayley, David H. *The New Blue Line: Innovation in Six American Cities.* New York: The Free Press, 1986.

Sulton, Anne Thomas. *Inner-City Crime Control: Can Community Institutions Contribute?* Washington: The Police Foundation, 1990.

Taft, Philip B., Jr., *Fighting Fear: The Baltimore County C.O.P.E. Project.* Washington: Police Executive Research Forum, 1986.

Trojanowicz, Robert C. "Evaluating a Neighborhood Foot Patrol Program: The Flint, Michigan, Project." In *Community Crime Prevention: Does It Work?* edited by Dennis P. Rosenbaum, 157–78. Beverly Hills: Sage Publications, 1986.

Wycoff, Mary Ann. "The Benefits of Community Policing: Evidence and Conjecture." In *Community Policing: Rhetoric or Reality,* edited by Jack R. Greene and Stephen D. Mastrofski, 103–120. New York: Praeger Publishers, 1991.

Yin, Robert K. "Community Crime Prevention: A Synthesis of Eleven Evaluations." In *Community Crime Prevention: Does It Work?* edited by Dennis P. Rosenbaum, 294–308. Beverly Hills: Sage Publications, 1986.

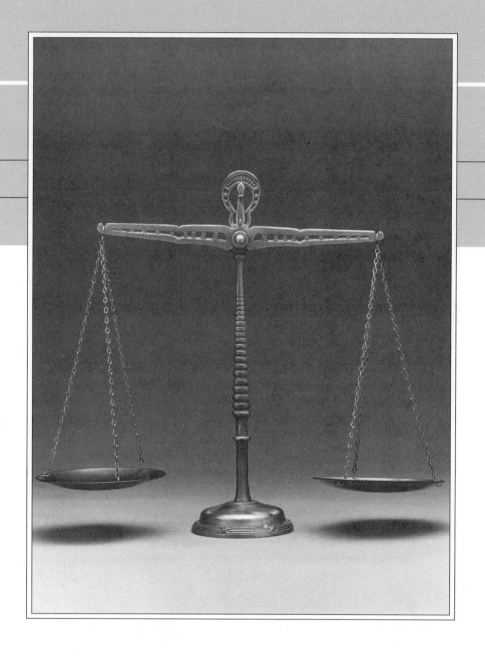

CRIMINAL JUSTICE
PROGRAMS

To perfect society, liberty is necessary to develop the faculties, both intellectual and moral, . . . but to preserve society it is necessary to guard the community against injustice, violence, and from anarchy within, and against attacks from without.

—John C. Calhoun

DO YOU KNOW

- What changes have occurred in the criminal justice system in the past decade?
- What the greatest obstacle to change within police agencies might be?
- What benefits might be derived from improving police-community relations?
- What opportunities are provided by calls for service?
- What services police might offer citizens?
- How effective citizen-police ride-alongs have been?
- What police-based programs have proven effective?
- What court-based programs have proven effective?
- What corrections-based programs have proven effective?
- What components of the criminal justice system can help reduce the crime problem?

INTRODUCTION

The criminal justice system includes law enforcement, the courts, and corrections. The way our courts and correctional facilities operate directly affects law enforcement. A major challenge to the criminal justice system is balancing liberty and security. As our society has changed, so must the criminal justice system that serves it. Many of the trends that affect the criminal justice system directly affect the type of programs police departments should implement to improve community relations.

Trends in the criminal justice system include:

- Emphasis on police service to the community rather than fighting crime.
- Greater responsibility and discretion for line officers.
- Reliance on cooperative efforts of law enforcement, courts, and corrections to accomplish the goals of the criminal justice system.
- Belief in a justice model rather than a medical model when dealing with offenders.

As noted by Trojanowicz (1987, p. 177): "Though most young officers think their job will involve the 'gun-toting,' 'siren-wailing,' 'crook-chasing' portrayed in the media and reinforced by their academy training, they find on the job that they spend most of their time mediating disputes, stopping neighborhood fights, or responding to complaints about barking dogs. The majority of their work involves delivering services to the community, not law enforcement activities."

The police are the most visible component of the criminal justice system and have the most direct contact with the public. The day-to-day contacts of line officers are the most critical factor in police-community relations. As previously discussed, what occurs within courts and corrections facilities can also greatly affect police-community relations. It is vital that the three components of the system collaborate and develop programs to serve the needs of the public.

THE POLICE FUNCTION AND POLICE-COMMUNITY RELATIONS REVIEWED

In essence, everything the police do affects their relationship with the community. Even the uniforms they wear are a factor, as noted by Aaron (1992, p. 14): "Today, uniforms have become a tradition, but the role and image of the police has changed dramatically since the tradition began. Some research already indicates that by selecting uniforms which are not associated with the old military style of policing and past police brutality, police may appear less threatening to other citizens in the community." He (p. 15) stresses that: "The image portrayed by the police to citizens is an issue of growing importance as resources dwindle and more citizens are asked to cooperation in community-based crime preventing and policing efforts." Police often resist change regarding their uniforms and other issues.

RESISTANCE TO CHANGE

According to Wadman and Olson (1990, p. 55), the lowest hurdle toward change to a "community wellness" or community-oriented philosophy of policing is selling the approach to the public. The next lowest hurdle is convincing the rest of city government. They state that "the highest hurdle of all will be the organizational resistance of the police agency itself."

The greatest obstacle to change may be resistance from within the police agency itself.

Sparrow (1988, p. 1) uses the example of a truck driver to illustrate resistance to change:

The professional truck driver does not drive his 50-ton trailer-truck the same way that he drives his sports car. He avoids braking sharply. He treats corners with far greater respect. And he generally does not expect the same instant response from the trailer, with its load, that he enjoys in his car. The driver's failure to understand the implications and responsibilities of driving such a massive vehicle inevitably produces tragedy: if the driver tries to turn too sharply, the cab loses traction as the trailer's momentum overturns or jackknifes the vehicle.

Police organizations also have considerable momentum. Having a strong personal commitment to the values with which they have "grown up," police officers will find any hint of proposed change in the police culture extremely threatening. Moreover, those values are reflected in many apparently technical aspects of their jobs—systems for dispatching patrols, patrol officers constantly striving to be available for the next call, incident-logging criteria, etc. The chief executive who simply announces that community policing is now the order of the day, without a carefully designed plan for bringing about that change, stands in danger both of "losing traction" and of throwing his entire force into confusion.

Overcoming Resistance to Change

According to Sparrow (1988) resistance to change can be reduced by two kinds of imbalance within an organizational structure that can "render it susceptible to change": **directed imbalance** and **experimental imbalance.**

Directed Imbalance.   Sparrow uses another physical comparison to describe directed imbalance—that of riding a bicycle. Think of how, when riding a bicycle, your body unconsciously shifts in the opposite direction of a turn to be made. Without this shift in balance, you are likely to tip over. You are also likely to fall if you shift in preparation for a turn and then do *not turn*. Sparrow (1988, p. 3) suggests: "Directed imbalances within a police organization will be those imbalances that are created in anticipation of the proposed change in orientation. They will be the changes that make sense only under the assumption that the whole project will be implemented, and that it will radically alter organizational priorities." He gives the following examples of directed imbalance:

- Movement of the most talented and promising personnel into the newly defined jobs.
- Making it clear that the route to promotion lies within such jobs.
- Disbanding those squads that embody and add weight to the traditional values.
- Recategorizing the crime statistics according to their effect on the community.
- Redesigning the staff evaluation system to take account of contributions to the nature and quality of community life.
- Providing inservice training in problem-solving skills for veteran officers and managers.

- Altering the nature of the training given to new recruits to include problem-solving skills.
- Establishing new communication channels with other public services.
- Contracting for annual community surveys for a period of years.

Experimental Imbalance. Experimental imbalance, as the name implies, creates an atmosphere of trial and error and of risk-taking. It encourages officers at all levels to be creative and seek innovative ways to approach community problems. Sparrow notes (p. 4): "The resourcefulness of police officers, so long apparent in their unofficial behavior, can at last be put to the service of the department. Creativity blossoms in an experimental environment that is tolerant of unusual ideas."

CHANGES TO ANTICIPATE

Change is occurring as law enforcement agencies move toward community-oriented, problem-solving policing. One of the largest changes is the "customer orientation" described by Couper and Lobitz (1991, pp. 522–53):

> A customer orientation means listening to your customers. Customers may be citizens, elected officials, employees, or interest groups. . . . Listening to and being responsive to citizens should be a goal. There are, of course, a number of parameters in being responsive—the law, ethics, and budgetary constraints. In this new era of community policing, listening to the customer is a vital part of the job. It is a change. Professionals today no longer have the exclusive market on knowing what is best for their patients, clients, or customers. Today, people want to be heard and participate.

Hageman (1985) suggests that the Blake Mouton managerial grid theory also fits the options facing police officers as they deal with the public, as illustrated in Figure 13.1. A (1,1) style of policing indicates low concern for control or for citizens' rights. It would be a removed, "do not rock the boat," style of policing. A (1,9) style of policing indicates low concern for control, and high concern for citizens' rights. A (9,1) style, in contrast, would put little emphasis on citizens' rights and great emphasis on control. The grid illustrates the many options officers have when they perform their jobs.

The police work grid implies that different situations require different responses: "Sniper or hostage situations usually do not call for

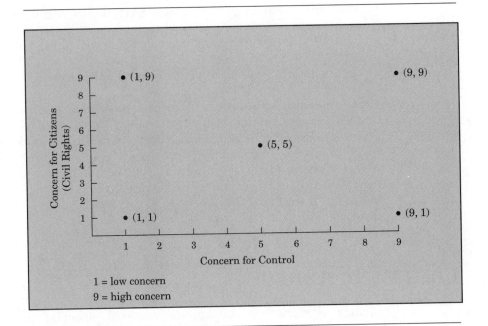

FIGURE 13.1 **Police Work Grid**

SOURCE: Reprinted with permission. Mary Jeanette Hageman. *Police-Community Relations,* 25. Beverly Hills: Sage Publications, 1985. © 1985 Sage Publications.

community surveys" (p. 26). Although the emphasis on community service is increasing, police are still expected to serve as protectors when necessary. The skill with which they fulfill this role greatly affects police-community relations.

Another basic way the police role varies because of community-oriented policing is the manner in which the police interact with the public. Snelson and Oettmeier (pp. 5–6) describe a number of objectives of the Houston Police Department's policing style, designed to facilitate interactive relationships between neighborhood residents and beat officers:

1. Establish trust and harmony between and among neighborhood residents and the beat officer by establishing a positive, cooperative, and productive relationship between both parties;

2. Exchange information between neighborhood residents and beat officers which will strengthen rapport and enhance neighborhood safety;

3. Respond to the problem of crime and criminal activity by maximizing the efficient utilization of available department and community resources in enforcing the law;

4. Identify and resolve neighborhood problems which will reduce the fear of crime and enhance the quality of life within the neighborhoods;

5. Establish and improve communication linkages and working relationships between and among divisional and departmental personnel;

6. Establish an effective management structure which utilizes divisional and community input to define service needs, direct operational commitments, and clarify responsibilities on behalf of division personnel and the public in order to more efficiently respond to the concerns of neighborhood residents;

7. Facilitate the acquisition, analysis, and utilization of information in order to identify neighborhood crime and non-crime problems capable of being resolved through mutual participation on behalf of police personnel and community residents;

8. Develop and implement programs, strategies, and/or activities to efficiently use beat officers' uncommitted patrol time;

9. Provide safe and orderly traffic flow through the neighborhoods by enforcing violations and reducing the number of traffic accidents; and

10. Identify and utilize employee incentives conducive to improving employee morale.

These objectives balance concern for the officers with concern for the community while balancing the officers' crime-fighting and service roles.

Benefits of Change

Wycoff (1991, p. 114) enumerates several benefits that are likely to result from this expanded view of policing. Officers should "have greater concern for citizens' problems, concern for victims, sense of independence, self-esteem, respect for their own skills, sense of 'ownership' of and responsibility for work, organizational commitment, and a more positive view of citizens and of the way in which citizens view the police."

Benefits of improved police-community relations might include greater police concern for citizens, including victims, as well as increased independence, self-esteem, and sense of ownership in the police function.

RESPONDING TO CALLS FOR SERVICE _____

A potential conflict exists between responding to calls for service and community policing efforts because calls for service use up much of the

In many jurisdictions, bike patrols are being used extensively.

time needed for problem identification and resolution efforts. Departments must set their priorities and determine if they will be driven by calls for service (reactive) or by a more problem-oriented approach (proactive). Regardless of the selected approach, the manner in which police respond to calls is a critical factor in enhancing police-community relations.

As stressed throughout this text, the one-on-one interaction between police officers and the citizens they serve is critical.

Responding to calls for service presents an excellent opportunity to foster good police-community relationships.

Officers' responses to service calls are critical to effective police-community relations; therefore it is important to assess how effectively officers do respond. Bondurant (1991, pp. 74–76) describes a citizen response questionnaire that is used in Plainsboro, New Jersey, to assess the effectiveness of officer performance in the field. The ten item questionnaire is mailed to citizens who request police service. Citizens are asked to respond yes or no to the following (p. 75):

1. Did the officer respond quickly to your call for service? Approximately how long did it take for the officer to respond after being called?

2. Was the officer courteous?
3. Was the officer neatly attired?
4. Did the officer identify himself by name? If not, do you think he should have?
5. Did the officer speak clearly? Were you able to understand him?
6. Were you satisfied with the service provided by the officer?
7. Did the officer appear knowledgeable?
8. Did he obtain all information that would seem pertinent under the circumstances of this contact?
9. If applicable, did you feel satisfied with the supplemental investigation conducted by the officer?
10. Upon completion of this police contact, did you feel satisfied with the general quality of the service rendered?
11. Additional comments:

Respondents are asked to sign, date, and mail the questionnaire back to the police department.

In addition to assessing how well officers respond to calls for service, most police departments have several other means to improve police-community relations. Indeed, any police department that adopts the community policing philosophy will make several internal changes and will also institute several community programs.

INNOVATIVE POLICE-BASED PROGRAMS

Some simple services that police departments might provide for the community cost little and require limited personnel. Other services, however, may involve programs that are relatively expensive and must be staffed by many officers. The services and programs described in the following pages are a small sample of options available to law enforcement agencies to enhance the police-community partnership.

The Houston Storefront Police Department

This experiment, evaluated by the Police Foundation and described briefly on pp. 348–49, included several services to the community that were relatively inexpensive and involved limited personnel yet accomplished significant results (Skogan and Wycoff, pp. 182–83).

Relatively inexpensive services include conducting monthly meetings, meeting with school administrators, conducting fingerprinting programs and blood pressure programs, participating in athletic contests, publishing newsletters, and providing ride-alongs.

The Houston Police Department held monthly meetings in a local church and discussed crime and other topics of community interest. Officers also met regularly with local school administrators to address the truancy problem. Their fingerprinting program for children began in the police department but was later moved to a local hamburger shop to reach more citizens. During the summer the department held softball, football, volleyball, and horseshoe competitions in which residents played against police officers. The department's ride-along program involved citizens selected by area churches and civic organizations to ride with an officer patrolling their neighborhood. Ride-alongs are one very popular, yet controversial means to improve police-community relations.

Ride-Along Programs

Ride-along programs are designed to give local citizens a chance to see what police work involves. According to Sharp (1990, p. 65), 96 percent of police departments polled across the country reported positive results from their ride-along programs and 88 percent of the officers involved agreed with the findings.

Ride-along programs are highly successful, with 96 percent reporting positive results.

A citizen rides along with the deputy sheriff to obtain a first-hand view of this important aspect of the criminal justice system.

Many ride-along programs permit any responsible juvenile or adult to participate, but other programs have restrictions and may limit ridership. Participation by officers in a ride-along program is usually voluntary. Whether riders are allowed to use still or video cameras during a ride-along varies from department to department. Many departments also require their riders to dress "appropriately."

Sometimes a ride-along does more than foster police-community relations. In Denver, for example, officers who take clergy as riders will have help in death notifications, suicide situations, sexual assault investigations, runaway situations, emotionally disturbed persons, substance abuse investigations, significant conflagrations, and child abuse victims (Sharp, p. 66).

Despite the numerous benefits of ride-along programs, Sharp (p. 67) notes: "There are departments which do not want to get involved in them for legitimate reasons such as insurance cost factors; liability considerations, concerns about the public's safety, officers not being in favor, administrative problems, the potential to be disruptive, and cost." He cites the statement of Corporal Wilson, Georgia Highway Patrol (p. 67):

> *The risk of injury to an untrained, nondepartmental civilian and the potential danger to our troopers resulting from the actions of an untrained, nondepartmental civilian will continue to contribute significantly to this department's decision not to sponsor civilian ride-along programs. An additional consideration is the unresolved question of civil liability of departmental members and the department.*

Many departments request those who participate in the ride-along program to sign a waiver that exempts the officer, the department, and the city from liability.

Model Police Programs

The National Symposium on Community Institutions and Inner-City Crime (the National Symposium) identified three police programs for inclusion in their project: East Dallas Community-Police and Refugee Affairs Office, the Detroit Junior Police Cadet Section, and the Houston Positive Interaction, Dispute Resolution, and Inhalant Abuse programs.

East Dallas Community-Police and Refugee Affairs Office. As noted by Sulton (1990, p. 69) the primary goal of this office is "to reduce crime by decreasing refugees' fear of police, easing their transition into American society, and increasing area residents' willingness to cooperate with police." The program addresses the needs of Asian refugees who often do not speak English, have limited job skills, do not understand the American culture, and may fear authority, including the police. Translation services is one of the office's primary focuses.

The office operates a storefront staffed by two officers, six community service officers, and 75 volunteers. Although initially opened to serve Asian immigrants, it has expanded its services to include all residents of East Dallas, including African-Americans, Hispanics, and Whites. The storefront provides not only food and clothing, but also fans, air conditioners, and other needed items. In addition, staff helps individuals find housing, jobs, and educational opportunities as well as makes referrals to appropriate social service agencies in the community.

The East Dallas Community-Police and Refugee Affairs Office operates a storefront that provides basic necessities to needy residents as well as assistance in finding housing, education, and jobs and referral to other agencies.

Sulton (1990, p. 72) notes that: "This program does not require police to abandon their traditional order maintenance and crime control functions, but enhances their ability to detect crime and make arrests through mutual cooperation." According to the founder of the office, Corporal Ron Coward (pp. 72–73):

The program must target the community in greatest need of services and work hand-in-hand with other community institutions that address the oppression of inadequate housing, unemployment, illiteracy, lack of recreational opportunities for youth, and other social problems. Every squad car does not have to be a rolling social service agency. . . . but some of the officers should be especially sensitive to varying needs of a multi-cultural population. You need experienced officers willing to aggressively work to improve the community and advocate on its behalf. The community must know that the police care. The storefront must be more than a tourist booth which simply directs needy residents to some other agency. And it cannot be centralized; each storefront must be tailored to the neighborhood in which it is located.

The exemplary nature of this program was noted by a site-team member (p. 72): "This program is built upon an enduring spirit of cooperation and caring that transcends racial and cultural barriers and affirms the belief that in a democracy police are more than guardians of law and order."

Detroit Police Department's Junior Police Cadet Section.   The program serves not only youth, but also the elderly in the community. Approximately 4,000 high school students and 100 college students participate in the program each year.

A mobile police station. Such facilities are often used effectively in neighborhoods with high crime rates.

Two services are provided by the Detroit Junior Police Cadets: school and community patrol and senior citizen escort.

In addition, the program seeks to prepare young people who want to pursue a career in law enforcement. It also operates several other projects, including one which stresses academic excellence.

Houston Police Department's Positive Interaction, Dispute Resolution, and Inhalant Abuse Programs. The Houston Police Department has developed three programs designed to improve police-community relations and to reduce crime and the fear of crime.

A Positive Interaction Program, Dispute Resolution Program, and an Inhalant Abuse Program have proven to be successful in Houston.

The *Positive Interaction Program* identifies community leaders who might join with the police to reduce crime and fear of crime and who might assist to mobilize communities in their crime prevention efforts. Basically, according to Sulton (p. 79), this program "organizes the organizers."

The *Dispute Resolution Program Implementation* is part of the Ingrando House Project which serves many African-Americans. Its purpose is to reduce or prevent violence between family members, friends, neighbors, and students by providing police officers trained in mediation and conflict resolution techniques.

The third program, the *Inhalant Abuse Program,* uses education and counseling to counter such harmful activities as glue sniffing. Program staff members educate other officers, school officials, social workers, and parents about the extent of the problem, how to detect it and how to prevent it. Although officers are trained counselors, when they encounter youths who are inhalant abusers, they generally refer them to an appropriate treatment agency.

Recommendations of the National Symposium for Police

The National Symposium recommends that police departments should (Sulton, pp. 107–108):

1. Make crime prevention a priority.
2. Work with other community institutions to improve the quality of life of inner-city residents.
3. Adopt a style of policing that: a) presents opportunities for police to reinforce the concept of neighborhood and become part of it by sharing residents' problems; and b) makes it possible for residents to work with police on order maintenance as well as crime problems.
4. Reduce the social distance between police and inner-city residents by organizing the department according to the needs of the community. Police departments should ascertain these needs through monthly meetings with police chief/community advisory committees and by recruiting and hiring minority group members sensitive to problems in the community.
5. Encourage use of civil remedies.
6. Enhance patrol officer crime prevention roles and provide the flexibility needed to develop innovative responses to inner-city problems.
7. Expand police training programs to include training in mediation techniques.

INNOVATIVE COURT PROGRAMS _____

The way courts address the accused has a direct impact on the crime problem and on community policing efforts. The National Symposium identified two model court programs: Albany, New York's Community Dispute Resolution Centers and Madison, Wisconsin's Deferred Prosecution/First Offenders Unit.

Model court programs include community dispute resolution centers and a deferred prosecution/first offenders unit.

Community Dispute Resolution Centers. The thirty-two dispute resolution centers are independent, community-based, nonprofit organizations contracted by the Unified Court System of the State of New York, Albany, to do the following (Sulton, p. 83):

1. Provide dispute resolution resources for local communities.
2. Prevent the escalation of disputes into more serious civil or criminal matters.
3. Relieve the courts of matters not requiring the formalities of judicial intervention.
4. Teach individuals how to resolve their problems through mediation.

Police officers, probation officers, judges, district attorneys, and legal aid offices can refer cases to a local dispute resolution center, or individuals may be self-referred. The mediation, conciliation, or arbitration services provided by the center are free. The Chief Judge of the State of New York, L. H. Cook, stated the usefulness of this approach (Sulton, p. 87):

> *The paths of dispute resolution are never set in concrete; they are for each age to establish for itself. But society, by its very nature and to avoid self destruction, requires adequate avenues to justice. In our time, mediation is one of them. . . . Mediation must in this decade be accorded its rightful place in society.*

The Deferred Prosecution/First Offenders Unit. This program, operated by the Dane County District Attorney's Office, Madison, Wisconsin, has as its purpose (Sulton, p. 88): "To prevent offenders' further involvements in crime by deferring prosecution upon the condition that they satisfactorily complete appropriate treatment and rehabilitation programs." The program recognizes the hazards of labeling individuals and the potential of treatment for first offenders who accept responsibility for their actions.

An offender's suitability for the program is based on several criteria including (Sulton, p. 90): the nature of the current offense, prior criminal record, admission of guilt, offender attitude, whether the offender is dangerous to self or community, likelihood of the offender repeating the crime, whether the offender will benefit from the treatment process, an agreement to participate in the treatment program prescribed, willingness to abide by the conditions of the diversion contract, and payment of a $10 monthly fee for each month of program participation.

The program uses a large network of social service agencies and public and private organizations. Because a "substantial portion" of program participants are shoplifters, the staff conducts a one-day Saturday workshop on retail theft. Another integral part of the program is voluntary community service, not as a means of punishment, but as a way to repay the community for the crime committed and to change the offender's behavior patterns. Among the benefits of this program, according to Sulton (p. 91), are:

> [C]onservation of police, prosecutorial, judicial, and correctional resources. . . . Only a small number of program participants have failed to complete their diversion contracts. As a result, police officers are not required to spend countless hours waiting to testify, prosecutors can devote their time to preparation of more serious and complex cases, court dockets are relieved, and scarce jail space is reserved for the most dangerous offenders.

> Program staff also noted several other benefits. For example, sanctions for criminal conduct are administered closer to the time when the offenses occurred. In addition, offenders' lives are minimally disrupted because they can continue to pursue their occupations and fulfill family obligations.

Recommendations of the National Symposium for the Courts

Recommendations of the National Symposium for the courts include the following (Sulton, p. 108):

1. Court officials should educate the public about the operations and limitations of juvenile and criminal justice agencies and invite citizens to visit courts and meet with judges.
2. When appropriate, prosecutors and judges should encourage criminal litigants to settle grievances outside court through mediation and other dispute resolution processes.
3. Judges should continue to tailor sentences to individual offenders rather than rely totally on sentencing guidelines. Sentencing guidelines may discourage judges from fashioning appropriate sentences when such sentences are warranted by the presence of highly unusual mitigating or aggravating circumstances.
4. Judges should use alternatives to incarceration, particularly when the offender is nonviolent. Community service, restitution, drug treatment, and house arrest can be effective sentences. When it is unlikely that the offender will victimize additional community members or that public order or safety

will be compromised, the least restrictive alternative should be selected.

5. Prosecutors, defense attorneys, and judges should encourage legislators to reevaluate statutory definitions of crimes. Legislative definitions of crimes frequently do not reflect the nature of the offense or extent of injuries to victims.

6. Judges' performance should be evaluated on the quality of decisions rendered rather than on the quantity of cases disposed. Judges frequently are criticized because of the backlog of cases on their dockets. However, many of the cases handled by judges present complex legal issues requiring a great deal of time and effort to resolve. When judges' decisions are affirmed on appeal, credit should be given for the quality of work performed.

7. Judges should work with community-based organizations and participate in activities to improve the quality of life of inner-city residents. For example, they can work to support community-based organizations by serving as members of the boards of directors, participating in public service events sponsored by the organizations, or providing advice on how the organization can work more effectively with criminal justice agencies.

AN INNOVATIVE CORRECTIONS PROGRAM

How corrections deals with those who are sentenced to jail or prison terms also affects the crime problem as well as community policing efforts. The National Symposium identified one model corrections program, the Volunteers in Parole program of the State Bar of California, San Francisco, California.

The model corrections program Volunteers in Parole provides a support system for young parolees and eases their transition from incarceration to productive citizenship.

This program is designed to ease the caseload of parole officers, many of whom may have caseloads of up to 150 parolees. As noted by Sulton (p. 93):

Many of the individuals supervised are youthful offenders without family, friends, permanent housing, employment, or other resources. These teenagers and young adults are uneducated and illiterate, unmarried parents of small children, struggling with drug or alcohol dependency, stigmatized by lengthy criminal records, suspicious, fearful, and uncertain. They frequently commit new crimes or violate the conditions of their parole because adequate support systems are unavailable.

The program, modeled after the Big Brothers and Big Sisters programs, pairs youthful parolees, ages fifteen to twenty-three, with attorneys who volunteer their time. Attorneys are used because, as noted by Sulton (pp. 93–94), they: "1) understand the legal system; 2) are familiar with community resources and have referral skills; 3) are experienced in dealing with bureaucracies; 4) are not intimidated by the sophistication of parolees; and 5) have an office where they can conveniently meet with parolees and privately discuss their concerns." In addition, attorneys have undergone a licensing procedure that should assure they are of good moral character, and they will be able to answer the numerous questions parolees may have about the criminal justice system, governmental agencies, leases, contracts, and other legal issues.

In addition to matching parolees with attorneys, the program conducts street law classes and informal lectures for the youthful parolees. Although no studies have been conducted on the effectiveness of the program, given the high cost of incarceration, according to Sulton (p. 96): "Should only a small number of the matches result in a reduction of the number of youth being returned to detention facilities or prisons,

Juvenile delinquents make their beds at a detention home.

the State of California probably saved millions of dollars by investing in this program."

Recommendations of the National Symposium for Corrections

Recommendations of the National Symposium related to corrections include the following (Sulton, pp. 109–10):

1. Correctional agencies, particularly community corrections, should provide opportunities for ex-offenders to fully participate in community life. Ex-offenders, who are a part of the crime problem, can become a part of its solution when provided encouragement and guidance by those charged with the responsibility of facilitating their reintegration into the community.
2. Because African-Americans are disproportionately represented as prison inmates, corrections should recruit and hire more African-Americans as corrections planners and correctional officials.
3. Alternatives to incarceration should be used whenever possible; imprisonment is very expensive, causes tremendous human suffering, and is not very effective at rehabilitation.
4. Funds earmarked to build adult prisons and to support the growing "correctional-industrial complex" should be reallocated and spent on programs that prevent youth involvement in crime.
5. Correctional agencies, particularly community corrections, should provide personal direction, guidance, and support services to ex-offenders. Typically, ex-offenders are supervised only via periodic telephone calls or office visits. Ex-offenders frequently need assistance in resolving personal problems that may be related to their involvement in crime. Correctional agencies may be the best source of this guidance because they have regular contact with ex-offenders and access to other social service agencies to which the ex-offender may be referred.
6. Prisons should prepare inmates for employment through training and work-release programs. The work release placements should be appropriate to the knowledge and skill levels of the offenders, and offenders should be adequately supervised to ensure public safety and prevent further criminal victimization.
7. Parole boards should require prison inmates to complete the equivalent of a high school education as a condition of parole, particularly where they have been sentenced to lengthy

prison terms and are capable of fulfilling this requirement. One must be able to read, write and count in order to participate in society. When offenders are illiterate, it is likely that they will recidivate. Therefore, the incentive of early release from prison should be used to encourage offenders to prepare themselves for participation in society.

8. Parole boards should discontinue the practice of returning parolees to prisons for technical violations of parole (e.g., changing jobs without notifying the parole officer) when no new crime has been committed.

9. Halfway houses should provide drug, family, and job counseling services to ex-offenders. These houses also should work with state agencies, community-based organizations, and inner-city residents to facilitate ex-offender participation in the community.

10. Juvenile justice agencies should establish diversion programs that permit nonviolent offenders to work in community service projects.

COORDINATED EFFORTS

What happens in each component of the criminal justice system directly affects the other components of the system.

A coordinated effort among law enforcement, courts, and corrections is required to effectively deal with the crime problem and to elicit the support of the community in doing so.

Over thirty years ago, such cooperation was successfully implemented in California (Price, pers. com., 1992):

In the 1960s the San Bernardino County California Sheriff's Department had an exchange program where a combined committee of police departments, sheriff's officers, prosecutors, probation and parole officers, corrections, court officers and educators exchanged personnel on a limited scale for one month. Cooperation between departments increased measurably after the exchanges. Members of each agency became more aware of the duties, responsibilities and problems of all of the other criminal justice agencies in the area as a direct result of the exchanges.

Summary

Trends in the criminal justice system include an emphasis on service rather than crime fighting, greater responsibility and discretion for line officers, reliance on cooperative efforts of law enforcement, courts, and corrections to accomplish the goals of the criminal justice system, and belief in a justice model rather than a medical model when dealing with offenders. The greatest obstacle to change in the criminal justice system may be resistance from within the police agency itself.

Benefits of improved police-community relations include greater police concern for citizens, including victims, as well as increased independence, self-esteem, and sense of ownership in the police function.

Responding to calls for service is an excellent opportunity to foster good community relationships. Ride-along programs are highly successful; 96 percent of the programs report positive results. The National Symposium identified three model police programs. The first, the East Dallas Community-Police and Refugee Affairs Office, operates a storefront that provides basic necessities to needy residents as well as assistance in finding housing, education, and jobs and referral to other agencies. Two services are provided by the Detroit Junior Police Cadets: school and community patrol and senior citizen escort. A Positive Interaction Program, Dispute Resolution Program, and an Inhalant Abuse Program have proven to be successful in Houston.

Model court programs include a community dispute resolution center and a deferred prosecution/first offenders unit. The model corrections program Volunteers in Parole provides a support system for young parolees and eases their transition from incarceration to productive citizenship.

A coordinated effort among law enforcement, courts, and corrections is required to effectively deal with the crime problem and to elicit the support of the community in doing so.

DISCUSSION QUESTIONS _____

1. What changes have been made in your police department in the last five years?
2. What police-community relations programs do you feel hold the most promise to accomplish the desired results?
3. What police-community relations programs does your police department participate in?
4. Does your department permit ride-alongs? If so, who can participate?
5. Do you believe the patrol officer's uniform should be changed? If so, how?
6. Do you feel the managerial grid "fits" the police situation? If so, how? If not, why not?
7. Do you feel mediation and arbitration are solutions to our crowded court dockets?

8. Do you believe first offenders should be treated differently than repeat offenders? Why or why not?
9. What alternatives to incarceration would you support? For whom?
10. Which recommendations would you support for the police, the courts, and corrections?

DEFINITIONS
Can you define these terms: directed imbalance, experimental imbalance.

REFERENCES

Aaron, Titus. "Police and the Uniform: We Need More Research." *Law and Order.* (April 1992): 14–15.

Bondurant, Elizabeth. "Citizen Response Questionnaire: A Valuable Evaluation Tool." *The Police Chief.* (November 1991): 74–76.

Couper, David C. and Lobitz, Sabine H. *Quality Policing: The Madison Experience.* Washington: Police Executive Research Forum, 1991.

Hageman, Mary Jeanette. *Police-Community Relations.* Beverly Hills: Sage Publications, 1985.

Price, Carroll S. Letter to author, July 1992, reviewing manuscript.

Sharp, Arthur G. "Ride-Along with Me." *Law and Order.* (October 1990): 65–69.

Skogan, Wesley G. and Wycoff, Mary Ann. "Storefront Police Offices: The Houston Field Test. In *Community Crime Prevention: Does It Work?* edited by Dennis P. Rosenbaum, 179–99. Beverly Hills: Sage Publications, 1986.

Snelson, J. W. and Oettmeier, T. N. *Operational Plan for the Westside Command Station.* Houston Police Department, 1987.

Sparrow, Malcolm K. *Perspectives on Policing: Implementing Community Policing.* Washington: U.S. Department of Justice, National Institute of Justice, November 1988.

Sulton, Anne Thomas. *Inner-City Crime Control: Can Community Institutions Contribute?* Washington: The Police Foundation, 1990.

Trojanowicz, Robert C. "Evaluating a Neighborhood Foot Patrol Program: The Flint, Michigan, Project." In *Community Crime Prevention: Does It Work?* edited by Dennis P. Rosenbaum, 157–78. Beverly Hills: Sage Publications, 1986.

Wadman, Robert C. and Olson, Robert K. *Community Wellness: A New Theory of Policing.* Washington: Police Executive Research Forum, 1990.

Wycoff, Mary Ann. "The Benefits of Community Policing: Evidence and Conjecture." In *Community Policing: Rhetoric or Reality* edited by Jack R. Greene and Stephen D. Mastrofski, 105–20. New York: Praeger Publishing, 1991.

PROGRAMS FOR YOUTH

If society wishes greater protection from juvenile crime, more attention has to be paid to the costly process of promoting moral order and of preventing crime.

—Lamar Empey,
criminologist (1978)

DO YOU KNOW

- What exemplary youth programs can promote positive police-community relations?
- What the focus of PALs is?
- What a police-school liaison program is? What its dual goals are?
- What the DARE program is?
- What group of professionals is of great importance in delinquency prevention programs?
- What youth program has been endorsed by the IACP?
- What the Teens on Patrol program is?
- What model programs for youth have been identified by the National Symposium on Community Institutions and Inner-City Crime Project?
- What a wizard is?

Many hope that the answers to crime, violence, and substance abuse in our society lie in the numerous preventive programs for our youth. If we can somehow reach children before they become involved in drugs and its resulting life of despair, crime, and poverty, perhaps we can prevent a significant amount of misery in our society and stem the escalating crime rate.

Given these hopes, it is especially tragic when one reads of events such as the January 17, 1989, killing of five elementary school pupils in a Stockton, California schoolyard by a gunman. As noted by Okaty (1991, p. 39): "Crime and terror in schools is a harsh condition facing children, teachers and parents at all levels of the educational sector." Making schools safe for students to attend is another challenge for police officers.

On a less sensational level, but equally important, the National School Safety Center, Pepperdine University, California, has identified several studies that link truancy to daytime crime. As noted by Okaty (p. 39): "Police administrators can be proactive in reducing community crime by working closely with schools and school districts to compare student absentee patterns and the neighborhoods where crimes are occurring."

Before reviewing specific programs for youth, consider how community policing and a problem-oriented approach can be used to address common problems police encounter with juveniles.

A PROBLEM-ORIENTED APPROACH FOR DEALING WITH PROBLEMS INVOLVING YOUTH

Police are often called to deal with groups of "rowdy" juveniles who are not breaking any laws but who are disturbing a neighborhood. Spelman and Eck (1992, p. 205) describe how police can use a problem-solving approach in such instances:

> *The quiet nights of a middle-class Newport News neighborhood were spoiled when groups of rowdy teenagers began to frequent the area on Fridays and Saturdays. There had been no violence, and*

the kids' primary offenses were loud music, horseplay, and occasional vandalism. But residents felt the teenagers were unpredictable, particularly since they came from the city's mostly Black southeast side, several miles away. The neighborhood became a regular stop for officers working the evening shift.

Sergeant Jim Hogan recognized that responding to these calls took time but accomplished little except to irritate everybody involved. One Friday night he asked the beat officer, Paul Summerfield, to look into the problem and develop a better solution.

Summerfield suspected that the source of the problem might be a roller skating rink. The rink had been trying to increase business by offering reduced rates and transportation on Friday and Saturday nights. As he drove north toward the rink later that night, Summerfield saw several large groups of youths walking south. Other kids were still hanging around the rink, which had closed shortly before. Summerfield talked to several of them and found that they were waiting for a bus. The others, he was told, had become impatient and begun the three-mile walk home. Then Summerfield talked to the rink owner. The owner told him he had leased the bus to pick up and drop off kids who lived far from the rink. But he said there was always more kids needing rides at the end of the night than the bus had picked up earlier.

When Officer Summerfield returned to the skating rink early the next evening, he saw about fifty youngsters get out of the bus rented by the skating rink. But he saw others get out of the public transit buses that stopped running at midnight, and he saw parents in pajamas drop their kids off, then turn around and go home. Clearly the rink's bus would be unable to take home all the kids who would be stranded at closing time.

Summerfield consulted Sergeant Hogan. They agreed that the skating rink owner should be asked to bus the kids home. Summerfield returned to the rink Monday and spoke with the owner. When informed of the size of the problem he had unwittingly created, the owner agreed to lease more buses. By the next weekend, the buses were in use and Summerfield and Hogan saw no kids walking home.

Elapsed time from problem identification to problem solution; one week. Resources used: about four hours of an officer's time. Results: fewer calls, happier kids, satisfied homeowners.

This is a prime example of managing a problem by marshalling the necessary resources rather than simply continuing to respond to the calls about the problem—the essence of community-oriented policing. In other

An officer explains bike safety to elementary school children.

instances, programs have been developed in an attempt to prevent problems from occurring.

TRADITIONAL PROGRAMS FOR YOUTH

Police interaction with youth and several programs that focus on their needs were discussed in Chapter 8. Youth have traditionally been included in police-community relations efforts in several ways.

Common programs aimed at youth are school safety programs, bicycle safety programs, the McGruff "Take a Bite out of Crime" program, the Officer Friendly program, police athletic leagues (PALs), the fingerprinting of young children, and police explorer programs.

In different localities, police have developed variations of many of these programs. The traditional *McGruff* as a crime prevention spokesperson program, for example, has expanded in some areas to include McGruff Houses, safe havens for young children. Another expansion is the McGruff crime dog robot developed by Robotronics. Operated by remote control, the robot winks, blinks, moves his hands and arms, tips and turns his head, and has a two-way wireless voice system allowing the operator to talk and listen.

Police departments have also expanded upon the PALs program.

The National Police Athletic League (**PAL**), now over fifty years old, was developed to provide opportunities for youth to interact with police officers in gyms or ballparks instead of in a juvenile detention hall.

The Portland Oregon Police Department has adapted the PALs program to deal with escalating gang violence and street sale of drugs. As noted by Austin and Braaten (1991, p. 36), the goals of the Portland-area PAL are to:

- Reduce the incidence of juvenile crime, substance abuse, and gang violence.
- Provide positive alternative activities for boys and girls.
- Guide boys and girls to make responsible decisions in life.
- Foster better understanding between youth and the police.

To accomplish their goals, the department has undertaken several activities. They have conducted a week-long Sport Quickness Day Camp for six hundred at-risk youth, that keeps them productively occupied for eight hours a day in boxing, wrestling, football, soccer, martial arts, basketball, racquetball, track and field, volleyball, and speed and quickness training.

The department also organizes events in which officers can participate with PALs youth, including a one-day fishing excursion, trips to Seattle Sea Hawks football games, and scholarships to summer camps held throughout the state. According to Austin and Braaten (p. 38): "Through PAL, we are helping these kids build self-esteem, meet life's challenges, interact with positive role models, enhance their physical sports abilities and make friends with police officers."

Officer Friendly programs are designed for lower grade school children and generally include a police officer who goes into classes to discuss good citizenship, responsibility, and general safety. The program uses coloring books and a special activity book that teachers can use with their regular social studies curriculum.

Pace (1991, p. 255–57) describes the Officer Friendly program in St. Louis, Missouri:

This program is designed to establish constructive understanding between children in the primary grades and police officers.

Public Affairs officers work with elementary school principals to establish a schedule for patrol officer visits. District commanders then assign the officer who patrols the area in which the school is located, to make two visits to each kindergarten through third

Officer Friendly *programs allow police officers to interact one-on-one with youngsters.*

grade classroom in the school. An officer's job and equipment is described as well as safety. He utilizes picture reading books and electric street signals in his talks. Each teacher receives a manual for ongoing programs.

Following the second visit, the officer provides Junior Citizenship certificates for the children.

The officers then conduct "rap" sessions with older children in the school to explain the police function and answers questions in order to establish rapport with them.

The traditional police explorers program, an advanced unit of the Boy Scouts of America, also serves many communities. In Mesa, Arizona, for example, thirty-five explorers have been trained in various aspects of police work such as fingerprinting, identification techniques, first aid, and firearms safety. The minimum age for the program is fifteen, and the youths must have superior motivation and skill. As noted by Lesce (1991, p. 98): "The program demands a serious mind-set and dedication to public service, not self-serving ego satisfaction."

Explorers have a three to six month probation; full membership is contingent on completing training and meeting proficiency standards as well as acceptable personal conduct. Lesce (p. 100) suggests that: "Explorer programs serve two purposes: favorable community relations and early recruitment for law enforcement agencies." Some departments, in fact, make even greater use of their explorer program. The Chandler Arizona Police Department, for example, used two eighteen-year-old Explorers in a sting operation involving a bar and liquor store's employees who sold alcohol to minors.

Many of the programs for juveniles involve the schools. Historically, the schools have been charged with instilling discipline in the students who attend.

Youth and the Schools

The principle of **in loco parentis,** meaning "in place of parents," gives schools the authority to act as a parent might in situations requiring discipline or need. As noted by Pace (1991, p. 255): "Teachers, next to parents, are society's most important transmitters of values, mores, and cultures." He stresses:

> *For many years, teachers, in internalizing their values, have been the most hostile group toward the police. Through their value system, they have consistently rated police officers low on acceptance scales. This is, in part, because police departments and school administrators have not maintained a proper liaison.*

According to Summerhays and Lindbloom (1989, p. 69): "Educators and law enforcement groups often have had difficulty in finding common ground for distinguishing between what is a crime and what is a disciplinary problem." They note:

> *Certainly, a law enforcement agency may not wish to be called to every minor theft or altercation in the classroom. . . . At the same time, it must be remembered that serious events do occur that call for police involvement; unfortunately, in many cases, the police are not summoned until it is too late. . . .*
>
> *For whatever reasons, it appears that approximately one in five school administrators has a serious problem when it comes to forming positive relationships with local law enforcement agencies.*

Summerhays and Lindbloom (p. 70) describe one program which strives to improve police-school relations, the National School Safety Center, which brings teams from throughout the country together for a week of instruction and interaction. Each team has four people from the same community: the chief of police or sheriff, the school superintendent, the district attorney, and the chief juvenile officer of the court. The teams spend the week working with each other on common problems.

POLICE-SCHOOL LIAISON PROGRAMS

In 1958 Flint, Michigan, developed a highly publicized delinquency prevention program involving joint efforts of school authorities, parents, social agencies, the juvenile court, businesses, and the police department. It became known as a school-liaison program and was widely replicated across the country.

A **police-school liaison program** places an officer into a school to work with school authorities, parents, and students, to prevent crime and antisocial behavior and to improve police-youth relationships.

Goals of most police-school liaison programs include the following:

- To reduce crime incidents involving school-age youth.
- To suppress by enforcement of the law any illegal threats that endanger the child's educational environment.
- To improve the attitudes of school-age youths and the police toward one another.

According to Drowns and Hess (1990, p. 360): "The techniques used by school liaison officers involve counseling children and their parents; referring them to social agencies to treat the root problems; referring them to drug and alcohol abuse agencies; and being in daily contact in the school to check the progress of behavior. Often school liaison officers deal with pre-delinquent and early delinquent youths with whom law enforcement would not have been involved under traditional programs."

Police-school liaison officers do not get involved in school politics or in enforcing school regulations. The school administrators are involved in these matters.

The joint goals of most police-school liaison programs are to prevent juvenile delinquency and to improve police-youth relations.

The police-school liaison programs can also do much to promote better relations among the police, school administrators, and teachers. According to Summerhays and Lindbloom (1989, p. 69): "Educators and law enforcement groups often have had difficulty in finding common ground for distinguishing between what is a crime and what is a disciplinary problem." They stress (p. 70):

There are a number of organizations that can focus attention on school-police relations and provide supportive programs both on the community and national levels. The International Association of Chiefs of Police, the National Association of Secondary School Principals and the National Association of School Boards, to name a few, should cooperate in finding ways to enhance school-police problem solving. The research conducted indicates a real need to foster better relationships and understanding among a significant portion of the nation's school administrators. In the long term, better understanding will help all of us to provide a safe learning environment for our children.

In a survey conducted in May 1988, a questionnaire was sent to all of the school district superintendents in the country, 13 percent responded. Of those responding, 60 percent reported a drug problem in their schools. Interestingly, as noted by Summerhays and Lindbloom (1989, p. 70): "Drugs, however, were not identified as a security or crime problem by the administrators." No matter how drug use is viewed, it is often a target of police educational programs. Often officers help develop and promote programs aimed at preventing drug and alcohol abuse.

PROGRAMS AIMED AT PREVENTING DRUG AND ALCOHOL ABUSE

Many police departments and schools work together to promote drug and alcohol abuse awareness. In Orange County, Florida, for example, the Sheriff's office broadcasts antidrug and antialcohol television programs directly into local elementary schools. According to Sarubbi (1991, pp. 41–42): "The video teaches children to deal with peer pressure and say 'No' by using the word STARS":

> S—See the problem.
> T—Think about your choices.
> A—Ask for help.
> R—Recognize the best choice.
> S—Makes you a STAR if you stick to your good choice.

The DARE Program

The Drug Abuse Resistance Education (DARE) program was developed jointly by the Los Angeles Police Department and the Los Angeles Unified School District.

The Drug Abuse Resistance Education (**DARE**) program is aimed at elementary age school children and seeks to teach them to "say no to drugs," to resist peer pressure, and to find alternatives to drug use.

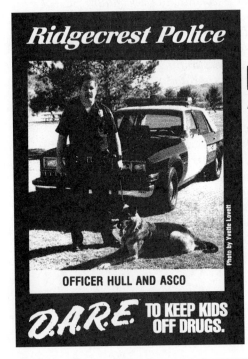

Ridgecrest Police

OFFICER HULL AND ASCO

Photo by Yvette Lovett

D.A.R.E. TO KEEP KIDS OFF DRUGS.

K-9 PROGRAM

Asco was Ridgecrest P.D.'s first Police Dog. Asco has been in service for three years. Asco was purchased by the citizens of Ridgecrest. Asco is a full-blooded German Shepherd. He was raised and trained in Germany.

SAFETY TIP   **9**

SMART KIDS D.A.R.E. TO SAY "NO!" Drugs can hurt you. Besides, it's against the law to use drugs. Don't let anyone talk you into drugs. You're a smart kid . . . keep it that way.

This card comes to you as a gift from your friends at the Ridgecrest Police Department and the City Council.

Produced by: McDag Productions, Inc.
P.O. Box 80826, Baton Rouge, LA 70898

FIGURE 14.1   Ridgecrest Police DARE card

The program uses a "self-esteem repair" approach consisting of seventeen classroom sessions taught by experienced police officers.

The City of Ridgecrest, California initiated a DARE program and wanted a public relations program to help promote it. Ridgecrest used cards similar to baseball cards, each featuring numerous officers in different settings. According to Narramore (1990, p. 23):

> The program is highly visible. We have put the DARE logo on everything possible. All of the students wear DARE T-shirts, their pencils say DARE, we even have DARE wrist bands. However, the newest and biggest success we have had in promoting the program are the new DARE cards.
>
> We even included photographs of the two police dogs and their handlers. Each card is numbered and has a safety tip on the reverse side of the card along with a job description of the person on the card, such as a definition of what a rangemaster does.

PEP Kids

PEP Kids is a program for parents, educators, police, and kids, who work together to face the challenge of substance abuse among youth. The program was jointly conceived by the Tucson police chief and the superintendent of Amphitheater schools. The program focuses on preparing youth to not be influenced by a peer who tries to pressure them into trying drugs. As noted by Paterson and Schmoker (1992, p. 282): "Students hear first-hand about health, on the one hand, and the horrors of arrest, the destructive effects of drugs on the mind and body on the other. These anecdotes, some fairly grisly, underscore the reality that decisions have consequences, some unintended."

They stress (p. 283): "PEP-Kids takes students beyond the cliches and into the real world they inhabit, where one day, alone or with friends, someone will offer them something they shouldn't accept. PEP-Kids prepares them for that moment."

Legislation Establishing Drug-Free Safe Zones Around Schools

Many states have passed legislation increasing the penalties for selling drugs around schools. They have also posted the areas and increased patrols during school hours.

The Flying Fuzz

Patrol Officer Dennis Guth, also known as "The Flying Fuzz," has seventy national drag racing records and has won the 1989 Drag Bike USA national championship. He is a fifteen year veteran of the Whitehall Township Pennsylvania Police Department and uses his drag bike and his racing records to reach out to youth. As noted by Krum (1990, p. 59): "During school demonstrations, Guth gets a message across to hundreds of youngsters every year. He speaks against the abuse of drugs and alcohol while lauding the positive aspects of athletics."

COP'RZ

Bork (1991, p. 29) notes: "The term 'beat cop' has been redefined by five Dayton, Ohio, police officers." These cops entertain students, grades kindergarten through nine, with rock and roll music, promoting the message: "Say No to Drugs!" Since forming in the spring of 1990 the officers have made more than fifty performances, entertaining approximately 50,000 children and challenging them to be drug free. According to Bork (p. 30), they hit the stage "in uniform—to the accompaniment of a shrieking siren, blazing blue lights, and pounding drums. . . . Encouraging audience participation, COP'RZ launches into 'We Will, We Will Rock You,' their version being, "We Will, We Will Say NO!'" They include in every program the National DARE theme song "Stand By Me," inviting the teachers to join them on stage.

Teachers are among the most important professionals involved in making delinquency prevention programs work.

As noted in Chapter 8, teachers greatly influence the youth with whom they work. Unfortunately, teachers often have negative attitudes about the police. Any efforts to improve relationships between teachers and officers should be applauded.

Confiscated Vehicles

Many police departments have confiscated unusual and expensive automobiles used by drug dealers and have integrated them into their anti-drug campaigns. The Miami Police Department, for example, confiscated a $70,000 luxury Porsche 911 Carrera and redesigned it as a mock patrol car. Officers painted on the side of the car in capital letters: THIS CAR CONFISCATED BY THE MPD STREET NARCOTICS UNIT.

In their program, "Operation Hot Wheels," the Miami Police Department also has two, thirty-three-foot long Gulfstream motor homes which have been redesigned as classrooms on wheels ("Vehicles Bought with Confiscated Monies," *Law and Order,* p. 35). Officers take the units to schools, parks, and other community functions to relay the message that crime and doing drugs do not pay.

Teenage Drinking Task Force

The sheriff in Jim Wells County in South Texas and the chief of police of Orange Grove, a community in the northeast corner of the county, joined forces to tackle the problem of underage drinking. Alone, neither had the personnel to conduct an effective sweep, but together, their first sweep resulted in nearly fifty citations to minors in possession of alcohol and a dozen driving while intoxicated citations.

The efforts of these departments began the South Texas ad hoc teenage drinking task force. The task force has since expanded to include agencies from Live Oak, Kleberg, Nueces, Duval, and Brooks counties as well as municipal forces from seven cities and towns. As noted by Reynolds (1991, p. 49): "The premise is simple—if you need help, call. Officers from whatever agencies have manpower to spare will be there to reinforce your officers. . . . Task force policy is either to cite and release juveniles and minors found in possession of alcohol, or to transport them to a central point, from which their parents are called to pick them up."

Reynolds (p. 50) suggests that "a valuable byproduct of the task force is the high visibility given to police during a sweep. This has resulted in significant decreases in crimes against property and family violence calls on nights the force is operating."

PROGRAMS TO PREVENT OR REDUCE CHILD ABUSE

The "good touch, bad touch" child abuse prevention program has been highly successful in some areas. In such programs an officer comes into elementary classrooms to teach children where it is and is not all right to be touched. Some officers tell children that no one should touch them where their bathing suit would be.

The "Soft Room"

Slahor (1992, p. 281) describes how the Palm Springs California Police Department set aside one room "just for kids" who for one reason or another were temporarily detained at the police station:

> *A tall chest of drawers in one corner contains donations of toys, small games, books, diapers, baby supplies, fruit juices, clothing, and other "necessaries" for infants, toddlers, and children. A small-sized table and chairs decorate the room, and a television is ready with donated videotapes of cartoons and children's stories to help a youngster wile away the time. Stuffed toys are stored on a hammock-like shelf up in one corner. A quilt and playpen are also available.*

> *The room is painted in bright, primary colors and decorated with large decals of Walt Disney characters. . . . It is anticipated that about 100 children a year will use the new "just for kids" room.*

Officer Ollie

This program, instituted by the Geneva Illinois Police Department, teaches very young children about preventing child abduction, skateboard and bicycle safety, latchkey and sexual abuse education. The Officer Ollie program is linked to the town's festivals and parades, with the Chamber of Commerce providing publicity. The director of the chamber notes (Hardy, 1990, pp. 19–20): "The Officer Ollie program lets the community know that the police department is aware, concerned, and involved in the community—not only as traditional officers, but also as a friend, willing to entertain and educate their children."

As noted by one officer (p. 21): "We're planting seeds with these children that the police are their friends, that we are there as helpers and not just ticket writers and arresters. If there's something going on they can come to us."

PROGRAMS FOCUSING ON BUILDING PERSONAL RELATIONSHIPS

Departments across the country have developed programs to allow students and police officers to get to know and understand each other better. The Denver Police Department, for example, has a program called "Brown Baggin' with the Blues," in which children have lunch with police officers.

The International Association of Chiefs of Police (IACP) has endorsed the Kops' n Kids program, a program bringing together children and officers to have fun.

As noted by Brown (1991, p. 6): "The program brings officers and children together—not to deliver anti-drug or anti-crime speeches, but to have fun." Officers come with their motorcycles and their K-9s for demonstrations; they have lunch; they form running clubs; they do whatever helps to present police as positive role models and to present law enforcement as a career option.

The Greeley Colorado Police Department has a similar program, "Adopt-an-Officer," in which police officers volunteer to be "adopted" by fourth and fifth grade students. They share meals, write letters, exchange cards, visit the police station, and, like the Kops' n Kids program, just have fun.

The Las Vegas Metropolitan Police has a unique program, "Shop with a Cop," which was designed to make the Christmas season happy for abused, neglected, and disadvantaged children. As noted in the program description: "They wore badges, not beards. They drove squad cars, not sleighs. And none of them had bellies that shook when they laughed like bowls full of jelly. But to dozens of underprivileged Las Vegas youngsters, these officers were Santa Claus." One hundred thirty police officers each took one underprivileged child on a shopping spree at the local K-Mart. In 1989, each child had $75 to spend, the money contributed by local businesses.

The Joplin Police Department has also developed an innovative approach to reduce conflicts between youth and police. It resulted from a local program pairing each school in the district with a local business. One school, however, the Alternative School serving approximately ninety students who had difficulty adjusting to traditional schools, had no partner. During the initial year of the partnership program, the principal of the Alternative School and the new Joplin chief of police developed a good working relationship through their mutual involvement in various civic programs. They concluded that the police department would be a natural business partner for the Alternative School. According to Wrightman and Coburn (1991, p. 38:)

> *The primary objective of this partnership was to provide the students with first-hand knowledge of a police officer's job through a positive encounter. Another goal was to let students see the officer as a caring individual whose job is service to others instead of the ultimate authority figure. It was felt this could only be accomplished by allowing individual relationships to be developed between students and officers. Individual ride-alongs helped break down the barriers of suspicion which existed both for the student and the officer. . . .*

> *In the three years this partnership program has been in existence, a formerly cautious, suspicious and doubting group of students and police officers have found acceptance with each other. . . . Attitudes have been changed and friendships developed. A greater understanding of the various lifestyles of the students and officers has been more closely examined, thereby contributing to a greater understanding of each partner's role in our community.*

YOUTH GANGS IN THE SCHOOLS

The National School Safety Center (1988, p. 25) publication *Gangs in Schools: Breaking Up Is Hard to Do* suggests: "A positive, consistent approach to discipline and conflict prevention can achieve long-term and far-reaching results and improve the overall school climate." The Center suggests several prevention and intervention strategies to reduce problems with gangs and gang members.

Behavior codes should be established and firmly and consistently enforced. These codes may include dress codes and bans on showing gang colors or using hand signals. On the positive side, schools should promote and reward friendliness and cooperation.

Graffiti removal should occur in schools immediately. Graffiti is not only unattractive, it enables gang members to advertise their turf and authority. In some instances photographs of the graffiti may aid certain police investigations. School officials should give remaining paint cans and paint brushes that might be used as evidence to the police. As an alternative to graffiti, students might be encouraged to design and paint murals in locations where graffiti is most likely to occur.

Conflict prevention strategies are also important to address the problem of gangs in school. Teachers should be trained to recognize and deal with gang members in nonconfrontational ways. Staff should identify all known gang members. Staff must try to build self-esteem and promote academic success for all students, including gang members.

Crisis management is another important part of dealing with gangs. The police department and school officials should have a plan in place for dealing with crises which might arise. Included in the plan should be means for communicating with the authorities, parents, and the public. The Center (pp. 33–34) recommends the following actions in a school crisis:

- Have a media policy worked out in advance. Spell out who will be the media spokesperson, and make it clear no one else should speak *officially* for the school or agency.
- Route all media inquiries to one person or, at least, to one office.
- Prepare an official statement responding to the particular crisis situation. Read from or distribute this statement when media inquiries are made. This will maintain consistency.
- Anticipate media questions and prepare and rehearse answers.
- Don't be afraid to say, "I don't know." This is better than lying or responding with the offensive phrase, "No comment." Volunteer to get the answer and follow up within a specified time.
- Start a rumor control center, if the situation warrants. Publish a number for media representatives to call if they hear a rumor or need information.
- Provide the newsmedia with updates as events unfold, even after the initial crisis is handled.
- Keep calm and maintain a professional manner. Once calm has returned, it is imperative to begin work that will prevent a recurrence of the crisis.

Community involvement is also needed to effectively reduce and prevent gang activity. Parents and the general public should be made aware of gangs operating in the community, as well as of popular heavy metal and punk bands. They should be encouraged to apply pressure to television and radio stations and to book stores and video stores to ban material that promotes use of alcohol, drugs, promiscuity, or devil worship.

Specific school and community programs that have been implemented to deal with gang activity are described in Appendix C.

COMMUNITY-BASED YOUTH PROGRAMS

When youth have activities to occupy their time, they are much less apt to get into trouble. Participation in clubs, theater, sports, and jobs can all be important. In Rochester, New York, each summer about one hundred youths are hired to keep order in the city's parks.

Rochester New York's Teens On Patrol program hires youth to patrol the city's parks and recreational areas in the summer.

Many youths employed to patrol parks in the summer pursue careers in the criminal justice field.

WILDERNESS PROGRAMS

Youth in Transition is a wilderness program in Santa Fe, New Mexico, sponsored by Southwest Wilderness Challenge, Inc. As noted in their brochure, the program is "dedicated to the development and reorientation of teenagers through significant wilderness experiences." It is for youth ages thirteen to eighteen who exhibit any of the following traits: bright, but unmotivated; low self-esteem; insecure, lacking confidence; withdrawn; rebellious; depressed; runaways; alcohol or drug use; manipulative; expelled, suspended, or dropped out, do not finish what they start.

Through a twenty-one day wilderness expedition under the guidance of experienced staff, youth live and travel approximately 130 miles through the mountains and deserts in wilderness areas of the Southwest. Among the "aboriginal living skills" students have the chance to learn are fire-making (with bow drill and hand drill); wild edible plant identification, collection, and preparation (seeds, roots, and berries); water collection; shelter construction; deadfalls, snares, and fish traps, tool-making (from stone, bone, and sinew); cordage-making (from natural materials); animal tracking, sign tracking, following trails and runs; basic first aid and health maintenance; group dynamics and cooperative living.

Anticipated changes after completion of the program include enhanced self-esteem; self-discovery (new talents and capacities discovered); self-confidence; dependability; leadership; determination; self-discipline; and resourcefulness.

Dr. Victor B. Cline, professor of psychology and author of *How to Make Your Child a Winner,* sent his son on the expedition and said of the experience:

> *When Russ was 14 we noticed he had a tendency toward shyness, a reluctance to express his inner feelings, a certain apartness from the family. He was very smart and doing well in school, but he was struggling to find his own identity and selfhood. He tended to be his own man and didn't accept suggestions from others, even his own parents. . . .*

At first, Russ didn't want to go. . . . But in the end he went, shuffling and reluctant, but he went. . . . We went to pick him up from the wilderness area, and I witnessed a sight that can never be erased from my mind. As Russ got off the truck . . . in his eyes and on his face I saw a look of supreme triumph. He seemed to be walking six feet off the ground. He had found himself.

MODEL PROGRAMS FOR YOUTH

The National Symposium on Community Institutions and Inner-City Crime Project (the National Symposium) has identified several projects focused on providing services for youth. Some of these projects were discussed in previous chapters.

Included in the model programs for youth are:

- The Children of the Night (Hollywood).
- House of UMOJA Boystown (Philadelphia).
- Community Youth Gang Services Project (Los Angeles).
- Junior Police Cadet Section (Detroit).
- The School Program to Educate and Control Drug Abuse (SPECDA) (New York).
- Cabrini-Green Youth Options Program (Chicago).

A discussion of the last two programs follows.

The School Program to Educate and Control Drug Abuse (SPEDCA). This program, a joint venture of the New York City Board of Education and New York City Police Department, seeks to apprehend drug dealers who sell drugs close to schools. It also seeks to reduce the demand for drugs by educating students about the dangers of alcohol and drug use, by helping them resist peer pressure, and by providing healthy alternatives.

The program has sixteen sessions, eight developed for fifth graders and eight for sixth graders. By 1987 this program had expanded to twenty-eight school districts and was using one hundred full time officers. According to police data, thousands of drug-dealer arrests have been made since the program began. In addition, a study conducted by the John Jay College of Criminal Justice found the following positive results (Sulton, 1990, p. 25): "The program has 1) increased student awareness of drugs and their dangers, 2) resulted in positive student attitudes toward SPECDA team members, and 3) encouraged students to remain drug free."

The Cabrini-Green Youth Options Program. Cabrini-Green is a public housing project for thousands of impoverished African-Americans. Sulton (p. 56) says of Cabrini-Green:

> *This decaying pocket of poverty has a reputation as being one of the most dangerous public housing projects in the United States. . . .*
>
> *Hundreds of second and third generation Cobra, Vice Lords, and El Rukn gang members roam the hallways and rooftops. Semi-automatic gunfire usually begins in the early afternoon and continues throughout the night. An average of three youngsters are killed each month as a result of gang-related violence. . . .*
>
> *Older, well-organized groups recruit younger members to compete in an environment of fear and mistrust, one which encourages economically rewarding criminal activity such as drug trafficking, burglary, and prostitution.*

The Cabrini-Green Youth Options Program is sponsored by the Chicago Urban League and the Al Carter Youth Foundation. The purpose of the program is to deter gang recruiting by providing attractive alternatives. It provides educational counseling and employment services for youth as well.

Recommendations by the National Symposium for the Schools

The National Symposium has made the following recommendations for schools (Sulton, p. 105):

1. *Schools and other community institutions should work to prevent youth from dropping out of school. They should stress the relevance of education as it pertains to employment opportunities, self-development, and one's ability to successfully negotiate his or her way through our complex social, economic, and political systems.*
2. *Schools should help students organize peer support groups or clubs that promote educational attainment, leadership development, and community service.*
3. *Schools should work with families and community-based groups to improve as well as to reinforce the importance and relevance of education.*
4. *Schools should establish advisory committees that comprise teachers, students, and parents who discuss and resolve school-related problems and develop alternative forms of discipline.*

5. *Schools should develop curricula that teach students about values, sexuality, career choices, drug abuse, practical law, conflict resolution without violence, mediation, and juvenile justice agencies.*

6. *Schools should teach students the disciplines of work as well as basic academic skills.*

7. *The federal government should encourage elementary and secondary schools to teach children life skills such as time management, goal setting, decision-making, nutrition, physical fitness, parenting, the dynamics of family and community, and nonviolent conflict resolution.*

8. *Educational and training programs should be developed for police officers and social service professionals. These programs should teach about cultural differences and prepare participants to respond to the special needs of various population segments. Research is needed to develop effective educational and training programs.*

COURTS AND CORRECTIONS PROGRAMS

In Indiana, courts and corrections work together to create a system that will accommodate juveniles' needs. In Marion County, Indiana, as in other areas across the country, the court faces juvenile crimes ranging from vandalism and shoplifting to murder. Fortunately, as noted by Payne and Lee (1990, pp. 100, 102):

> *Thanks to a unique public-private partnership and a broad spectrum of alternative programs, the county has opened a state-of-the-art detention center with fewer beds than the old one—an almost unheard-of phenomenon.*
>
> *The county's alternative programs range from a run-away shelter and a wilderness camp to electronic surveillance and community clean-up programs. Together, they weave the fabric of a juvenile justice system that comprehensively evaluates youths in an attempt to steer them away from crime. The programs give juveniles positive options designed to foster responsibility and help mold them into contributing members of society.*

The juvenile facility and alternative programs resulted from the work of a coalition formed of law enforcement officers, prosecutors, public defenders, community organizers, educators, probation officers, and members of the court. The coalition talked with everyone in any way involved in the juvenile justice system in the county, "from cooks to

A Dallas police officer meets with his explorer troop in the city's Little Asia district. This East Dallas Community and Refugee Affairs Center was named "Best Inner-City Crime Reduction Project in U.S." by the Police Foundation, Washington, DC, in 1987.

commissioners." They also toured other juvenile facilities and hired consultants. The 16.6 million dollar center opened in March 1989 and includes the following features (Payne and Lee, p. 105):

- a control desk opened to dayrooms that allows staff to watch and talk with the juveniles;
- private visitation areas for youths to spend time with parents, ministers, and officers of the court;
- an area for court and detention center staff;
- a secured sally port for cars and vans;
- interior courtyards for outdoor recreation and visiting;
- a full-size gymnasium; and
- video display screens in the intake waiting rooms advising juveniles of their rights and highlighting available public services.

According to Payne and Lee (p. 106): "Collaboration is the key to successfully planning and building a new facility and to developing alternative programs for young men and women in trouble." They outline the following dispositional alternative programs developed by the Marion Indiana system (pp. 103–04):

- *Project Challenge:* A six-week program aimed at breaking the behavior cycles that lead youths to trouble. It includes a three-week wilderness camp that encourages youths to trust themselves and their peers, and provides vocational, family, and individual counseling.

- *Ivy Tech:* A part of the state's technical school system that offers vocational education for troubled youths who are functionally illiterate or in need of remedial education or extra attention in the classroom. Students learn skills such as auto mechanics, welding, or how to use computers. Many students then find jobs in the community.

- *Electronic Surveillance:* For four years, electronic surveillance has allowed Marion County to make sure students are home when they are supposed to be. The devices allow them to assume responsibility while ensuring community safety.

- *Run, Don't Run:* Aimed at youths who have literally run from encounters with law enforcement officers. Developed by the juvenile court with the Indianapolis Police Department and the Marion County Sheriff's Department, the program is intended to establish respect between young offenders and law enforcement officials. Youths learn from police officers and a judge or magistrate how fleeing, resisting and striking police officers influences the officers' actions.

- *Visions:* Designed for the serious first referral or repeat offender who comes into contact with the court system. Youths are admitted to the juvenile detention center for one night, followed by a morning lesson about the juvenile justice system. That afternoon juveniles tour the Indiana Boys/Girls School and the Marion County Jail.

- *Operation Kids CAN (Care About Neighborhoods):* Began in the summer of 1987, when more than 200 youths on probation picked up 3.5 tons of neighborhood trash. The program has now joined forces with the Indianapolis Clean City Committee. Youths spend mornings learning about the juvenile justice system. Then they work in structured community service projects such as cleaning vacant lots and picking up garbage.

- *Garden Project:* Youths and their parents plant vegetables and flowers during the summer. The program shifts in winter to craft projects.

- *National Corrective Training Institute:* Instructors have small group discussions with youths charged with misdemeanors. They talk with children about values, attitudes, and behavior.

- *Paint It Clean:* Requires youths associated with destructive gang activities to paint over gang graffiti in local neighborhoods, parks, and buildings. Under the supervision of court staff, Paint It Clean helps eliminate gang claims to territory and allows communities to reclaim their neighborhoods.

- *Summer Youth Program:* Gives youths the chance to go canoeing, horseback riding, camping, hiking, caving, and on a field trip to the Indiana Amusement Park.

- *Basketball:* For eleven years the court and the Twilight Optimist Club have sponsored a basketball league for youths. This collaboration gives juveniles the chance to participate in structured recreation with positive role models.
- *Near Peer Tutoring:* Targets junior high school probationers having trouble in at least one class. High school honor students and adult volunteers tutor youths weekly at neighborhood probation offices.

Three programs under the auspices of the Texas Juvenile Probation Commission's Office have reached out effectively to troubled youth: Williamson County's "Don't Choose Crime" program, Jefferson County's Foster Grandparent program, and Hidalgo County's Juvenile Court Conference Committee Volunteer program.

The *"Don't Choose Crime"* program is aimed at children from prekindergarten through grade twelve to teach them to avoid drugs and delinquency. Young children are given coloring books that illustrate the consequences of crime. Youth in grades four through twelve attend audio-visual presentations, receive a bookmark listing crimes and their penalties, and also receive book covers, news stories, and posters. As noted by Briscoe (1990, p. 92): "More than 4,500 birthday cards have been distributed to 12th grade students warning them that, under Texas law, adulthood begins at age 17."

Several school districts in Texas take students to the detention center for a tour. In addition, the district judge, members of the district attorney's office, the adult probation department, and the court clerk's office have staged mock trials for students.

Jefferson County's *Foster Grandparent* program focuses on high-risk juveniles with emotional problems or who have been physically abused or neglected. Senior citizens are given forty hours of training and then work with children in detention. The foster grandparents tutor students, talk with them about problems, counsel them, teach them arts and crafts or to play musical instruments.

Hidaglo County's *Juvenile Court Conference Committee Volunteer* program is a "neighbors helping neighbors" program. This program forms conference committees of local citizens who work with children who seem headed for serious trouble with the law. Conferences are held with the child and his or her parents, and the committee then makes a decision as to what would be best for the child involved. The parent and child are asked to sign a four-month contract with the committee which may include counseling, community service work, writing an essay, being tutored, referral to another agency, writing a letter of apology, a tour of the county jail or detention center, or any number of other possible activities.

As noted by Briscoe, deputy executive director of the Texas Juvenile Probation Commission (p. 95): "If we are ever going to manage the problems of crime and juvenile delinquency, we must involve citizens and reach beyond our traditional jurisdictional boundaries. Professionals alone can't do it. We must be creative, and we must form alliances with the public. These three programs are good examples of local departments doing just that."

A CALL FOR WIZARDS

Although the preceding projects and programs are successful and valuable to the participants, keep in mind the comments of Beyer (1991, p. 166):

> *Most effective programs cannot be replicated. What comes to my mind when someone asks me about effective programs are not organization models—instead I see the faces of the talented wizards who have created them. . . .*
>
> *I don't believe in successful treatment approaches per se. It is how the program's philosophy is put into action that matters.*

Wizards are those insightful, motivated leaders who can maximize a program's effectiveness.

Part of a wizard's magic is in selecting and training staff who truly love young people and can understand their values but who can also impart their own and the community's values. They do not label the youths with whom they work; they celebrate the diversity among the youths in any given program. As noted by Beyer (p. 174):

> *Wizards' great genius is their appreciation of the chemistry between the staff and the young people. You can see the loving relationship between staff and youth in any effective program: the hand of an actor on a young person's shoulder, the look of achievement as a youth docks a boat, the pride of a young person taking a good grade to a tutor. . . .*
>
> *Wizards are the ultimate motivators. They are not bound by training or habit to one approach. They do what works. Their programs are driven by the needs of the young people.*

Summary

Common programs aimed at youth are school safety programs, bicycle safety programs, the McGruff "Take a Bite out of Crime" program, the Officer Friendly program, police athletic leagues (PALs), the fingerprinting of young children, and police explorer programs.

The National Police Athletic League (PAL), now over fifty years old, was developed to provide opportunities for youth to interact with police officers in gyms or ballparks instead of in juvenile detention hall. A police-school liaison program places an officer into a school to work with school authorities, parents, and students, to prevent crime and antisocial behavior and to improve police-youth relationships. The joint goals of most police-school liaison programs are to prevent juvenile delinquency and to improve police-youth relations.

The Drug Abuse Resistance Education (DARE) program is aimed at elementary age school children and seeks to teach them to "say no to drugs," to resist peer pressure, and to find alternatives to drug use. Teachers are among the most important professionals in making delinquency prevention programs work.

The IACP has endorsed the Kops' n Kids program, a program bringing together children and officers to have fun. Rochester New York's Teens On Patrol program hires youth to patrol the city's parks and recreational areas in the summer. Included in the model programs for youth are the following programs: The Children of the Night (Hollywood), House of UMOJA Boystown (Philadelphia), Community Youth Gang Services Project (Los Angeles), Junior Police Cadet Section (Detroit), the School Program to Educate and Control Drug Abuse (SPECDA) (New York), and the Cabrini-Green Youth Options Program (Chicago).

Despite the existence of numerous exemplary programs, communities cannot simply copy them. The most successful programs are run by "wizards," insightful, motivated leaders who can maximize a program's effectiveness.

DISCUSSION QUESTIONS

1. Which of the programs for youth do you feel are most effective?
2. What programs for youth are available in your community?
3. Does your community have a police-school liaison program?
4. Why do school administrators not consider drugs a security or crime problem?
5. What other major differences in philosophy often exist between school administrators and police?
6. When you were young, were you exposed to McGruff? If so, do you remember what you thought of him?
7. Do you think officers in police-school liaison programs should be uniformed or not? What are the advantages of wearing a uniform? The disadvantages?
8. On which age group do you think police-school programs should focus? Why?

9. Which of the strategies to combat gang activity in schools do you think seem most workable?
10. What are the advantages and disadvantages of expelling disruptive gang members from school?

DEFINITIONS
Can you define these terms: DARE, *in loco parentis,* PAL, police-school liaison program.

REFERENCES

Austin, Dave and Braaten, Jane. "Turning Lives Around: Portland Youth Find a New PAL." *The Police Chief.* (May 1991): 36–38.

Beyer, Marty. "First, You Find a Wizard: The Best Juvenile Programs Start with Visionary Leaders." *Corrections Today.* (April 1991): 166, 172–74.

Bork, Patricia. "COP'RZ." *Law and Order.* (December 1991): 29–32.

Briscoe, Judy Culpepper. "In Texas: Reaching Out to Help Troubled Youths." *Corrections Today.* (October 1990): 90–95.

Brown, Lee P. "President's Message: Making the Problems of Youth a National Priority." *The Police Chief.* (June 1991): 6.

Drowns, Robert W. and Hess, Kären M. *Juvenile Justice.* St. Paul: West Publishing Company, 1990.

Hardy, Lynette. "Geneva, Illinois' Officer Ollie." *Law and Order.* (December 1990): 18–22.

Krum, Brad. "Flying Fuzz." *Law and Order.* (September 1990): 58–59.

Lesce, Tony. "Police Explorers: A Learning Experience." *Law and Order.* (September 1991): 97–100.

Narramore, Randy. "Cards for Kids." *Law and Order.* (December 1990): 23.

National School Safety Center. *Gangs in Schools: Breaking Up Is Hard to Do.* Malibu: Pepperdine University Press, 1988.

Okaty, George J. "Kids at School/Kids at Risk: Cooperation Needed to Address Unique Aspects of Crime Prevention on Campus." *The Police Chief.* (May 1991): 39–41.

Pace, Denny F. *Community Relations Concepts.* Placerville: Custom Publishing Company, 1991.

Paterson, James and Schmoker, Mike. "P.E.P. Kids: A Substance Abuse Prevention Partnership." *Law and Order.* (January 1992): 280–83.

Payne, James W. and Lee, Joe E. "In Indiana: A System Designed to Accommodate Juveniles' Needs." *Corrections Today.* (October 1990): 100, 102–03.

Reynolds, Phil. "Teen-Age Drinking Task Force." *Law and Order.* (December 1991): 49–50.

Sarubbi, Doug. "Orange County Sheriff's Office Broadcasts Anti-Drug/Alcohol Television Programs Directly Into Local Schools." *Law and Order.* (December 1991): 41–42.

"Shop with a Cop." *Law and Order.* (December 1990): 42.

Slahor, Stephenie. "Just for Kids." *Law and Order.* (January 1992): 281.

Spelman, William and Eck, John E. "Sitting Ducks, Ravenous Wolves, and Helping Hands: New Approaches to Urban Policing." In *Source Book: Community-Oriented Policing: An Alternative Strategy.* 201–09. Washington: ICMA, May 1992.

Sulton, Anne Thomas. *Inner-City Crime Control: Can Community Institutions Contribute?* Washington: The Police Foundation, 1990.

Summerhays, J. Jay and Lindbloom, Kenneth D. "The Need for Better Police-School Relations." *The Police Chief.* (November 1989): 69–70.

"Vehicles Bought with Confiscated Monies Help Miami Officers Reach Children." *Law and Order.* (December 1991): 35.

Wrightman, Michael and Coburn, Jim. "Reducing Youth/Police Conflicts: Joplin's Innovative Approach." *Law and Order.* (December 1991): 37–38.

"Youth in Transition," (brochure). Southwest Wilderness Challenge, Inc.

RESOURCES

National Association of Secondary School Principals (NASSP), 1904 Association Drive, Reston, VA 22091; (703) 860-0200.

National Association of School Boards (NSBA), 1680 Duke Street, Alexandria, VA 22314; (703) 838-6722.

National and local Parent Teachers Associations (PTAs). National PTA, 700 North Rush Street, Chicago, IL 60611-2571; (312) 787-0977.

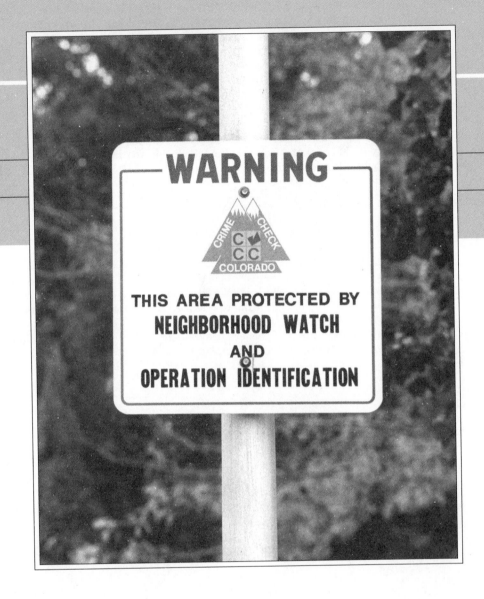

CRIME PREVENTION PROGRAMS: COLLABORATIVE EFFORTS

In the last analysis, the most promising and so the most important method of dealing with crime is by preventing it—by ameliorating the conditions of life that drive people to commit crime and that undermine the restraining rules and institutions erected by society against anti-social conduct.

—**President's Commission on Law Enforcement and Administration of Justice, 1967.**

DO YOU KNOW

- What synergism is and how it relates to crime prevention efforts?
- What crime prevention programs are commonly implemented?
- Who the Guardian Angels are?
- What types of special crime watches have been used?
- What types of institutions have developed model crime prevention programs?
- How volunteers are used in crime prevention?
- What the four R's of volunteer management are?
- What organizations concentrate their efforts on community crime prevention?
- What the two primary messages of most auto-theft programs are?
- What the CAT program is?
- What programs have been implemented to combat the drug problem in neighborhoods?

INTRODUCTION

Whose job is it to prevent crime? Many Americans, including the police, believe crime prevention is the responsibility of the police. Many of the programs already discussed seek to prevent crime, including many of those aimed at youth. When crime surges in a community, the usual public response is to demand that more officers be hired. Citizens often believe that a visible police presence will deter and reduce crime, although most studies indicate that this is not the case. For example, the classic study, *Kansas City Preventive Patrol Experiment* (Klockars 1983, p. 160), found: "The overwhelming evidence is that decreasing or increasing routine preventive patrol within the range tested in this experiment had no effect on crime, citizen fear of crime, community attitudes toward the police on the delivery of police services, police response time or traffic accidents."

Almost twenty-five years ago, the FBI's *Uniform Crime Reports* (1975) noted:

> *Criminal justice professionals readily and repeatedly admit that, in the absence of citizen assistance, neither more manpower, nor improved technology, nor additional money will enable law enforcement to shoulder the monumental burden of combating crime in America.*

The broad nature of policing in the 1990s highlights the critical contributions citizens, community agencies, and organizations can make to combat crime. For communities to thrive, citizens need a sense of neighborhood and to work together as a team. The resulting synergism can accomplish much more than isolated individual efforts.

Synergism occurs when individuals channel their energies toward a common purpose and accomplish what they could not accomplish alone.

The technical definition of *synergism* is "the simultaneous actions of separate entities which together have greater total effect than the sum of their individual efforts." As noted by Buchholz and Roth (1987, p. 2):

> *Athletics provides a multitude of examples [of synergism], particularly team sports such as basketball, football, soccer,*

rowing, relay races, hockey, etc. It is not only the individual athletes' abilities, but their work as a team that produces winners.

Other good examples of synergism come from the music world. Recall the power and energy produced by a top-notch marching band or symphony orchestra. It is up to each individual to know his or her part. There may be some solos, but ultimately what is important is how it all sounds together.

The police and the citizens they serve must realize that their combined efforts *are* greater than the sum of their individual efforts on behalf of the community.

Traditional Approaches to Crime Prevention

When crime prevention became popular in the late 1960s and early 1970s, many communities undertook similar types of programs.

Among the most commonly implemented crime prevention programs have been street lighting projects, property marking projects, security survey projects, citizen patrol projects, and crime reporting, neighborhood watch, or block projects.

Lurigio and Rosenbaum (1986, p. 22) note:

The enthusiastic embracing of community crime prevention is perhaps most apparent at the grass-roots level, where practitioners acclaim the utility of the efforts through popular press articles and numerous homespun program publications, newsletters, and guidebooks that also serve to assist interested communities in the planning and implementation of programs. . . . The following published declarations of success are typical:

1) A 1982 study by the Northwest Neighborhood federation in Chicago found that in 10 months, a neighborhood-watch program there had reduced crime 12%.

2) The Figgie Report on crime reduction indicated that the neighborhood-watch program in Detroit reduced burglary by 60% in a target community, and that serious crime fell 58% overall.

3) An investigation in Sangamon County, Illinois, which has formed 253 neighborhood-watch groups, found that some have achieved as much as an 85% reduction in crime rates.

4) *A multifaceted crime prevention project in San Diego, California, claimed a 21% reduction in burglary, a 50% drop in petty thefts, 173% decline in vandalism, and a 50% reduction in auto thefts.*

5) *Crime prevention efforts in a public housing development in Charlotte, North Carolina, reportedly led to more calls for police service, improved police-community relations, a diminution in residents' fear of crime, and a 32% decrease in all non-assaultive offenses.*

Such claims of success should, however, be carefully examined. Critics often claim that the evaluations are flawed. Indeed, research within communities is extremely difficult because:

- Measuring what *did not happen* is nearly impossible.
- Crime is usually under-reported.
- A reduction in reported crime could be the result of the crime prevention program or because the responsible criminal or criminals left town, went to jail on some other charge, or died, and so on.
- Crime can be influenced by everything from seasonal and weather changes, school truancy rates, and the flu, to road construction or even a change in a bus stop location. A drop in the crime rate does not necessarily mean a crime prevention program is working.

In addition, many of these programs are evaluated by people who have no training or experience in appropriate research methods and, consequently, they sometimes produce flawed results.

Some also argue that crime is not prevented by programs like Neighborhood Watch but instead it is displaced to neighborhoods where the residents are not as likely to report suspicious activity to the police. Even if this is true, such programs do raise community awareness and have a "chilling effect" on criminals who are inhibited by those who watch and call the police.

Use of crime data to evaluate crime prevention projects poses special problems. Crime data, obviously, is limited to *reported* crimes. Practitioners are aware of the *dark side of crime,* that is, the huge amount of crime that is *unreported.* When projects are instituted to enlist the community in preventing crime, the citizens' heightened awareness and involvement often results in an *increase in reported crime,* but this does *not* mean that crime itself has actually increased.

During the following discussion consider the difficulties in evaluating crime prevention projects or, indeed, any project involving many diverse individuals and problems.

Street Lighting Projects

Since ancient times, lighting has been one means to deter and detect crime. Street lighting projects through environmental design (CPTED) efforts are often an important part of crime prevention. Most street lighting projects seek to not only improve the likelihood of deterring and detecting crime, but also to improve the safety of law-abiding citizens. Available research indicates that street lighting does *not* decrease the incidence of crime in participating target areas but that it is useful to reduce citizens' fear of crime and increase their feelings of security. As noted by Lurigio and Rosenbaum (1986, p. 29): "It is not likely, however, that improved street lighting, by itself, will be effective against crime in the absence of the conscious and active support of both citizens (in reporting what they observe) and police (in responding and conducting patrols)."

Property Identification Projects

Often referred to as "Operation Identification" or "O-I" projects, property identification is aimed at deterring burglary and at returning property that is stolen when deterrence fails. Most property identification projects provide citizens with instructions, a marking tool, and a unique number to be applied to all valuable items within a household. Stickers are provided to homeowners to display on windows and doors warning possible burglars that the residents have marked their valuables and they are on record with the police.

In addition to its deterrent effect, the property identification program also helps police track the source of stolen goods and return stolen property to its rightful owners.

It is often difficult to get people to participate in the program, however. As noted by Lurigio and Rosenbaum (p. 25): "The sponsors of O-I have been largely unable to achieve a satisfactory level of citizen participation in the program (on the average, only 10% of the targeted households were enrolled.)" In addition, although the burglary rate dropped for those enrolled in the program, it did not drop citywide. There is no evidence available to suggest a difference in the number of apprehended or convicted burglars in communities that do or do not participate in the program.

Crime Prevention Security Surveys

Crime prevention security surveys are also usually an integral part of projects that focus on the environmental design of facilities and on "target hardening" as a means to deter or prevent crime. As noted by Crowe (1992, p. 22A):

> *CPTED is based on the theory that the proper design and effective use of the built environment can lead to a reduction in the incidence and fear of crime and an improvement in the quality of life. Years of experiments and field applications have demonstrated that CPTED works in all environments—that is, it applies to*

commercial, residential, transportation, recreational, and institutional environments.

It has worked on scales as small as a single room and as large as an entire community.

Surveys used to determine the effectiveness of the existing "environmental design" are usually conducted by police officers specially trained in this area. They do comprehensive on-site inspection of homes, apartments, and businesses. Of particular interest are doors, windows, locks, lighting, and shrubbery that might be used to a burglar's advantage. The officer offers specific suggestions on how a location might be made more secure. As noted by Lurigio and Rosenbaum (p. 25): "Security survey projects seem to exert a measurable effect on reducing victimizations among survey recipients and on improving police-community relations." They also note that the best results are accomplished when systems are in place to assist in implementing the recommendations and to conduct a follow-up review to determine compliance.

Citizen Patrol Projects

Many variations of citizen patrol exist in the United States. Some are directed at a specific problem such as crack houses and sale of drugs in a neighborhood. Others are aimed at general crime prevention and enhanced citizen safety. Citizen patrols may operate throughout a community or may be located within a specific building or complex of buildings such as tenement houses.

Lurigio and Rosenbaum (pp. 26–27) suggest that citizen patrol projects "enjoy resounding support from local police and community residents." They suggest: "The most successful patrols are affiliated with a larger community or neighborhood organization, are conscientious in sustaining a working relationship with law enforcement, and are flexible enough to engage in non-crime prevention activities when patrolling is patently unnecessary."

One hazard of citizen patrols is the possibility of vigilantism which has a long, often proud, history in the United States and, indeed, in the history of law enforcement and criminal justice. Now this hazard is quite serious because of the increase of readily available handguns in our country.

Probably the best known citizen patrol is the **Guardian Angels.** According to Clede (1990, p. 37): "The Alliance of Guardian Angels, Inc. is a non-profit, all volunteer organization whose purpose is to fight crime and provide positive role models for young children ... Angels now number more than 5,000 individual members."

The Guardian Angels are private citizen patrols who seek to deter crime and to provide a positive role model for young children.

A member of the Guardian Angels addresses a group of citizens concerned about rising crime and gang violence in their community.

The Guardian Angels operate in sixty-seven cities in the United States as well as Canada and Mexico. As noted by Greenberg (1991, p. 42): "The Angels wear bright red berets and T-shirts imprinted with a flapping wing and badge insignia. They carry a pad, pen, whistle and—sometimes—handcuffs. Although they carry no weapons, they do attempt to arrest felony suspects and hold them for the police."

In New York City, there is another type of private citizen patrol, called the Veterans Civilian Observation Patrol or V-COPS. According to Clark (1991, p. 8): "Each member is a homeless veteran of the U.S. armed forces who has volunteered his time and energy not only to help prevent crime in the neighborhoods, but also to aid in his recovery from drug abuse or alcoholism and to regain a sense of self-esteem."

Ironically, the V-COPS were born out of neighborhood problem. In 1988 the Borden Avenue Veterans Residence was opened by the Salvation Army to serve homeless veterans. Neighbors complained about noise and drinking at the shelter, but only a very small number of those living there were actually causing the problem. The police officer assigned to defuse the situation conceived the idea of the V-COPS, and it quickly became popular. About two hundred homeless veterans have participated in the program since then.

V-COPS patrol bank areas on the days Social Security and welfare checks arrive, and the grateful bank officials often provide them with lunch. As noted by one V-COP (Clark, p. 8): "Our presence deters [criminals] from coming around the neighborhood. They know who we are. They know we're veterans. They think we're probably psycho or Rambo, and they walk away."

When on duty, V-COPS wear T-shirts with their emblem and march through neighborhoods military-style, silently, using hand signals. If the V-COPS find trouble or suspicious circumstances, they notify one of their group stationed in the precinct house who monitors their radio transmissions. This person then notifies on-duty patrol officers who respond.

Communities who want to develop a citizen street patrol will find assistance in a brochure developed by the Neighborhood Crime Prevention Council. The guide discusses how to recruit volunteers, how to structure patrols, and what actions to take if one witnesses a crime. Citizen arrest procedures, a watch log, and job descriptions are included.

Citizen Crime Reporting, Neighborhood, or Block Programs

Citizen crime reporting programs (CCRP) help to organize neighborhoods as "mutual aid societies" and as the "eyes and ears" of the police. According to Garofalo and McLeod (1988, p. 1): "Thousands of Neighborhood Watch programs exist in the United States, and it is fair to describe them as the backbone of the Nation's community crime prevention effort." Typically local residents hold meetings of such programs in their homes or apartments. During the meetings, neighbors get to know each other and what is normal activity for their neighborhood. They receive educational information about crime prevention from the local police department and are told how to contact the police if they see something suspicious.

Signs are posted throughout the neighborhood warning possible offenders of the program. Often the programs provide safe houses for children to use if they encounter danger on their way to or from school.

Some programs work to enhance citizens' reporting capability. Whistlestop programs, for example, provide citizens with whistles which they can blow if they are threatened or see something requiring police intervention. Anyone hearing the whistle is to immediately call the police. Whistlestop programs are the modern-day version of the "hue and cry."

Some programs enlist the aid of ham radio operators who can report suspicious or illegal activity directly to the police without using public telephone lines. Other programs have implemented special hot lines whereby citizens can call a specific number with crime information and perhaps receive a monetary reward.

According to Lurigio and Rosenbaum (p. 28): "There is a derth of hard evidence demonstrating that crime reporting projects increase the level of surveillance in an area or the frequency and quality of citizen's reports regarding suspicious or illegal activities."

McLean (1991, p. 58) describes the citizen's watch program in Honolulu:

Organized as fixed-location neighborhood watches, a remarkable 26,000 homes in nearly 300 separate neighborhoods are a direct extension of the Honolulu Police Department. If you factor in the 2.3 people per home in the Honolulu city/county jurisdiction, it's safe to say there are probably 58,000 sets of eyes and ears.

- *Honolulu PD's senior citizen watch has members in 44 registered groups within the county. They total roughly 830 individuals.*
- *Business security watches, now being organized,number 321 commercial establishments, including the sprawling Ala Moana Shopping Center with 156 members.*
- *The Neighborhood Security Watch is growing by 600 homes per month, with no end in sight.*
- *Some 450 cars, trucks and buses have drivers who are, in a manner of speaking, "riding shotgun" with their cellulars and radios—trained and ready to accurately report crimes in progress.*

Table 15.1 illustrates the types of activities engaged in by Neighborhood Watch programs and the relative popularity of each.

Very few of the programs concentrate only on the "neighborhood watch." Project Operation Identification and home security surveys are by far the most common activities of Neighborhood Watch programs. Street lighting programs, crime tip hot lines, and physical environmental concerns are also quite common.

SPECIAL CRIME WATCH PROGRAMS

In addition to the traditional types of crime watch programs commonly implemented throughout the country, some communities have developed more specialized types of crime watch programs.

Specialized crime watch programs include mobile crime watch, youth crime watch, business crime watch, Realtor watch, and carrier alert.

Honolulu's mobile crime watch seeks to enlist the aid of motorists who have two-way communication equipment in their vehicles such as CBs, car telephones, or cellular telephones. Volunteers attend a short orientation session that trains them to better observe and report suspicious activity. Participants are also given Mobile Watch decals to place on

TABLE 15.1
Activities Engaged in by Neighborhood Watch Programs (based on program survey responses)

Activity	Number	Percent
Neighborhood Watch only	49	8.9
Crime Prevention Specific		
Project Operation Identification	425	80.6
Home security surveys	357	67.9
Street lighting improvement	183	34.7
Block parenting	144	27.3
Organized surveillance	66	12.0
Traffic alteration	37	7.0
Emergency telephones	24	4.6
Project Whistle Stop	18	3.4
Specialized informal surveillance	18	3.4
Escort service	12	2.3
Hired guards	11	2.1
Environmental design	7	1.3
Lock provision/installation	4	0.7
Self defense/rape prevention	3	0.5
Crime Related		
Crime tip hotline	197	37.5
Victim witness assistance	101	19.2
Court watch	17	3.2
Telephone chain	7	1.3
Child fingerprinting	2	0.4
Community Oriented		
Physical environmental concerns	201	38.1
Insurance premium deduction survey	20	3.6
Quality of life	9	1.6
Medical emergency	4	0.7

SOURCE: James Garofalo and Maureen McLeod. *Improving the Use and Effectiveness of Neighborhood Watch Programs.* U.S. Department of Justice, National Institute of Justice/Research in Action Series. April 1988: 2.

their vehicles. They are advised to call 911 if they hear screaming, gunshots, breaking glass, or loud explosive noises; if they see someone breaking into a house or car; if they observe a car driven in a dangerous or erratic manner; if they observe a person on the ground apparently unconscious; if they see anyone brandishing a gun or knife; or if they see an individual staggering, out of control, or threatening others.

They are also trained to recognize and report other unusual behaviors such as:

- A child who appears to be lost.
- Anyone being forced into a vehicle, especially a child or female.
- Cars cruising erratically and repetitively near schools, parks, and playgrounds.
- A person running, especially if carrying something of value.
- Parked, occupied vehicles at unusual hours near potential robbery sites.
- More than normal traffic in and out of a house or commercial establishment.
- Someone going door-to-door or passing through backyards.
- Persons loitering around schools, parks, secluded areas, or in the neighborhood.

Pace (1991, p. 266) describes three other specialized watch programs implemented by the Miami-Dade Metro Police Department:

Youth Crime Watch: This program is available to all elementary and secondary students who will be trained in crime prevention and in observing and reporting incidents in their schools. Additionally, the youths may initiate and develop their own programs in order to make their neighborhoods safer.

Business Crime Watch: A general meeting of all businesses is held, similar to the "Primary Meeting." Crime prevention and crime watch training, however, applies to businesses, offices, and stores rather than to residences.

Realtor Watch: Realtors throughout the county are trained to "crime watch" during their working hours in the neighborhoods and commercial areas in which they are selling.

Another specialized type of crime watch is the *Carrier Alert* program, initiated by the United States Postal Service. In this program letter carriers are asked to become aware of elderly citizens or citizens with special needs on their routes and to look out for them. They are to report any lack of activity or suspicious activity at their homes to the police.

Most successful community-based programs that focus on crime prevention or safety issues have a close partnership with law enforcement. The community and law enforcement have vital components to offer the other, making cooperation between the two highly desirable. It is difficult to imagine, for instance, an effective community-based Crime Watch program without input or cooperation from the local police agency. Crime Watch programs are built on the premise of mutual aid—citizens and police working together.

NATIONAL NIGHT OUT

National Night Out is a program originated in Tempe, Arizona, and sponsored by the National Association of Town Watch and the Philips Lighting Company. Held in August, this nation-wide program encourages neighborhoods to turn on their porch lights, go outside, and meet their neighbors. One crime prevention association's newsletter states: "The best deterrents for crime are good lighting and watchful, caring neighbors. The porch or yard lights are partly symbolic, partly crime prevention, but the neighborliness is the most important."

During the August 7, 1990, National Night Out a special satellite crossed the country and photographed all the lights in its path. Neighborhood Watch programs are encouraged to plan a party or event during National Night Out.

MODEL PROGRAMS

The National Symposium on Community Institutions and Inner-City Crime Project has identified several model crime prevention programs.

Model crime prevention programs have been developed by a hospital auxiliary, churches, foundations, businesses, and civic groups.

BELLVIEW HOSPITAL AUXILIARY, NEW YORK—Special Project on Training of Professionals in Sexual Exploitation Prevention of the Developmentally Disabled. The advisory committee of the project consists of crime victims, rehabilitation professionals, and disabled individuals. Each year the project conducts seven or eight training sessions for twenty-five to thirty human service and criminal justice professionals. The training focuses on prevention of sexual exploitation, emphasizing that disabled people can be independent, assertive, and able to defend themselves. Trainers are taught several techniques the disabled can use to avoid victimization or to cope with it should it occur. According to Sulton (1990, p. 29): "The project encourages local professionals to think about ways in which individuals and organizations can establish a local network of medical, psychological, and legal services to which the disabled can turn before or after they have been abused . . . [promoting and facilitating] a local self-help approach to service delivery and education that continues after the training session ends."

PONCE, PUERTO RICO—Centro Sister Isolina Ferre Programa Del Dispensario. This church-based program seeks to help the poor of Puerto Rico's second largest city through "education, advocacy, and revitalization at both the individual and community levels" (Sulton, p. 30). The center was founded in 1968 and is governed by a board of directors. It conducts educational programs, job-training programs, advocacy programs, and community revitalization in the form of small business development.

The advocacy component seeks to foster community unity and spirit. Advocates are community residents who help "open doors to opportunities" for other residents. They represent troubled youth dealing with the justice system. They teach parents about their responsibilities and parenting skills. They also provide counseling to abused children, encourage handicapped children to participate in society to the fullest extent possible, and encourage all children to remain in school.

LUTHERAN METROPOLITAN MINISTRIES ASSOCIATION OF CLEVELAND, OHIO—Community Re-Entry Program. This church-sponsored, community-based corrections program focuses on "reintegration" of offenders through employment. Sulton (pp. 35–36) describes the concepts on which Community Re-Entry is based:

1. People more readily act their way into a new kind of thinking, than think their way into a new kind of acting.
2. Through community service one is able to explore one's talents and become more productive.
3. Offenders must be integrated into the community for the good of society and themselves.
4. People should be allowed to exercise self-determination.

Components of the program include Care Teams discussed in Chapter 7, where ex-offenders help the elderly living in low-income, high-rise apartment buildings. The Denise McNair New Life Center is a storefront operation directed by ex-offenders that provides court-related advice, intervenes in family crisis situations, makes referrals to other community services and agencies, and conducts home visits.

A Community Detention program is sometimes used in place of incarceration. During the day offenders do community service or work at their jobs, but they spend the night at the center. The program has also created jobs, operating such businesses as Paint Plus, Maintenance Plus, Fresh Lunch/Fresh Start, Creative Printing, and the Wick Band. Yet another component of the program is the School Care Team, which provides drug and violence prevention counseling to high school students. Ex-offenders visit schools and talk with youth about the dangers of drug abuse and violence.

CHICAGO, ILLINOIS—Sunbow Foundation, Inc. This program is based on the belief that poor women should be trained for well-paying nontraditional jobs, specifically jobs in the construction field. The program is directed by an advisory board consisting of representatives from social services, building construction, and the criminal justice system. Site visit staff learned that 91 percent of the women enrolled in the program completed it and that 88 percent obtained jobs with Chicago-area construction and cable companies. As noted by Sulton (p. 43): "The program familiarized participants with drafting, blueprints, construction math, masonry, plumbing, electrical work, HVAC, and the use and care of hand and power tools. Program participants attended workshops on safety, first aid, fitness, career planning, and human relations."

NEW YORK—Wildcat Service Corporation.   Wildcat is a private, nonprofit transitional employment program that seeks to "break the cycles of poverty and welfare dependency by hiring and training the chronically unemployed for subsidized jobs and moving them into the regular workforce" (Sulton, p. 46). Approximately 2,000 individuals participate each year, the majority being African-American or Hispanic.

The program operates like a traditional temporary help or job placement agency. In addition to this basic program, the Wildcat Service Corporation operates a Youth Literacy and Work Experience Program for juvenile offenders; an Enhanced Work Experience Youth Program for those receiving public assistance or from low-income families; a Clerical Work Experience/Classroom Training Program for adults on public assistance or who are unemployed; a Clerk-Typist Training Program for adults on public assistance; and a Supported Work Program for offenders currently in New York City-based state correctional institutions who are in work release programs and within six months of parole.

WASHINGTON, D.C.—Around the Corner to the World (ACW).
This program is located in Adams Morgan which is, according to Sulton (p. 51): "the most densely populated and ethnically diverse neighborhood in our nation's capital." She notes:

> *Around the Corner to the World is a neighborhood-based, grassroots response to the displacement, lost sense of community, and crime occurring in Adams Morgan. . . .*
>
> *ACW's primary goal is to stabilize and revitalize Adams Morgan through youth leadership development and economic development.*
>
> *ACW emphasizes personal empowerment (confidence and self-esteem), community empowerment (reinforcement of basic institutional relationships), and means, and capacity to live positively and independent of destructive forces. It promotes self-sufficiency and economic development by teaching marketable skills and providing jobs to neighborhood residents.*

NEWARK, N.J.—Soul-O-House Drug Abuse Program. Soul-O-House is an outpatient, community-based drug prevention and rehabilitation center which seeks to reduce drug abuse and crime by helping citizens achieve productive, meaningful lives. According to Sulton (p. 67): "Program participants are counseled from an African-American perspective within an extended family. . . . Knowledge of one's culture and history and cultural pride are associated with positive self-concept." The program operates a latchkey program for elementary school children, sponsors parent meetings, health seminars on AIDS, field trips, and athletic events for area residents.

USING VOLUNTEERS

Many police departments make extensive use of volunteers. In fact, according to Hageman (1985, p. 134):

> *This is the age of active citizen involvement. Citizens participate in public relations groups, in political pressure groups, on citizen review boards or advisory boards, in crime prevention programs, and on operational level interaction groups. Citizens also volunteer their services in myriad other agencies. Although there are pros and cons to the use of volunteers and citizen participation, the con arguments would only limit citizen participation, not eradicate it. Perhaps our society has reached a level of understanding that acknowledges that consumers, even consumers of an administration of justice service, have the right to a voice in decision making (it's their tax dollars, after all). Citizens' opinions are valued, even though an agency might not be legally able to adhere to a citizen's wish.*

The importance of community volunteers is stressed by Leavy (1992, p. 69): "Volunteer resource pools, if enthusiastically used, can bring an enormous cachet of diversified expertise into a given situation. These volunteers are generally enthusiastic, committed and eager to contribute to the task. . . . Volunteer talent is a gift which if not fostered and utilized will be lost forever. Law enforcement cannot afford to lose the benefits a pool of volunteers can provide. The answer very simply is: USE THEM (to the maximum)—OR LOSE THEM."

Volunteers may serve as reserve officers, auxiliary patrol, community service officers, or on an as-needed basis.

Reserve officers, auxiliary patrol, or community service officers usually wear uniforms and badges, but are unarmed. They are trained to perform specific functions that assist the uniformed patrol officers. They may be used to patrol watching for suspicious activity, to direct traffic, to conduct interviews with victims of and witnesses to crimes, and to provide crime-prevention education at neighborhood watch meetings, civic groups, churches, and schools.

Some communities use a volunteer officer program. According to Weinblatt (1991, p. 19), in some Massachusetts districts, volunteer officers are trained, armed, and certified by the state. Volunteer officers alleviate severe personnel shortages in some areas. The program allows the department to have two-officer squads and also serves as a pre-screening for potential paid officers. Weinblatt suggests: "Many volunteer officers are young people looking to make a career out of law enforcement and see volunteering as a way to get a foot in the door and test the waters."

Community service officers (CSOs), according to Hageman (1985, p. 131), are uniformed but unarmed, are usually between age seventeen and twenty-one and are often from a minority group. CSOs may work with youths to prevent delinquency, refer citizen complaints to the appropriate agency, and investigate minor thefts. They are usually heavily involved in public relations activities as well. Some CSOs are paid, but much less than police officers. Explorer programs, discussed in Chapter 14, and police cadet programs are other sources for volunteers.

Often departments ask professionals such as physicians, teachers, and ministers, to volunteer their services, sometimes as expert witnesses. In Tempe, the Volunteers in Policing program has grown from three volunteers to 120. Their volunteer management philosophy is based on what they call the "Four R's."

The four R's of volunteer management are research, recruitment, retention, and recognition.

"No Mere Paper-Pushers" (1991, p. 9) quotes the volunteer coordinator, Judy Bottorf, as saying: "Volunteers are really community-based policing, because they are in the community every day, they bring a different perspective. They have special problem-solving skills and feedback that we can use." The chief of police feels that the more than 1,000 volunteer hours a month are an excellent return on the investment they made in establishing Bottorf's position.

One of the Volunteers in Policing programs, the Motorist Assist Program, helps stranded motorists and also assists in directing traffic at accident scenes. Volunteers in this program can also write civil citations for parking violations in handicapped zones and fire lanes.

Often volunteers perform office-type functions in police departments. Volunteers might perform crime analysis, conduct tours, or answer telephone messages. They might also provide assistance to police at crime prevention programs and Neighborhood Watch meetings. Many departments use the AARP volunteer program, capitalizing on the experience and free time of the elderly citizens of the community.

Advantages of Using Volunteers

Hageman (1985, pp. 132–33) suggests several advantages of using volunteers in police work. Volunteers provide a vital communication link between the citizens and the "establishment," including the police department. They can help establish the creditability of the department's public relations and educational efforts. Volunteers provide additional sources of information and perspectives. Hageman says (p. 133): "Citizens as paraprofessionals can be equated with a tremendous reservoir of energy extremely useful for emergencies. They can alleviate critical shortages of paid professional personnel while serving as a recruitment pool for future positions."

Disadvantages of Using Volunteers

Using volunteers does, however, cause certain problems. In fact, some police officers feel that volunteers are "more trouble than they are worth." Hageman (p. 133) lists the following possible problems:

1) *People who are "joiners" or have time and/or money often lack sensitivity to minorities. Thus, they may perpetuate a bias instead of decreasing interclass hostilities and misunderstandings.*
2) *Citizen advisory committees lack direct policy-setting responsibilities.*
3) *Some citizens desire profit and gain for themselves. Thus, they develop programs that are mere window dressing, so as not to change the status quo.*
4) *Some citizens lack professional qualifications and training.*
5) *Since volunteers receive no pay, they cannot be docked or penalized for early withdrawal from the volunteer program.*
6) *Citizens lack awareness of the criminal justice system in general and specific agencies in particular.*
7) *Because of the use of volunteers and/or citizen participation, some communities and politicians fail to take responsibility for solving the larger social problem and/or refuse to hire adequate numbers of personnel or pay better wages.*

In addition, some police unions have reacted negatively to volunteers who are sometimes viewed as competitors for police jobs. Reserve officers, in particular, tend to cause patrol officers to feel their jobs are threatened by those willing to do police jobs for free. Departments should take care to be certain that the objectives of volunteer use are understood by the salaried police officers. Officers should know that programs that use volunteers are those that could not otherwise exist due to lack of personnel and funding.

ORGANIZATIONS FOCUSED ON CRIME PREVENTION

Among the most visible organizations focused on crime are citizen crime prevention associations, Crime Stoppers, and MADD.

Citizen Crime Prevention Associations

Among the many activities undertaken by citizen crime prevention associations are the following:

- Paying for crime tips.
- Funding for police-crime prevention programs.
- Supporting police canine programs.
- Raising awareness in the community through crime prevention seminars, newsletters, cable TV shows, and booths.
- Providing Teddy Bears for kids.
- Raising money through sources such as:
    Business contributions;
    Membership fees;
    Charitable gambling; and
    Sales of alarms, mace, "Call Police" signs (usually sold as a service to community, not to raise any substantial money).
- Funding specific programs such as rewards to community members who call the hot line with crime information.

Crime Stoppers

Crime Stoppers is a non-profit program involving citizens, the media, and the police. Local programs offer anonymity and cash rewards to individuals who furnish to police information that leads to the arrest and indictment of felony offenders. Each program is governed by a local board of directors made up of citizens from a cross-section of the community, the businesses of the community, and law enforcement. The reward money comes from tax-deductible donations and grants from local businesses, foundations, and individuals.

When a crime-related call is received by Crime Stoppers, it is logged in with the date, time, and a summary of the information given by the caller. Callers are given code numbers to be used on all subsequent calls by the same person regarding that particular case. Each week, one unsolved crime is selected for special treatment by the media. Over 850 programs throughout the United States, Canada, Australia, England, and West Africa are members of Crime Stoppers International.

Mothers Against Drunk Driving (MADD)

Mothers Against Drunk Driving (MADD) is a non-profit, grassroots organization with over 400 chapters nationwide. Its membership is open to anyone: victims, concerned citizens, law and safety workers, and health professionals. As noted in their literature: "The mission of Mothers Against Drunk Driving is to stop drunk driving and to support victims of this violent crime."

MADD was founded in California in 1980 after Candy Lightner's thirteen-year-old daughter was killed by a hit-and-run driver. The driver had been out of jail on bail for only two days for another hit-and-run drunk driving crash. He had three previous drunk driving arrests and two convictions. But he was allowed to plea bargain to vehicular manslaughter. His two year prison sentence was spent not in prison, but in a work camp and later a halfway house.

At a vigil sponsored by Mothers Against Drunk Driving, as a mother tells of her daughter who was killed by a drunk driver, her husband raises a picture of their daughter.

MADD differentiates between accidents and crashes:

Those injured and killed in drunk driving collisions are not "accident victims." The crash caused by an impaired driver is a violent crime. Drunk driving involves two choices: to drink AND to drive. The thousands of deaths and injuries caused each year by impaired driving can be prevented . . . they are not "accidental."

MADD seeks to raise public awareness through community programs such as Operation Prom/Graduation, their Poster/Essay Contest, their "Tie One on for Safety" Project Red Ribbon campaign, and a Designated Driver program. Their national newsletter, *MADD In Action,* is sent to members and supporters. MADD also promotes legislation to strengthen existing laws and adopt new ones. In addition, MADD provides victim services. Victims and their families may call 800-GET-MADD for emotional support and guidance through the criminal justice system. Annual candle-light vigils are held nationwide to allow victims to share their grief with others who have suffered due to drunk driving.

A current goal of MADD is to reduce by 20 percent alcohol-related traffic fatalities by the year 2000. To accomplish this goal, they are implementing measures in five major areas: youth issues, enforcement strategies, stronger sanctions, responsible marketing and service, and self-sufficiency (funding for enforcement through DWI fines, fees, and other assessments).

PROGRAMS AIMED AT PREVENTING AUTO THEFT

Many police departments furnish citizens with information on how to prevent auto theft. Information may be provided in the form of pamphlets, newspaper stories, PSAs on television, or speeches made to civic organizations. Such programs usually include tips such as the following from Honolulu's brochure:

- Never leave your keys in the ignition, not even at home or in a parking lot. It is an open invitation to theft.
- Hiding spare keys under the carpeting or over a sun visor is about as clever as leaving a house key under a doormat. Thieves know all the obvious places to look.
- Do not leave luggage, packages, or other easily removed items in view inside your automobile. Lock your property in the trunk. Doctors should always conceal their bags while away from their vehicles.

- Automobile thieves frequent streets and parking areas in the vicinities of public gatherings. Do not take needless risks by leaving valuables in your car when it is not necessary to be transporting them.
- Avoid transferring items to the trunk of a vehicle at a location where it is to be parked. A thief may be watching. Checkbooks, credit cards, or other credentials which a thief could use should not be left in the car.
- At night park in a lighted area, preferably close to a corner where a potential thief may realize that he is more likely to be observed. (Thefts of automobile accessories have increased greatly since the introduction of bucket seats, car stereos, and special wheels. These items, as well as hubcaps and other parts, should be marked as an aid to identification. Thousands of dollars worth of automobile parts are sold at auction every year by the Police Department because the rightful owners could not be located.)
- If your car is broken into or stolen, inform the police of the loss immediately. Stolen vehicles frequently are used in the commission of other crimes.

The two main messages of anti-car theft programs are:

- Do not leave the keys in the car ignition.
- Lock the car.

These messages are conveyed in a variety of ways from stickers to put on dashboards to posters warning that leaving keys in the ignition is a violation of the law if the car is parked on public property. In addition, leaving one's keys in the ignition is an invitation to theft, could become a contributing cause to some innocent person's injury or death, and could raise the owner's insurance rates.

The CAT Program

New York City has developed an anti-auto theft program that enlists the aid of motorists.

The Combat Auto Theft (**CAT**) program allows the police to stop any car marked with a special decal between 1 a.m. and 5 a.m.

The program is more a crime prevention program than a law enforcement strategy. Hildreth (p. 92) describes the following key elements of the program:

- Participation is strictly voluntary. Car owners sign a consent form affirming that they do not normally drive between 1 a.m. and 5 a.m., the peak auto theft hours.

- Car owners are given a tamper-proof CAT Program decal to be affixed prominently on the inside of the car's rear window.

Those who participate in the program waive their rights against search and seizure protection. According to Hildreth (p. 93), New York's three-year-old CAT Program has registered 37,326 cars, of which only sixty-seven have been stolen. Further, says Hildreth: "New York City authorities have estimated that cars not enrolled in the CAT Program are 48 times more likely to be stolen than those that are protected by the program."

PROGRAMS TO DETER PROSTITUTION _____

The Des Moines Police Department encourages citizens to send "Dear John" letters to registered owners of vehicles involved in prostitution. Citizens are told they can obtain the owner's name, address, make, year, and color of the vehicle by taking the license number to the Iowa Department of Transportation. The information is free. Citizens are also given a sample letter they can send to the registered owner, like that which appears in Figure 15.1. Citizens are also instructed to send copies of the letter to the county attorney and to the vice squad.

COLLABORATIVE EFFORTS TO COMBAT THE DRUG PROBLEM _____

"U.S. Illegal Drug Tab Exceeds $40 Billion" (1991) reads a *Law Enforcement News* headline. According to the article, in 1990 Americans spent:

$17.5 billion for cocaine;
$12.3 billion for heroin;
$8.8 billion for marijuana; and
$2.0 billion for hallucinogens, amphetamines and other drugs.

New York Rep. Charles Rangel, a member of the House Committee on Narcotics Abuse, believes the figures are too low. He estimates that the figure is closer to $100 billion a year (p. 1). In addition, as noted in "Automating the War against Drug Dealers" (1991, p. 107): "When you realize that upwards of 87% of all felony crimes committed in the United States today are drug related, you know why President Bush calls drugs 'the gravest domestic threat facing our nation today.'"

Communities have instituted many grassroots efforts to combat drug dealing. In Des Moines, for example, the police have provided

Date: _____

_____

_____

_____

_____

Mr. and/or Mrs. _____ :

Your _____ was seen picking up a
(DESCRIPTION OF VEHICLE)

prostitute in the vicinity of _____ in
(AREA)

Des Moines on _____ , at approximately_____ .
(DATE)   (TIME)

We hope you realize that by participating in such behavior you risk criminal prosecution, as well as exposing yourself — and possibly your family — to public humiliation and a host of diseases including the deadly AIDS virus.

Prostitution is unacceptable and it will not be tolerated anymore in our neighborhood. A detailed description of your vehicle, complete with the license number, has been circulated to area residents.

Sincerely,

North Side Neighbors

cc: James Smith
    Polk County Attorney

    Vice Squad
    Des Moines Police Department

FIGURE 15.1   Sample "Dear John" Letter

SOURCE: Reprinted by permission. Des Moines Police, *"Drugs: A Municipal Approach, A Community Handbook,"* 15.

citizens with a list of suspicious activities and common indicators of residential drug trafficking, illustrated in Figure 15.2. Police ask that citizens who suspect drug trafficking occurring in their neighborhoods contact the vice/narcotics control unit.

In Minneapolis, Minnesota, police and property owners are using black and gold "No trespassing" signs in inner-city neighborhoods. "The

---

1. A high volume of foot and/or vehicle traffic to and from a residence at late or unusual hours.
2. Periodic visitors who stay at the residence for very brief periods of time.
3. Alterations of property by the tenants, including the following:
   a. Covering windows and patio doors with materials other than curtains or drapes;
   b. Barricading windows or doors;
   c. Placing dead bolt locks on interior doors; and
   d. Disconnecting fire alarms.
4. Consistent payment of rent and security deposits with U.S. currency, especially small denominations of cash. (Large amounts of 20 dollar bills are commonly seized from drug dealers.)
5. The presence of drug paraphernalia in or around the residence, including, but not limited to, glass pipes, syringes, propane torches, paper or tinfoil bindles, folded shiny-slick paper (snow seals), large quantities of plastic baggies, scales, money wrappers, and small glass vials.
6. The presence of unusual odors coming from the interior of the residence, especially the odor of pungent chemical substances and/or burning materials.
7. The presence of firearms, other than sporting firearms, including fully automatic weapons, assault weapons, sawed off shotguns, machine pistols, handguns, and related ammunition and holsters.
8. The presence of tenant's possessions and furnishings which are inconsistent with the known income level of the tenant. This would include, but is not limited to, the following:
   a. New and/or expensive vehicles;
   b. Expensive jewelry and clothing; and
   c. Expensive household furnishings, stereo systems, and other large entertainment systems.
9. Tenants who are overly nervous and apprehensive about the landlord visiting the residence.

Any of the indicators, by itself, may not be reason to suspect drug trafficking. However, when combined with other indicators, they may be reason to suspect drug trafficking. If you suspect drug trafficking in your neighborhood, please contact the Des Moines Police Vice/Narcotic's Control Unit at 283-4883. "The

---

FIGURE 15.2.   Suspicious Activity and Common Indicators of Residential Drug Trafficking

SOURCE: Reprinted by permission. Des Moines Police, *"Drugs: A Municipal Approach, A Community Handbook,"* 26.

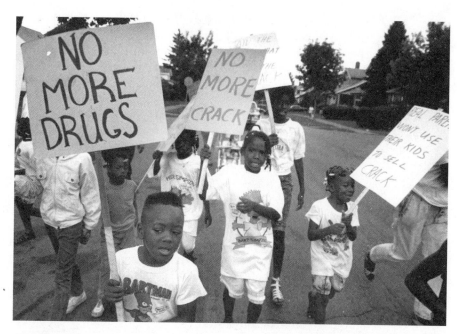

Children from an east side Detroit neighborhood march against crack houses in their neighborhood.

distinctive signs," according to Gendler (1991, p. 1B), "mark a new program intended to improve residents' security and deter street-level drug dealing by telling officers that they can enter the properties to question loiterers without a call from the property owner." This expands the power of the police greatly and removes from landlords the sometimes threatening responsibility of signing a citizen's arrest form before the police can act.

In another area of the city, a group called HOPE (Homes on Portland Enterprise) marched near known crack-houses, carrying signs and demanding that the dealers leave the neighborhood. As noted by Grow (1992, p. 1A): "Living in a crack neighborhood means living in fear of both the bad guys (those involved in drugs) and the good guys (police). It means telling your child she can't play in the little park next door. It means friends won't come to visit. It means carrying a knife while waiting for the bus."

In March 1992, a group of women decided to take their neighborhood back from the drug dealers. They painted signs and marched near the crack houses. Grow states (p. 1A): "They make an unusual group of drug warriors, these women marching with their kids. They've got no money, no political clout. They're scared to death. But they're determined to make their dreams come alive again. They're determined to live in a safe neighborhood." The march received much media attention and appears to have been successful.

Across the river, the city of St. Paul also enlisted the aid of residents to force an alliance to fight drug dealers. The program, called FORCE (Focusing Our Resources on Community Empowerment), centered on getting longtime residents to permit narcotics officers to use their homes to monitor drug sales in the neighborhood. According to Lonetree (1992, p. 5B):

> The FORCE team would work with a network of block club leaders to target drug dealers and to force the removal of, or improvements to ramshackle drug houses. Ramsey County would provide child protection services for youths found in drug houses. The Institute on Black Chemical Abuse also would advocate treatment programs for drug-addicted people who are caught selling or buying drugs.

Another grassroots effort has taken place in Price, Utah, a community with 10,000 people. The family services, school district, police, and mental health professionals have established a volunteer interagency committee known as SODAA (Stop Our Drug & Alcohol Abuse). This committee coordinates prevention and education programs and strives to eliminate duplication of efforts.

The committee developed and promoted a Substance Abuse Awareness Sabbath. They developed a five-page informational factsheet and identified all churches in the community. They then distributed the factsheets through the forty-four churches which represent nineteen denominations. As noted by Shilaos (1990, p. 43), each church was asked to:

- Duplicate and distribute a copy of the handout to every adult member.
- Devote part of their Sabbath to substance abuse awareness.

The local newspaper also dedicated an entire page to the campaign. Every church that participated in the Substance Abuse Awareness Sabbath received recognition in the article.

Another very successful crime prevention program was developed in Wilson, North Carolina. Their program, "Operation Broken Window," was rooted in the broken window philosophy discussed earlier. The 500 block in Wilson was their "broken window," an open-air drug market widely known as a place where drugs could be easily bought. Undercover police operations had been unsuccessful in reducing the problem. The Wilson Police Department turned to problem-oriented policing as a possible solution. According to Younce (1992, p. 67), in the planning process, "the department used all of the available resources of the city, including direct input from citizens who worked and lived in the target area."

The department formulated a four-pronged attack: undercover operations, increased uniform police presence with more officers and a satellite police station in the target area, two K-9 units assigned to drug interdiction at the local bus station, and attention to social and environmental conditions. Younce (pp. 668–69) notes: "Social conditions that facilitated the drug sales in the target area were identified. Grass was cut, trash was removed. Street lights were installed, repaired, or replaced. Buildings were inspected for code violations, and the owners were notified to correct the problems. Low lying areas were filled with dirt to prevent water from standing, and abandoned properties frequented by drug users were boarded up and secured."

Operation Broken Window was a success. The drug dealers left, and crime rates went down. An important side benefit also occurred, as Yonce noted (p. 69):

> An important by-product of the operation was a fundamental change in the attitudes of officers within the department concerning the target area. As a result of the long hours that many invested in the area, their attitude is now one of partnership and ownership, and a resolve not to allow the dealers back in. Additionally, the attitudes of the residents, business people, and citizens, improved toward the police as a result of their efforts in this critical area.

> However the yardstick by which we measure the success of this type of operation is how the people in the area feel. In a local newspaper article praising the actions of the city in returning the streets to the people, residents reported that they were able to walk the streets again and sit on their front porches. Four businesses known to be associated with the illegal drug trade closed during the operation—and, importantly, two new legitimate businesses moved into the area.

In another approach dealing with the drug problem, the FBI has reassigned approximately three hundred agents formerly assigned to duty in areas within the Communist regimes in Eastern Europe to help in the "war against drugs and gangs." According to an associated press release (1992, p. 7A), the FBI has some important tools to contribute, including: "broader powers to use wiretaps and seize drug dealers' property, an ability to prosecute under federal laws on extortion, racketeering and interstate crime, and longer prison terms for some crimes."

Another effort that has received national attention is the Justice Department's **Weed and Seed** program. This program is a community-based, multi-agency approach to fighting drug use, violent crime, and gang activity in high crime neighborhoods. The goal is to "weed out" crime and then "seed" the neighborhoods with a variety of crime and drug prevention programs. Sixteen cities received approximately $500,000 in 1992 and will receive the same amount in 1993 if Congress appropriates the funds. The sixteen cities that the Justice Department chose for the program are Atlanta, Boston, Charleston, Chicago, Denver, Fort Worth, Los Angeles, Madison, Philadelphia, Pittsburgh, Richmond, San Antonio, San Diego, Seattle, Washington, and Wilmington.

Dealing with Drug Problems in Public Housing

Dealing with the drug problem in public housing requires the collaborative efforts of the police, public housing authorities, other agencies, and, most importantly, the residents themselves. Initiatives to deal with the problem have been identified by Weisel (1990, pp. 99–112).

Strategies to deal with the drug problem include improving the physical environment, removing offenders, reducing the demand for drugs, improving intelligence, and empowering residents.

Although aimed specifically at public housing, with modification the same strategies would also work in many inner-city neighborhoods.

Improving the Physical Environment. Improving indoor and exterior lighting has been successfully used in some projects. Clean-up efforts in trash-strewn lots which provide easy hiding places for drugs have also been successful. As noted by Weisel (1990, p. 100): "In many cities, including Chicago, police have worked with housing officials to develop access control for buildings. By limiting entrances and exits to one per building, non-residents can be kept outside." Some housing projects have developed identification cards for their residents so that outsiders can be readily observed.

Removing Offenders. Increased efforts at *enforcing laws* against dealing drugs and *increasing prosecution* are also deterrents to drug dealers. Sometimes the housing authority makes an apartment available to the local police department in which to set up an office. This visible police presence can be a strong deterrent. It can also provide residents with a feeling of security as well as concrete evidence that the city is working on the problem.

Some housing agencies, residents, and police departments have worked to create drug-free zones (*DFZs*) similar to those used around schools. Patrol efforts are concentrated in DFZs and being arrested for drug dealing carries increased penalties. Other cities, such as Fort Lauderdale, Tampa, and Louisville, have targeted small geographic areas known as *Oases*. As noted by Weisel (p. 102): "The Oasis Program ... is an approach that includes analyzing slum areas, building a coalition with community groups and police, and developing drug-free oases as an initial step toward a safer community. The oases are intended

Students at a Minneapolis high school examine a 1988 high-performance Calloway Corvette valued at $65,000. The police confiscated the car from a drug dealer and converted it into a police car.

to have a domino effect over time until the larger community becomes revitalized."

Asset seizures of drug dealers is another strategy frequently used by police. Police departments use federal or state forfeiture laws that allow them to seize property and assets of drug dealers, including drugs, cars, boats, airplanes, mobile homes, land, and cash. Asset seizures not only punish the offenders, but also send a strong message to the youth of the community who may be quite impressed with the material possessions that drug dealers flaunt.

Ison (1991, p. 12A) notes: "The government's take last year totaled nearly $500 million nationally. That's a twenty fold increase since the criminal forfeiture program started in 1985. About $450 million was returned to law enforcement agencies to fight crime."

According to Ison: "The Justice Department's goal is twofold. One is to punish drug traffickers and other criminals by hitting them in the pocketbook. The second goal is to pour proceeds from the seized assets back into law enforcement. In effect, the government is using the crooks' own booty to finance the war against other crooks."

Police may also use *lease enforcement.* Beginning in April 1989, the Department of Housing and Urban Development (HUD) has required that leases include an explicit provision permitting eviction if any member of a household engages in drug-related criminal activity.

Finally police have found that, simply *making drug dealing inconvenient* may be an effective deterrent. San Diego police, for example, discovered that drug dealers were using public telephones on certain street corners. The police worked with the telephone company to fix the telephones so that they could be used only for outgoing calls, thereby stopping outsiders from calling in orders for drugs.

Reducing the Demand. Another approach to the drug problem is to focus on those who use drugs. Some police departments have used *sting operations* during which undercover police agents sell drugs and then arrest those who buy them. These operations have sometimes been criticized as unethical or even an illegal form of entrapment. Police must exercise extreme care if they use such operations as a strategy to reduce the drug problem.

Educating users may be a more fruitful and perhaps more ethical approach to the drug problem. School programs such as DARE can help youth to resist peer pressure to experiment with drugs. *Providing diversion or alternatives* to finding acceptance or excitement through drug use may also help. Providing community recreational programs, improving ballfields and parks, installing a basketball court, or sponsoring athletic contests are all important additions to a community in its fight against drugs.

Providing treatment and rehabilitation for drug users is sometimes also an effective strategy. Often residents are not aware of the existence of such treatment facilities. In many communities, however, such facilities do not exist.

Improving Intelligence. If police can enlist citizens to provide information about drug dealing to the police, much can be accomplished. Most residents in public housing know where drug deals are made. Many also believe, however, that the police either do not care or are actually corrupt because they arrest few dealers. When dealers are arrested, they are often back on the street within hours. Residents should be educated about the difficulties of prosecuting drug dealers and the need for evidence.

Some departments conduct *community surveys* in low income neighborhoods to learn about how residents view the drug problem. Some departments have established *tip lines* where residents can provide information anonymously.

Improved reporting can be accomplished in a number of ways, as described by Weisel (1990, p. 110):

> In Philadelphia, police developed a radio bypass of police communication so that beat officers could be telephoned directly by citizens for calls that would have been assigned a low priority by police dispatch.

> Police can also improve the information they receive about problems in other ways. Intelligence can be increased by unusual procedures. Police have been known to interview arrestees to obtain

inside information on how certain criminal activities are conducted. In other agencies, arrestees have been interviewed in jail with a jail debriefing form. This kind of data is useful as police continue to document the link between drugs and criminal activity.

Housing personnel are often the closest to drug problems in public housing. These housing personnel can be trained to identify drugs or drug dealing behaviors, and cooperate with police in following up on complaints.

Intelligence information can also be improved by facilitating the communication between narcotics investigators and patrol officers. For example, in Atlanta, a narcotics supervisor recognized that patrol and narcotics had historically used a different radio frequency and were unable to communicate. The problem was quickly corrected.

Empowering Residents.   Many police agencies have focused on the broader needs of residents of low-income housing. In Tulsa, for example, officers believed that limited job opportunities were a problem for youth living in public housing. The officers now steer youths into Job Corps, a training and job service program that is an alternative to the traditional high school. Weisel (p. 98) cautions:

Police should always remember that the problems in many of these poor neighborhoods have been there for many years and are deeply rooted in poverty and other enduring social problems. There are real limits to what the police can actually accomplish. . . .

Thus, it is important to set modest objectives and take pride in even very small successes in troubled areas. Because drug problems are particularly complex and enduring problems in poor neighborhoods, modest successes are very important. These small successes are instrumental in improving the quality of life for the people who reside in the drug-ravaged areas. If police try to reduce the harms caused by drug dealing in a specific area, great strides can be made in terms of improving the lives of the law-abiding citizens who call the community home.

A COMPREHENSIVE, COORDINATED COMMUNITY APPROACH

The Des Moines Police Department has developed a *Community Involvement Handbook* developed jointly by the police department, the United

Way, and over thirty-five neighborhood groups. The handbook serves as a resource of information as well as a guide for action. It is intended to help neighborhood groups become active and start making a difference. Called the "municipal approach," the program has four "prongs": community involvement, enforcement, prevention/education, and treatment. Portions of the handbook have been translated into Spanish, Vietnamese, Cambodian, and Laotion. The handbook covers such topics as:

- When to call the police.
- "Dear John" letters.
- Street lighting and residential security lighting.
- Trash and litter.
- Working with good landlords.
- Working with businesses in your area.
- Boarding up abandoned houses.
- Forming neighborhood associations.
- Neighborhood block walks.
- Red ribbons (symbolizing drug-free environments).
- Cutting down shrubbery.
- Rallies and marches.
- Occupying parks and streets.
- Newsletters.

This practical guide might serve as a model for other police departments that wish to involve the community in not only the fight against drugs but also against crime and violence.

Summary

Synergism occurs when individuals channel their energies toward a common purpose and accomplish what they could not accomplish alone. Among the most commonly implemented crime prevention programs have been street lighting projects, property marking projects, security survey projects, citizen patrol projects, and crime reporting, neighborhood watch, or block projects.

The Guardian Angels are private citizen patrols who seek to deter crime and to provide a positive role model for young children. Specialized crime watch programs include youth crime watch, business crime watch, Realtor watch, and carrier alert.

Model crime prevention programs have been developed by a hospital auxiliary, churches, foundations, businesses, and civic groups. Volunteers may serve as reserve officers, auxiliary patrol, community service officers, or on an as-needed basis. The four R's of volunteer management are research, recruitment, retention, and recognition.

Among the most visible organizations focused on crime are citizen crime prevention associations, Crime Stoppers, and MADD. The two main messages of anti-car theft programs are (1) do not leave the keys in the ignition and (2) lock the car. The Combat Auto Theft program allows the police to stop any car marked with a special decal between 1 a.m. and 5 a.m.

Strategies to deal with the drug problem include improving the physical environment, removing offenders, reducing the demand for drugs, improving intelligence, and empowering residents.

DISCUSSION QUESTIONS

1. What examples of synergy have you been a part of or witnessed?
2. What crime prevention programs are in your community? Have you participated in any of them?
3. Which of the programs discussed in this chapter seem most exemplary to you? Why?
4. Do you have an Operation Identification program in your community? If so, have you participated? If not, why not?
5. Do you feel the Guardian Angels and similar volunteer citizen patrol groups serve a valuable function?
6. Do you favor the use of volunteers within the police department? If so, in what capacities?
7. Does your police department use volunteers? If so, how?
8. How effective do you think the FBI agents will be as they join local efforts to combat the drug and gang problem? What factors will be important?
9. Do you have any "broken windows" in your community? If so, how would you characterize them?
10. What steps might be taken to repair a community's "broken windows" and protect against having them broken again?

DEFINITIONS

Can you define these terms: CAT, Guardian Angels, synergism, weed and seed.

REFERENCES

Associated Press. "FBI Brings Spy Catching Skills Into War Against Gangs." Minneapolis *Star Tribune*. (January 16, 1992): 7A.

"Automating the War Against Drug Dealers." *Law and Order*. (November 1991): 107.

Buchholz, Steve and Roth, Thomas. *Creating the High-Performance Team*. New York: John Wiley and Sons, Inc., 1987.

Clark, Jacob R. "New Look for Military Model: Homeless Vets Patrolling NYC." *Law Enforcement News*. (September 30, 1991): 8–9.

Clede, Bill. "Guardian Angels: Bane or Blessing?" *Law and Order*. (December 1990): 37–39.

Crowe, Timothy D. "The Secure Store: A Clean, Well-Lighted Place." *Security Management.* (March 1992): 22A–24A.

Federal Bureau of Investigation. *Uniform Crime Reports.* Washington: U.S. Department of Justice, September, 1975.

Garofalo, James and McLeod, Maureen. *National Institute of Justice Research in Action: Improving the Use and Effectiveness of Neighborhood Watch Programs.* Washington: U.S. Department of Justice, National Institute of Justice, April 1988.

Gendler, Neal. "Signs Give Extra Power to Police in Inner City." Minneapolis *Star Tribune.* (September 28, 1991): 1B, 5B.

Greenberg, Martin Alan. "Volunteer Police: The People's Choice for Safer Communities." *The Police Chief.* (May 1991): 42–44.

Grow, Doug. "Drug Warriors Try to Take Portland Ave. Back from Crack Dealers." Minneapolis *Star Tribune.* (February 17, 1992): 1A, 16A.

Hageman, Mary Jeanette. *Police-Community Relations.* Beverly Hills: Sage Publications, 1985.

Hildreth, Reed. "The CAT Program." *Law and Order.* (May 1990): 92–93.

Ison, Chris. "Tables Turned: U.S. Government Uses Criminals' Assets to Finance War Against Drugs." Minneapolis *Star Tribune.* (July 29, 1991): 1A, 12A.

Klockars, Carl B. *Thinking about Police: Contemporary Readings.* New York: McGraw-Hill, 1983.

Leavy, James G. "Community Resources: Volunteers and Special Officers." *Law and Order.* (February 1992): 69.

Lonetree, Anthony. "St. Paul Police, Residents Forge Alliance to Fight Drug Dealers." *Star Tribune.* (July 16, 1992): 5B.

Lurigio, Arthur J. and Rosenbaum, Dennis P. "Evaluation Research in Community Crime Prevention: A Critical Look at the Field," In *Community Crime Prevention: Does It Work?* edited by Dennis P. Rosenbaum, 19–44. Beverly Hills: Sage Publications, 1986.

McLean, Herbert E. "Watching Out for Honolulu." *Law and Order.* (June 1991): 58–62.

Neighborhood Crime Prevention Council. *Developing a Street Patrol—A Guide For Neighborhood Crime Prevention.* Boston: Justice Resource Institute, 1985.

Pace, Denny F. *Community Relations Concepts.* Placerville: Custom Publishing Company, 1991.

Shilaos, Aleck K. "Substance Abuse Awareness Sabbath." *Law and Order.* (December 1990): 43.

Sulton, Anne Thomas. *Inner-City Crime Control: Can Community Institutions Contribute?* Washington: The Police Foundation, 1990.

Tempe Community Relations Office. "No Mere Paper-Pushers, Tempe Police Volunteers Are Making a Difference." *Law Enforcement News.* (November 30, 1991): 9, 15.

"U.S. Illegal Drug Tab Exceeds $40 Billion." *Law Enforcement News.* (June 15/30, 1991): 1, 5.

Weisel, Deborah Lamm. *Tackling Drug Problems in Public Housing: A Guide for Police.* Washington: Police Executive Research Forum.

Weinblatt, Richard B. "The Birth of a Volunteer Officer Program." *Law and Order.* (December 1991): 19–20.

Yonce, Thomas C. " 'Broken Window' Stops Drug Sales." *Law and Order.* (April 1992): 67–70.

PROBLEM-ORIENTED POLICING IN CONTEXT

A problem well stated is a problem half solved.
—Charles Kettering.

DO YOU KNOW

- Who is credited with originating problem-oriented policing?
- What the first step in Goldstein's problem-oriented policing is?
- What four stages of problem solving are used in Newport News?
- What the magnet phenomenon is?
- What three areas problem analysis considers?
- How efficiency and effectiveness differ? Which is emphasized by community-oriented policing?
- What crime-specific planning is?
- What mental locks should be avoided?
- What killer phrases are?

In Chapter 1, problem-oriented policing was introduced as a trend of the future, perhaps replacing the professional model of policing that has dominated the last two decades. Throughout the text, the diversity of individuals with whom police officers work as well as the complexity of the problems with which they must deal have been emphasized. Successfully dealing with our diverse and complex population requires more than the efforts and expertise of the police department or even the entire criminal justice system. It requires a coordinated effort of citizens, agencies, organizations, and the criminal justice system. The following discussion presents problem-oriented policing as one approach to effective policing that uses the community's vast resources.

Problem-oriented policing involves identifying problems and making decisions about how best to deal with them. A **problem** is a deviation from what is desired, a difficulty. A **decision** is a judgment or conclusion. Making a decision is the act of selecting from among alternatives. An all-important first step in problem-oriented policing is to identify problems in a community.

COMMUNITY-ORIENTED POLICING AND PROBLEM SOLVING

Many practitioners equate community-oriented policing and problem solving. As noted by Wilson and Kelling (1989, p. 49): "Community-oriented policing means changing the daily work of the police to include investigating problems as well as incidents. It means defining as a problem whatever a significant body of public opinion regards as a threat to community order. It means working with the good guys, and not just against the bad guys." Wilson and Kelling suggest that community-oriented policing requires the police mission to be redefined "to help the police become accustomed to fixing broken windows as well as arresting window-breakers."

Eck and Spelman (1987, p. xv) define problem-oriented policing as follows: "**Problem-oriented policing** is a department-wide strategy aimed at solving persistent community problems. Police identify, analyze, and respond to the underlying circumstances that create incidents." The differences between traditional, incident-driven, reactive policing

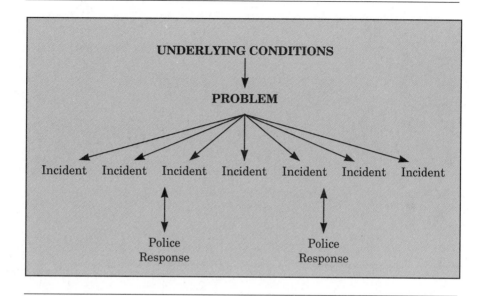

FIGURE 16.1 Incident-Driven Policing

SOURCE: Printed with permission by PERF. John E. Eck and William Spelman. *Problem Solving: Problem-Oriented Policing in Newport News.* Washington: Police Executive Research Forum, 1987: 4-1987. © Police Executive Research Forum.

and the newer, problem-driven, proactive policing are illustrated in Figures 16.1 and 16.2.

As noted by Eck and Spelman (1987, p. xix): The National Institute of Justice requires that problem-solving systems follow five basic principles:

- Officers of all ranks and from all units should be able to use the system as part of their daily routine.
- The system must encourage the use of a broad range of information, including but not limited to conventional police data.
- The system should encourage a broad range of solutions, including but not limited to the criminal justice process.
- The system should require no additional resources and no special units.
- Finally, any large police agency must be able to apply it.

Herman Goldstein is credited with originating problem-oriented policing.

Goldstein (1990, pp. 14–15) cites five concerns that have most strongly influenced the development of problem-oriented policing:

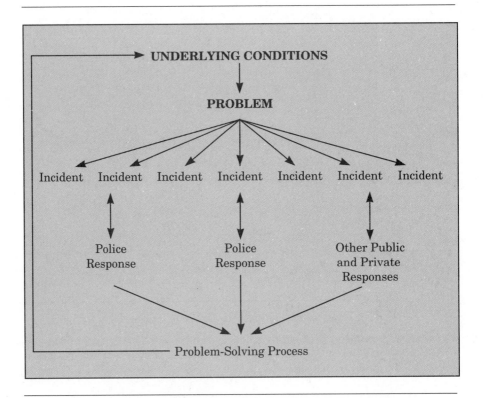

FIGURE 16.2   Problem-Oriented Policing

SOURCE: Printed with permission by PERF. John E. Eck and William Spelman.
Problem Solving: Problem-Oriented Policing in Newport News. Washington: Police
Executive Research Forum, 1987: 4-1987. © Police Executive Research Forum.

1. The police field is preoccupied with management, internal
    procedures, and efficiency to the exclusion of appropriate
    concern for effectiveness in dealing with substantive
    problems.
2. The police devote most of their resources to responding to
    calls from citizens, reserving too small a percentage of their
    time and energy for acting on their own initiative to prevent
    or reduce community problems.
3. The community is a major resource with an enormous
    potential, largely untapped, for reducing the number and
    magnitude of problems that otherwise become the business of
    the police.
4. Within their agencies, police have readily available to them
    another huge resource: their rank-and-file officers, whose time
    and talent have not been used effectively.

5. Efforts to improve policing have often failed because they have not been adequately related to the overall dynamics and complexity of the police organization. Adjustments in policies and organizational structure are required to accommodate and support change.

Problem-oriented policing was developed in response to these concerns. Consider again, the first concern that influenced the development of problem-oriented policing, that of efficiency and effectiveness.

EFFICIENCY AND EFFECTIVENESS

Efficiency involves the minimization of waste, expense, or unnecessary effort. Efficiency results in a high ratio of output to input. Efficiency is doing things right. **Effectiveness** has to do with producing the desired result or end goal. Effectiveness is doing the right thing. Ideally, both efficiency and effectiveness are present in policing.

Calls coming to a 911 dispatcher provide raw data from which problems might be identified.

Efficiency, doing things right, has been the traditional emphasis in law enforcement. Effectiveness, doing the right things, is the emphasis in community-oriented policing.

Unfortunately, too often police departments have emphasized efficiency, for example, rapid response to calls, number of citations issued, and the like, than what will produce the desired outcomes of the department.

According to Goldstein (p. 32): "In its broadest context, problem-oriented policing is a comprehensive plan for improving policing in which the high priority attached to addressing substantive problems shapes the police agency, influencing all changes in personnel, organization, and procedures."

This focus on substantive problems (effectiveness) rather than on the smooth functioning of the organization (efficiency) is a radical change which is difficult for some departments to make. Those departments which have made the shift in focus have accomplished excellent results. The focus on effectiveness is the foundation of and, in Goldstein's approach, the first step toward problem-oriented policing.

ADDRESSING SUBSTANTIVE PROBLEMS

Traditionally police have responded to incidents, handled them as effectively as possible, and then moved on to the next call. This fragmented approach to policing conceals patterns of incidents that may be symptomatic of deeper problems. Says Goldstein (p. 33): "The first step in problem-oriented policing is to move beyond just handling incidents. It calls for recognizing that incidents are often merely overt symptoms of problems."

The first step in problem-oriented policing is to group incidents as problems.

The basic elements in Goldstein's problem-solving approach combine steps a police department can take and theoretical assumptions to make the steps work. They include the following (pp. 32–49):

- Grouping incidents as problems.
- Focusing on substantive problems as the heart of policing.
- Effectiveness as the ultimate goal.
- The need for systematic inquiry.
- Disaggregating and accurately labeling problems.
- Analysis of the multiple interests in problems.

A citizen patrol member calls his volunteer center. Citizens are a major resource, with great, largely untapped potential to help reduce neighborhood problems.

- Capturing and critiquing the current response.
- An uninhibited search for a tailor-made response.
- Adopting a proactive stance.
- Strengthening the decision-making processes and increasing accountability.
- Evaluating results of newly implemented responses.

Many departments have developed problem-solving approaches that incorporate these basic elements.

A FOUR-STAGE PROBLEM-SOLVING PROCESS

Eck and Spelman (1987, p. 42) describe the four-stage problem-solving process used in the Newport News Police Department.

Four stages of problem solving are scanning, analysis, response, and assessment.

Scanning refers to identifying the problem. Analysis is learning the problem's causes, scope, and effects. Response is acting to alleviate the problem, that is selecting the alternative solution or solutions to try. Assessment is determining if the response worked. Table 16.1 illustrates potential sources of information for identifying problems.

To assist in problem analysis, the Newport News Police Department developed a problem analysis guide that lists topic headings police should consider in assessing problems, illustrated in Table 16.2.

Problem analysis considers the individuals involved, the incidents, and the responses.

TABLE 16.1
Potential Sources of Information for Identifying Problems

Crime Analysis Unit—Time trends and patterns (time of day, day of week, monthly, seasonal, and other cyclical events), and patterns of similar events (offender descriptions, victim characteristics, locations, physical settings, and other circumstances).

Patrol—Recurring calls, bad areas, active offenders, victim types, complaints from citizens.

Investigations—Recurring crimes, active offenders, victim difficulties, complaints from citizens.

Crime Prevention—Physical conditions, potential victims, complaints from citizens.

Vice—Drug dealing, illegal alcohol sales, gambling, prostitution, organized crime.

Communications—Call types, repeat calls from same location, temporal peaks in calls for service.

Chief's Office—Letters and calls from citizens, concerns of elected officials, concerns from city manager's office.

Other Law Enforcement Agencies—Multi-jurisdictional concerns.

Elected Officials—Concerns and complaints.

Local Government Agencies—Plans that could influence crimes, common difficulties, complaints from citizens.

Schools—Juvenile concerns, vandalism, employee safety.

Community Leaders—Problems of constituents.

Business Groups—Problems of commerce and development.

Neighborhood Watch—Local problems regarding disorder, crime, and other complaints.

Newspapers and Other News Media—Indications of problems not detected from other sources, problems in other jurisdictions that could occur in any city.

Community Surveys—Problems of citizens in general.

SOURCE: Printed with permission by PERF. John E. Eck and William Spelman. *Problem Solving: Problem-Oriented Policing in Newport News.* Washington: Police Executive Research Forum, 1987: 46. © 1987 Police Executive Research Forum.

TABLE 16.2
The Problem Analysis Guide (List of topic headings)

Actors
  Victims
    Life style
    Security measures taken
    Victimization history
  Offenders
    Identity and physical description
    Life style, education, employment history
    Criminal history
  Third parties
    Personal data
    Connection to victimization
Incidents
  Sequence of events
    Events preceding act
    Event itself
    Events following criminal act
  Physical context
    Time
    Location
    Access control and surveillance
  Social context
    Likelihood and probable actions of witnesses
    Apparent attitude of residents toward neighborhood
  Immediate results of incidents
    Harm done to victim
    Gain to offender
    Legal issues
Responses
  Community
    Neighborhood affected by problem
    City as a whole
    People outside the city
  Institutional
    Criminal justice system
    Other public agencies
    Mass media
    Business sector
  Seriousness
    Public perceptions
    Perception of others

SOURCE: Printed with permission by PERF. John E. Eck and William
Spelman. *Problem Solving: Problem-Oriented Policing in Newport News.*
Washington: Police Executive Research Forum, 1987: xxi. © 1987 Police
Executive Research Forum.

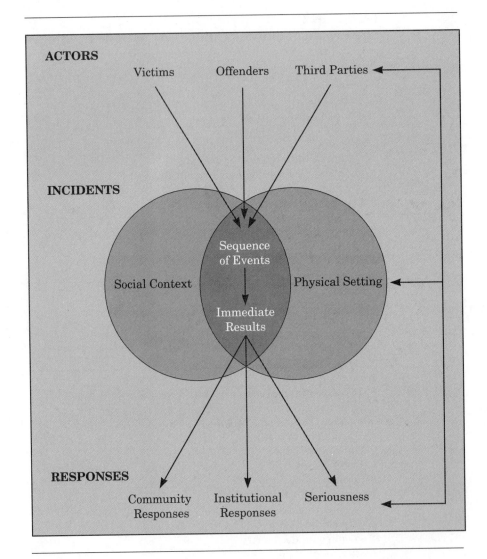

FIGURE 16.3   Problem-Analysis Guide

SOURCE: Printed with permission by PERF. John E. Eck and William Spelman. *Problem Solving: Problem-Oriented Policing in Newport News.* Washington: Police Executive Research Forum, 1987: 55. © 1987 Police Executive Research Forum.

Illustrated in Figure 16.3, their graphic representation of this problem-analysis guide highlights the complex interaction of individuals, incidents, and responses occurring within a social context and a physical setting.

The problems Newport News Police identified and how they approached them are discussed later in the chapter. Based on the Newport

News experience, Eck and Spelman (1987, p. 3) offer twelve suggestions as to what a problem-oriented policing agency should do:

1. Focus on problems of concern to the public.
2. Zero in on effectiveness as the primary concern.
3. Be proactive.
4. Be committed to systematic inquiry as the first step in solving substantive problems.
5. Encourage use of rigorous methods in making inquiries.
6. Make full use of the data in police files and the experience of police personnel.
7. Group like incidents together so that they can be addressed as a common problem.
8. Avoid using overly broad labels in grouping incidents so separate problems can be identified.
9. Encourage a broad and uninhibited search for solutions.
10. Acknowledge the limits of the criminal justice system as a response to problems.
11. Identify multiple interests in any one problem and weigh them when analyzing the value of different responses.
12. Be committed to taking some risks in responding to problems.

Note the similarities between these suggestions and the basic elements of problem-oriented policing set forth by Goldstein on pp. 468–69.

When identifying problems, it is important to be aware of the *magnet phenomenon.*

The **magnet phenomenon** occurs when a phone number or address is associated with a crime simply because it was a convenient number or address to use.

A **magnet telephone** is one which is available when no other telephones are, for example, a telephone in a convenience store which is open all night and on weekends. Victims of or witnesses to a crime in the area may use that telephone to report the crime, even though the store was not the scene of the crime. Similarly, a **magnet address** is one which is easy for people to give, for example, a high school or a theater.

Buerger (1992, p. 127) describes how this phenomenon operated in a problem-solving approach being used by the Minneapolis Police Department with the city's bus depot:

After analyzing the calls, it became apparent that the depot was also a magnet address because it is easy for a caller to identify: "I need help; I am across the street from the Greyhound station." The dispatcher then entered the message to meet a party across from the Greyhound depot, and used that as the address-of-record for that call.

When specific crimes are identified during the first stage of problem solving, crime-specific planning may be appropriate.

PROBLEM-ORIENTED POLICING AND CRIME-SPECIFIC PLANNING

To maintain effective police-community partnerships, police must also fulfill their crime-fighting role. Police can approach this role with many of the problem-solving skills just discussed, using crime-specific planning. Cummings (1990, p. 63) notes: "While similar to problem-oriented policing in its process, crime-specific planning is more specific in that it approaches criminal justice problems by considering underlying problems that are categorized by the type of offense." Crime-specific planning involves reviewing the following factors (Cummings, p. 63):

1. Seriousness of the offense.
2. Frequency of the occurrence.
3. Public concern.
4. Impact on the community.
5. The drain on resources of the criminal justice system.
6. The susceptibility of each crime to control.
7. Whether the crime is one of opportunity or calculation.
8. The degree of concentration required to develop plans for the perpetration of the crime.
9. The *modus operandi* and patterns.
10. The violent characteristics that may be present.
11. The property that may be taken or damaged.
12. The victim's response.
13. The community's response.
14. The system's response.
15. The actual target.
16. Characteristics of the target.
17. When the target is attacked.
18. How the target is attacked.
19. Where the target is located in the environment.
20. The number of potential targets in each area.
21. The accessibility of the targets.
22. Transportation patterns surrounding the targets.
23. Offender characteristics.

Crime-specific planning uses the principles of problem-oriented policing to focus on identified crime problems.

A careful analysis of these factors will provide the basis for problem-solving and deriving alternatives for approaching each specific crime problem. As noted by Cummings (p. 64): "Both problem-oriented policing and crime-specific planning are preferable to the reactive strategies of the past. However, police departments should implement problem-oriented policing *before* crime-specific planning. . . . Problem-oriented policing works because it takes into account the underlying economic, social and environmental factors that contribute to crime."

COMMON MISTAKES IN PROBLEM SOLVING

As noted by Bennett and Hess (1992, pp. 145–46): "Common mistakes in problem solving and decision making include spending too much energy on unimportant details, failing to resolve important issues, being secretive about true feelings, having a closed mind, and not expressing ideas. . . . Inability to decide, putting decisions off to the last minute, failing to set deadlines, and using unreliable sources of information are other common errors in problem solving and decision making." Timm (1984, pp. 434–36) expands upon this list and believes the following mistakes are commonly made during problem solving and decision making:

- Making decisions when no decision is needed.
- Making multiple decisions about the same problem.
- Finding the right decision for the wrong problem; that is, dealing with symptoms rather than causes.
- Failing to follow through on implementation.
- Failing to consider the costs.
- Using disorganized decision processes.
- Delaying a decision that must be made.
- Making decisions while angry or excited.

Each of these common mistakes in problem solving and decision making has its positive counterpart. For example, rather than making decisions while angry or excited—make decisions calmly when you are in control of the situation. Bennett and Hess (1992, p. 146) offer the following checklist against which to evaluate decisions:

Is the decision:

- Consistent with the agency's mission, goals and objectives?
- A long-term solution?
- Cost-effective?
- Legal?
- Ethical?
- Practical?
- Acceptable to those responsible for implementing it?

Problem Solving and Creativity

Several structured approaches to problem-oriented policing have been discussed. These approaches will be less than effective, however, unless creativity is incorporated into the approach. **Creativity** is a process of breaking old connections and making useful new connections. It is often synonymous with **innovation.** von Oech (1983, p. 7) stresses: "The creative mind has the power to transform one thing into another. By changing perspective and playing with our knowledge and experience, we can make the ordinary extraordinary and the unusual commonplace. *Discovery consists of looking at the same thing as everyone else and thinking something different.*"

Thinking Outside the Dots

The following exercise (Figure 16.4) is frequently used in problem-solving seminars. Try to complete the exercise. If you cannot connect the dots, turn to Appendix D for the solution. Now, those of you who could connect the dots and those of you who had to look at the solution share the same knowledge: "You sometimes have to go outside the perimeters." As noted by von Oech (1983, p. 24): "Nothing is more dangerous than an idea if it is the only one you have." He describes several **mental locks,** or ways of thinking that prevent creativity, to be avoided.

Mental locks that prevent creative thinking include:

- The right answer.
- That's not logical.
- Follow the rules.
- Be practical.
- Avoid ambiguity.

- To err is wrong.
- Play is frivolous.
- That's not my area.
- Don't be foolish.
- I'm not creative.

The Right Answer.   von Oech (1983, p. 22) notes that most people will take over 26,000 tests before completing their education. He suggests: "Children enter elementary school as question marks and leave as periods."

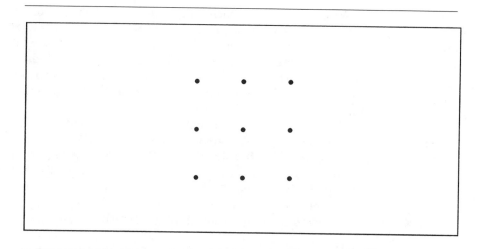

FIGURE 16.4   Nine-Dot Exercise Instructions: Using four straight lines, connect the 9 dots. You may start wherever you wish, but do not lift your pencil from the paper.

That's Not Logical.   Sometimes logic limits creativity. Both creative and logical thinking are usually needed for the toughest problems.

Follow the Rules.   How often do parents admonish their very young children to "stay in the lines" when they color or tell them that they cannot color the people in their coloring book purple? Although patterns and rules *can* help in problem solving, they can also hinder the process.

Be Practical.   People have the unique and useful ability to imagine, to dream. As Walt Disney was fond of saying, "If you can dream it, you can do it." Practicality is also important when seeking solutions. However, when problem-solving, practicality can limit creative solutions. von Oech (p. 54) calls the realm of the possible a "germinal seedbed." He encourages people to ask "what if" questions to stimulate the imagination.

Avoid Ambiguity.   von Oech (pp. 76–78) presents the following illustration:

Exercise: In the following line of letters, cross out six letters so that the remaining letters without altering their sequence, will spell a familiar English word.

B S A I N X L E A T N T E A R S

Try the exercise.

Many people approach this problem by focusing on the fact that there are sixteen letters here. People think that if they cross out six, they will have a ten-letter word, and they concentrate on which letters to cross out. In fact, one man who had a computer fed the problem in, confident that he would have the answer momentarily. Imagine his surprise when the computer generated a thirty-foot-long printout of possible solutions.

The minute he saw the list, he realized he had asked the computer the wrong question. The greatest computer in the world cannot resolve the wrong problem. To solve the problem, ask yourself, "What else could 'cross out six letters' mean?" von Oech (p. 78) suggests that instead of crossing out six letters, you literally crossed out the "S," the "I," the "X," the "L," and the "E," and so on. If you try this approach, you will be left with the word *banana*. When thinking creatively, ambiguity can help.

To Err Is Wrong. This fallacy is similar to the mental trap about "right answers." Risk taking is a necessary part of progress. To err is wrong only if you do not learn from the "mistake." Henry Ford once said, "Failure is the opportunity to begin again more intelligently."

Play Is Frivolous. People tend to take themselves too seriously. Take time out to play in your mental playground. Solutions to problems often come when you least expect them. Give them time in your "germinal seedbed" while you enjoy yourself doing something that gives you pleasure.

That's Not My Area. Our society has become so complex that specialization is often necessary. Sometimes, however, someone who is outside a specific field but who is genuinely interested in and perhaps affected by a problem can suggest the most brilliant alternative. This is, in fact, often true of citizens. Alternatives to crime-related problems may be generated by non-law enforcement professionals if given an opportunity.

Don't Be Foolish. Relax, have fun and brainstorm, allow all ideas to percolate—even those that may seem ridiculous. Men who dreamed of flying were considered foolish.

I'm Not Creative. As the saying goes: "If you think you can or if you think you can't, you're right." Never demean yourself or your abilities, including your ability to be creative. You would not be this far into this text if you were not a capable individual. You have absorbed a great deal of information and you have years of experience to relate to that information. If you wish you can approach policing in creative ways.

Once you have considered "how to unlock your mind for innovation," consider next how others might deter you—or you might be deterring others—from creative solutions.

Killer Phrases

Killer phrases are judgmental, critical statements that are put-downs. Killer phrases stifle creativity.

Among the most common killer phrases are the following (Buchholz and Roth, p. 136): "That's too radical. It's contrary to policy. That's not our area. It won't fit within the deadline. We'll never get help. That's too much hassle. It just won't work. It's too obvious. Get real. Be practical. Costs too much. We've never done it that way before. Get serious."

Avoid such phrases when you are thinking to yourself and in your discussions with others if you want creative solutions to the numerous problems you will encounter in policing. The alternative solutions to problems are waiting to be "discovered."

Recall the discussion of "wizardry" in the last chapter. There are no magic solutions to policing problems, and there is no single best approach. Knowledge plus creativity and a little bit of wizardry can make for terrific police-community partnerships and the possibility for police and the public to solve problems together.

PROBLEM-ORIENTED POLICING AT WORK

The theoretical foundation of problem-oriented policing in Newport News was discussed earlier in this chapter. During the problem identification process, the following problems became evident (Eck and Spelman, 1987, p. 44):

- Groups of workers from a large industrial complex engaged in drug dealing, drug usage, and drinking during their lunch break.
- Thefts from vehicles in the downtown parking areas.
- Prostitution and robberies in District 1.
- Burglaries in New Briarfield Apartments.
- Business burglaries in District 9.
- Confrontations between students from rival high schools.
- Jefferson Avenue traffic accidents.
- Serial crimes.
- Disorder problem in a small area of bars and a motel, near a military base.
- Traffic congestion in the downtown area when day shift workers leave the industrial area.
- Non-reporting of suspicious circumstances by citizen witnesses.

- Disturbances around and near a meeting area of people looking for dates.
- Groups of youths drinking, using marijuana, making noise and littering near a residential community.

Table 16.3 illustrates how police categorized the problems so they could be analyzed.

The way the department addressed the problem of commercial burglaries illustrates the problem-solving approach. The patrol officers

TABLE 16.3
Types of Problems

	Citywide	Neighborhood
Crime problems	Domestic homicides Gas station driveoffs Assaults on police officers	Personal robberies (Central business district) Commercial burglaries (Jefferson Avenue business district) Vacant buildings (Central business district) Residential burglaries (New Briarfield Apts) Residential burglaries (Glenn Gardens Apts) Larcenies (Beechmont Gardens Apts) Thefts from autos (Newport News Shipbuilding) Drug dealing (32d and Chestnut)
Disorder problems	Runaway youths Driving under the influence Disturbances at convenience stores	Rowdy youths (Peninsula Skating Rink) Shot houses (Aqua Vista Apts) Disturbances (Marshall Avenue 7-Eleven) Dirt bikes (Newmarket Creek) Disturbances (Village Square Shopping Center)

SOURCE: Reprinted with permission by PERF. John E. Eck and William Spelman. *Problem Solving: Problem-Oriented Policing in Newport News.* Washington: Police Executive Research Forum, 1987: 82. © 1987 Police Executive Research Forum.

surveyed the area and found that some major streets had been barricaded due to a major highway construction project. This resulted in limited vehicle traffic, limited police patrol at night, and a large increase in nighttime burglaries. To alleviate these problems, patrol officers were instructed to leave their squads and patrol the area on foot at night. The officers also persuaded the merchants to clean up the piles of trash and debris which could easily conceal the activities of burglars.

Besides dealing with the environment, Sgt. Quail, the officer in charge, also analyzed the specific problem (p. 83):

> *He collected offense reports of burglaries committed in the area. To help identify geographic patterns, he plotted them on a detailed spot map. To identify M.O. and repeat offender patterns, Quail recorded a description of the suspects, time of commission, type of property taken, and similar information on a specially designed form. Finally, he suspected that some of the offenders were using vacant apartments located above some of the businesses to conceal stolen property; he began to investigate this possibility.*

These efforts resulted in the apprehension of several burglars and a decrease in the burglary rate. When the construction was completed and the barriers removed, the burglaries decreased further. Since construction is frequent, Sgt. Quail began to develop a policy and procedure statement so that police and city agencies could communicate better regarding construction projects, street closing, and potential burglary problems.

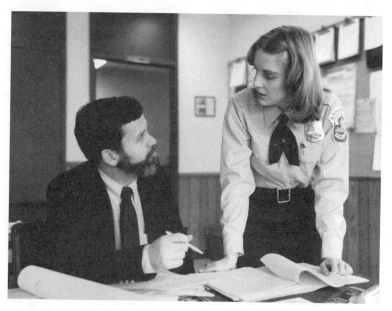

A Washington D.C. police officer talks with a citizen representative of a neighborhood safety organization.

The Tulsa Police Department has also adopted the problem-oriented approach to policing. Smith (1990, p. 62) notes that "Cuff' em and stuff 'em" is no longer their approach, quoting their chief of police who says: "We try to look at the whole problem. Prevention is as important as apprehension." Their approach, according to Smith, involves the following steps (p. 63):

- Identify the problem and analyze it to see if its cause is environmental, social, physical, ages of residents, economics, or a symptom of something else that is wrong.
- Set a goal and determine a direction on how to respond. Is there something that needs to be eliminated, reduced, or just improved? Sometimes the problem does not have to be totally eliminated to be successful.
- Analyze the result of the approach taken to see what worked and what didn't—and if changes should be made.

When the Tulsa Police Department shifted to this approach, they began to group their incident data to look for patterns. By doing so, they found that they had received sixty to eighty calls from one woman in thirty days. The calls had been answered by different officers on different shifts, and no one realized how much time was spent responding to her calls. They investigated the situation and found that the woman was lonely and had a drinking problem. They got her involved in some of the community's social service agencies and since that time have not received a single call from her.

Not all problems were solved as easily, however. When they assessed the drug problem in a local housing project, a solution involved much more probing. The department found that the residents were extremely frightened, that violence was so prevalent that fire and ambulance services were afraid to answer calls there, and that the Housing Authority considered the drug problem the landlord's concern—not police business. The police persisted, however, and discovered some serious problems. First, many residents did not have telephones, and therefore had no means of communication with the outside world. Adding foot and horse patrol brought the officers and the outside world to them. Project managers and foot patrols were provided with radios or beepers so they could maintain contact with each other.

Another related problem was lack of transportation for the great majority of the residents. Police enlisted the aid of the Community Partnership, a social service agency, which was able to help with the problem. As a result, several residents were able to attend school, vocational programs, or get jobs.

The Baltimore County department has also implemented problem-oriented policing. In 1981, they first implemented the approach, called Community Oriented Police Enforcement or COPE. The department's basic mission at that time was to fight the fear of crime by addressing the social problems that caused it. According to Taft (1986, p. 10): " 'Citizen Oriented Police Enforcement' officers would engage in intensive patrol, develop close contacts with citizens, conduct 'fear surveys' (door-to-door canvassing to identify concerns) and use any means within their power to quell fear."

One early success was when COPE officers saw the potential for violence between two groups of black and white students who used adjacent bus stops. COPE officers convinced the County Board of Education to move one stop to a new location, eliminating the daily confrontations between the two groups.

In 1983, two COPE officers were called to Garden Village, warned to expect trouble because the citizens there hated the police. Using the problem-solving approach to the crime and violence existing in Garden Village, the officers conducted fear surveys, compiled crime statistics, took pictures of deteriorating areas, and measured distances from housing projects to playgrounds. They then brainstormed for solutions to deal with the various problems they had uncovered. According to Taft (1986, p. 15):

> *Using statistics to show that most Garden Village crime occurred after dark, the pair convinced Baltimore Gas and Electric to repair the broken street lights. Using photographs of potholes and cracked pavement, they persuaded the county roads department to patch up Garden Village's alleyways. Using the dimensions of other basketball courts and playgrounds, they badgered county park and recreation officials until a dormant rehabilitation and construction project was approved for a local park.*

In another instance, officers were called to help with a panhandling problem that had gotten out of hand in Dundalk, a small neighborhood on the outskirts of Baltimore. Although vagrants had inhabited Dundalk for over twenty years, they had recently become a serious problem, accosting local shoppers for money to buy liquor. Plainclothes COPE officers helped the officers from that precinct make nineteen arrests, which reduced the panhandling. The officers knew, however, that the underlying problem was still there. Using the problem-solving approach, they accomplished the following (Taft, p. 18):

> *The officers convinced the county to trim shrubs and add lights in the park where panhandlers loitered. They helped the Chamber distribute 15,000 copies of a "Stop Panhandling" flyer . . . and visited liquor store owners to remind them that selling liquor to an intoxicated person is illegal. They researched panhandling laws from different cities and drafted a new version for Baltimore County, one that would make such aggressive panhandling a criminal offense.*

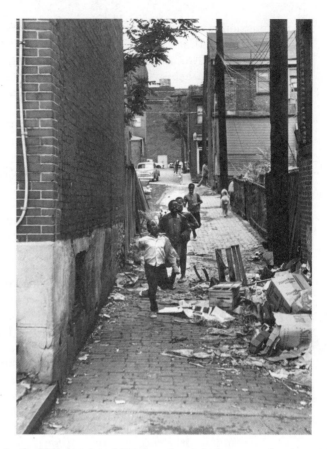

This alley in the Hill district of Pittsburgh might become a key target for a problem-oriented police department.

> *But Fox and Grupp [the two COPE officers] knew that even stiffer jail sentences would not prevent the vagrants from returning. So they turned their attention to a more radical solution: establishing Baltimore County's first detoxification and rehabilitation center.*

They also succeeded in setting up a task force on the homeless, which continues to examine the remaining problems. As noted by Officer Fox (Taft, p. 19): "We changed the environment. We changed public attitudes. We verified the need for a detoxification facility. We asked for a task force and got it. COPE works."

According to Taft (p. 22): "The success of COPE suggests that modern police can play an even more active role than their historical counterparts—that in today's complex society police can, if they so choose, become active agents of change by identifying social problems and bringing to bear public and private resources to solve them."

BENEFITS OF PROBLEM-ORIENTED POLICING

Kelling and Moore (1991, p. 19) suggest: "Police officers enjoy operating with a holistic approach to their work; they have the capacity to do it successfully; they can work with citizens and other agencies to solve problems; and citizens seem to appreciate working with police."

As noted by Bittner (1986, p. 30), problem-oriented policing is not really a radical new idea:

> *Problem-oriented policing is firmly rooted in the practical outlook of the 'street cop.'... Experienced, skilled and judicious officers have always known that, for example, the likelihood of violent teenage conflict in public housing depends upon the layout of the walkways, the locations of entrances and exits, and the distribution of transportation facilities. The best officers have always geared their capacities to intervene to the existence of such conditions. Problem-oriented policing ... builds on the wisdom and on the perception of necessities as seen by these officers."*

Bittner is speaking of the problem-oriented COPE project, but his comments can be applied in a much broader context. He notes: "It is the great strength of the COPE project that it makes explicit what was implicit and unrecognized in street practice; it makes routine what was exceptional." He concludes (p. 31): "I look forward to the day when the entire police profession recognizes problem-solving as a regular part of the job."

Summary

Herman Goldstein is credited with originating problem-oriented policing. One concern of such an orientation is differentiating between efficiency and effectiveness. Efficiency, doing things right, has been the traditional emphasis in law enforcement. Effectiveness, doing the right things, is the emphasis in community-oriented policing.

The first step in problem-oriented policing is to group incidents as problems. Four stages of problem solving are scanning, analysis, response, and assessment. Problem analysis considers the individuals involved, the incidents, and the responses. Such analysis should take into account the magnet phenomenon. This phenomenon occurs when a phone number or address is associated with a crime simply because it was a convenient number or address to use.

Crime-specific planning uses the principles of problem-oriented policing to focus on identified crime problems. Both crime-specific planning and problem-oriented policing can be more effective if those working on the problem can approach it creatively. Mental locks that prevent creativity include the right answer, that's not logical, follow the rules, be practical, avoid ambiguity, to err is wrong, play is frivolous, that's not my area, don't be foolish, and I'm not creative. Killer phrases are judgmental, critical statements that serve as put-downs and stifle creativity.

DISCUSSION QUESTIONS

1. How do you approach problems? Do you have a systematic approach?
2. Do you think problem-oriented policing takes more time than the traditional method?
3. Does your department use problem-oriented policing?
4. Do you consider yourself to be creative? What helps you to be so? What hinders you?
5. What difficulties can you foresee for a department that uses problem-oriented policing?
6. How do problem-oriented policing and crime-specific planning differ?
7. Considering the list of mental locks on page 476, do you find yourself thinking in any of these ways? If so, what can you do to unlock your creativity?
8. In what kinds of problems do you think a problem-solving approach would be most effective?
9. How do community policing and problem-oriented policing compare and contrast? Can you use both?
10. How does the information in Section 2, "Building Relationships," affect the information in this section, "Projects and Programs: Coordinated Efforts"?

DEFINITIONS
Can you define these terms: creativity, crime-specific planning, decision, effectiveness, efficiency, innovation, killer phrases, magnet address, magnet phenomenon, magnet phone, mental locks, problem, problem-oriented policing.

REFERENCES

Bennett, Wayne W. and Hess, Kären M. *Management & Supervision in Law Enforcement.* St. Paul: West Publishing Company, 1992.

Bittner, Egon. "Afterword." In *Fighting Fear: The Baltimore County COPE Project,* 30–31. Washington: Police Executive Research Forum, February 1986.

Buchholz, Steve and Roth, Thomas. *Creating the High-Performance Team.* New York: John Wiley and Sons, 1987.

Buerger, Michael E. ed. *The Crime Prevention Casebook: Securing High Crime Locations.* Washington: Crime Control Institute, 1992.

Cummings, D. Brian. "Problem-Oriented Policing and Crime-Specific Planning." *The Police Chief.* (March 1990): 63–64.

Eck, John E. and Spelman, William. *Problem-Solving: Problem-Oriented Policing in Newport News.* Washington: The Police Executive Research Forum, 1987.

Goldstein, Herman. *Problem-Oriented Policing.* New York: McGraw-Hill Publishing Company, 1990.

Kelling, George L. and Moore, Mark H. "From Political Reform to Community: The Evolving Strategy of Police." In *Community Policing: Rhetoric or Reality,* edited by Jack R. Greene and Stephen D. Mastrofski, 3–25. New York: Praeger Publications, 1991.

Smith, Charlotte Anne. "Tulsa PD Uses Multiple Solutions." *Law and Order.* (September 1990): 62–66.

Taft, Philip B., Jr. *Fighting Fear: The Baltimore County COPE Project.* Washington: Police Executive Research Forum, February 1986.

Timm, Paul R. *Supervision.* St. Paul: West Publishing Company, 1984.

von Oech, Roger. *A Whack on the Side of the Head.* New York: Warner Books, 1983.

Wilson, James Q. and Kelling, George L. "Making Neighborhoods Safe." *The Atlantic Monthly.* (February 1989): 46–52.

APPENDIX A

BRIEF DESCRIPTIONS OF REPRESENTATIVE GANGS

B–BOY

AFFILIATES: NONE

COLORS: NONE
REPRESENT: NONE
SYMBOLS/TERMS: BOMBERS
BUBBLE LETTERS
THROW-UPS
CHARACTERS
CREWS
HIP HOP
KINGS
TAGS
TOYS

Typical Examples of Graffiti:

Brief History:

This group consists of talented juveniles and young adults who share a common interest in "tagging" and "graffiti." Publicity surrounding New York City subway art introduced a variety of visual styles in the 1970s which have since been popularized in such European cities as Amsterdam, Barcelona, Berlin, Bruhl, Copenhagen, Paris, Sydney, and Vienna.

Members are committed to specific forms of self-expression and strive to display their statements in public places. Some are known to take their ideas from such publications as *Subway Art* (1984) and *Spraycan Art* (1987).

DISCIPLES

Affiliates: Black Disciples
Black Gangster Disciples
Black Gangsters
Simon City Royals—white
Crips

Colors: Blue/White and Blue/Black
Represent: Right
"All is One"
Folks
Symbols: Six Point Star
Pitchforks
Sword
Winged Heart

Typical Examples of Graffiti:

Brief History:

Based primarily in Chicago, the Disciples are known variously as the Black Gangster Disciples, Black Disciples, or Black Gangsters. This group has the reputation of being one of the most feared and highly organized black street gangs.

Recruitment by hard-core members is selective and sophisticated, particularily in the prison setting. Allegiance to the "nation" is demanded and frequently tested. Members have rank and must follow a chain of command.

This group is frequently engaged in drug wars, and the members with rank are often heavily armed.

LATIN KINGS

Affiliates: Latin Saints   Colors: Gold/Black/Red
            Vice Lords   Represent: None
            Bloods   Symbols: Three Point Crown
                                          Five Point Crown

Typical Examples of Graffiti:

Brief History:

Latin Kings are typically young Hispanics who have settled in inner-city neighborhoods. Members are intensely loyal and follow codes of conduct which have been handed down orally within some families for generations. The chain of command is informal, and members remain close socially.

Latin Kings have been common in some Latino neighborhoods in Los Angeles since the 1940s. Today, Latin Kings exist in most large cities with Hispanic communities. Criminal activity varies among groups depending on neighborhood circumstances and the needs of the more powerful individuals in each group.

CLUB/NATURALS/CRUE

Affiliates: None

Colors: None
Represent: None
Symbols: Letter "N"

Typical Examples of Graffiti:

Brief History:
Native Americans are members of this group. The group structure is somewhat casual, and individuals display strong social bonds.

Individuals in this group tend to be neatly dressed and "natural" with few outward identifiers. Members are often associated with illegal drug activity and auto theft.

VICE LORDS

Affiliates: Latin Kings
Conservative Vice Lords
Insane Vice Lords
4 Corner Hustlers
Micky Cobra Stones
War Lords
El-Rukns
Bloods

Colors: Red/Black
Blk/Gold
Represent: Left
"All is Well"
People
Symbols: Five Point Star
Martini Glass
Crescent
Pyramid
Top Hat
Cane

Typical Examples of Graffiti:

Brief History:

There are nineteen subfactions of this group in the City of Chicago as well as in the Illinois prison system. Vice Lords have existed in Minneapolis and Chicago since the 1950s, and the group now has factions throughout the South.

The membership tends to be young, and recruitment is aggressive in schools and on the streets. The imagery of this group tends to glamorize a life-style centered on drugs and predatory crime. The behavior patterns of the young members are patterned after the older and bolder Vice Lord members.

CULT–ORIENTED

Affiliation: Stoners

Colors: None
Represent: None
Symbols/Terms: Pentagram
Hexagram
Inverted Cross
Cross of Nero
"A" in Circle (Anarchy)
Black/White Candles
Goat's Head
Sign of Beast (666)
Swastika

Typical Examples of Graffiti:

Brief History:
While not commonly regarded as a street gang, cult-oriented youth tend to band together and participate in anti-social behavior which can conflict with others. The practice of Satanism has been combined with drugs and an interest in "heavy metal" music to produce bizarre behavior in some individuals.

Drug-induced rituals are popular and known to include systematic mutilations, grave robbing, and desecration of religious places. Furthermore, some cult-oriented activity has included murder.

APPENDIX B

DATA ON CRIME VICTIMS' COMPENSATION AND ASSISTANCE

Crime Victims Compensation Awards

STATE	GRT. NO 90-VC-GX-	FY 86 $23,594,000 (39)	FY 87 $28,296,000 (40)	FY 88 $38,600,000 (38)	FY 89 $44,647,429 (42)	FY 90 $46,527,000 (42)
Alabama	0001	0	79,000	237,000	405,000	603,000
Alaska	0002	283,000	246,000	143,000	164,000	161,000
Arizona	0004	0	0	0	60,000	93,000
Arkansas	0005	0	0	0	0	0
California	0006	5,185,000	6,353,000	16,691,000	13,610,000	15,444,000
Colorado	0008	472,000	703,000	740,000	1,211,000	1,175,000
Connecticut	0009	442,000	478,000	509,000	431,000	422,000
Delaware	0010	123,000	172,000	165,000	173,000	267,000
Dist. Columbia	0011	85,000	112,000	80,000	167,000	122,000
Florida	0012	1,493,000	1,872,000	1,808,000	2,250,000	2,022,000
Georgia	0013	0	0	0	0	0
Hawaii	0015	150,000	165,000	179,000	142,000	214,000
Idaho	0016	0	0	0	25,000	125,000
Illinois	0017	1,242,000	921,000	921,000	1,025,000	820,000
Indiana	0018	117,000	147,000	0	434,000	734,000
Iowa	0019	57,000	106,000	155,000	212,000	203,000
Kansas	0020	116,000	131,000	134,000	189,000	146,000
Kentucky	0021	213,000	212,000	197,000	344,000	270,000
Louisiana	0022	77,000	114,000	222,000	326,000	220,000
Maine	0023	0	0	0	0	0
Maryland	0024	433,000	785,000	855,000	1,014,000	1,179,000
Massachusetts	0025	387,000	321,000	353,000	634,000	1,096,000
Michigan	0026	699,000	686,000	654,000	780,000	774,000
Minnesota	0027	190,000	284,000	276,000	466,000	496,000
Mississippi	0028	0	0	0	0	0
Missouri	0029	266,000	355,000	373,000	567,000	615,000
Montana	0030	129,000	136,000	118,000	67,429	0
Nebraska	0031	31,000	38,000	0	0	0
Nevada	0032	106,000	93,000	0	0	0
New Hampshire	0033	0	0	0	0	0
New Jersey	0034	1,243,000	1,910,000	1,332,000	2,080,000	1,159,000
New Mexico	0035	65,000	83,000	73,000	145,000	144,000
New York	0036	2,434,000	2,597,000	2,655,000	3,200,000	3,076,000
North Carolina	0037	0	0	0	0	225,000
North Dakota	0038	32,000	27,000	22,000	68,000	48,000
Ohio	0039	2,369,000	2,056,000	1,106,000	1,713,000	2,543,000
Oklahoma	0040	187,000	241,000	214,000	238,000	269,000
Oregon	0041	261,000	285,000	340,000	514,000	462,000
Pennsylvania	0042	888,000	776,000	701,000	798,000	662,000
Rhode Island	0044	123,000	231,000	277,000	340,000	443,000
South Carolina	0045	173,000	234,000	403,000	423,000	505,000

STATE	GRT. NO 90-VC-GX-	FY 86 $23,594,000 (39)	FY 87 $28,296,000 (40)	FY 88 $38,600,000 (38)	FY 89 $44,647,429 (42)	FY 90 $46,527,000 (42)
South Dakota	0046	0	0	0	0	0
Tennessee	0047	495,000	1,278,000	928,000	1,402,000	638,000
Texas	0048	1,472,000	2,223,000	3,193,000	6,023,000	6,068,000
Utah	0049	0	0	0	47,000	342,000
Vermont	0050	0	0	0	0	0
Virgin Islands	0078	62,000	26,000	73,000	26,000	25,000
Virginia	0051	186,000	280,000	349,000	578,000	274,000
Washington	0053	970,000	1,108,000	1,180,000	1,573,000	1,870,000
West Virginia	0054	53,000	64,000	593,000	423,000	173,000
Wisconsin	0055	285,000	368,000	322,000	336,000	365,000
Wyoming	0056	0	0	29,000	24,000	35,000

SOURCE: U.S. Department of Justice, Office for Victims of Crime. *Office for Victims of Crime: A Report to Congress, April 1990,* Washington: U.S. Government Printing Office. 1990: Appendix B–1.

Victim Assistance Allocations

STATES	GRT. NO 90-VA- GX-	FY 86 $41,270,000 (57)	FY 87 $30,772,000 (57)	FY 88 $34,888,000 (57)	FY 89 $43,492,000 (59)	FY 90 $64,818,500 (57)	FY 91 $65,674,500 (57)
Alabama	0001	700,000	526,000	592,000	729,000	1,077,000	1,086,000
Alaska	0002	175,000	153,000	165,000	224,000	268,000	270,000
Arizona	0004	559,000	426,000	503,000	630,000	939,000	958,000
Arkansas	0005	453,000	351,000	387,000	489,000	692,000	697,000
California	0006	3,953,000	2,832,000	3,372,000	4,073,375	6,552,000	6,757,000
Colorado	0008	578,000	439,000	496,000	617,000	896,000	904,000
Connecticut	0009	574,000	436,000	486,000	605,000	881,000	887,000
Delaware	0010	192,000	165,000	177,000	241,000	299,000	303,000
Dist. Columbia	0011	194,000	166,000	176,000	238,000	291,000	287,000
Florida	0012	1,751,000	1,270,000	1,516,000	1,855,000	2,939,000	3,030,000
Georgia	0013	978,000	722,000	840,000	1,032,000	1,584,000	1,613,000
Hawaii	0015	256,000	211,000	229,000	304,000	398,000	403,000
Idaho	0016	251,000	207,000	221,000	292,000	377,000	381,000
Illinois	0017	1,831,000	1,327,000	1,501,000	1,793,000	2,776,000	2,800,000
Indiana	0018	927,000	686,000	768,000	934,000	1,406,000	1,422,000
Iowa	0019	538,000	410,000	445,000	552,000	791,000	796,000
Kansas	0020	467,000	360,000	398,000	501,000	714,000	721,000
Kentucky	0021	660,000	497,000	553,000	679,000	993,000	997,000
Louisiana	0022	771,000	576,000	646,000	783,000	1,147,000	1,146,000
Maine	0023	274,000	223,000	242,000	318,000	422,000	428,000
Maryland	0024	754,000	564,000	642,000	793,000	1,195,000	1,217,000
Massachusetts	0025	972,000	718,000	807,000	980,000	1,482,000	1,494,000
Michigan	0026	1,465,000	1,068,000	1,209,000	1,455,000	2,239,000	2,257,000
Minnesota	0027	726,000	544,000	612,000	752,000	1,124,000	1,139,000
Mississippi	0028	491,000	377,000	418,000	522,000	742,000	745,000
Missouri	0029	853,000	634,000	715,000	874,000	1,312,000	1,323,000
Montana	0030	224,000	188,000	199,000	265,000	332,000	333,000
Nebraska	0031	342,000	271,000	294,000	376,000	512,000	517,000
Nevada	0032	237,000	197,000	217,000	293,000	388,000	403,000
New Hampshire	0033	247,000	204,000	224,000	300,000	395,00	402,00
New Jersey	0034	1,230,000	901,000	1,024,000	1,238,000	1,896,000	1,909,000
New Mexico	0035	314,000	252,000	279,000	363,000	491,000	498,000
New York	0036	2,767,000	1,991,000	2,256,000	2,678,000	4,199,000	4,230,000
North Carolina	0037	1,027,000	757,000	868,000	1,060,000	1,617,000	1,644,000
North Dakota	0038	203,000	173,000	182,000	245,000	301,000	300,000
Ohio	0039	1,717,000	1,247,000	1,404,000	1,680,000	2,604,000	2,629,000
Oklahoma	0040	596,000	452,000	501,000	614,000	883,000	882,750
Oregon	0041	502,000	385,000	427,000	536,000	776,000	791,000
Pennsylvania	0042	1,890,000	1,369,000	1,542,000	1,843,000	2,864,000	2,886,000
Rhode Island	0044	245,000	203,000	218,000	290,000	375,450	377,000
South Carolina	0045	596,000	452,000	510,000	636,000	935,000	949,000
South Dakota	0046	206,000	175,000	186,000	251,000	311,000	312,000
Tennessee	0047	809,000	603,000	683,000	839,000	1,257,000	1,273,000
Texas	0048	2,505,000	1,805,000	2,124,000	2,531,000	3,958,000	4,012,000
Utah	0049	348,000	276,000	302,000	388,000	532,000	538,000
Vermont	0050	180,000	157,000	166,000	228,000	276,000	279,000
Virginia	0051	948,000	701,000	802,000	987,000	1,510,000	1,537,000
Washington	0053	754,000	564,000	642,000	794,000	1,201,000	1,232,000
West Virginia	0054	394,000	308,000	332,000	419,000	574,000	573,000
Wisconsin	0055	817,000	608,000	681,000	832,000	1,248,000	1,256,000
Wyoming	0056	177,000	155,000	161,000	220,000	258,000	257,000

STATES	GRT. NO 90-VA- GX-	FY 86 $41,270,000 (57)	FY 87 $30,772,000 (57)	FY 88 $34,888,000 (57)	FY 89 $43,492,000 (59)	FY 90 $64,818,500 (57)	FY 91 $65,674,500 (57)
Puerto Rico	0072	591,000	448,000	497,000	617,000	894,000	898,000
Virgin Islands	0078	16,000	11,000	13,000	165,000	173,000	172,000
Guam	0066	18,000	12,000	15,000	169,000	180,000	182,000
American Sa- moa	0060	5,000	4,000	5,000	155,000	159,000	159,000
N. Mariana Isl.	0069	3,000	2,000	2,000	153,000	155,000	155,000
Trust Territor.		19,000	13,000	16,000	0	0	0
Micronesia	0064	0	0	0	25,500	0	0
Marshall Isl.		0	0	0	10,625	0	0
Palau	0070	0	0	0	25,500	28,050	27,750

SOURCE: U.S. Department of Justice, Office for Victims of Crime. *Office for Victims of Crime: A Report to Congress, April 1990,* Washington: U.S. Government Printing Office. 1990: Appendix G–1.

Appendix C

Programs for Youth

The following programs were identified and described by the National School Safety Center in their publication *Gangs in Schools: Breaking Up Is Hard To Do,* copyright 1988, Pepperdine University Press. The Center has granted permission to reprint their descriptions of the programs.

Each program was contacted and requested to update the information on their specific effort. The descriptions which follow are a combination of the National School Safety Center's descriptions and the specific projects' updates. Addresses and telephone numbers are current as of the spring of 1993.

Andrew Glover Youth Program

100 Center St.
Manhattan Criminal Court, Room 1541
New York, NY 10013
212/349-6381

A privately funded organization, the Andrew Glover Youth Program works to protect neighborhoods in New York's Lower East Side from crime. Another objective of the Program is to steer youth away from negative and illegal activities. The Program serves a large number of black and Hispanic young people by working with police, courts, youth services, and social services to provide counseling, gang mediation, family counseling, and housing assistance.

Youth workers are in contact with kids where they spend most of their time: on the streets. The youth workers also live in the community and are available for assistance twenty-four hours a day. The program was named after a local police officer who cared about and tried to help youth and who was shot to death in the line of duty by teenagers.

B.U.I.L.D. (Broader Urban Involvement and Leadership Development)

1223 N. Milwaukee Ave.
Chicago, IL 60622
312/227-2880

Non-profit B.U.I.L.D. works with gang members on the streets, trying to involve them in athletic or social recreational events and to encourage them to participate in education and job training programs. Many of the streetworkers are "graduates" of street gangs who the organization assisted.

B.U.I.L.D. also runs a prevention program for twenty-eight junior high school students identified as at-risk for joining gangs by school and police authorities. The program includes a weekly class session and after-school activities to teach kids about the dangers of joining gangs and offers positive alternative activities. The project is supported by Chicago's social, civic, and corporate sectors.

Center for Urban Expression (C.U.E.)
The Dorchester Youth Collaborative
1514A Dorchester Ave.
Dorchester, MA 02122
617/228-1748

The Center for Urban Expression steers youth into structured, goal-oriented activities with a special focus on community organizing. The Common Ground prevention club, sponsored by the Center, brings youths of diverse ethnic backgrounds together to work on a variety of projects and performances.

Community service teams may shovel snow or clean garages for community residents; others may become involved in youth leadership programs. Common Ground groups have given song/rap performances in six states and have become very visible locally through their anti-drug audio and video public service media announcements.

Chicago Intervention Network
Department of Human Services
Youth Delinquency Prevention Division
510 N. Peshtigo Court, Section 5B
Chicago, IL 60611-4375
312/744-0881 or 312/744-1820

The Chicago Intervention Network works with students of all ages and provides the schools with the following programs and services: (1) early intervention and prevention curriculum, including activities in anger management, impulse control, and empathy training; (2) twenty-week delinquency prevention sessions in eighty schools; (3) attitude development sessions covering self-esteem, resisting peer pressure, and understanding and managing conflict; (4) Safe School Zone Law presentations; (5) School Watch programs; Truancy follow-up; (6) assessments on gang problems in and around schools; (7) mediation and prevention of gang violence; (8) technical assistance and information for teachers and parents on how to identify gang activity through symbols, colors, and signs; (9) help in securing Safe School Zone signs for schools; and (10) individual and group counselling for challenged youth.

Gang Awareness Resource Program (GARP)
The California State Office of Criminal Justice Planning provided grant funds for the Gang Awareness Resource Program (GARP). The Program is now in its fourth year. It places an Operation Safe Streets gang investigator deputy on the Carson High School campus in a highly visible "resident" capacity. The investigator serves the high school, as

well as feeder junior high and elementary schools, through the following services: training and instruction of faculty, administrators, school police, parks and recreation personnel, community groups, parents, and civic officials on gang awareness, and coordination of information between schools and between law enforcement and schools. The investigator also establishes a partnership with the business sector for their support in the effort to eliminate street gang violence.

The bridge which GARP has built between law enforcement and the schools (both faculty and students) has led to enhanced communications, reduced gang versus gang incidents, and resulted in diminished gang activity on or about the high school campus. The GARP staff has developed and published a gang awareness pamphlet for community distribution and a pocket gang directory for school administrators and police.

The GARP deputy is in daily contact with many gang members and, as a result, has arrested many for crimes committed not only on the campuses, but also in the community. He has identified hundreds of new gang members who have not, as yet, entered the criminal justice system. He has assisted in the solution of many other crimes based upon his day-to-day contacts with students throughout the Carson city schools. The GARP deputy has made hundreds of gang awareness presentations before school staff, student assemblies, and community groups. As a consequence, both school campuses and the community benefit from reduced gang violence.

Gang Crime Section
Chicago Police Department
1121 South State Street
Chicago, IL 60605
312/747-6328

The first formal gang unit in the Chicago Police Department was formed in 1967. Known by various names over the years (Gang Intelligence Unit, Gang Crimes Investigations Division, Narcotics and Gangs Unit, and Gang Crimes Enforcement Division), it became the Gang Crime Section in 1984 and has retained that name since.

The Gang Crime Section is composed of tactical (uniformed) police and detective level Gang Crime Specialists (plain clothes) police officers. Specialists conduct follow-up investigations on gang-related incidents while tactical personnel conduct directed patrol missions in areas of the city experiencing increased gang activity.

The activity of all active street gangs is monitored by gang specialists and reported on periodically. With each arrest the files of known gang members is updated. Computer analysis of reported gang incidents and statistical analysis of arrest activity and weapon seizures is prepared by administrative personnel. The results of this analysis are used to initiate directed-missions in the most active areas of the city.

House of Umoja (Unity)
1410 N. Frazier St.
Philadelphia, PA 19131
215/473-5893

Known as the first urban "Boys' Town," the house has taken in more than 2,500 youths since it began in 1968. At the time of the House of Umoja's inception, the deadliest phenomenon facing the youth of Philadelphia was gang warfare. The concern of Falaka and David Fattah over their own son's involvement led them to open their home in West Philadelphia to gang members. The House of Umoja quickly developed into a communal living facility, geared toward keeping young men off the streets and giving them the education and life skills necessary to enter into society and the work force. Realizing that for many of these youths, a street gang acts as a surrogate family, providing a sense of belonging and self-worth, the Fattahs created a family system of their own.

The House of Umoja Boystown has since become one of the most acclaimed and successful youth service programs in the country. Now occupying most of the original block of Frazier Street, the stated purpose of the house is to "provide a non-traditional, community-based experience which offers a positive learning environment for young men who lack a sufficient family support structure." Umoja provides not only the basic amenities of food and shelter, but also educational and emotional support often lacking even in the most "stable" of American families.

The house's outreach program has sponsored the Black Youth Olympics, cultural exchange programs with boys from Belfast, Ireland, and local cultural programs. In the wake of the first Rodney King verdict in Los Angeles, Umoja cooperated with the Quaker Friends Society to call for peaceful response. The House also speaks on behalf of the community at local meetings, city hearings, or any gathering where a concerned voice is required.

The Paramount Plan: Alternatives to Gang Membership
Human Services Department
City of Paramount
16400 Colorado Ave.
Paramount, CA 90723
213/531-3503

The highly regarded Paramount Plan stresses disapproval of gang membership while working to eliminate the future gang membership base and to diminish the influence of gangs. The program sponsors neighborhood meetings and provides anti-gang curricula and posters on request. Community meetings are led by bilingual leaders and are held in neighborhoods identified by the sheriff's office as "under gang influence." The community meetings are aimed at parents and preteens.

A fifth-grade anti-gang curriculum was introduced in the Paramount Unified School District in 1982 that emphasized constructive activities available in the neighborhood.

Say Yes, Incorporated
3840 Crenshaw Blvd., Suite 217
Los Angeles, CA 90008
213/295-5551

This program offers crisis intervention, field monitoring, and workshops for school staffs. The workshops teach staff about the gangs operating in the neighborhood and describe gang characteristics and problems.

Say Yes teams monitor selected athletic events to stop violence in its formative stages. These teams supplement regular school, security, and law enforcement personnel. The staff also monitors elementary, junior, and senior high schools, provides rap sessions, and sponsors Neighborhood Watch, athletic, and summer job programs.

U.S. Department of Justice Community Relations Service
5550 Friendship Blvd., Suite 330
Chevy Chase, MD 20815
301/492-5929

This service specializes in conciliating and mediating race-related conflicts in any context—for example, on school campuses, between police and minority communities, and in housing developments. The Community Relations Service has been called in to ease tense transitions in school desegregations in Boston and New York and other related incidents. There are Community Relations Service regional offices in Boston, New York, Philadelphia, Atlanta, Chicago, Kansas City (Missouri), Denver, Dallas, Seattle, and San Francisco. There are also field offices in Detroit, Houston, and Miami. Telephone numbers of branch offices should be listed under the U.S. Department of Justice, Community Relations Service in local telephone directories.

The Community Relations Service has a hot line that can be used to report incidents of racial harassment and hate violence and to request conflict resolution assistance. The telephone number is 1-800-347-HATE.

Youth Development, Inc. Gang Intervention Program
6301 Central Ave. N.W.
Albuquerque, NM 87105
505/831-6038

Youth Development, Inc. (YDI) is a social services organization offering more than thirty different programs to assist children, youth, and families. The different components offer education, residential, counseling, corrections, prevention, recreation, and employment assistance to at-risk youth and their families.

The YDI Gang Intervention Program works on three levels: prevention, diversion, and intervention. Puppetry, theater, presentations, and educational programs focus on preventing gang violence and activities. Diversion involves directing at-risk youth into positive activities and behaviors, while the intervention component works with gang members and court-ordered youth to stop self-destructive behavior.

A major project is a regular ten-week workshop for court-ordered gang members. Youths participate in community activities such as feeding the homeless, team building events such as a ropes course, and educational programs including visiting a medium security prison. Each youth also has a counselor who works intensively with him or her on a one-to-one basis during the ten-week program.

The Gang Intervention program is successful because it focuses on working with the youths as individuals, rather than as gang members. Also the YDI program is not against gangs per se, but against gang violence and illegal activities.

Appendix D

Solution to the Nine–Dot Exercise

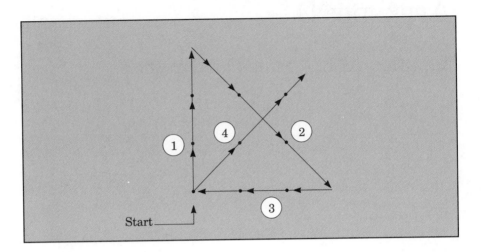

GLOSSARY

Number in parentheses indicates the chapter in which the term is introduced.

acculturation a society takes in or assimilates another culture. Also called *assimilation*. (5)

AARP American Association for Retired Persons. (7)

AD Alzheimer's disease. (7)

ADA refers to the Americans with Disabilities Act. (6)

allocution speaking before a judge or a court. (10)

Alzheimer's disease a progressive, irreversible brain disease affecting four million elderly Americans. The classic symptom is loss of memory. (7)

American Dream anyone can become rich and powerful if they work hard enough. (5)

Ameslam stands for American Sign Language, the preferred communication mode for the majority of deaf individuals. (6)

assimilation a society takes in or assimilates another culture. Also called *acculturation*. (5)

attention deficit hyperactivity disorder a common disruptive behavior disorder of children characterized by heightened motor activity (fidgeting and squirming), short attention span, distractibility, impulsiveness, and lack of self-control. (8)

bias a prejudice that inhibits objectivity. Bias can evolve into hate. (4)

bias crime any act or attempted act to cause physical injury, emotional suffering, or property damage through intimidation, harassment, racial or ethnic slurs and bigoted epithets, vandalism, force, or the threat of force, motivated all or in part by hostility to the victim's real or perceived race, ethnicity, religion, or sexual orientation. Also called *hate crime*. (5)

Big D's of juvenile justice refers to diversion, decriminalization, deinstitutionalization, and due process. (8)

body language messages conveyed by how a person looks, moves, and gestures. (4)

broken window phenomenon suggests that if it appears no one cares about the community as indicated by broken windows not being repaired, disorder and crime will thrive. (2)

CAT Combat Auto Theft, a program that gives the police the authority to stop any car marked with a special decal between 1 A.M. and 5 A.M. (15)

catastrophic reaction occurs when a situation overloads an individual's mental ability to act rationally and he or she reverts to impulsive behavior. Associated with Alzheimer's disease. (7)

cognitive restructuring a coping mechanism in which victims reinterpret their experience to ameliorate the adverse effects of the incident. (9)

communication the transfer of information and understanding from one person to another. (4)

communication process involves a sender, a message, a channel, a receiver, and sometimes feedback. (4)

community refers to the specific geographic area served by a police department or law enforcement agency and the individuals, organizations, and agencies within that area. (2)

community policing a philosophy or orientation that emphasizes working with citizens to solve crime-related problems and prevent crime. (1)

community relations see *public relations*. (1)

community wellness emphasizes a proactive police-community partnership to prevent crime. (1)

CPTED crime prevention through environmental design—altering the physical environment to enhance safety. (12)

crack children children who were exposed to cocaine while in the womb. (8)

creativity a process of breaking old connections and making useful new connections. Often synonymous with innovation. (16)

crime-specific planning uses the principles of problem-oriented policing to focus on identified crime problems. (16)

crisis behavior results when a person has a temporary breakdown in coping skills. (6)

cross-sectional analysis a research method whereby data is analyzed by area rather than by individuals responding. (12)

culpability any action of the victim that in some measure may contribute to the victimization. (10)

cultural conflict a theory that suggests that diverse cultures sharing the same territory will compete with and attempt to exploit one another. (5)

cultural pluralism a theory that suggests there are many melting pots. Some groups fuse into one pot, other groups into another. (5)

cultural window a person's world-view through which he or she interprets events. (5)

culturally literate possessing the basic information needed to thrive in one's society. (5)

culture a collection of artifacts, tools, ways of living, and a language common to a fairly large group of people, all passed on to the next generation with few changes. (5)

DARE Drug Abuse Resistance Education program aimed at elementary age school children, seeking to teach them to "say no to drugs." (14)

deaf persons having hearing loss to such a degree they cannot understand spoken words. (6)

decision a judgment or conclusion. (16)

decriminalization refers to the efforts to make status offenses noncriminal actions. Has also been used in attempts to legalize marijuana. (8)

deinstitutionalization refers to the release of thousands of mentally ill individuals into society to be cared for by family or a special network of support services. (6) Also refers to efforts to release incarcerated youth through parole and community programs. (8)

delusion (paranoid) disorder   illness characterized by nonbizarre delusions focused on a single theme or a series of connected themes. Common themes include persecution, jealousy, and grandiosity. (6)

demographics   the characteristics of a human population or community. (2)

directed imbalance   those imbalances within an organization that are created in anticipation of a proposed change in orientation. (13)

disability   a physical or mental impairment that substantially limits one or more of an individual's major life activities. (6)

discretion   freedom to make choices among possible courses of action or inaction—to arrest or not arrest, for example. (3)

discrimination   showing a preference or prejudice in treating individuals or groups. Discrimination is a behavior based on an attitude or prejudice. (4)

diversion   turning a youth away from the criminal justice system, rerouting him or her to another agency or program. (2) Finding alternatives to placing juveniles into detention facilities. (8)

due process   the rights guaranteed by the Fifth Amendment: notice of a hearing, full information regarding the charges made, the opportunity to present evidence in self-defense before an impartial judge or jury, and to be presumed innocent until proven guilty by legally obtained evidence. (8)

EBD   emotionally/behaviorally disturbed. (8)

effectiveness   producing the desired result or goal. Doing the right things. (16)

efficiency   minimizing waste, expense, or unnecessary effort. Results in a high ratio of output to input. Doing things right. (16)

elder abuse   includes physical and emotional abuse, financial exploitation, and general neglect. (7)

empathy   truly understanding another person. (4)

empirical study   research based on observation or practical experience. (12)

epilepsy   a disease of the central nervous system which results in seizures. (6)

ethnocentrism   the opinion that one's own way of life is better than all others. (5)

experimental imbalance   an atmosphere of trial and error, or risk taking. (13)

extensional world   the world that comes to us through experience. (4)

fetal alcohol syndrome   (FAS) children who suffer from the effects of their mother consuming alcohol while pregnant. Effects include impulsivity, poor communication skills, and inability to predict consequences or to use appropriate judgment in daily life. Small children may be very active and easily distracted. Adolescents may be frustrated and depressed. (8)

formal power structure   includes those with wealth and political influence: federal, state, and local agencies and governments, commissions, regulatory agencies, and power groups. (2)

four-minute barrier   the point in an initial meeting at which most people have formed a positive or negative opinion about someone. (4)

gang a somewhat organized group of some duration with a special interest in violence for status-providing purposes. See also *street gang* and *youth gang*. (9)

ghetto an area of a city usually inhabited by individuals of the same race or ethnic background who live in poverty and social disorganization. (2)

ghetto syndrome a vicious circle of failure: poverty, poor education, joblessness, low motivation to work, welfare, and poverty. (5)

graffiti writing on buildings and walls. Used by gangs to mark their turf. (9)

granny bashing physically abusing the elderly. (7)

granny dumping abandoning of the elderly. (7)

graying of America a metaphor reflecting the fact that our population is aging. (7)

Guardian Angles private citizen patrols who seek to deter crime and to provide a positive role model for young children. (15)

hate crime any act or attempted act to cause physical injury, emotional suffering, or property damage through intimidation, harassment, racial or ethnic slurs and bigoted epithets, vandalism, force, or the threat of force, motivated all or in part by hostility to the victim's real or perceived race, ethnicity, religion, or sexual orientation. Also called *bias crime*. (5)

hearing impaired refers to individuals who have some residual hearing, that is, sounds may be audible, but not clear. Words are not just softer, they are garbled. Also called *hard of hearing*. (6)

heterogeneous involving things (including people) which are unlike, dissimilar, different. The opposite of homogeneous. (2)

homogeneous involving things (including people) which are basically similar, alike. The opposite of heterogeneous. (2)

hue and cry the ancient practice of citizens calling out if they saw a wrongdoing, summoning all citizens within earshot to join in pursuing and capturing the wrong-doer. (1)

hyphenated American tendency to include ethnic background in a person's nationality, for example, Italian-American, Polish-American, illustrating America's tendency to pluralism or a multicultural approach. (5)

in loco parentis acting "in place of parents"; gives the schools the authority to act as a parent might in situations requiring discipline or need. (14)

incident an event calling for some sort of police assistance. (1)

informal power structure includes religious groups, wealthy subgroups, ethnic groups, political groups, and public interest groups. (2)

innovation a new way of doing something, often synonymous with creativity. (16)

jargon the technical language of a profession. (4)

justice model views lawbreakers as responsible for their own actions. Sometimes called the punishment model. In comparison to the medical or welfare model. (2) (8)

killer phrases judgmental, critical statements that serve as put-downs. They stifle creativity. (16)

kinesics the study of body movement. (4)

Language Line a service providing translation in 143 languages twenty-four hours a day, seven days a week. (5)

learning disability one or more significant deficits in the essential learning processes. (8)

magnet address an address which is easy for people to give and consequently it often is mistakenly associated with reported crimes. (16)

magnet phenomenon occurs when a phone number or address is associated with a crime simply because it was a convenient number or address to use. (16)

magnet telephone one which is available when no other telephones are and consequently it is often mistakenly associated with reported crimes. (16)

medical model sees those who break the law as victims of society, not responsible for their own actions. Sometimes called the welfare model. In comparison to the justice or punishment model. (2)

mental health the ability to integrate one's self with one's environment. (6)

mental illness a severe disturbance in thinking, feeling, and relating that results in substantially diminished capacity to cope with life's ordinary demands. (6)

mental locks ways of thinking that prevent creativity. (16)

mental retardation normal intellectual development fails to occur. Significant subaverage general intellectual functioning resulting in, or associated with, defects or impairments in adaptive behavior, such as personal independence and social responsibility, with onset by age 18. (6)

mission statement a written declaration of purpose. (3)

mood disorders severe depression, mania, or cycles of depression and mania. (6)

multi-cultural trap occurs when people get so involved with their own cultural concerns they ignore the rest of the society in which they live. (5)

negative contacts unpleasant interactions between the police and the public. They may or may not deal with criminal activity. (3)

neighborhood-oriented policing (NOP) a philosophy of policing stressing a responsive style of policing dependent on quality day-to-day interactions between the police and the public. (1)

networking building and keeping of professional relationships for mutual interest and mutual help. (4)

networks the complex pathways of human interaction that guide and direct an individual's perception, motivation, and behavior. (4)

NIMBY syndrome "Not in *my* backyard." It is fine to have a half-way house—across town, not in my backyard. (2)

nonverbal communication includes everything other than the actual words in a message: tone, pitch, and pacing. (4)

"Norman Rockwell" family a working father, a housewife mother, and two children of school age—only six percent of U.S. households today. (8)

one pot jurisdictional approach treating children who are abused or neglected, those who are status offenders, and those who are truly criminal all the same. (8)

PAL police athletic league, developed to provide opportunities for youth to interact with police officers in gyms or ballparks instead of in juvenile detention hall. (14)

panel analysis a research method where data is analyzed by individuals responding rather than by area. (12)

paradox a seemingly contradictory statement that may, nonetheless, be true; for example, the less one has, the less one has to lose. (3)

parens patriae refers to the government's responsibility to take care of minors and others who cannot legally take care of themselves. (8)

patronage system politicians rewarded those who voted for them with jobs or special privileges. Also called the *spoils system*. (1)

perception what is seen; the process of giving meaning or organization to experience. (4)

personality disorder inflexible and maladaptive personality traits and significant impairment in social and occupational functioning. (6)

phenomenological point of view stresses the fact that reality is different for each individual. (4)

plea bargaining a practice in which prosecutors will charge a less serious crime in exchange for a guilty plea, thus eliminating the time and expense of a trial. (2)

police-community relations (PCR) the relationship existing between the police and the citizens, organizations, and agencies they serve and protect. (1)

police-school liaison program places an officer, uniformed or not, into a school to work with school authorities, parents, and students, to prevent crime and antisocial behavior, and to improve police-youth relationships. (14)

post traumatic stress disorder (PTSD) a persistent reexperiencing of a traumatic event through intrusive memories, dreams, and a variety of anxiety-related symptoms. (10)

poverty syndrome includes inadequate housing, inadequate education, inadequate jobs, and a resentment of those who control the social system. (5)

preference selecting someone or something over another. (4)

prejudice a negative judgment not based on fact, an irrational, preconceived negative opinion. An attitude that may result in discriminatory behavior. (4)

primacy effect the tendency to form impressions of people quickly. (4)

primary victims those actually harmed by an incident. (10)

privatization using private security officers or agencies to provide services typically considered to be law enforcement functions. (2)

proactive anticipating problems and seeking solutions to these problems. The opposite of *reactive*. (1)

problem a deviation from what is desired; a difficulty. (16)

problem-oriented policing (POP) focuses on grouping incidents to identify problems and then determine possible underlying causes. (1) A department-wide strategy aimed at solving persistent community problems. (16)

professional model emphasized crime control by preventive automobile patrol coupled with rapid response to calls. The predominant policing model of the 1970s and 1980s. (1)

Progressive Era also called the *Reform Era*. Emphasized preventive automobile patrol and rapid response to calls for service. (1)

PSA public service announcement. (12)

psychotic symptoms demonstrate a significant loss of contact with reality and include illogical thought, incoherent speech, disorientation, extreme mood fluctuation, social withdrawal, hallucinations and delusions, and neglect of family and occupational obligations. (6)

public relations efforts geared at raising the image of the police and the police organization. (1)

qualitative evaluation such evaluations are more descriptive and less statistical. The opposite of quantitative evaluation. (12)

reactive responding after the fact, for example, responding to calls for service. The opposite of *proactive*. (1)

recidivism a tendency to relapse into a former pattern of behavior, especially criminal habits. (2)

reciprocity a cooperative interchange. Each party in the effort has something to offer and also something to gain from the relationship. (12)

representing a means to show allegiance or opposition through clothing. Uses an imaginary line drawn vertically through the body. (9)

schizophrenia a deterioration in one's personality to the point where feelings, thoughts, and behavior are not coherent. (6)

second injury occurs to victims when they are treated badly by professionals who should be helping them, including police officers and the entire criminal justice system. (10)

secondary victims those who are indirectly affected by a trauma. (10)

seizure a sudden, uncontrolled event or episode of excessive electrical activity in the brain. It may alter behavior, consciousness, movement, perception, and/or sensation. Does not always involve a stiffening or jerking of the body. (6)

selective enforcement the use of police discretion, deciding to concentrate on specific crimes such as drug dealing and to downplay other crimes such as white collar crime. (3)

self-fulfilling prophecy believing self-talk or what others say about you and causing it to come true. (4)

semantic environment the way words are used and the way they are interpreted shape beliefs, prejudices, ideals, and aspirations. They constitute the moral and intellectual atmosphere in which a person lives. (4)

semantics the study of meaning. (4)

sensorium that part of the brain that interprets what the eye takes in. (4)

social contract a theory in law which suggests that for everyone to receive justice, each person must give up some individual freedom. (2)

spoils system politicians rewarded those who voted for them with jobs or special privileges. Also called the *patronage system*. (1)

statistically significant a predetermined level at which the results would not occur by chance. The most common level is .05 meaning the results would occur by chance no more than five times in one hundred. (12)

status offenses actions by a juvenile that would not be a crime if committed by an adult, for example, truancy or smoking cigarettes. (8)

stereotyping assuming all people within a specific group are the same, lacking individuality. (4)

street gang a group of people who form an allegiance based on various social needs and engage in acts injurious to public health and public morals. The preferred term of most local law enforcement agencies. (9)

street justice occurs when police officers use their discretionary powers to simply talk to youth who are status offenders rather than taking them into custody. (8)

symbiotic a relationship in which those involved depend upon each other for existence. (11)

symbolic process the process by which people can arbitrarily make certain things stand for other things. (4)

syndrome of crime a group of signs, causes, and symptoms that occur together to foster specific crimes. (2)

synergism occurs when individuals channel their energies toward a common purpose and accomplish what none of them alone could accomplish. (15)

TAB temporarily able-bodied. (6)

TDD telecommunication device for the deaf. (6)

thin blue line the distancing of the police from the public served. (1)

TOP Teens on Patrol, program in Rochester, New York, that hires youths to patrol the city's parks and recreational areas in the summer. (14)

turf territory occupied by a gang, often marked by graffiti. (9)

verbal world the world that comes to us through words. (4)

victim impact statement (VIS) a written report describing in detail the full effect of a crime on the victim. May influence the sentence passed by the judge. (10)

victim service programs provide crisis counseling, shelter, and other specialized treatment. (10)

victim statement of opinion (VSO) victim's opinion of what an offender's sentence should be. (10)

victim/witness assistance programs seek to provide assistance to victims and witnesses as they move through the judicial process. (10)

victimization being harmed or made to suffer. (10)

victimology the study of crime victims; includes the concepts of vulnerability and culpability. (10)

vulnerability   suggests that certain groups of people are more susceptible to being victimized because of demographics rather than anything they control as individuals. (10)

weed and seed   a community-based, multi-agency approach to fighting drug use, violent crime, and gang activity in high crime neighborhoods. The goal is to "weed out" crime and then "seed" the neighborhoods with a variety of crime and drug prevention programs. (15)

welfare model   view that children are basically good and in need of help. (8)

youth gang   a self-formed association of peers, bound together by mutual interests, with identifiable leadership, well-developed lines of authority, and other organizational features, who act in concert to achieve a specific purpose or purposes which generally include the conduct of illegal activity and control over a particular territory, facility, or type of enterprise. (9)

Author Index

Subject Index

Photo Credits